Colin Atkins

Christmas 1993.

THE HIGH MOUNTAINS OF THE ALPS

Willi Burkhardt

(above) The Fiescherhorn and Grünhorn groups with the Finsteraarhorn beyond in a view across the Ewigschneefeld from the summit ridge of the Mönch.

THE HIGH
OF

Helmut Dumler
Willi P. Burkhardt

MOUNTAINS THE ALPS

Diadem Books
The Mountaineers

British Library Cataloguing in Publication Data
Dumler, Helmut
High Mountains of the Alps. Vol.1:
4000m Peaks
I. Title II. Burkhardt, Willi P.
796.5
ISBN 0-906371-43-0

Library of Congress Cataloging in Publication Data
Dumler, Helmut
[Viertausender der Alpen. English]
The high mountains of the Alps / Helmut Dumler and Willi P. Burkhardt; with additional photos by John Allen, Richard Goedeke, Wil Hurford, Bill O'Connor, Jim Teesdale, Dave Wynne-Jones and others.
p. cm.
Includes index.
ISBN 0-89886-378-3
1. Mountaineering – Alps – Guidebooks. 2. Skis and skiing – Guidebooks. 3. Alps – Guidebooks. I. Burkhardt, Willi P. II. Title
GV199.44.A4D8813 1994
796.5'22'094947 – dc 20

Published simultaneously in Great Britain and the United States by Diadem Books, London and The Mountaineers, Seattle.

All trade enquiries: in Great Britain, Europe, Commonwealth (except Canada) to Hodder/Headline plc, Mill Road, Dunton Green, Sevenoaks, Kent; in the U.S.A. and Canada to The Mountaineers, 1011 SW Klickitat Way, Seattle, WA 98134, U.S.A.

Colour separations by Chroma Graphics, Singapore and Ecran Offset, Croydon.
Photoset by Vitaset, Paddock Wood.
Printed and bound in Italy by L.E.G.O., Vicenza.
(Printer Trento)

Title photo (pages 2-3): The North Faces of the Eiger, the Mönch and the Jungfrau at dawn. Contents photo (pages 4-5): Liskamm, Pollux and Castor from the Breithorn Pass. Preface photo (page 6): The view east from the Aiguille du Midi to Grand Combin. Photos: Willi Burkhardt

Contents

Preface

Karl Blodig and Four-Thousand-Metre Peak Collecting

Karl Blodig was the climber who first popularised the four-thousand-metre peak climbing idea which is now a growing passion for many keen mountaineers in Europe. He was born in Vienna in 1859 and spent his childhood in Graz from where he made his first notable climb (Triglav) at the age of fifteen. Five years later he made an early ascent of the East Face of Monte Rosa with the Swiss guide Christian Ranggetiner. In 1882, after gaining his doctorate in optical medical science, he made guideless ascents of the Zumsteinspitze, the Dufourspitze and the Weisshorn with Louis Friedmann and, after a spell working abroad, set up his practice as an oculist in Bregenz in 1885.

Thereafter his record of 4000m peaks climbed was as follows:

1890 Barre des Écrins, Mont Blanc (both with Ludwig Purtscheller).
1892 Jungfrau, Mönch, Finsteraarhorn, Aletschhorn.
1895 Dom, Breithorn, Liskamm, Matterhorn traverse.
1898 Gross Grünhorn, Täschhorn, Dent Blanche (again with Purtscheller).
1899 Grandes Jorasses, Dent du Géant, Aiguille de Bionnassay (again with Purtscheller, who shortly afterwards had an accident on the Dru and a few months later succumbed to influenza).
1900 Lagginhorn, Fletschhorn (considered a four-thousander until 1950).
1901 Lenzspitze, with the Alpine artist Edward Theodore Compton.
1902 Strahlhorn, Rimpfischhorn, as well as numerous four-thousanders during the next few years including, in 1903, the Lauteraarhorn and the first traverse of the Rochefort Ridge with Max Horten.
1911 The first ascent of the Brouillard Arête on Mont Blanc with Humphrey Owen Jones, Geoffrey Winthrop Young and Josef Knubel.

There followed the First World War, and an injury in the Bernese Alps. In 1932 at the age of 73 he made a solo ascent of the Grande Rocheuse and Aiguille du Jardin – numbers seventy-five and seventy-six in his personal table of four-thousanders.

By this time others had overtaken Blodig* but his name was forever associated with the activity after the publication of *Die Viertausender der Alpen* in 1923. A second edition in 1928 was followed by two reprints. The book was republished in 1968 by Rudolf Rother in Munich with major revisions by Helmut Dumler. Dumler also wrote the 1989 edition which was illustrated by the photographs of Willi Paul Burkhardt.

*Blodig's claim to be the first man to climb all the 4000ers rests on the list of qualifying peaks as of 1911.

The English language rights were acquired by Diadem Books, whose editor, Ken Wilson, redesigned the book adding new historical material and over one hundred and fifty new photographs.

The list of peaks is now a subject of intense debate. In his recent guidebook, *The Alpine 4000m Peaks by the Classic Routes*, Richard Goedeke identifies a total of 150 peaks and tops. This new version of the Blodig/Dumler book highlights sixty main peaks to which Goedeke adds Punta Barreti to make a total of sixty-one which can be taken as the conventional list from an Austro/German perspective. Some British and French mountaineers have noted that if the minor Monte Rosa peaks are to be included the summits of Mont Blanc, the Grandes Jorasses and Grand Combin have equally valid claims. The sharp pinnacles of the Diable Ridge are also considered to merit peak status. Such disparity may be no bad thing for this is surely not an activity about which to become obsessive – it is the alpine odyssey that is important, rather than slavish list-ticking.

'It will be said he was a keen climber and an enthusiastic spokesman for the beauties of the Alps'; thus Blodig formulated his own epitaph, so to speak, before he passed away on 7 September 1956 at the age of ninety-seven. The interest he generated is now a growing passion for many bringing with it a love and respect for one of the finest mountain ranges in the world, and a deeper understanding of the historical roots of a magnificent pastime.

Karl Blodig as a young man and in old age.

Piz Bernina *4049 m*

Bernina! The word awakens an association of ideas: ice and snow; dazzlingly white blades of névé; coarse-scaled glacial arêtes; ridges and walls; deep-frozen splendour of the sublime Eastern Alps. The Piz Bernina merges with the 3995 metre Piz Bianco, or Piz Alv, to form a single entity – the only four thousander in the Eastern arc of the Alps. Whether viewed from Piz Morteratsch, from Diavolezza (across the Bellavista Terrace), from Piz Corvatsch or from the Tschierva Hut, when the great ridge glows with the last of the sunlight, Piz Bernina portrays a constant and unmistakable allure.

The name is said to have been passed on from the valley to the heights, in the opinion of Walther Flaig, the chronicler of the range, citing Aegidius Tschudi who, as early as 1555, mentions a 'Chiantum Bernina' (the hamlet of Bernina Häuser). The first ascent of this complex mountain was made on 13 September 1850 by the Swiss surveyor Johann Coaz with Jon and Lorenz Ragut Tscharner. They took a route through the 'Labyrinth' of the Morteratsch Glacier and then climbed the East Ridge from the Forcella Crast'Agüzza, reaching the summit at 6 p.m. Today's Normal Route, the South Ridge or Spallagrat, was climbed in 1866 by that ubiquitious English alpinist Francis Fox Tuckett – a Bristol businessman, with Frederick Augustus Yeats Brown and guides Christian Almer and Franz Andermatten. Their expedition, an extended traverse of the range, began at midnight from Foppa to the south, gained the summit at 11 a.m., and ended at Pontresina at 3 p.m.

The North Ridge or Biancograt (Crast' Alva in the Romansch tongue of the natives of Engadine), from the Fuorcla Prievlusa to the summit of the Piz Alv, was climbed on 12 August 1876 by Henri Cordier (France) and Thomas Middlemore (England) with the Swiss guides, Johann Jaun and Kaspar Maurer. However, they did not continue from Piz Alv to the main summit of the mountain. The deep indentation of the Berninascharte which lay ahead struck such fear into them that they preferred to climb back down the Biancograt. Two years later, to the day, the Berlin scientist and politician Dr Paul Güssfeldt accomplished the traverse across to the Piz Bernina – and thus the first complete ascent – under the guardianship of the Pontresina guides Hans Grass and Johann Cross. On 15 March 1929, Carl Collmus trudged up the wintry Biancograt with Kaspar and Ulrich Grass. Also of interest was Hermann Buhl's six-hour ascent and descent of the Piz Bernina from the Boval Hut in 1950 to win a wager of 200 Swiss francs. He descended the Biancograt's 500m snow crest in an astonishing fifteen minutes and arrived back at the hut with not a minute to spare. In the early summer of 1973, the diminutive South Tyrolean chimney sweep, Heini Holzer, descended the Biancograt on skis, taking just one hour to reach the Tschierva Hut with a storm raging all around him. Sadly, four years later, when attempting a ski descent of the far more difficult North-East Face of the neighbouring Piz Roseg, 'Tiny Heini', as he was affectionately known by all, fell to his death.

The Biancograt

According to a poll conducted among well-travelled mountaineers, this immaculate blade of névé is considered among the finest ridge routes of its kind in the Alps. It is also the best route of ascent on the Piz Bernina and, when combined with a descent of the Spallagrat, is the most exemplary of all mountain traverses. The climb divides neatly into four quite different sections: the

The Outlying Peaks

Three isolated four-thousanders stand apart from the main ranges of the Western Alps: Piz Bernina, Gran Paradiso and Barre des Écrins. Piz Bernina is part of the Eastern Alps, in the Romansch region on the borders of Switzerland and Italy, yet the scale of this heavily-glaciated range gives it a power and presence more reminiscent of the Western Alps. The Gran Paradiso is firmly and fully rooted in Italian soil, the highest summit of the Graian range south of Mont Blanc. More than one hundred kilometres south-west of Mont Blanc, the Barre des Écrins crowns the savagely beautiful Dauphiné massif. Each of these outlying ranges have their own very special alpine character, in welcome contrast to the hurly-burly of the main alpine regions. Yet the principal peaks bear comparison with any in the greater ranges and their satellites are scarcely less challenging.

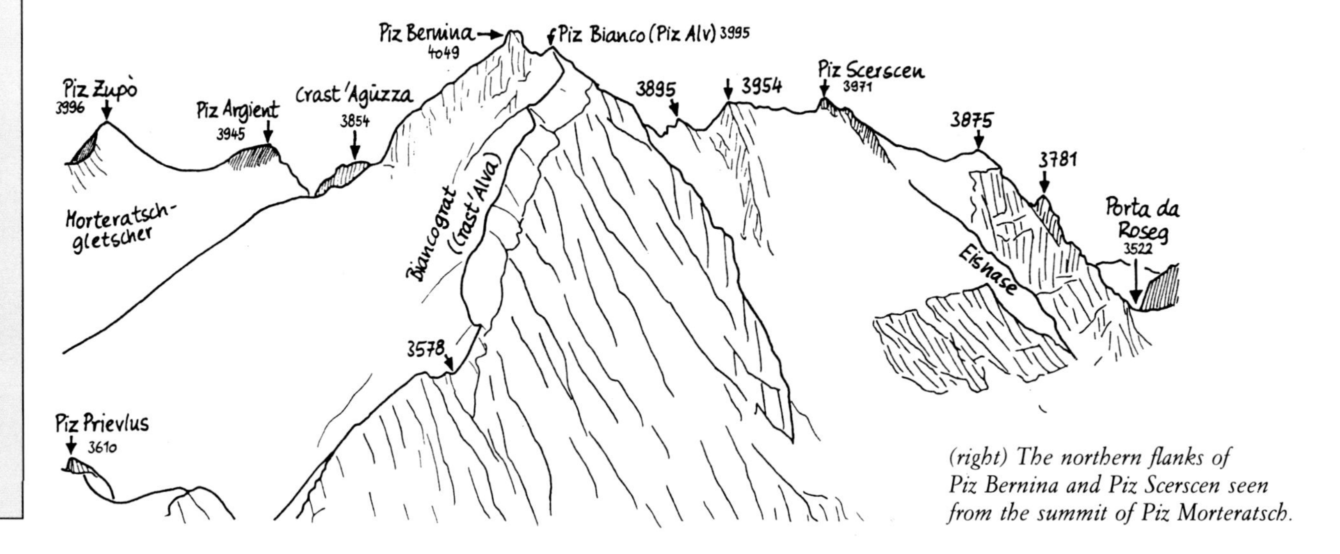

(right) The northern flanks of Piz Bernina and Piz Scerscen seen from the summit of Piz Morteratsch.

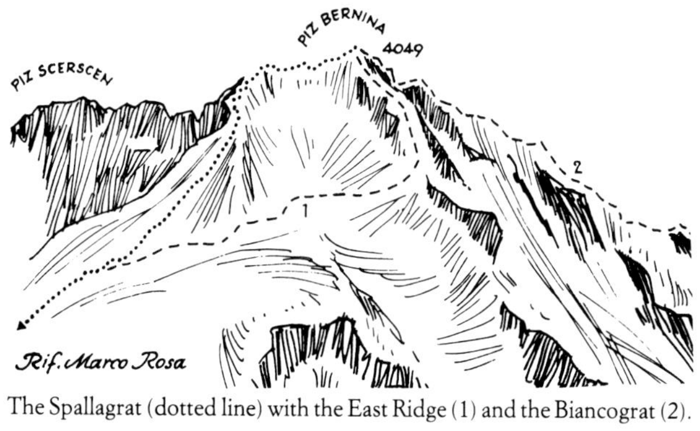

The Spallagrat (dotted line) with the East Ridge (1) and the Biancograt (2).

(left) Piz Bernina's East Face from the Fortezzagrat.

(below left) Descending from the Bellavista Terrace towards Piz Bernina.

(below) At the col beyond the Fuorcla Prievlusa – at the start of the Biancograt.

Bill O'Connor

Bill O'Connor

Colin Foord

(above) Looking down the Biancograt from a steep section half-way up the ridge. The Tschierva Glacier is in shadow on the left.

approach from the Tschierva Hut to Fuorcla Prievlusa; the rock ridge to the start of the snow arête and the Biancograt itself; the passage across the Berninascharte from Piz Alv to the summit.

On the continuation down the Spallagrat to the Marco e Rosa Huts, one also crosses La Spalla (4020m), the southern shoulder (Spalla) of the massif.

The Normal Route (the Spallagrat)

Though easier, this is a less coveted route of ascent than the Biancograt because of its long approach, but it makes an ideal ski expedition. One skins up to the plinth at the foot of the Spallagrat and after the walk along the summit arête – only the width of a boot in places – 1900m of ski descent is the reward. However even in winter there is serious crevasse danger so it is safest to

VALLEY BASES

Pontresina 1805m. In the highest lateral valley of the Engadine between Samedan and the Bernina Pass. Hotels, inns, pensions. Youth Hostel *tel* 082/ 6 72 23. Good railway and bus services.

HUTS/OTHER BASES

Plauns Campsite 3.5km from Morteratsch on the road to the Bernina Pass, open from the beginning of June to the end of September *tel* 082/ 6 62 85.

Hotel Morteratsch 1896m. On the Bernina Railway, 2km from the Bernina road *tel* 082/ 6 62 85. 84 places.

Tschierva Hut 2573m. SAC. Above the northern side of the Tschierva Glacier. 100 places. Staffed at Easter and Whitsuntide and from mid-June to October *tel* 082/ 6 71 88. 3½ hours from Pontresina by the Rosegtal.

Rifugio Marco e Rosa De Marchi 3599m/3609m. CAI. two huts 300m west of the Forcella Crast'Agüzza. Staffed from July to mid-September *tel* 0342/ 21 23 70. 65 places. The old hut is open all year. 5 hours from the Boval Hut via the 'Buuch', similar time from the Diavolezza. Alternatively from Lanzada in Italy take the road to Campo Moro (23km), 4 hours to *Rifugio Marinelli-Bombardieri*(2813m. CAI. 218 places. *tel* 0342/ 45 14 94), then a further 2½ hours to the hut.

Boval Hut 2495m. SAC. Above the western edge of the Morteratsch Glacier. 100 places. Staffed at Easter and Whitsuntide and from June to October *tel* 082/ 6 64 03. 2½ hours from Hotel Morteratsch via Chunetta. Winter approach over the Morteratsch Glacier.

Diavolezza Huts 2973m. Private. 170 places. Staffed from June to mid-October and December to April *tel* 082/ 6 62 05. Near the top station of the Diavolezza ski-lift; valley station Bernina Sud (2050m)

the Diavolezza ski-lift; valley station Bernina Sud (2050m) reached by rail and bus services, inn accommodation, open from mid-June to mid-October and December to April *tel* 082/ 6 64 05.

NORMAL ROUTE

South Ridge (Spallagrat) PD II and I. 3 hours from the Marco e Rosa Hut. 450mH. Mixed climbing to start (cables), then an exposed snow ridge. *As a ski tour:* For experienced ski-mountaineers only! Take the Fortezza Ridge (from either Boval or Diavolezza) and gain the Bellavista Terrace via the 'Buuch' or 'through the Loch' (crevasse danger everywhere) and continue to the Forcella Crast'Agüzza.
4-6 hours to the Marco e Rosa Hut. Leave skis at the foot of the ridge.

RIDGES AND FACES

Biancograt AD III (sections), II, I. To 45°. 7 hours from the Tschierva Hut to Piz Alv summit. 1 hour across to Piz Bernina (in normal conditions). 2 hours to descend Spallagrat to Marco e Rosa Hut. 1500mH. Mixed climbing, rock and a long ice ridge.

East Ridge PD II. 3 hours from the Marco e Rosa Hut, 450mH. Mixed – a useful alternative to the Spallagrat.

North-East Face AD+. To 55°. 12 hours from foot of route. 1300mH. Of the four dangerous approaches to the upper face only the Gurgel (gully) can be advised. A night approach obligatory. The upper face can be reached from the East Ridge.

MAPS/GUIDEBOOKS

Landeskarte der Schweiz 1:50,000 Sheet 5013 *Oberengadin* or 1:25,000 Sheet 1277 *Piz Bernina. Bernina Alps* by Robin Collomb (West Col); *The Alpine 4000m Peaks by the Classic Routes* by Richard Goedeke (Diadem/Menasha).

Colin Foord

(above) *Near the summit of Piz Bernina after traversing the shattered ridge from Piz Alv past the double notch of the Berninascharte – a section can become quite difficult when snow-covered.*

rope up. The same warning applies for mountaineers descending from the Marco e Rosa Huts in summer when it is usually best to go via the 'Buuch' rather than by the more serious Labyrinth ice-fall to gain the lower Morteratsch Glacier.

The traverse of Piz Bernina can be further embellished by adding the traverse of the Piz Palü, starting from the Fuorcla Bellavista, over the Spinasgrat, to the Diavolezza Hut. This also has the advantage of removing the aforementioned Morteratsch Glacier descent.

The Stairway to Heaven

My own recollection of the Biancograt, written many years ago, still seems very real:

'As we crouched, cowering, on the top of the Piz Morteratsch, I might have known it. The monument of snow, the Biancograt – "the Stairway to Heaven" – loomed in front of us through simmering dirty greyness which had weighed upon us for days.

'And now we stand before it, the line which has long been our desire. The sunlight bestows upon it the magic of which we have dreamt. There is no longer anything alien about this mountain, for the pictures which drew me here have lent it a kindred spirit. Always the same pictures: a snow-white line of light and shadow piercing the heavens, a glistening arrow fired into space. The gently arched ridge is very narrow to begin with – to the left lie crevasses, to the right a precipitous slope. As we take the first steps in the new snow, sensations multiply. Forgotten are the laborious night-time approach to the col and the scraping of crampons on the icy rocks of the ridge. These first steps are made in profound reverence, feeling for balance, setting one foot down in front of the other until, attuned to the rhythms, we push on with vitality, caught up in the euphoria of the route. One should move slowly on this ridge, stand and stare, enjoy it to the full.

'We had the best possible conditions and immaculate weather – a deep, cloudless blue. I have experienced many extreme ice climbs but never before, nor since, such a ridge. What followed remains only at the very edge of my consciousness – reverse-climbing down into the Notch, up to the summit, careful strides on the soft new snow of the Spallagrat, and the night spent in the jumbled boulders outside the overcrowded hut. The glow of that "Stairway to Heaven", however, lasts much longer. It will last a lifetime.'

Bill O'Connor

(above) *Descending the Spallagrat (South-East Ridge) with Piz Zupò in the background.*

Gran Paradiso *4061m*

Framed by the upper Aosta Valley to the north and the plains of the River Po to the south-east is the broad sweep of the Graian Alps. The highest peak of the range is Gran Paradiso which, after the Barre des Écrins, is the second southernmost four-thousander in the Alps.

The range has retained much of its original character, due to the founding of the National Park of the same name in which large areas have survived intact, saved from exploitation and the consequent man-made ravages.

'For here the name is not empty sound and fury, here it is a ringing cry, a glaring flame blazing heavenward from a white sacrificial pyre, summoning you to prayer in the church of the mountains,' enthused the 'Kaiser Pope' Franz Nieberl (1878-1968) at the mature age of fifty.

The mountain lies atop the central ridge of the range, about twenty kilometres south of Aosta, its shoulders cloaked in glacial snows with only the craggy pinnacles of the tops protruding. On the north side, a col separates it from the Piccolo Paradiso (3921m), and to the south, the Colle del Gran Paradiso marks it off from the rest of the range. In the north, branching off from the Aosta Valley, two valleys provide the approaches to the mountain – Val Savaranche and Val di Gogne-Valnontey, the former being the more important. The paths from the Valnontey to the Gran Paradiso are substantially longer and the uphill approaches to the huts and bivouacs considerably more arduous than the usual route from Pont at the upper end of Val Savaranche.

The Gran Paradiso offers a range of magnificent views, for on a clear day one can see 300km out over the

(below) High on the Normal Route, at the saddle by the pinnacle of the Becca di Moncorve.

Richard Gibbens

Richard Gibbens

(above) Looking south, beyond an intervening top, to Il Roc (4026m) from the col on the summit ridge.

VALLEY BASES

Pont 1954m. In the upper Val Savaranche. Bus service. The Albergo Gran Paradiso campsite is situated at the roadhead, The road to Val Savaranche leaves the Aosta valley at Villeneuve (17km west of Aosta).

HUTS/OTHER BASES

Rifugio Vittorio Emanuel II 2775m. CAI. West of the Gran Paradiso on a high plateau. 143 places. Staffed from 25 April to 25 September (inexpensive full-board arrangement) *tel* 0165/ 9 57 10. Winter room with 41 places in the old hut. 3 hours from Pont.

NORMAL ROUTE

West Flank F+ II (one pitch). 5 hours from the hut. 1300mH. Mainly a glacier tour with rock on the summit ridge.
As a ski tour: follow the summer route to the bergschrund (3½-4 hours). Crampons and axes (for the summit slope) can be borrowed at the hut.

RIDGES AND FACES

From the East PD+ II (sections). 5 hours from Bivacco Pol. 7 900mH. Mixed.
East Face AD+ To 50°. 5 hours from Bivacco Pol. 350mH from foot of face. Ice.
North-East Ridge PD+ III. 5 hours from Bivacco Pol. 900mH. Mixed climbing follows a difficult approach across the Tribulazione Glacier.
North-West Face D+ To 50°. 600mH from foot of face. 5 hours from the Victor Emanuel Hut. A classic route – an ice face then mixed climbing. The Diemberger Variant is a pure ice route. The 'Direttissima' gives climbing to 70°.

MAPS/GUIDEBOOKS

Kompass-Wanderkarte 1:50,000 Sheet 86 *Gran Paradiso. Graians East* by Robin Collomb (West Col); *The Alpine 4000m Peaks by the Classic Routes* by Richard Goedeke (Diadem/Menasha).

plains of the River Po to the Mediterranean. To the north-east, the Matterhorn, Monte Rosa, Dent d'Hérens and others can be made out, while the southern precipices of Mont Blanc appear to the north-west, with the Barre des Écrins to the south-west.

The Normal Route

Gran Paradiso was first climbed in 1860 by the British mountaineers John Jermyn Cowell and W. Dundas, guided by the Chamonix men Michel Payot and Jean Tairraz. The ascent was made in bitterly cold conditions and was not without incident, Tairraz having a twenty-foot fall which was arrested by Dundas, and Payot, after a prodigious period of step-cutting, arriving on the summit with near frostbitten hands. In poor visibility and near storm conditions they quit the top in haste and glissaded and ran down in just three hours. Next day, in order to enjoy the view, Cowell and Payot repeated the ascent.

'To please Payot, I counted carefully the number of steps he had cut the day before. The grand total was 1275, a score of which he was not a little proud, it being, he said, the greatest number that had ever been accomplished by a Chamouni man in one day.' The ascent took them five hours, four fewer than the day before – an indication of the handicap that absence of crampons imposed on the pioneers.

The twenty-two year old Cowell also made two further first ascents in the range in that year and the following year was a member of the party that made the first ascent of Nordend. Sadly he died three years later from an illness contracted in Italy after his Monte Rosa climb.

On Gran Paradiso the route followed was essentially the same as the current Normal Route, which these days starts from the Rifugio Vittorio Emanuel II, an incongruous affair reminiscent of an aircraft hangar with its ugly aluminium roof. The hut is comfortable, however, and well situated to view the icy cathedral of the Ciarforon, but the lie of the land prevents any view of the Gran Paradiso prior to the climb.

The Normal Route is a long but predominately non-technical climb up the west-flowing Paradiso Glacier and, as a rule, the path is broad and well-marked. The mountain is thus considered one of the easiest four-thousanders. To reach the glacier a boulder labyrinth directly behind the hut has to be negotiated. Here the path is less obvious so, as a pre-dawn start is advisable, it is best to reconnoitre this section the day before. Steinbock and wild sheep may occasionally be spotted *en route*, the latter seeking the cool of the new snows.

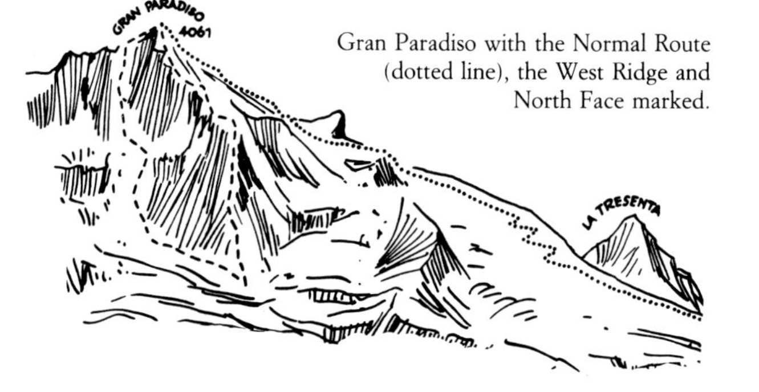

Gran Paradiso with the Normal Route (dotted line), the West Ridge and North Face marked.

Near the top, a ten-metre pitch (II) must be overcome to gain the white Madonna statue that adorns the summit area, though she does not mark the highest point. This is several metres higher across a blocky rock ridge which is easily crossed in a few minutes. However, if this traverse is heavily snowed-up or icy, my advice is to steer clear of it!

Gran Paradiso as a Ski Excursion

Although the Gran Paradiso enjoys a lengthy summer season, almost as many mountaineers climb it on skis during the months of May and June, a feat first accomplished at the end of the 1913 winter season by Paul Preuss and W. von Bergnuth. Since then, despite the absence of ski-lifts, it has developed into an out-and-out ski-peak, even though the slog up to the hut is often longer, with the little road from Pont not always cleared of snow (officially, the Val Savaranche is closed for the winter from November to June). But the effort is well worth while with a downhill run of 2000m from the summit.

The National Park

This makes a visit to this area more rewarding than to the more commercialised valleys elsewhere in the Alps. When, in 1922, King Vittorio Emanuel III, the last King of Italy, presented the hunting reserve of his predecessor to the State of Italy, this gesture marked the de facto founding of the Gran Paradiso National Park. With an area of 56,000 hectares, responsibility for its supervision falls to around sixty people in the Park and the Paradiso Garden of Alpine Plants, opened in 1956 up in the Valnont, exhibits a cross-section of the varied flora of the area.

The colonies of steinbock in the National Park have achieved a degree of fame, with experts estimating their numbers as c4000, dispersed in herds throughout the protected area. Many can be observed around the Rifugio Vittorio Sella (2584m), where they seem to congregate. It is best to spend a night at the huts – formerly two royal hunting lodges – and rise before dawn to take a half-hour stroll up the valley where, in the grey hours of morning, the animals can be watched and photographed from close quarters.

(right) Grivola and Gran Paradiso dominate the Eastern Graian Alps when viewed from the Mont Blanc range.

Barre des Écrins *4101 m*

Some 50km south-east of Grenoble, and within easy reach of Briançon lies the *Parc National des Écrins* in the Dauphiné, the name commonly applied to all the French Alps between Mont Blanc and Provence. Established in 1973, the park is a sparsely vegetated region scoured by glaciers, with the Massif des Écrins forming the dominant mountain group – its major summit being Barre des Écrins.

The mountain was first climbed in 1864 by a strong party, comprising the leading English alpinists Edward Whymper and Adolphus Warburton Moore with their equally famous guides Michel Croz (France) and Christian Almer (Switzerland), by a route up the North-East Ridge and a descent by the west. By this way the main summit is reached first. Beyond this a russet crown of jagged granite needles forms Pic Lory (4086m), the main satellite top, while beyond Brèche Lory (3974m) is the Dôme de Neige (4015m), which is much valued in winter by ski-mountaineers. Yet the main summit should really be the final objective of a ski excursion (leave skis at the foot of the West Ridge) as it provides views over the entire range, with the Cottian Alps and Monte Viso to the south-east and Mont Blanc and the Gran Paradiso discernible in the distance. The arduous ascent is richly rewarded with a downhill run of many thousands of metres across the white drapery of the West Flank and on down the Glacier Blanc.

Apart from the West Ridge route it is possible to reach the summit up the fall-line, following in the footsteps of the American-born William Augustus Brevoort Coolidge, that obsessive student of all matters alpine, with his guides Christian and Ulrich Almer and Christian Gertsch. They climbed straight up from the upper edge of the glacier while making the third ascent of the peak on 4 June 1870. For a traverse of the mountain, the North-East Ridge rising from the Brèche des Écrins provides a suitable opening gambit, leaving the West Ridge as the route of descent. It must be said that this combination – that taken by the first ascent party – is a mixed climb, more demanding than the normal West Ridge approach, with passages of grade II to III rock climbing.

John Allen

The icy South Face of Barre des Écrins flanked by the South-West Ridge of Pic Lory (left) and the South Pillar that rises directly to the summit (right).

The Normal Route

All these routes start in the north-east and north from the Refuge des Écrins which occupies a belvedere-like position perched above the Glacier Blanc. In August this is often packed with walkers and tourists and the mountaineering fraternity is increasingly found encamped amid the chaotic boulders which surround the hut.

From the hut, the line of the Normal Route can be seen in its entirety. A left-to-right dog-leg takes the climber through the icefalls and across the upper glacier plateau to gain the Brèche Lory at the foot of the summit bastion and the West Ridge. The bergschrund just below the brèche has caused many to pause since the ladder for aid, advocated by Edward Whymper, is unlikely to be among the items of luggage.

On the West Ridge, after a couple of steep pitches on

the exposed rocky crest, the angle relents and once the Pic Lory has been attained there are no further obstacles worthy of mention before the summit.

The ski ascent in winter conditions, both on the mountain and on the approach to the hut, is more or less the same as the summer route but the skis must be shouldered for the first steep step after the Refuge Cézanne. The rising traverse to the higher hut is avalanche-prone in the afternoons and on the climb itself harscheisen (ski crampons) could be useful on the occasional steep sections of the North Flank.

Approaches from La Bérarde

The western approach from La Bérarde, through the Val des Etançons, the Vallon de la Bonne Pierre and across the glacier of the same name, is more troublesome and five hours are needed to gain the Col des Écrins (3367m). Although the couloir below the saddle is partially protected by cables, the last section provides a pitch of tricky climbing. From the Col there remains a further two hours of climbing to gain the summit.

La Bérarde is also convenient for the Refuge Temple-Écrins (2410m) which is the base of operations for the South Face. Decried as loose and prone to stonefall, the route has sections of III rock and mixed climbing. In his book *Augenblicke – oben*, Richard Goedeke has this to say of it:

'After the moraines and the glacier begins the airy climbing on juggy rock which here and there demands a little re-arranging. Snow and ice follow and, depending on the conditions and the route chosen, some mixed climbing as well. [nevertheless] . . . a possibility for a glorious traverse of the mountain.'

For the South Pillar route, the Cézanne Hut is rather more favourably sited, being roughly one hour closer to the start of the climbing. The first ascent fell to one of the

The summer and winter route (dotted line) from the Glacier Blanc, up the North Flank and the West Ridge. To the right of the start of the ridge is the Dôme de Neige des Écrins.

Willi Burkhardt

John Allen

John Allen

(*left*) *The North-East Ridge of Barre des Écrins from Brèche de Écrins.*

(*right*) *Approaching the summit from Pic Lory.*

most prominent French alpinists of the post-war era, Jean Franco, who accomplished it on 15 August 1944 with his wife Jeanne. Franco, born in 1914 in Nice, was a noted director of the celebrated *Ecole Nationale de Ski et d'Alpinisme* at Chamonix and was one of those who made the first ascent of Makalu (8481m) in 1955. He was killed in a car accident in 1971.

Whymper's Observations

The driving force behind the first ascent of the peak was the London wood engraver and illustrator Edward Whymper (1840-1911). Whymper was one of the most colourful figures of the 'Golden Age' of Alpine mountaineering. On his early visits to the Alps, he perhaps felt rather ill at ease in the exclusive circle of his countrymen, who were predominantly intellectuals from the upper class of Victorian England. Who can say whether or not it was just this social difference which wound the mainspring of his incredibly successful career as an alpinist – the pinnacle of his achievement being the ascent of the Matterhorn in 1865. Often stubborn and despotic, coldly calculating on the mountain, he now and then betrayed a dry, typically English sense of humour, an example of which is found in his account of the first ascent of the Barre des Écrins in his classic book *Scrambles Amongst The Alps*:

'The night passed over without anything worth mention, but we had occasion to observe in the morning an instance of the curious evaporation that is frequently noticeable in the High Alps. On the previous night we had hung up on a knob of rock our mackintosh bag containing five bottles of Rodier's bad wine. In the morning, although the stopper appeared to have been in all night, about four-fifths had evaporated. It was strange; my friends had not taken any, neither had I, and the guides each declared that they had not seen anyone touch the bag. In fact it was clear that there was no explanation of the phenomenon but in the dryness of the air. Still it is remarkable that the dryness of the air (or the evaporation

(*left*) *The South-West Ridge of Barre des Écrins seen from the summit of Dôme de Neige des Écrins.*

Wil Hurford

VALLEY BASES

Ailefroide 1503m. A cluster of hotels in the Vallouise, 18km north-west of the Durance Valley, from where the approach road (closed December to April) branches off 16km south of Briançon. Bus service. Campsite *tel* 92 23 3200.

La Bérarde 1711m. A mountain village 26km south-east of La Clapier in the Romanche Valley, from where the road branches off. The use of the approach road is timetable-controlled (officially closed between November to May). Bus service to Grenoble (74km).

HUTS/OTHER BASES

Refuge Cézanne 1874m. A hotel situated on the boulderfield of the Pré de Madame Carle at the head of the Vallouise. 5km by road from Ailefroide (closed November to May).

Refuge des Écrins 3170m. CAF. On a rocky spur 70m above the northern edge of the Glacier Blanc. 100 places. Staffed during the skiing season and in the summer months. 2½ hours (short *via ferrata*) to Refuge du Glacier Blanc (2550m), 4½ hours in total.

Refuge Temple-Écrins 2410m. CAF. South-west of the Barre des Écrins on the northern bank of the Vallon-de-la-Pilatte stream. 88 places. Staffed in summer. 3 hours from La Bérarde.

NORMAL ROUTE

North Face, West Ridge PD+ II, I. To 40½. 6 hours from the Écrins hut. 1000mH. A glacier tour to below the West Ridge, then mixed climbing. *As a ski tour:* As for the summer route (ski depot at the bergschrund).

RIDGES/FACES

North-East Ridge AD III, II. To 50°, 2 hours/440mH from Brèche des Écrins. Mixed climbing.

South Pillar TD V+ and V (sections), IV, III. 9 hours/1100mH from foot of route. A classic rock climb.

MAPS/GUIDEBOOKS

Didier and Richard 1:50,000 Sheet 6 *Massif et Parc Nationales Écrins*; IGN 1:25,000 Top 25 Sheet 3436ET *Meije/Pelvoux*; Institut Géographique National 1:50,000, Sheets *La Grave* and *Christophe en Oisans*. *Écrins Massif* by John Brailsford (Alpine Club). *The Alpine 4000m Peaks by the Classic Routes* by Richard Goedeke (Diadem/Menasha).

of wine) is always greatest when a stranger is in one's party. The dryness caused by the presence of even a single Chamonix porter is sometimes so great that not four-fifths but the entire quantity disappears. For a time I found difficulty in combating this phenomenon, but at last discovered that if I used the wine-flask as a pillow during the night, the evaporation was completely stopped.'

Whymper's account of the climb and particularly his celebrated illustration of 'Almer's Leap' may have involved a degree of dramatic licence. Many years later this 'Leap' was discounted by Coolidge (in his obituary to Christian Almer – not that in *A.J.* but, perhaps significantly, the one written for the *S.A.C. Jahrbuch*) as a virtual invention concocted to spice up the book. The matter rapidly degenerated into a savage and very public dispute between the two. Alpine Club notables were drawn in and vilified and libel was threatened though later withdrawn. It was a telling illustration of the stubbornness of two men who remain among the dominating personalities of the Victorian mountaineering era and, ironically, maintained a good working relationship until Whymper's death.

The Bernese Alps

The Bernese Alps are adorned by nine independent summits above the four-thousand metre mark. Despite its title, most of the range is in the Canton Valais with the Schreckhorn and Lauteraarhorn as the only four-thousanders located entirely on Bernese soil. The border between the two cantons runs, logically enough, along a natural watershed – from Les Diablerets in the west, by the crest of the main ridge to the Mönch and thence over the Finsteraarhorn to the Grimsel Pass. The outer topographical boundary of the range is the Rhône Valley to the south, and in the north by a line drawn from Aigle, through Adelboden to Lake Thun and thence by the Hasital to the Grimsel. A north/south axis from Kandersteg, across the Gemmi Pass to Leukerbad, divides the chalks and Jurassic limestones of the western section of range from the igneous and crystalline rocks of the higher peaks to the east. The highest summit of the range is the Finsteraarhorn (4273m) at the extreme eastern end. When measured against the summits of the Pennine Alps the Bernese Alps appear almost second-rate, whereas in terms of actual height above the valleys they are far more impressive. Zermatt, for example, lies some 600m higher than Grindelwald. Admittedly the Bernese Alps cannot boast such an unusual mountain as the Matterhorn or such a commanding massif as the Monte Rosa but the chain of North Faces between Eiger and the Lauterbrunnen Breithorn, the Konkordia ice plateau (Konkordiaplatz) and the Aletsch Glacier are unique features that lend the range its individual character. The other great ranges seem more exploited too, whereas here, though the ubiquitous ski-lifts, cable-cars and railways ply the flanks, the interior retains a savage wildness.

The Bernese Oberland, often wrongly equated with the Bernese Alps, is the sub-alpine region of the Canton Berne, separate from the gigantic formations of the true Bernese Alps to the south. The Oberland does, however, offer the most glorious spectacle of this range. In his book *The Playground of Europe* Leslie Stephen, viewing the range from the Oberland, enthused, 'No earthly object that I have seen approaches in grandeur to the stupendous mountain wall whose battlements overhang the villages of Lauterbrunnen and Grindelwald'. These sentiments had genuine meaning in the last century. Protected by its great ice and rock walls to the north and by its massive glaciers to the south and east, the Bernese Alps should still present this satisfyingly complete and challenging character. But the Jungfrau Railway has stolen its inner mystery forever, opening it to tourists, skiers and mountaineers alike, whilst latterly helicopters have removed some of the underlying commitment required for its great face climbs. Nevertheless, the Bernese Alps still preserve a unique character that effortlessly shrugs off the puny attempts of 'civilization' to demean it.

(left) The Bernese Alps seen from the east across the Grimsel Pass to the Finsteraarhorn and the Lauteraarhorn

Willi Burkhardt

(left) The Mönch and the Eiger at the head of the Grindelwald Fiescher Glacier in a view from the East.

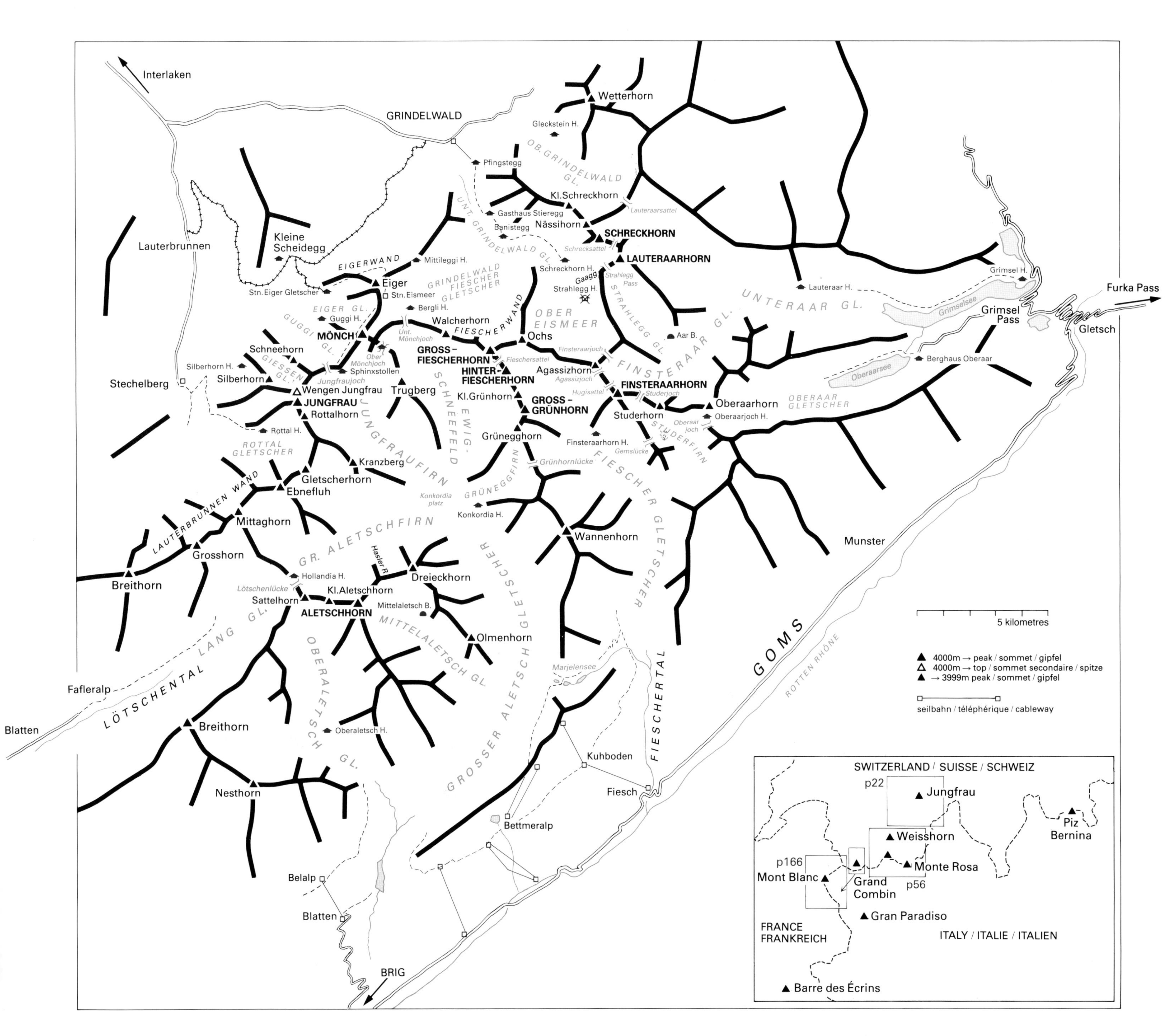

Interlaken
GRINDELWALD
Wetterhorn
Gleckstein H.
Pfingstegg
Kl.Schreckhorn
Gasthaus Stieregg
Banistegg
Nässihorn
SCHRECKHORN
LAUTERAARHORN
Lauteraarsattel
Schrecksattel
Lauterbrunnen
Kleine Scheidegg
EIGERWAND
Mittileggi H.
Stn.Eiger Gletscher
Eiger
Stn.Eismeer
Bergli H.
Schreckhorn H.
Strahlegg H.
Strahlegg Pass
Gaagg
Lauteraar H.
Grimsel H.
Furka Pass
Grimsel Pass
Gletsch
Grimselsee
UNTERAAR GL.
EIGER GL.
Guggi H.
MÖNCH
Walcherhorn
FIESCHERWAND
Ochs
OBER EISMEER
Aar B.
Schneehorn
Silberhorn H.
Stechelberg
Silberhorn
Sphinxstollen
Jungfraujoch
Wengen Jungfrau
JUNGFRAU
Rottalhorn
Rottal H.
Trugberg
GROSS-FIESCHERHORN
Fieschersattel
HINTER-FIESCHERHORN
Kl.Grünhorn
GROSS-GRÜNHORN
Agassizhorn
Agassizjoch
Finsteraarjoch
Hugisattel
FINSTERAARHORN
Studerjoch
Studerhorn
Oberaarhorn
Oberaarjoch H.
Oberaarjoch
Berghaus Oberaar
Oberaarsee
OBERAAR GLETSCHER
FINSTERAAR GL.
STUDERFIRN
Grünegghorn
Finsteraarhorn H.
Gemslücke
Grünhornlücke
ROTTAL GLETSCHER
Kranzberg
Gletscherhorn
Ebnefluh
JUNGFRAUFIRN
EWIG-SCHNEEFELD
Konkordia platz
Konkordia H.
GRÜNEGGFIRN
FIESCHER GLETSCHER
LAUTERBRUNNEN WAND
Mittaghorn
Grosshorn
Breithorn
GR. ALETSCHFIRN
Hasler R.
Dreieckhorn
Hollandia H.
Lötschenlücke
Kl.Aletschhorn
Sattelhorn
ALETSCHHORN
Mittelaletsch B.
MITTELALETSCH GL.
Olmenhorn
Wannenhorn
Munster
LANG GL.
LÖTSCHENTAL
Fafleralp
Blatten
Breithorn
Nesthorn
OBERALETSCH GL.
Oberaletsch H.
GROSSER ALETSCH GLETSCHER
Marjelensee
FIESCHERTAL
Kuhboden
Fiesch
Bettmeralp
Belalp
Blatten
BRIG
GOMS
ROTTEN RHÔNE
5 kilometres
4000m → peak / sommet / gipfel
4000m → top / sommet secondaire / spitze
→ 3999m peak / sommet / gipfel
seilbahn / téléphérique / cableway
SWITZERLAND / SUISSE / SCHWEIZ
p22
Jungfrau
Weisshorn
Piz Bernina
p166
Mont Blanc
Grand Combin
Monte Rosa
p56
Gran Paradiso
FRANCE FRANKREICH
ITALY / ITALIE / ITALIEN
Barre des Écrins

Jungfrau *4158 m*

The Jungfrau is the most important peak of the great northern wall of the range and the third highest mountain in the Bernese Alps, named because her snow-cloaked 2000m northern slope, when viewed from a distance in a diffuse light, has the appearance of a maiden's veil. This stately mountain flank is best admired from the small peaks above Kleine Scheidegg – impressive and complex, it is richly decorated in ice and snow: below the summit of the Wengen Jungfrau the shadowy Nordwand forms a sombre backdrop for evocative dazzling snow peaks which divide a series of remote névé basins that nourish the Giessen, Guggi and Kuhlauen glaciers.

Nor, indeed, is the south-west side of the mountain bereft of high Alpine allure, for here nature is represented in her wildest and most unsullied form by the Rottal amphitheatre that includes the ice-clad Gletscherhorn and Ebnefluh. The 700m eastern flank is less arresting, but is quite difficult, as evidenced by the shocking accident statistics on the Normal Route. In late summer and autumn gaping crevasses and bare ice on the direct approach to the Rottalsattel force a detour on to the North-East Spur of the Rottalhorn.

The Meyers and the First Ascent

The Jungfrau was first climbed on 3 August 1811 by Johann Rudolf and Hieronymus Meyer, sons of the Swiss topographer Johann Rudolf Meyer of Aarau, accompanied by two Valais chamois hunters (thought to be Aloys Volker and Joseph Bortes). They approached from the south-west by way of the Lötschental and from a camp above the Grosser Aletschfirn gained the summit in the early afternoon of their third day out. Their route is thought to have gone up the Kranzbergfirn and over the Lauihorn and Rottalhorn to the Rottalsattel and the summit.

A chronicler described the final section:

'The last part of their ascent led over a keen ice arête on which they seated themselves *a cheval* and carefully, half-sitting, half-climbing, slid upwards. . . . The summit point measured about twelve feet in diameter, which bears no relation to the shape of the Jungfrau summit as perceived by later ascensionists . . . and is explained by the fact that a mighty swathe of crusted snow must have adhered to the otherwise sharp crest of the summit ridge.'

The vagueness of their account led to critical speculation, and to settle the matter Gottlieb Meyer, son of the J.R. Meyer who had made the first ascent, climbed the mountain again in September 1812 (with Bortes and Volker), approaching by the Aletsch Glacier and probably following today's Normal Route. A flag was erected on the summit and was seen from Strahlegg.*

The Jungfrau by Sledge

The first winter ascent, in 1872, was made in a rather unconventional manner by the American lady mountaineer, Miss Meta Brevoort. When she stepped on to the summit on 22 January, accompanied by her nephew and protégé W.A.B. Coolidge, a high-alpine sledge ride lay behind her. The sledge was drawn by six guides. The conveyance remained behind on the Jungfraufirn and Miss Brevoort completed the remaining journey on foot, in the company of – among others – Tschingel, the soon-to-be-famous mountaineering Beagle bitch which Christian

*These events (plus expert analysis) are detailed in William Longman's history of early Jungfrau ascents in an addendum to the *A.J.* VIII Addendum p49.

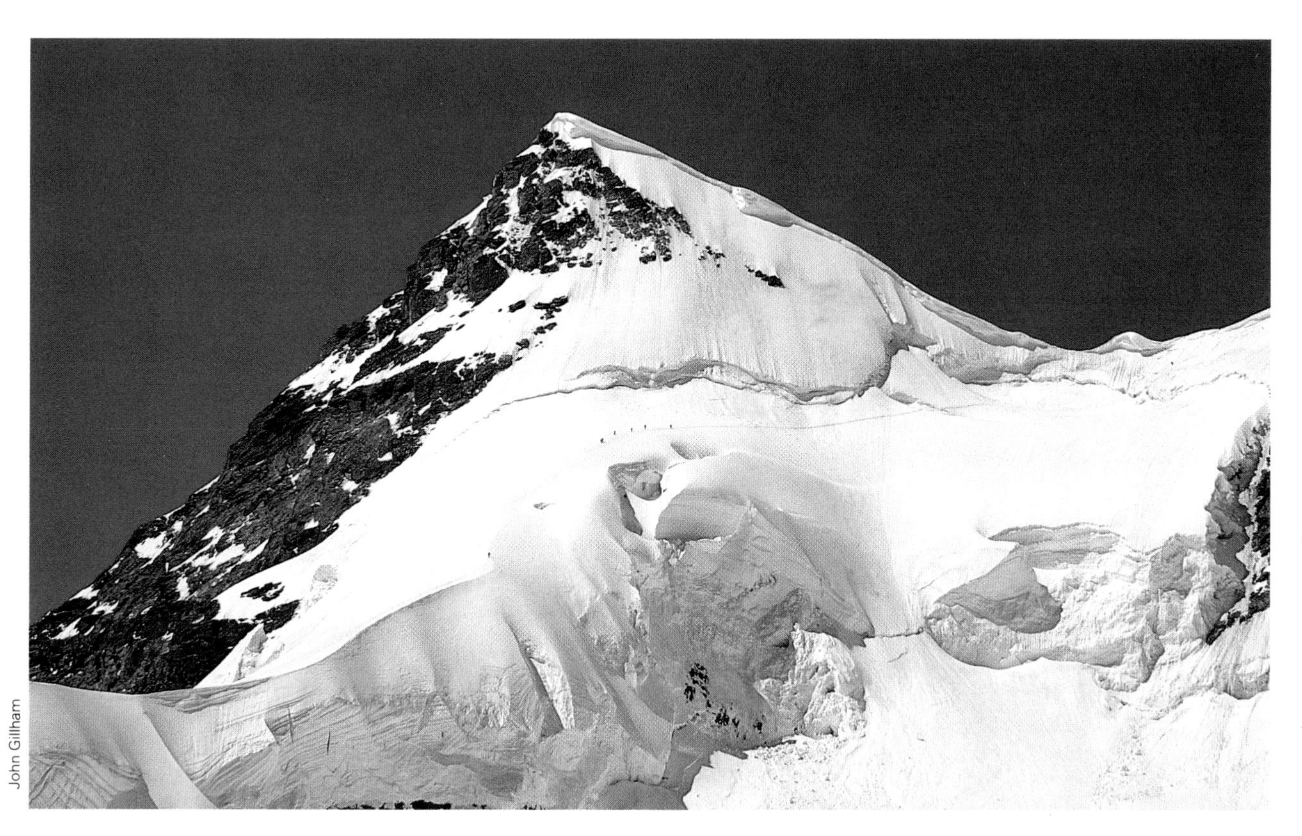

John Gillham

Climbers traversing below the Rottalhorn to link North-East Spur to the Rottalsattel. The Normal Route (probably that taken in 1812) takes the obvious direct line over the bergschrund.

Willi Burkhardt

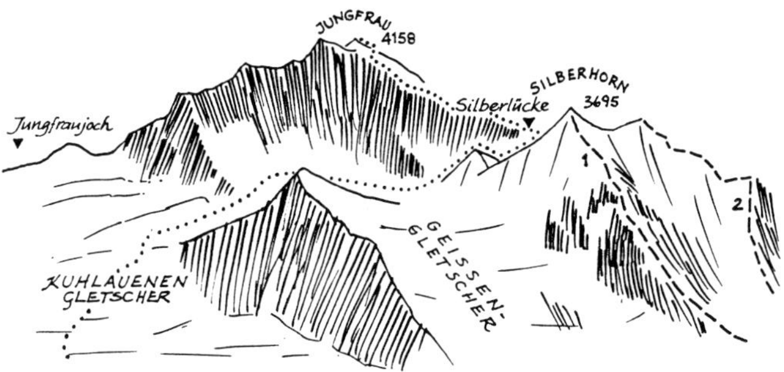

The Guggi Route (dotted line) was the Normal Route before the Jungfraujoch railway was built. The North-West Ridge of the Silberhorn (1) and the Rotbrett Ridge (2) are also marked.

Almer had given to Coolidge. To this day it probably still holds the record for canine alpinism, with thirty summits and thirty-six alpine passes to its credit, including the first unassisted canine ascent of Mont Blanc.

The Normal Route

Had the ingenious project instigated by Zürich entrepreneur Adolf Guyer-Zeller been realised, the terminus of the Jungfrau Railway would now be situated at the summit of the Jungfrau with an elevator deep in the bowels of the mountain. Luckily the First World War hindered the completion of the final section beyond Jungfraujoch. So the Maiden remained inviolate, which is just as well, for on some days the railway carries as many as 4000 passengers to the highest railway station in Europe.

The railway lures mountaineers to attempt a three-hour dash to the summit. This sounds very inviting, yet it ignores the acclimatization necessary. Many unprepared climbers labour on up, gasping for breath and intensely preoccupied with themselves. Hence the disproportionately high number of deaths. The falls occur on the rising traverse from the Rottalsattel to the rocks of the summit structure, and when the climb is iced up it is best to fix protection on this section. Even the route up to the Rottalsattel should not be underestimated. In perfect conditions it can be climbed direct but, when the alternative way by the North-East Spur of the Rottalhorn is chosen, there may be avalanche risk on the steep slope leading across to the col. Skiers, in particular, should be mindful of this.

From the Rottalsattel an hour is needed to attain the summit. On the western side of the crest of the ridge a total of fourteen iron stakes at 20m-40m intervals serve as running belays. A 35° névé slope then leads up to the summit crags.

The Guggi Route

One of the most interesting routes on the Jungfrau is the intricate Guggi Route which works a cunning line through the hanging glaciers of the North Flank. This is an itinerary of some difficulty that is frequently impractical because of crevasse problems. It was first climbed in 1865 by two Englishmen, Sir George Young and the Rev. Hereford Brooke George (the inaugural editor of the *Alpine Journal*) with guides and porters led by Christian Almer. The ascent was something of a *tour de force* for the period, a ladder being carried to bridge the bigger crevasses. However, in the absence of the Jungfrau Railway, it was soon the established Normal Route on the mountain. Latterly it has frequently been impractical due to the crevasse problems, but in good conditions it must rate as one of the most interesting ice excursions in the Alps as the route crosses the northern slopes over the ice peaks of the Schneehorn and Klein Silberhorn to gain the Silberlücke, and from there follows the Silbergrätli to the summit.

Routes from Lauterbrunnen

The search for a shorter route up the Jungfrau led to the western flank undergoing sustained investigation from the 1860s. Here the mountain appears formidable with long approach marches to gain the Rottal basin or the plinth of the Silberhorn. The West Couloir of the Rottalsattel was climbed in 1864 by a party comprising Reginald John Somerled Macdonald, Florence Craufurd Grove and Leslie Stephen with Melchior and Jakob Anderegg, and Johann Bischof. An accident here in 1872, when Bischof and another guide perished in an avalanche, removed any popularity it had gained as an ascent route.

The standard route from Rottal became the Inner Rottal Ridge which was climbed in 1885 (Fritz von Allmen with the guides Graf, Brunner, Schlunegger, H. von Allmen and Stager).

The elegant North-West Ridge of the Silberhorn was climbed in 1865 by the Rev. James John Hornby (later to become headmaster of Eton College) and Rev. Thomas Henry Philpot with Christian and Ulrich Almer, Johann Bischof and Christian Lauener (they descended by the

(right) The view east from the Schilthorn across the Stechelberg to the Eiger, the Mönch and the Jungfrau.

Giessen Glacier). The adjoining Rotbrett Ridge was climbed on 23 September 1887 by Henry Seymour King with Ambros Supersaxo and Louis (Ludwig) Zurbrücken in bitterly cold conditions. They crossed the summit of the Jungfrau at nightfall and the descent of the Normal Route in a biting wind turned into an epic trial, with a forced bivouac, and then, the following morning, much step-cutting down the blue ice to reach the Jungfraufirn.

Four months later Mrs E.P. Jackson and Emil Boss with Ulrich Almer and Johann Kaufmann made a winter traverse of the Jungfrau, ascending the East Face and descending to the Silberlücke where they were aided by some of Supersaxo's steps. On reaching the Guggi Glacier they too were overtaken by darkness and forced to bivouac. This was the final climb of Mrs Jackson's remarkable ten-day winter campaign, described by *A.J.* editor, Coolidge, as 'Such a series of great ascents in winter has hitherto been accomplished by no English climber and will long remain unsurpassed'. But the forced bivouac took its toll: Mrs Jackson retained 'severe frostbite in the feet followed by much suffering and the amputation of some of the toes',† injuries that brought her remarkable mountaineering career to an abrupt end.

The North-East Ridge

The Wengen Jungfrau (4089m), has a justified claim to be treated as more than a minor top. It can be reached by a short trip from the summit but the best way is to cross it during an ascent of the 1.5km North-East Ridge, a wonderful rock and mixed climb with pitches of IV on the exposed upper slabs. Ironically, in view of this comment, the first passage of the ridge was made in 1903 in *descent* by Charles Francis Meade with the guides Ulrich and Heinrich Führer. They crossed the summit just after 6 a.m. and then took fourteen hours to descend the ridge

†From *Men, Women and Mountains* by Sir Claud Schuster (p62). No mention was made of these injuries in the *A.J.* report on the climb, an omission possibly prompted by the public disquiet in Great Britain (not least in Royal circles) about a spate of mountaineering accidents at this time.

(below left) An aerial view of the West Face of the Jungfrau showing the West Couloir of the Rottalsattel with the Inner Rottal Ridge to its left.

(below) View on the Normal Route – above the Rottalsattel and on the summit.

Willi Burkhardt

Bill O'Connor

Richard Goedeke

In good conditions the usual line of ascent (dotted line) runs from the Jungfraujoch via the Rottalsattel to the main summit. Other routes are East Face – Levers/Rubi Route (1), the North-East Ridge (2), and the alternative Normal Route up the North-East Spur of the Rottalhorn (3) (see photograph on page 30).

with many long abseils on what must have been a venture of total commitment. After gaining the base of the crucial upper step Meade began to feel confident of the outcome:

'It was a relief thus early [9 a.m.] to get Ulrich's opinion that we must succeed in our attempt. At any rate a glance back up the way we had come was enough to convince us that retreat was already not to be thought of. Indeed, a great alpine ridge seen end on and at close quarters presents one of the ghastliest pictures of utter inaccessibility imaginable.

'. . . those who have never mountaineered will never know that a hard climb in the High Alps is one of the most soul stirring experiences that a man can undergo.'

The climb was ascended eight years later by Hauptmann A. Weber and Hans Schlunegger and climbed solo in 1923 by Joseph Georges *le Skieur* in four hours and in the 1950s in just two hours by Hermann Buhl.

Willi Burkhardt

(right) The western flank of the Jungfrau towering above the Rottal Glacier basin with the shadowy North Face of the Gletscherhorn on the right. The route to the Silberhorn Hut crosses the slopes below the cliffs of the Rotbrett on the left.

VALLEY BASES

Grindelwald 1034m. In the Bernese Oberland. Hotels, guest houses, pensions, campsite. Youth Hostel *tel* 036/ 53 10 09. Good rail and bus connections. 20km from Interlaken.
Lauterbrunnen 769m. In the valley of the same name. Hotels, guest houses, pensions. Large covered car-park at station.
Jungfraujoch 3454m. Self-service restaurant with seating for 200 (no overnight stays) just east of the actual col (3475m). Terminus of the railways from Grindelwald and Lauterbrunnen. First train about 7 a.m. Journey time 1¾ hours. Overnight accommodation at: *Kleine Scheidegg Station Buffet* (70 places) *tel* 036/ 55 11 51: *Bellevue* at Kleine Scheidegg (120 beds) *tel* 036/ 55 12 12; *Eigergletscher Hotel* by the station (60 places) *tel* 036/ 55 22 21.
Stechelberg 910m. The last village in the Lauterbrunnen Valley. Guest houses, pensions. Post Bus.

HUTS/OTHER BASES

Mönchjoch Hut/Guggi Hut see Mönch p31.
Silberhorn Hut 2663m. SAC. At the base of the Rotbrett Ridge. Unstaffed but open all year. 12 places. 5 hours from Wengeralp Station, 6 hours from Stechelberg – both approaches avalanche prone.
Rottal Hut 2755m. SAC. To the north of the Rottal Glacier. 46 places. Staffed on summer weekends *tel* 036/ 55 24 45. 6 hours from Stechelberg.

NORMAL ROUTE

South-East Ridge PD+ II, I. To 35-40°. 4 hours from the Jungfraujoch. 700mH. Glacier approach, snow and ice, then mixed ground. *As a ski tour:* As for the alternative summer route to a ski depot in the glacier basin east of the Rottalhorn. Continue on foot via the Rottalsattel to the summit.

RIDGES AND FACES

South-West (Inner Rottal) Ridge AD III, II. Iron stakes and fixed ropes at various points. 6 hours from the Rottal Hut. 1400mH. Mixed.
North-West (Rotbrett) Ridge D IV-(sections), III, II. Fixed ropes on 3 sections, sundry iron stakes. 8 hours from the Silberhorn Hut. 1500mH. Mixed.
North Flank (Guggi Route) D+ II–. To 50° with a short passage at 55° on crux pitch. 10 hours from the Guggi Hut (descent to the Guggi Glacier protected by steel cables). 1400mH. Mainly snow and ice with some mixed.
North-East Ridge D+ IV (two pitches), III, II. 10 hours from the Jungfraujoch. 750mH. Mixed and rock.
North-West Face TD IV (sections). To 55°. 11 hours from the Silberhorn Hut. 1500mH. Ice and mixed ground.

MAPS/GUIDEBOOKS

Landeskarte der Schweiz 1:50,000 Sheet 5004 *Berner Oberland* for all the main range. Small sections of approach are on: Sheet 264 for Lötschental, Belalp, Bettmer and Fiesch; Sheets 255 and 265 for Grimselsee. *Bernese Alps Central* by Robin Collomb (Alpine Club): *The Alpine 4000m Peaks by the Classic Routes* by Richard Goedeke (Diadem/Menasha).

Mönch *4099 m*

The ice cold barricade of the North Faces of Eiger, Mönch and Jungfrau is surely unique within the Alpine regions. Nowhere else does such a statuesque rank of mountains rear themselves directly above areas of habitation. The focal point of this triptych is the Mönch, its summit set astride the cantons of Berne and Valais. It is the fourth highest peak of the Bernese Alps and, despite its imposing visage, its closeness to the Jungfrau Railway makes it the most-climbed four-thousander. While the valley-side precipice of the Mönch is numbered amongst the great North Faces of the Western Alps, the southern flank, which faces the Jungfraufirn, exhibits a more moderate form. Here is situated the short but elegant ridge taken by the Normal Route.

Whichever climb is chosen the views from the mountain are uniformly splendid – both extensive and contrasting. To the north lies the fairytale Lauterbrunnen Valley, the alpine pastures carpeted in green. There, too, are the towns of Mürren and Grindelwald, appearing as toy villages. To the south the eye is drawn to the sheer endlessness of dazzling glaciers and majestically defiant fortresses of ice. Before 1912, the approach required an extended day's walk, usually by a traverse across the southern slopes of the Eiger. In that year the Jungfrau Railway was completed after twenty-one years of steady construction work on its 9.3km length, a miracle of technology even today.

The first ascent party comprised Dr Siegmund Porges, from Vienna, guided by the Grindelwald men Christian Almer and Ulrich and Christian Kaufmann. After a bivouac near the Ober Mönchjoch they climbed the mountain on 15 August 1857, apparently by a route directly up the East Ridge. Today's easier Normal Route up the South-East Spur was credited to Reginald Macdonald with Almer and Melchior Anderegg (1863). However, Macdonald's account* based on Almer's observations at the time, suggests that Porges' party may have taken (either in ascent or descent) today's Normal Route.

Alternatives to the Normal Route

Should the Normal Route prove to be swarming with parties, the South-West Ridge offers an excellent alternative. This was first climbed in 1875 by Rev. F.T. Wethered

**A.J.* I p423

(left) The North-West Face of the Mönch cloaked in winter snow.

(right) Mönch seen from the Jungfrau with the Nollen in profile on the left, the South-West Ridge rising above the Jungfraujoch in the centre, and the South-East Ridge (Normal Route) forming the right-hand skyline.

Willi Burkhardt

John Allen

with Christian Almer and Christian Roth. This is a mixed climb, rather more difficult than the Normal Route, but an ideal prelude to a traverse of the mountain, using the Normal Route for descent. Somewhat more exacting is the ice-climbing of the South Face, while even more mountaineering skill and fitness are demanded by the classic North-West Buttress of the mountain, whose crucial section, an ice-bulge known as the 'Nollen', is steeper than the 'Eisnase' of the Piz Scersen in the Bernina, but nevertheless forms a satisfying centrepiece for a route of great scenic charm.

The North Face or, to be more exact, the 1000m North Face Rib, first climbed by Hans Lauper and Max Liniger in 1921, is less frequented. Featuring steep ice (to 60°) and rock pitches to V– it is sustained, but relatively free from objective dangers. By contrast the austere North-West Face is one of the most serious in the Alps. It was first climbed on its right side in 1934 by Mrs Hutton-Rudolf with the very experienced guide Adolf Rubi and Peter Inäbnit. The most direct line – exposed to constant stonefall in most seasons – was finally overcome between 23-26 December 1976 by the British alpinists Dick Renshaw and Dave Wilkinson.

The Normal Route

The South-East Ridge, though short, contains difficulties on both rock and ice, notably a very sharp and exposed ice arête near the summit which demands steadiness, particularly in softening snow. There have been some nasty accidents here. When the rocks are iced over or the summit ridge heavily corniced the mountain shows its teeth, this irrespective of possible problems caused by the altitude for those using the railway, which can partially be redressed by a night spent at the Mönchjoch Hut.

The Lötschen Ski Tour

This is extolled as the finest and, at 32km, probably the longest glacier skiing outing in the Alps and is an ideal spring expedition. The Mönch can easily be climbed as a prelude, after which the descent begins from the Ober Mönchjoch at the head of the Ewigschneefeld (the Field of Eternal Snows). Just thirty minutes skiing is needed to reach Konkordiaplatz. From here, a three-hour plod up the Aletschfirn leads to the Lötschenlücke, where the crowning glory awaits – the 1500m descent down the Lötschental.

(left) On the South-West Ridge of the Mönch with the Sphinx and the Jungfrau in the background.

Willi Burkhardt

(left) *An aerial view of the North-West Face (in shadow) and West Face of the Mönch divided by the North-West Spur with its ice bulge – the Nollen. Beyond the Sphinx on the right the Jungfraufirn feeds the distant Aletsch Glacier.*

Four Men and a Ladder on the Eisnollen

The ice on the so-called 'Nollen' is often glistening blue, smooth and hard. In spite of this the difficult section, barely ten metres high, offers no great problem when tackled with twelve-point crampons and modern ice tools, and often retains old steps. Nowadays nobody would contemplate the tactics of the first ascent party who carried up a ladder to overcome the crucial bulge. The initiator of this undertaking was twenty-eight year old Edmund von Fellenberg, a mining engineer and scholar from Berne, and, by all contemporary accounts, a man fired with ambition. The eight-metre wooden ladder was, of course, rather unwieldy on the mountain. The leader of the party, Christian Gertsch, whose task it was both to carry the ladder and hack broad steps in the ice, soon fell unconscious and chalk-white to the ground, as related by von Fellenberg: 'After the poor man had vomited profusely and imbibed vigorously of our hoffmannstropfen† he declared himself ready to dare a further attempt. Yet the harassed Gertsch did not hold out for much longer and was sent back to Wengenalp with the ladder.'

Somehow von Fellenberg and his guides Christian Michel and Peter Egger must then have subdued the 'Nollen', and, after a bivouac, they raised the Swiss flag on the Mönch at 3.30 p.m. on 13 July 1866.

†Herbal sedative. Homeopathic sedative drops containing plant extracts such as valerian root.

The West Face

This is the little-noticed 1200m face overlooking the Guggi Glacier. Here the most modern ice climbing and mixed climbing skills are required to tackle the Central and Faden Couloirs. 'Winter to early summer, possibly late autumn,' Kaspar Ochsner designates as the most favourable times of the year. In 1982, accompanied by Peter Apegglen and Michael Gruber, he conquered the seemingly madcap route up the slender ice hose in two stages, to produce what is probably the hardest climb on the mountain.

From the Sphinx Gallery the Normal Route (dotted line) leads across to the South-East arm of the East Ridge, which it follows to the summit. Other routes are the South Face (1) and the South-West Ridge (2).

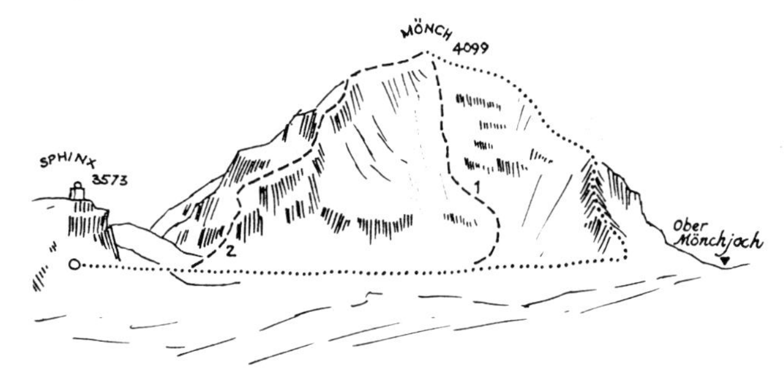

VALLEY BASES

Grindelwald see Jungfrau p27

HUTS/OTHER BASES

Mönchjoch Hut 3630m. Private. On the Ober Mönchjoch below the East Spur of the Mönch. 125 places. Staffed in April and May and from the end of June to September *tel* 036/ 71 34 72. 1 hour from Jungfraujoch.

Guggi Hut 2792m. SAC. On the North-West Spur of the Mönch, between the Eiger and Guggi Glaciers. 30 places. Staffed from July to August and at weekends in September (for the sale of drinks). 3 hours from Eigergletscher Station (2320m).

Jungfraujoch see Jungfrau p27.

NORMAL ROUTE

South-East Ridge/East Ridge PD To 45°. Sections of II. 3 hours from the Mönchjoch Hut. 450mH. Mixed.

RIDGES AND FACES

South-West Ridge AD– III, II. 4 hours from the Jungfraujoch. 650mH. Mixed (mainly rock).

South Face D+ To 50°. 4 hours/450mH from foot of the face. Ice – an early start after a good freeze essential.

North-East Face D To 57°. 3 hours/350mH from start. An ice route.

North-West Spur (Eisnollen) D To 66° (10m section), 50° (80m). 7 hours from Guggi Hut. 1300mH. Rocky scrambling to Point 3112 (2 hours), then névé and ice.

North Face Rib (Lauper Route) D+/TD V– (one section), III, II. To 60°. 13 hours from Guggi Hut. 1000mH from the foot of the face. Mixed climbing and a long icefield.

MAPS/GUIDEBOOKS

Landeskarte der Schweiz 1:50,000 Sheet 5004 *Berner Oberland* for all the main range. Small sections of approach are on: Sheet 264 for Lötschental, Belalp, Bettmer and Fiesch: Sheets 255 and 265 for Grimselsee. *Bernese Alps East* by Robin Collomb (Alpine Club), *The Alpine 4000m Peaks by the Classic Routes* by Richard Goedeke (Diadem/Menasha).

Aletschhorn *4195 m*

It was forty-eight years after the first ascent of the Jungfrau that this aloof pyramid was obliged to submit to the will of Man. The irony is that the Jungfrau climb involved an expedition of greater length and difficulty and the pioneers actually camped below the Aletschhorn, a higher peak, *en route*. Possibly the obvious difficulties on the northern flank stifled any interest. It was finally climbed from the Mittelaletsch Glacier on 18 June 1859 by Francis Fox Tuckett, Johann Josef (J.J.) Bennen, Victor Tairraz and Peter Bohren. Tuckett's entertaining account of the climb in *Peak, Passes and Glaciers* Vol. II displays a passion for climbing that led to ascents of 269 peaks and 687 passes. He was also an assiduous scientific observer and made barometric calculations during the climb and on the summit in the teeth of an icy gale. 'The wind of such violence as almost to carry off one's legs, driving snow, and twenty degrees Fahrenheit of frost, are not quite the companions one would select for examination of so vast a landscape . . . but . . . I unhesitatingly maintain that there is a joy in these measurings of the strength of nature in her wildest moods, a quiet sense of work done, in the teeth of the opposition . . .'

These sentiments were soon to be put to an even sterner test. On the way down, at the Aletschjoch, Tuckett paid off Bennen, and with Bohren and Tairraz began a descent of the North Face, hoping to make a short cut to the Lötschental. A short distance below the cornice . . . :

'My attention was attracted by a sudden exclamation from Victor, who appeared to stagger and all but lose his balance . . . a layer of snow, ten inches to a foot in thickness, had given way exactly beneath his feet, and first gently, and then fleet as an arrow, went gliding down, with that unpleasant sound somewhat resembling the escape of steam which is so trying on the nerves of the bravest man when he knows its full and true significance. At first a mass of eighty to one hundred yards in breadth . . . gave way, but the contagion spread, and . . . the slopes left and right of us, for an extent of at least half a mile, were in movement, and, like a frozen Niagara went crashing down the ice precipices and séracs that still lay between us and the Aletsch Glacier.' Chastened, they carefully and rapidly returned to the ridge, and retraced their steps back to the Mittelaletsch, a good deal wiser about 'the strength of nature in her wildest moods'.

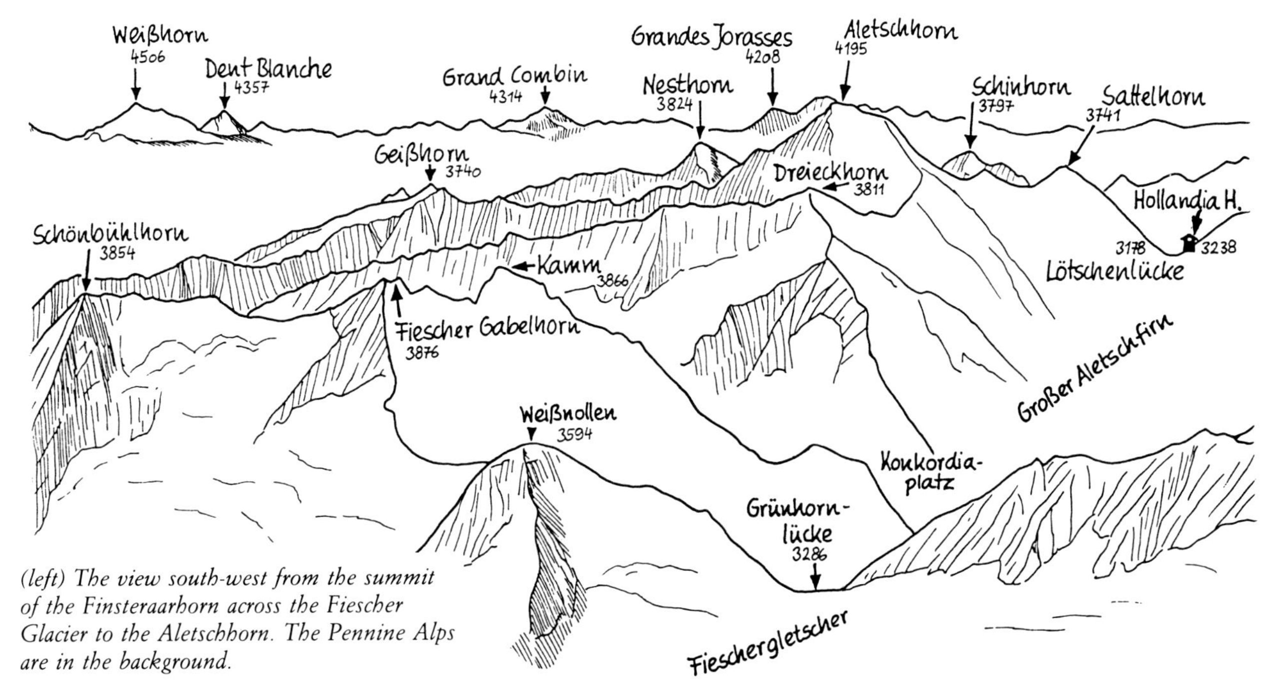

(left) The view south-west from the summit of the Finsteraarhorn across the Fiescher Glacier to the Aletschhorn. The Pennine Alps are in the background.

Three Normal Routes

Viewed from the Lötschenlücke or from Konkordiaplatz, the Aletschhorn presents a broad 1100m North Face of brooding ice which casts gloomy shadows over the harsh polar scenery of the Grosser Aletschfirn. On the south side, though less imposing and gloomy, lies a similar landscape. Here, the Mittelaletsch and Oberaletsch glaciers reach out to claw at the offshoots of the mountain's craggy ridges. The usual routes to the summit are from the south-west (the Oberaletsch Hut) and south-east (Mittelaletsch Bivouac). The easiest way from the north, the Hasler Rib, takes the left-hand side of the North Face. The route is named after Gustav Hasler (who sponsored the building of the Konkordia Hut) to commemorate his first winter ascent on 26 January 1904, but the likely first ascent of the rib was in 1888 by C. Lüscher and guides.

From Mittelaletsch

The construction of the Mittelaletsch Bivouac in 1977 brought the original south-east approach back into the limelight and provides the shortest climb to the top from a hut. Striking off at first towards the Aletschjoch, it then continues via the occasionally corniced North-West Ridge, to finish up a 40° slope to the false summit at 4086m, poised above the North Face.

The hut is also valuable for ski-mountaineers, for whom the Mittelaletsch route has a long tradition – in the spring of 1918 the first ski ascent of the mountain was accomplished from the south-east by Hans Lauper, F. Egger and Henri Rey. On a ski ascent it is customary to proceed on foot from the Aletschjoch.

From Oberaletsch

It should be borne in mind that the approach to the Mittelaletsch Bivouac is, in fact, a route in itself. Before

Doug Scott

Wil Hurford

Wil Hurford

this refuge was built most ascents were made up the South-West Rib from the Oberaletsch Hut. This is a long but usually quite amenable mixed route, with a section of II on the rise to the summit, but in bad conditions, with the couloir iced up, it can become most unpleasant. This ascent also allows a traverse of the mountain with a descent down the Mittelaletsch Glacier.

Another point in favour of the south-west approach is that the Oberaletsch Hut boasts a full service of meals and drinks and occupies a splendid position amid impressive surroundings.

The North Face

The easiest climb from the north (from the Konkordia Hut) is by the 700m Hasler Rib. This is a sustained mixed climb, the most difficult of the Normal Routes on the Aletschhorn, set in a fine position, sandwiched between the sérac zones. It has 45° ice slopes and sections of grade II to III climbing up the long brittle rock rib which leads to the North-East Ridge, just above the Aletschjoch. Thus perched, there are still 500m in vertical height separating one from the top.

For alpinists infatuated with ice faces, the 1100m section of the North Face offers rich scope for activity. There are several routes, three on the central area of the face. All are dangerous in their lower sections and quite steep, though less steep higher up. The main snow and ice line (Blanchet/Rubi/Mooser, 1925), starts up a steep ice fall which can be impassible if the larger crevasses are not bridged with avalanche debris. The more direct route to the right, established by Ludwig Steinauer and H. Ellner in 1935, combined with the middle part of the 1925 route, is said to offer the best line.

The Aletschhorn Traverse

Probably the most rewarding expedition on the mountain is the traverse, starting from the Lötschenlücke with a 45° snow and ice rib to the Sattelhorn (or, rather easier, by a choice of routes from the Oberaletsch Glacier). The climb then crosses the Kleines Aletschhorn, Aletschhorn and Dreieckhorn before descending to Konkordia. This gives fifteen hours of snow and ice climbing, with isolated passages at 50° and grade III rock climbing.

(top left) The North Face of the Aletschhorn seen beyond the Kranzberg in a view from the Mönchjoch Hut.

(far left) Looking down the South-East Ridge of the Aletschhorn with the Oberaletsch Glacier in the background.

(near left) Crossing the Kleines Aletschhorn on an ascent of the West Ridge of the Aletschhorn.

The Aletsch Glacier – Alpine Perfection

The Aletsch Glacier embodies, as no other, a primeval glacial world. About 24km long, it extends from the uppermost snowfields of the Jungfraufirn to Massaschlucht (1520m). It is 3.8km at its widest point and has a total area of 86 sq.km. The main flow is nourished by four enormous névé/glacier basins – the Grosser Aletschfirn, the Jungfraufirn, the Ewigschneefeld and the Grüneggfirn. They meet at Konkordiaplatz (2800m). Measurements conducted here in 1958 put the thickness of the ice at 900 metres at its deepest point – at the edges it is still as deep as 500m, a phenomenon unique in Europe. South of Konkordia, the Aletsch flows 16km to its snout at an approximate rate of 55cm a day or roughly 200m a year. Despite a yearly névé build-up of up to five metres at the Jungfraujoch, it has receded almost 500m during the past thirty years. The level of the surface has apparently dropped too, as a result of this shrinkage, for a century ago the ice reached to the Konkordia Hut.

John Allen

(above) At Konkordiaplatz – looking south-west up the Grosser Aletschfirn to the Aletschhorn and Lötschenlücke.

(below) The view north-west up the Aletsch Glacier to Konkordiaplatz with the Jungfrau and the Mönch in the distance.

Willi Burkhardt

VALLEY BASES

Grindelwald see Jungfrau p27
Fiesch 1050m. In the Rhône Valley. Hotels, inns, pensions. Railway station with Post Bus connections.
Blatten 1322m. A village 9km north of Brig in the Rhône Valley (Post Bus connections). Hotel, pensions.
Bettmeralp 1950m. On a plateau above Bettmer (Rhône Valley). Reached by a 10km road (passable in winter) and cable-car *tel* 028/27 23 51. Hotels, inns, pensions. Bunkhouses: *Matterhornblick tel* 028/ 27 26 39; *Venusblick tel* 028/ 27 13 96.
Fafleralp 1788m. At the end of the Lötschental road (large car park), 23km from Rhône Valley (nearest station Gampen-Steg) with Post Bus connections (in winter, only as far as Blatten). 2 hotels.

HUTS AND OTHER BASES

Oberaletsch Hut 2640m. SAC. At the lower end of the West Ridge of the Gross-Fusshorn, above the eastern side of the Oberaletsch Glacier. 60 places. Staffed from 15 June to 15 September. *tel* 028/ 27 17 67. 3½ hours from Belalp cable-car station, 2091m (valley station in Blatten).
Mittelaletsch Bivouac 3013m. SAC. A small hut at western foot of the Kleines Dreieckhorn, above the east sideof the Mittelaletsch Glacier. 14 places. No cooking facilities or wood – 5 hours from Bettmeralp. Winter path from Moosflue lift (2335m) – 6 hours. Avalanche danger on the north-west slopes of the Olmenhorn.
Konkordia Huts 2840m. SAC. 100m above the Konkordia ice plateau. 130 places. Staffed from end of March to end of September *tel* 036/ 55 13 94. 2½ hours from Jungfraujoch. 5 hours from the middle station at Kuhbodenstafel (2221m), via the Marjelensee. In winter, the drag lift to the Talligrat, 2610m and a ski descent to the Marjelensee can save time.
Jungfraujoch see Jungfrau p27
Hollandia Hut 3238m. SAC. On the ridge above the Lötschenlücke (3178m). 106 places. Staffed from 1 April to 31 May and from 1 July to 31 August *tel* 028/ 49 11 35. 7 hours from Fafleralp.

NORMAL ROUTES

North (Hasler) Rib AD+ Sections of III and II. To 50°. 7 hours/1150mH from start of route. Mixed climbing, free from objective dangers.
South-West Rib PD+ II (on summit rise). 8 hours from the Oberaletsch Hut. 1600mH. *As a ski expedition:* follow the Oberaletsch Glacier to (c.2800m) beyond the lower reaches of the South-West Ridge then work right, to join the summer track. Leave skis below the steepening on the SW Ridge.
South-East Flank and North-East Ridge PD 4½ hours from the Mittelaletsch Bivouac Hut. 1200mH. A glacier tour.

RIDGES AND FACES

South-East Ridge AD– II. 8 hours from the Oberaletsch Hut. 1600mH. Mixed.
West-North-West Ridge AD+ III (sections). To 50°. 10 hours from the Lötschenlücke. 1100mH. Mixed.
North Face TD To 45°, summit wall 50° – the crux is a 10m ice barrier 400m below summit. 8 hours/1100mH from start of route. A sustained ice climb.

MAPS/GUIDEBOOKS

See Jungfrau p27

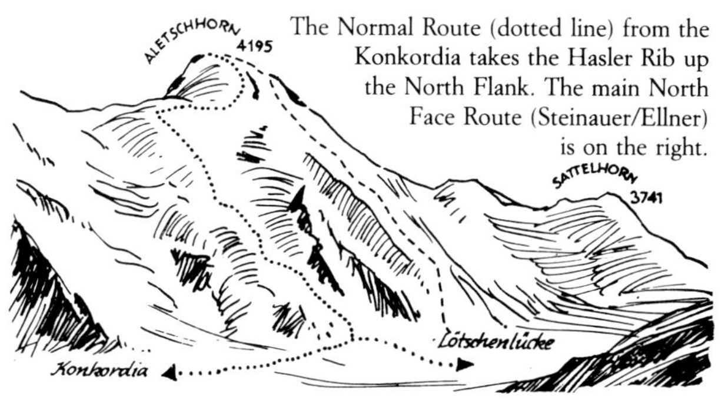

The Normal Route (dotted line) from the Konkordia takes the Hasler Rib up the North Flank. The main North Face Route (Steinauer/Ellner) is on the right.

Schreckhorn *4078 m*

Running north-west to south-east and reaching into the clouds – or so it seems – the ten-kilometre Schreckhorn chain forms the centrepiece of the eponymous group of mountains and culminates in the Schreckhorn, with the curiously similar but diminutive Klein Schreckhorn (3494m) to its north-west.

Walther Flaig described it as: 'the most thoroughbred, savage and feared peak of the group.' One has to concur with this assessment and the Schreckhorn should be regarded as the most difficult four-thousander in the Bernese Alps.

The name of the mountain – 'Schreck' or terror horn expresses its exact nature, not as a derivative of the German 'schrecklich', meaning 'horrifying, atrocious' (for that would be to do the mountain an injustice) but more in the sense of 'abschreckend' or 'forbidding', a description which at once triggers fascination and thus, paradoxically, holds the power of attraction.

The challenge of the Schreckhorn lies in its framework of three prominent ridges. The walls between these ridges – West Face, North-East Face, South Face – are, with the exception of the latter, barely worthy of mention. The South Pillar however (Karl Blach, Karl Reiss, 1955; Werner Munter, F. and D. Schmied, 1964) has been described as by Hans Grossen as 'the finest rock route on a Bernese four-thousander.'

Since the first ascent on 16 August 1861 by the English writer and intellectual Leslie Stephen, with Grindelwald men Christian and Peter Michel and Ulrich Kaufmann, this has been a prized objective for ardent alpinists. Their route, which remained the normal route of ascent for half a century, took the upper Schreck Couloir to the Schrecksattel and then followed the South-East Ridge, but nowadays it is rarely climbed. This is due partly to its difficulty, with ice as steep as 50° in the 350m couloir, and partly to the objective dangers which have steadily increased as the snow cover has lessened. These can be partially avoided by the Amatter Variation, but considerable risks remain.

These days, the best way from the Schreckfirn follows in the tracks of the 1902 party. The very experienced British trio of John Wicks (a businessman, after whom the Bâton Wicks on the Grands Charmoz was named), Edward Bradby (a solicitor) and Claude Wilson (a doctor), astutely noted the possibilites of the apparently steep, but actually very solid and safe South-West Ridge. They duly climbed this fine route (unguided) without problems on 26 July 1902 and thus opened up the present day Normal Route. Facing the sun, the route clears quickly after bad weather and it is also very useful as a descent route for those making a traverse of the mountain by way of either the North-West or South-East ridges. Even more ambitiously the route could begin a traverse from the Schreckhorn to the Lauteraarhorn – a marathon expedition that takes between thirteen and sixteen hours.

(left) The western flanks of the Schreckhorn and the Lauteraarhorn seen from the foot of the Mittelleggi Ridge on the Eiger.

The Andersongrat or North-West Ridge, was named after its first ascensionist, John Stafford Anderson, who was accompanied by George Percival Baker and the leading guides Ulrich Almer and Aloys Pollinger (7 August 1883). This gives an enthralling and varied climb, always presuming that one is a match for the conditions encountered upon it. The foot of the ridge is best approached from the Lauteraar Hut, across the Lauteraar Glacier and over the Nassijoch (or, more challengingly, via the Gleckstein Hut and the Lauteraarsattel). It is the most exacting of the Schreckhorn's ridge routes and at least eight hours are required for its ascent.

Ascending the South-West Ridge

The establishment of the new Schreckhorn Hut (1981) in an easily accessible position slightly above the long-derelict Schwarzegg Hut, and as a replacement for the Strahlegg Hut which was destroyed by an avalanche, has resulted in an even greater stream of tourists than before making their way up to the Oberes Eismeer. The majority of residents on busy weekends are usually bound for Strahlegghorn, but the remainder will be Schreckhorn aspirants. In the wee small hours they search for the tracks marking the path over the rocky backbone of the 'Gaagg', climbing to the start of the névé at an altitude of about 3150m. From the hut it is about three hours to this point which, ideally, should be reached by dawn. From the uppermost basin of the Schreckfirn one proceeds below the fall-line of the South Face, keeping to the left, to arrive at a prominent ramp which slants up to a shoulder on the South-West Ridge. Crossing the bergschrund can prove to be a headache. Once this has been negotiated the first rock pitches are on iron-hard gneiss, after which the ramp leads to the shoulder (sometimes involving some quite tricky rock pitches). Above the shoulder soars the South-West Ridge, which gives immaculate climbing on sound rock, the steepest section usually being turned on the left. The ridge narrows as it approaches the South-West summit from where the route crosses the connecting ridge – at times, particularly after a fresh fall of snow, a rather ticklish affair – to the monolith on the rounded dome of the highest point, decorated with a cap of snow, to complete a splendid route.

The story of the 'Elliottswengli'

Of the few who climb the upper Schreck Couloir to the Schrecksattel and from here tackle the South-East Ridge, fewer still are acquainted with the story of the 'Elliottswengli', the ice slope beyond the Schrecksattel where the first pinnacle on the ridge is turned on the right, a passage now equipped with iron stakes. Here the ambitious English alpinist the Rev. Julius Marshall Elliott fell to his death. A year earlier Elliott had made the psychologically important second ascent of the Matterhorn's Hörnli Ridge with his guides, Peter Knubel and Joseph-Marie Lochmatter. On 26 July 1869, in the company of Franz Biner from Zermatt and Joseph Lauber, and followed by two others, Elliott attempted the Schreckhorn. The trio had been together on many routes so, on Elliott's decision, they climbed unroped and soon drew ahead of the following party. From the Schrecksattel the Rev. P.W. Phipps and Peter Baumann watched their progress as they moved off the ice slope onto the pitch known today as the 'Elliottswengli'. Here Elliott lost his purchase while springing from the snow to the rock. In a flash Biner grabbed at him, seizing him by the arm, but his precarious stance prevented Biner from holding on. Elliott slid down the snow slopes and into the abyss, falling hundreds of metres to the Lauteraar Glacier. His body was recovered the following day from a very dangerous position by a team of Grindelwald guides.

This accident led to an serious debate about the practice of climbing unroped in the Alps.*

A.J. IV p373

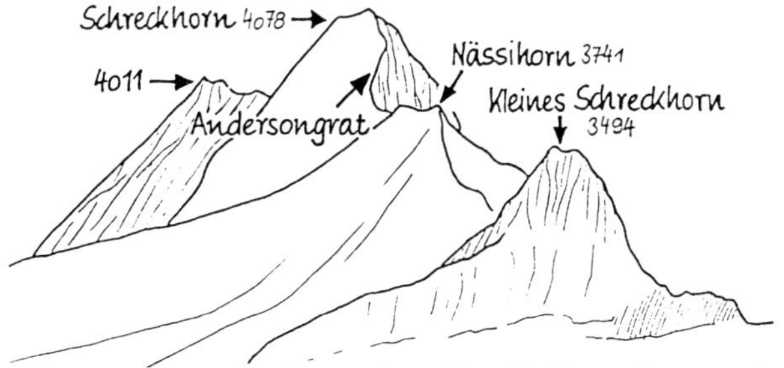

(right) A view up the Oberer Grindelwald Glacier basin to the northern flank of the Schreckhorn.

Willi Burkhardt

The Schreckhorn from the south showing the Normal Route (dotted line) to the South-West Ridge with the South Pillar (1), the South Face Couloir (2) and the upper Schreck Couloir variant (3).

(left) The South Face of the Schreckhorn. The South-West Buttress forms the left skyline, its steepest section offering perfect rock (below).

Wil Hurford

Schreckhorn Notes

VALLEY BASES

Grindelwald see Jungfrau p27

Grimsel Hospice 1980m. A hotel at the reservoir of the same name, open from end of June to end of September *tel* 036/ 73 12 31. 60km from Interlaken. Post Bus connections from Meiringen and Oberwald.

HUTS AND OTHER BASES

Schreckhorn Hut 2520m. SAC. At Schwarzegg above the Oberes Eismeer. 90 places. Staffed from mid-June to September *tel* 036/ 55 10 25. From the top station (1391m) of the Grindelwald/ Pfingstegg cableway – 1½ hours to the *Gasthaus Stieregg* (1650m. 18 places, *tel* 036/ 53 17 66). Continue via Banisegg (1807m) with stretches of *via ferrata*, to the site of the former Schwarzegg Hut and thence to the Schreckhorn Hut. 5 hours from Pfingstegg. One of the most enjoyable hut walks in the Bernese Alps.

Gleckstein Hut 2317m. SAC. Above the northern side of the Grindelwald Glacier, north-west of the Schreckhorn. 90 places. Staffed from mid-June to September *tel* 036/ 53 11 40. 4 hours from Hotel Wetterhorn (1223m) (4km from Grindelwald, road and buses) – some sections cable-protected.

Lauteraar Hut 2392m. SAC. At the foot (south) of the Hienderstock, on the true left-hand side of the Unteraar Glacier. 50 places. Staffed from mid-June to end September *tel* 036/ 73 11 10. Follow the north shore of the Grimselsee to the Unteraar Glacier (2 hours). Cross the glacier (marker poles) to the hut. 5 hours from Grimsel Hospice.

NORMAL ROUTE

South-West Ridge AD+ III (sections), II. 7 hours from the Schreckhorn Hut. 1600mH. A glacier approach, then predominantly rock and mixed ground.

RIDGES AND FACES

Schreck Couloir/South-East Ridge PD+ II. To 50° in upper Schreck Couloir. 8 hours from Schreckhorn Hut. 1600mH. Mixed.

South Pillar D V (for 80m), IV+, IV and easier. 7 hours/600mH from foot of face. 10 hours from Schreckhorn Hut

North-West Ridge (Andersongrat) AD III. 8 hours from Lauteraar Hut via Nassijoch. 1700mH. Glacier climbing to final rock ridge.

North-East Arête AD+ IV (sections), III, II. 4 hours/500mH from foot of face. 8 hours from Lauteraar Hut. Mixed.

North-East Face D+ To 53°. 6 hours/550mH from base of route. Mainly ice with mixed climbing to finish.

MAPS/GUIDEBOOKS

See Mönch p31

Lauteraarhorn Notes

VALLEY BASES

Grimsel Hospice see Schreckhorn p39.

HUTS AND OTHER BASES

Aar Bivouac 2731m. SAC. On the south-east slopes of the Lauteraarhorn and Rothörn, above the eastern edge of the Strahlegg Glacier before the point of confluence with the Finsteraar Glacier. No cooker or utensils. 7 hours from Grimsel Hospice.

Lauteraar Hut/Schreckhorn Hut see Schreckhorn p39.

NORMAL ROUTE

South Face Couloir/South-East Ridge AD+ Sections of II on South-East Ridge. To 35° on South Face Couloir. 6 hours from Aar Bivouac. 1350mH. Predominantly an ice route.

RIDGES AND FACES

South-West Ridge D+ V– (one pitch), IV, III. 5 hours/700mH from the Strahlegg Pass. With a traverse round the difficult summit formation to South-East Ridge: AD+ III, II. 4 hours. Mixed climbing.

North-West Ridge (Lauteraargrat) D IV-, III+ and III. 5 hours from Schrecksattel. 1km long/130mH.

MAPS/GUIDEBOOKS

See Mönch p31.

Lauteraarhorn *4042 m*

This second-highest mountain in the Schreckhorn group attracts little attention. It is mediocre in form with a comparably mediocre ascent. Furthermore, and this applies equally to the Schreckhorn, there is little scope here for the skier. One dignity must be accorded to the mountain in that it is positioned amidst a splendidly scenic landscape with outstanding summit views, particularly of the Finsteraarhorn. The first ascent on 8 August 1842 was made by today's Normal Route from the Strahlegg Glacier, by the Nuremburg glaciologists Edouard Desor and Christian Girard and the Zürich professor Arnold Escher von Linth. Their guides were Melchior Bannholzer and Jakob Leuthold, Chief Guide of Grindelwald, supported by Johann Madutz, Fahner and D. Brigger. The scientists were conducting a systematic study of the glaciers of the Bernese Alps from a bivouac HQ beneath a boulder on the medial moraines of the Unteraar Glacier, jokingly christened 'Hotel des Neuchatelois'.

The rocky South-West Ridge, with its difficult (IV+) finishing section was climbed on 5 October 1900 by E.F.L. Fankhauser with Christian Jossi. The route up to the final section is no harder than III and the 'Band' link between that and the South-East Ridge was discovered at some stage (date unclear), thus creating a more convenient Normal Route from Grindelwald, avoiding the traverse of the Strahlegg Pass.

Nonetheless in the years that followed, the Lauteraarhorn seldom received visitors, a situation which persisted until the completion of the Aar Bivouac in 1976.

Women on the Lauteraarhorn

Female climbers have featured strongly in the mountain's history. The first winter ascent, on 5 January 1888, was made by Mrs E.P. Jackson, with Emil Boss and guides Ulrich Almer and Johann Kaufmann (in the following period this party also climbed the Fiescherhorn and traversed the Jungfrau).

Also of note was the occasion of the first traverse of the North-West Ridge on 24 January 1902 which produced a celebrated example of alpine rivalry. Gertrude Bell and her guides Ulrich and Heinrich Führer had plans to traverse the ridge, but they found themselves in competition with Fräulein H. Kuntze with her guides P. and R. Bernet. The Kuntze party ascended from the Schrecksattel and the Bell party descended from the

(right) A view up the Strahlegg Glacier from the summit of the Oberaarhorn. The Schreckhorn and the Lauteraarhorn dominate the head of the glacier.

John Allen

Dave Wynne-Jones

(left) A view up the South Face Couloir of the Lauteraarhorn from the head of the Strahlegg Glacier.

summit. They crossed *en route*, the meeting reportedly being 'not greeted with enthusiasm'.

This connecting ridge between the Lauteraarhorn and Schreckhorn, roughly one kilometre in length, boasts the minor top P.4011 at the point where the East Face Rib joins the ridge.

The Ascent from the Aar Bivouac

This refuge is situated so close to the Lauteraarhorn that the Normal Route, by way of the South Face Couloir and the uppermost section of the South-East Ridge, can be accomplished in a few hours. However, after an ascent, even the most speedy alpinists would be pressed to descend the glacier highways quickly enough to catch the last ferry of the day (4 p.m.) across the Grimselsee. Notwithstanding this, an early start is advisable, for the névé in the couloir should be firm for both ascent and descent, and the stonefall risk begins early. Should the ridge above this broad gully be hung with cornices, further projectiles are possible, even when one keeps to the rocky rib which bounds the couloir on the left.

As a rule, one climbs unroped to the junction with the South-East Ridge; from here, however, on the coarse gneiss of the airy arête, belays are necessary.

The Wrestler at the Schwarzegg Hut

In the early days the little Schwarzegg Hut on the Schreckhorn served as the most important base of operations in the area. On 16 August 1903, forty-three year old Karl Blodig, Viennese by birth, but by then practising as an optician in Bregenz, set off from Grindelwald with his guide, Feldner, to climb the Lauteraarhorn. They spent the night in the very cramped Schwarzegg Hut as Blodig recalled:

'The Bernese guides present turned out to be most unlikeable chaps. . . . After a few small and not so small skirmishes, which had been started wilfully by the guides, I explained to them that we were . . . members of the SAC and therefore patrons of the guides corps; furthermore, that we enjoyed the rights accorded to us as hosts of the establishment and would defend them . . .; that I had come here to climb my sixty-first four-thousander; that I was a prize-winning gymnast and wrestler and that I felt disposed to answer the next vulgar remark with a punch'.

Luckily for the Swiss, it remained a verbal altercation. They were, of course, unaware of the fact that the Austrian had once incapacitated three of their colleagues with a deft display of wrestling holds. A group of elegant Zermatt guides had been goading his own guide, Christian Ranggetiner, about his shabby attire. Ranggetiner had endured the barbs with equanimity, but warned. 'Just wait until tomorrow when the master gets back from the Weisshorn, he'll give you what for!' When Blodig arrived at Zermatt, he removed his jacket and laid out three of the local guides. The others withdrew sheepishly from the fray.

The Normal Route (dotted line) by the South Face Couloir with the South-East Ridge (1) and the South-East Ridge (2).

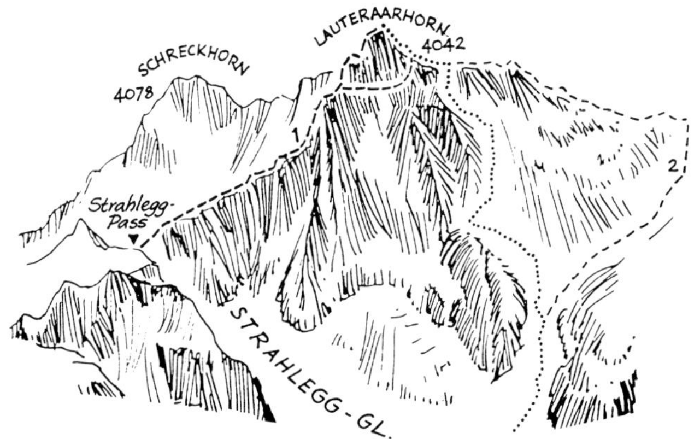

(right) The Schreckhorn and the Lauteraarhorn seen from the summit of the Finsteraarhorn.

Dave Wynne-Jones

(right) On the Lauteraarhorn's South-East Ridge. The Lauteraar Glacier leads down to the Grimselsee on the left.

Gross-Fiescherhorn *4048m*

and Hinter-Fiescherhorn 4025m

To the observer at Grindelwald, the Gross-Fiescherhorn, seen beyond the vertiginous North-East Ridge of the Eiger, presents a stunning four-kilometre ice rampart. The central buttress of this precipice measures 1250m at the point of the summit fall-line of the Gross-Fiescherhorn. Surrounding the mountain are the mighty glacial flows: to the west, the tame Ewigschneefeld; to the north, the gaping crevasses of the Grindelwald Fiescher Glacier; to the south-east, the main (Valais) Fiescher Glacier grinds its way down sixteen kilometres to the Fieschertal and the Rhône Valley, with an area of 33 sq.km, the third largest glacier in Switzerland.

The Gross-Fiescherhorn is a mountain with several dissimilar countenances. Firstly, there is the above-mentioned Fiescherwand, one of the most daunting faces in the Alps. Then, poles apart, there is the graceful natural beauty of the snow slopes eastern flank, perched above the Fiescher Glacier, whereas the south-west and western aspects above the Ewigschneefeld have a more craggy appearance. It was from the Ewigschneefeld that, on 23 July 1862, the first, ascent party, comprising the Englishmen Adolphus Warburton Moore and Rev. Hereford Brooke George and their Grindelwald guides Christian Almer and Ulrich Kaufmann, set out to attain the summit by way of the South-West Ridge, the route still used as today's Normal Route.

The Fiescherwand

Naturally enough, it was the northern aspect which initially drew attention to the Gross-Fiescherhorn, yet in those days, when Alpine mountaineering was just beginning, no one dared contemplate an ascent of the Fiescherwand – a face threatened by great balconies of seemingly unstable ice. Since then, several routes have been made here, the safest being the line climbed in 1947 by the Swiss, Dolf Reist (later to make the second ascent of Everest), Ernst Reiss and E. Sollberger.

(left) The Fiescherwand can be studied from the approach path to the Mittelleggi Hut on the Eiger. Ochs dominates the left side of the wall and the Gross-Fiescherhorn is above the highest central section.

Ski possibilities

Though the Fiescherwand is much-feared, the mountain's easier facets make it popular as a ski venue. The two normal routes approached from any of the main huts are ideal targets for the ski-mountaineer. Few fine spring days pass that do not see parties on the summit and at Easter and Whitsuntide it even gets crowded. The Gross-Fiescherhorn also enjoys an excellent reputation among summer mountaineers, due to the low degree of difficulty on its normal routes and its central location in the Bernese Alps.

South-East Ridge or Traverse?

Until the end of the seventies the Finsteraarhorn Hut and the Konkordia Huts were the best bases for the Normal Routes on the Gross-Fiescherhorn. Ski-mountaineers generally preferred the Finsteraarhorn Hut for approaching the Fieschersattel, a practice still common today. In late summer, however, the Fiescher Glacier often develops belts of crevasses which are difficult to negotiate.

With the inauguration of the Mönchjoch Hut, the Gross-Fiescherhorn became a convenient target from this mountain refuge. From the Ober Mönchjoch, where the hut stands, the Normal Route suffers a loss in height of only 300m on the descent of the Ewigschneefeld before the actual line of ascent begins, whereas, to reach this point from Konkordia involves an uphill slog of almost 500m.

The favourable location of the Mönchjoch Hut and its easy accessibility from Jungfraujoch means that the Bergli Hut is no longer popular as a base, the walk-in requiring ten hours from Grindelwald or a complicated three-hour approach from Eismeer Station.

The real meat of the Normal Route is supplied by the South-East Ridge – 130m in vertical height and 700m long – with which one is confronted as soon as the Fieschersattel is reached. This final climb can occasionally prove dangerous, namely when parties on the brittle craggy zone above loosen and drop rocks. At such times it is best to avoid the fall-line and make a rising traverse to the right. The reliable gneiss of the ridge itself gives intervals of stimulating climbing at grades I and II. There is, however, a better route. The quality of the Fieschergrat, starting from Unter Mönchjoch, is an open secret amongst experienced alpinists. The Walcherhorn (3692m) is a subsidiary summit crossed to gain the corniced crest of the North-West Ridge of the Fiescherhorn, which leads elegantly to the summit in a splendidly exposed position. This ascent is usually no more difficult than the route from the south-east, but it does involve a 50° ice pitch which, when the ice is smooth and hard, calls for perfect cramponing technique and ice screw protection. Moreover, the bergschrund at the Unter Mönchjoch can queer the pitch at the outset. This wonderful ridge provides the ideal prelude to a traverse of the Gross-Fiescherhorn – an excursion rich in adventure, descent being by way of the South-East Ridge. Often the path struck from the Mönchjoch Hut leads up the West Flank to the névé at P.3613, thus missing out the Walcherhorn. However, since the above-mentioned ice pitch still bars the way above this, the Fieschergrat Intégral is still a better proposition. If it's worth doing, it's worth doing properly!

The Lötschentour Ski Descent

For ski-mountaineers, there is the additional attraction of the wonderful 32km Lötschentour, the grandest and most lengthy glacier run in the whole of the Alps (described in the Mönch chapter p31). From Lötschenlücke, the 1500m drop down to Fafleralp follows.

The Ice Routes of the Fiescherwand

The first attempts on the face were recorded by chroniclers as early as 1926. The Berlin climber Kehl, on the rope of the Grindelwald guide Fritz Amatter, pushed the route a good 250m until they were stopped by the slabby, verglassed rocks.

Some time previously, in 1924, the Japanese climber

(right) Climbers approaching the final slopes of the Gross-Fiescherhorn after a traverse of the North-West Ridge.

Yuko Maki, accompanied by Englishmen Frank Smythe and John Percy Farrar, had made a critical appraisal of the face, noting a possible line of ascent by way of the rock spur leading directly up to P.3804 on the North-West Ridge. This was then used by the Swiss pair Walter Amstutz and Peter von Schumacher on their fifteen-hour ascent of the 1000m North Rib on 3 August 1926. Yet the North Rib merely marks the boundary of the actual Fiescherwand and the problem of climbing the face still awaited a solution.

The problem was then taken up by the Munich civil engineer Wilhelm (Willi) Welzenbach, born in 1900 and one of the best-known and experienced alpinists, already famed as an expert on ice faces. Although he had 'a limitless horror of those precipices', the true perpendicular line direct to the top of the Fiescherwand could not be banished from his thoughts. In 1926, however, a disease of the joints put an end to these flights of fancy – he remained in a Swiss clinic until the summer of 1927. It appeared that this crippling illness spelt the end of Welzenbach's climbing, but he slowly worked his way back to fitness and, in 1929, with Heinz Tillmann, he repeated the North Rib in 8½ hours.

A year later, on 5 September 1930, the pair returned to tackle the main part of the face. They started directly below the summit and on the lower part of the face were continually threatened by the two great ice cliffs on the upper face. On the lower rock and mixed section, with Tillmann in the lead, they reeled off rope-length after rope-length, moving steadily forwards, fortified by their long experience of climbing on vicious mixed ground. Nothing disturbed their composure; there was no rush, safety being weighed against haste.

'It was gone midday by the time we reached the end of the rib and stood at the foot of the icefield embedded in the face at this point. Above us, rock and ice loomed up at an impossibly steep angle to dizzy heights. Only to the right did a route through the ring of cliff seem feasible.

'I now went first to relieve Tillmann who had led thus far. . . . We belayed each rope length carefully, gaining ground but slowly. Due to the warm weather, stones began to break off higher up the face and whizzed down the steep slopes past us, vanishing among the cliffs a few rope lengths below.'

During the course of the afternoon it began to snow,

John Allen

Willi Burkhardt

(right) The North-West Ridge of the Gross-Fiescherhorn with the Ewigschneefeld on the right.

yet they pressed on and completed the face after twelve hours of climbing, just as it was growing dark. The Fiescherwand had been climbed.

Welzenbach (describing the route while they descended from the Bergli Hut the following day) observed:

'. . . again we scrutinised its cracks and gullies, its slabby walls and fluted ice. But this time not with the eye of a hunter, endeavouring to discover its secrets, but rather with the eye of a connoisseur, proudly satisfied at having solved the problems of this face.'*

THE HINTER-FIESCHERHORN

Although the Hinter-Fiescherhorn does not rise conspicuously from the ridge which links the Gross-Fiescherhorn to the Gross-Grünhorn, it deserves respect as a four-thousander as several routes, which are wholly unconnected with its bigger brother, converge upon the mountain. Nevertheless its ascent can be easily combined with that of the Gross-Fiescherhorn, either as a two-pronged itinerary from the Fieschersattel, or as part of an extended traverse of the group. The peak is also a very tempting objective for ski-mountaineers.

The first ascent was in 1864 by Edmund von Fellenberg, with guides Peter Inäbnit and Ulrich Kaufmann, who took the present day Normal Route by the Ewigschneefeld and the Fieschersattel. From the summit, the North-West Ridge drops to the col of the Fieschersattel while the South-East Ridge falls away to the Klein-Grünhornlücke. This latter col can also be reached on skis from the Ewigschneefeld but the South-East Ridge is rather more difficult than the usual North-West Ridge route. This also holds true for the South-West Rib which represents a natural line of ascent even though it finishes at P.3891 on the South-East Ridge. This is a route for individualists and is also recommended as a ski tour, the planks being left roughly 100m below the gendarme which is then turned on the left-hand side to gain a notch on the South-East Ridge below the summit formation.

Extreme mountaineers will be attracted to the South-East Face, which offers 800m of mixed climbing.

*From *Weizenbach's Climbs* by Eric Roberts (West Col, 1980).

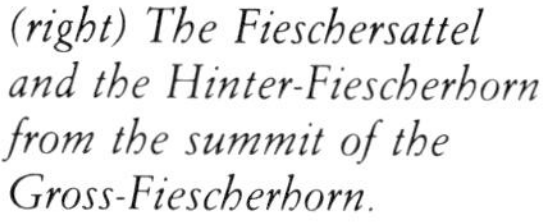
(right) The Fieschersattel and the Hinter-Fiescherhorn from the summit of the Gross-Fiescherhorn.

The Konkordia Huts

During the summer of 1976, the capacity of the upper Konkordia Hut was increased from 36 to 84 beds. This is one of the finest alpine huts, situated in a unique position in the centre of the Bernese Alps. It is not unlike a polar base with extensive glacier views in virtually all directions. Another point of interest for those who wish to stay at the huts is the final climb of 400 steps from Konkordiaplatz, which represents most of the glacial decline during the last 150 years!

Normal Routes on the Hinter-Fiescherhorn

The easiest ascent of the Hinter-Fiescherhorn is by way of the Fieschersattel, with a final 100m hop up the North-West Ridge. For this route the Mönchjoch Hut is the best base but for the South-East Ridge ascent, via the Klein-Grünhornlücke, the Konkordia Huts are more favourably sited. Ski-mountaineers will doubtless decide to mount their 'attack' from the Finsteraarhorn Hut, traversing off to the left before reaching the Fieschersattel and on to the arched névé of the North-East Ridge which, in the right conditions, permits the use of skis right up to the summit. This route can then be used for a 1000m ski descent which, with perfect visibility and trustworthy route-finding, can be made unroped.

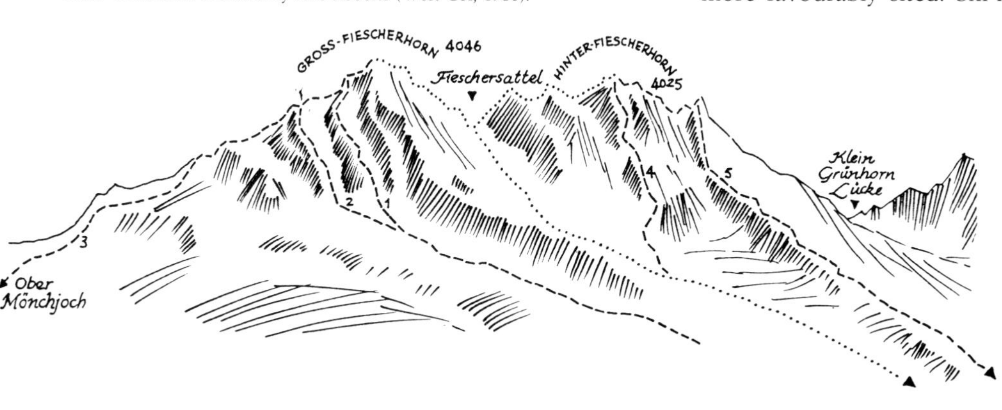

The easiest route (dotted line) gains the Fieschersattel and continues up the South-East Ridge, this also being the easiest route to the Hinter-Fiescherhorn. Other routes marked are, on the Fiescherhorn: the West Face (1), the West Face/North-West Ridge (2), the North-West Ridge intégral (3); and on Hinter-Fiescherhorn: the West Face (4), the South-West Rib (5).

Fiescherhorn Traverse

The noted Austrian mountaineer Ludwig Purtscheller wrote graphically about his traverse of the Fiescherhorn group:

Willi Burkhardt

(left) The upper south-eastern névé basin of the Gross-Fiescherhorn seen from the Finsteraarhorn. The Mönch and the Eiger are in the background with Ochs on the right.

'The panorama which unfolds from the summit of the Gross-Fiescherhorn, the scenic grandeur, the charm and gracefulness of the valley backdrops and the stunning visual contrasts are outshone by hardly any other high peak in the Bernese Alps. Our summit shares with the Jungfrau the same wonderful view of the verdant foot-hills and plateaux; with the Aletschhorn, a similar glimpse into the heart of the Bernese Alps; with the Finsteraar-horn, the same severe Arctic landscape. Most impressive, too, is the view down to Grindelwald, lying 1000m below our feet, meadows bathed in golden sunlight, white-washed houses beckoning like a welcoming wave from some alluring Paradise. The richness and splendour of this canvas can merely be hinted at here. A lengthier sojourn was surely required, yet we stayed for only a short time at the summit, for it was our intention to visit the Hinter-Fiescherhorn also and to make a longer halt there. Thus, after a five-minute pause, we set off again and steered a course for our second objective away across the ridge. Initially, things went tolerably well but, as the way became more heavily corniced and the breaches in the ridge impassable with overhanging masses of snow, we decided to climb down towards the névé slopes on our left, which were admittedly very steep and split by a gaping bergschrund, and then, roughly 100 metres beneath the corniced ridge and keeping to the western edge of the commodious snow depression extending to the Ochs Fiescher-horn, to aim once again for the Hinter-Fiescherhorn above. This was accomplished without any great loss of time, despite the deep, soaking-wet snow, and towards 11 a.m. we stood on the second summit. Of great interest was the retrospective view of the main summit, rising extremely sharply, and sight of the tracks which our foot-steps had inscribed across the ridge and the north-east flank of the mountain.'

VALLEY BASES

Grindelwald see Jungfrau p27.

Berghaus Oberaar 2338m. Private. On the Oberaarsee dam, open July to end of September *tel* 036/ 73 11 15. Winter room (telephone) always open. 6km from Grimsel Pass (traffic via private road (traffic light system).

Fiesch see Aletschhorn p35.

HUTS AND OTHER BASES

Mönchjoch Hut see Mönch p31.

Konkordia Huts see Aletschhorn p35.

Finsteraarhorn Hut 3048m. SAC. On the south-east slope of the Gross-Fiescherhorn above the north-east side of the Fiescher Glacier. 115 places. Staffed from April to mid-September *tel* 036/ 55 29 55. 5 hours from Jungfraujoch via Grünhornlücke (good on skis), 2½ hours from Konkordia via Grünhornlücke. 9 hours from the Grimsel Pass or Berghaus Oberaar via Oberaarjoch Hut (5½ hours). 9 hours from Fiesch, up the heavily-crevassed Fiescher Glacier.

NORMAL ROUTES ON GROSS-FIESCHERHORN

Ewigschneefeld/Fieschersattel/South-East Ridge PD II, I. 5 hours from Mönchjoch or Konkordia. 800mH from Ewigschneefeld. A glacier tour to the col, then mixed climbing. *As a ski tour:* Leave skis at the bergschrund below the Fieschersattel.

Fiescher Glacier/Fieschersattel/South-East Ridge PD II, I. 6 hours from Finsteraarhorn Hut 1050mH. A glacier tour to Fieschersattel, then mixed climbing. *As a ski tour:* Leave skis at the Fieschersattel.

RIDGES AND FACES ON GROSS-FIESCHERHORN

Fieschergrat AD II. To 50°. 3 hours from Unter Mönchjoch. 600mH. Mixed climbing with ice and névé. Cornice dangers.

Ewigschneefeld/North-West Ridge PD+ To 50°. 4½ hours from the Mönchjoch Hut. 650mH from Ewigschneefeld. Névé and glacier.

North Rib TD+ IV, III. 10 hours/1000mH from base of route. A sustained mixed climb.

North Face ED IV, III. To 65° on mixed ground, to 60° on summit icefield. 11 hours/1250m from the base of the route. One of the most difficult and serious north faces in the Alps.

NORMAL ROUTES ON HINTER-FIESCHERHORN

Ewigschneefeld/Fieschersattel/North-West Ridge PD– I. 4 hours from Mönchjoch or Konkordia. 800mH from Ewigschneefeld. A glacier tour to the col, then mixed climbing. *As a ski tour:* Leave skis at the bergschrund below the col.

Fiescher Glacier/North-West Ridge PD To 35°. 5 hours from Finsteraarhorn Hut. A glacier tour.

RIDGES AND FACES

South-East Ridge PD II (sections). 4 hours/850mH from Ewigschneefeld. A glacier tour to the Klein-Grünhornlücke, then mixed climbing.

South-West Rib PD II(sections). 4 hours/600mH from Ewigschneefeld. A glacier tour then mixed climbing.

MAPS AND GUIDEBOOKS

See Mönch p31

John Allen

Gross-Grünhorn *4043 m*

It is the rock – amphibolite, containing green hornblende (amphibole) – which has lent its name to the Grunhörn group, situated on the ridge south of the Fiescherhorn group. The Gross-Grünhorn is the main top between the cols of the Klein-Grünhornlücke and the Grünhornlücke, the ridge being flanked to the west by the snows of the Ewigschneefeld, and to the south and east by the Grüneggfirn and the Fiescher Glacier respectively. At 3860m the Grünegghorn is also worthy of attention; the peak is crossed on the normal route to the Gross-Grünhorn and, furthermore, ranks as a ski-mountaineering excursion of some repute. The Klein-Grünhorn is merely a protuberance on the connecting ridge to the Hinter-Fiescherhorn.

The Gross-Grünhorn is the closest four-thousand metre peak to the Konkordia Huts, yet none of the routes from there can be dismissed as easy: the Normal Route has sections of II and III and the North-West Ridge (the ideal start for a traverse of the mountain), isolated pitches of IV–. Nevertheless, ski-mountaineers, aided by heavy snow cover, can tackle the peak from the Ewigschneefeld, where the glaciers reach almost to the summit of the mountain.

The Normal Route is inconveniently placed for an attempt from the Finsteraarhorn Hut, since the approach to the col at the start of the South-West Ridge is more difficult than from the Konkordia approach. In such circumstances it is best to cross the Grünhornlucke first and pick up the Konkordia approach to the col on the Grüneggfirn. A far better option, if based at the

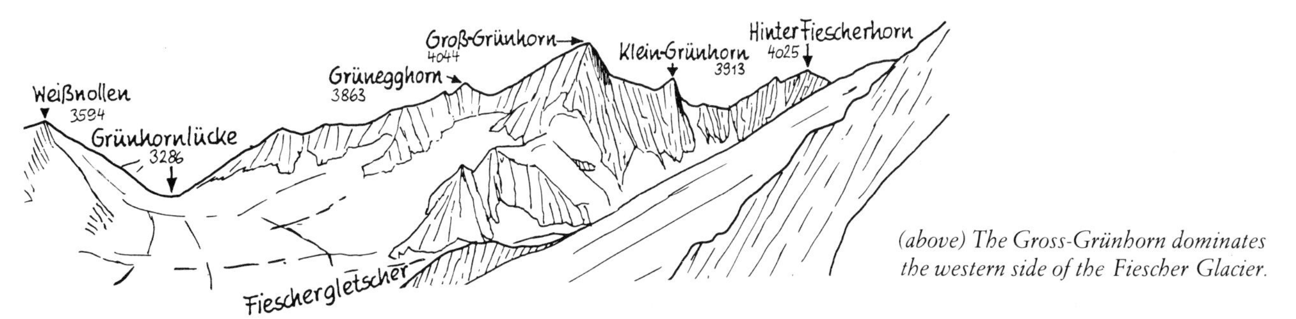

(above) The Gross-Grünhorn dominates the western side of the Fiescher Glacier.

John Allen

John Allen

(above) The Konkordia Huts now stand high above Konkordiaplatz after 150 years of glacial retreat.

Finsteraarhorn Hut (and the rocks are free of snow), is the classic South-East Ridge/South-East Face route. Another option, though considerably harder, is the East Pillar which is comparable in both difficulty and quality to the South Pillar of the Schreckhorn.

From the Konkordia Huts

In earlier days parties climbed the Gross-Grünhorn from the Ewigschneefeld by the West Flank to the saddle at the foot of the South-West Ridge, but the route is complicated by the zone of tortuous crevasses, and endangered by séracs, and nowadays is mainly used by ski-mountaineers operating in more favourable seasons. Even they must contend with the danger from falling blocks of ice on the climb to the saddle.

In summer the best way is by the Grüneggfirn over the Grünegghorn, though here the névé slope to the south-west spine of the Grünegghorn is angled at some-

John Allen

(right) Descending the western slopes of the Gross-Grünhorn towards the Ewigschneefeld and Konkordiaplatz.

(left) The East Face of the Gross-Grünhorn forms a tempting objective when seen from the Finsteraarhorn Hut.

thing approaching 50° and gives a spicy rising traverse. A rock ridge leads from the west top (3787m) to the main summit of the Grünegghorn, 70m higher. The descent to the col before the final rise to the Gross-Grünhorn is also rocky and the South-West Ridge provides 250m of rock climbing as a finale, where it is best to keep slightly to the left of the ridge line.

The History of the Gross-Grünhorn

On 7 August 1865, the Bernese mineralogist and expert on the Bernese Alps, Edmund von Fellenberg, and his guides, Peter Egger, Peter Michel and Peter Inäbnit, reached the summit in very bad weather, by a route from the Ewigschneefeld. In those days, with the glaciers deeper and with generally heavier snow conditions, this route may well have been easier than today's much-crevassed version. Their attempt the previous year, by the Grüneggfirn, had stopped at P.3810 on the Grünegghorn where they built a cairn (the final few metres of that peak being completed in 1903 by Gustav Hasler and R. Bernet). The second ascent was made in 1886 by W.A.B. Coolidge with Christian and Rudolf Almer (sons of the great guide), and the third by a party led by the German Gustav Euringer in August 1893 – both repeats following the Ewigschneefeld approach.

During the following years, those seeking new ground concentrated their efforts on the ridges. On 26 August 1913, Baron Dietrich von Bethmann-Hollweg, accompanied by the Valais men Oskar and Othmar Supersaxo, made the noteworthy first ascent of the South-East Ridge/South-East Face route. A later party achieved a route on the right-hand section of the North-East Face. The West Face fell to the Dutchman Ger von der Leck in 1958 and on 27 August 1967 the Swiss Christoph Blum and Ueli Frei climbed the East Pillar, which is described by experts as 'one of the most beautiful high-alpine rock routes of the Bernese Alps'.

The history book of the Gross-Grünhorn does not close with this event. Interesting chapters are still to be written – North-East and South-East faces still (1993) await ascents. The 'last great problem' is the 700m North-East Face, whose lower two-thirds feature steep mixed ground (average angle 60°) capped, in the upper section, by a band of cliffs. The South-East Face Direct is more than 500m high, but appears less difficult.

Rudolf Rother

(above) The Gross-Grünhorn from the Gross-Fiescherhorn.

Gross-Grünhorn, with the Normal Route (dotted line) via the Grünegghorn with the North-West Ridge (1)

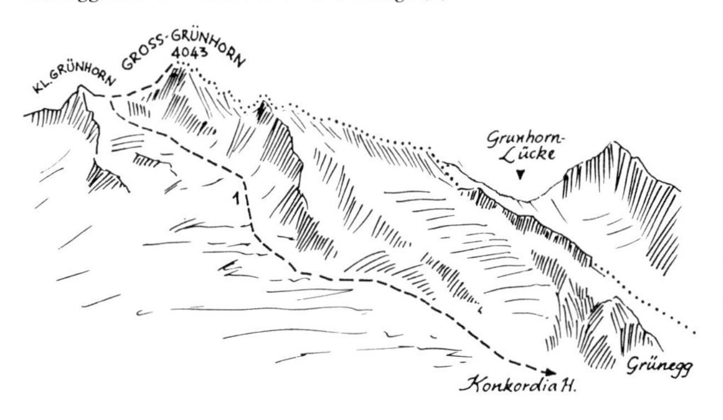

VALLEY BASES
Grindelwald see Mönch p31
Berghaus Oberaar/Fiesch see Fiescherhorn p46

HUTS AND OTHER BASES
Mönchjoch Hut see Mönch p31
Konkordia Huts see Aletschhorn p35
Finsteraarhorn Hut see Fiescherhorn p46

NORMAL ROUTE
Gruneggborn/South-West Ridge PD+ III– (one pitch), II and easier. To 45° with one section at 50°. 6 hours from the Konkordia Huts. 1300mH. A glacier tour, then mixed and rock. *As a ski tour:* from Konkordia, follow the east side of the Ewigschneefeld to the craggy South-West Spur (P.3135) of the Grünegghorn. Turn sharp left shortly before this and then trend rightwards (north-east) across the heavily crevassed glacier until beneath the western precipices of the mountain. From here, bear south-east up two steep slopes to the col on the South-West Ridge. Deposit skis here. Climb the ridge to the summit. 7 hours from Konkordia.

RIDGES AND FACES
North-West Ridge AD IV– (sections), III. 7 hours from Konkordia. 1300mH. A glacier approach, then rock and mixed climbing.
South-East Ridge/South-East Face AD III. 5 hours from the Finsteraarhorn Hut. 1000H. Mixed climbing then rock.
East Pillar D V– (10m pitch), VI+, III. 8 hours from the Finsteraarhorn Huts. 650mH from foot of face. An alpine rock climb.

MAPS/GUIDEBOOKS
See Mönch p31.

Finsteraarhorn *4273 m*

Hemmed in by the Fiescher Glacier, the snows of the Studerfirn and the Finsteraar Glacier, there soars the cruciform hornblende and gneiss framework of the highest Bernese peak. It is the purity of line of the Finsteraarhorn which is its finest characteristic; a keenly angular north-facing cone that provides a visage to inspire the most jaded Alpinist. From the western prospect, viewed from the vicinity of the Gross-Grünhorn, it appears as an elongated arête, comprising the North-West and South-East Ridges. On this side the névé claws high at the mountain's flanks, allowing climbers obvious ascent routes from the strategically situated Finsteraarhorn Hut located above the Fiescher Glacier. The Normal Route from here, combining the South-West Face and the upper North-West Ridge, is a feasible route for an ascent with skis where it often possible to reach the Hugisattel (4100m) thus allowing a 1000m ski descent back to the Finsteraarhorn Hut. The Normal Route continues from the Hugisattel, climbing the uppermost rise of the airy and delightful North-West Ridge.

The intégral ascent of the North-West Ridge is a long but worthwhile expedition for more experienced mountaineers. It is the most logical route from Grindelwald using the Schreckhorn Hut, but this way involves a long and quite serious ascent to gain the crest at the Agassizjoch from where the stepped ridge rises impressively to the summit.

The South-East Ridge

This is the longest ridge on a Bernese four-thousander, measuring 2½ kilometres from the Gemslücke, although only the last third is generally climbed (this being reached from the Finsteraarhorn Hut) from the cleft above the Third Tower. Above this the main difficulties are 'The Slab', only a few metres high but sparsely furnished with holds (fixed rope often in place) followed by a 12m chimney pitch.

First Ascent Controversy

The disputed first ascent of the mountain was by the South-East Ridge (reached by a mixed rib from the Studerfirn) on 16 August 1812 by Arnold Abbühl, Joseph Bortes and Aloys Volker, guides of Johann Rudolf Meyer, scion of the wealthy Meyer family of Aurau, and at that time a twenty-year old student at Tübingen University. Meyer's father had taken part in the Jungfrau ascent of the previous year. When the four gained the ridge, Meyer, who was exhausted, remained behind while his guides advanced. Later the first ascent was claimed.

Jim Teesdale

(right) Above the Hugisattel on the final section of the North-West Ridge of the Finsteraarhorn.

To many the name of the glaciologist Franz Joseph Hugi will always be linked with the first ascent of Finsteraarhorn (just like de Saussure and Mont Blanc), and the 'Hugisattel' is now an official geographical feature. The saddle was first reached in 1828 by Hugi and his guides Christian Lauener, Arnold Dändler, Arnold Abbühl, Jakob Leuthold and Johann Währen, but the party retreated from the final ridge in the face of bad weather and a cornice incident. On 10 August 1829, Hugi returned with Leuthold and Währen, who pushed the route up the North-West Ridge to the top, while Hugi and others remained slightly below. In 1828 Hugi had taken the opportunity to question Abbühl about the 1812 ascent but had found him vague and unconvincing and, when his guides apparently found no sign of an earlier ascent on the summit, Hugi formally contested Meyer's claim. There followed one of the most protracted controversies in alpine history. The matter was eventually argued out in great detail in 1913 in an article by John Percy Farrar in the *Alpine Journal** in which he concluded that Meyer's claim was false, but innocently so, and that the guides had probably reached a high shoulder of the ridge, turning back well short of the summit. Farrar pointed out that this alone would have been an outstanding climb for the period, especially on a first attempt.

Thus the first ascent belongs to Hugi's party from which Leuthold emerges as the driving force – 'able, intrepid and very intelligent' according to a later employer.

The 1828 attempt was not without its drama as Hugi described in his book *Naturhistorische Alpenreise*: 'Arnold Dändler was just in front of me, with a long pole which he held out over the crest of the ridge. As he was pulling himself thus across the declivity, he lost his footing. At one jump I grabbed the other end of the pole, whereupon the snow beneath me broke asunder. Barely two feet thick, it had been blown by the wind across the

**A.J.* XXVII, pp263-300. The article 'The First Ascent of the Finsteraarhorn; A Re-examination' is a masterpiece of mountaineering analysis with every aspect of the controversy examined in detail by a man with an intimate knowledge of the mountain.

invisible crest of the rocks to form a five or six feet wide build up on the other side. And there I was, more than four thousand feet up, hanging free from the pole almost vertically above the Finsteraar Glacier, whilst Dändler dangled out over the snow cliffs on the other side. Had our fragile see-saw broken, Dändler would have flown unchecked across the snow and down to the Vieschermeer to the west while I would have fallen eastwards to the Aarmeer. The opening in which I was hanging grew larger and I was able to examine the snow crust, perched in mid-air, and through the hole see the Finsteraar Glacier'.

Difficult Climbing above Four Thousand Metres

The additional attraction of the Normal Route lies in the fact that new peaks keep appearing the higher one climbs. First pause for breath at the Breakfast Ledge, 3616m, a notch on the ridge. To the south-west, across the col of the Grünhornlücke, the Aletschhorn can be seen. The Pennine Alps and Mont Blanc come into view. Beyond the Fiescher Glacier, the East Pillar of the Gross-Grünhorn thrusts upwards.

From the Finsteraarhorn Hut the summit is best reached via the Hugisattel and the North-West Ridge (dotted line).

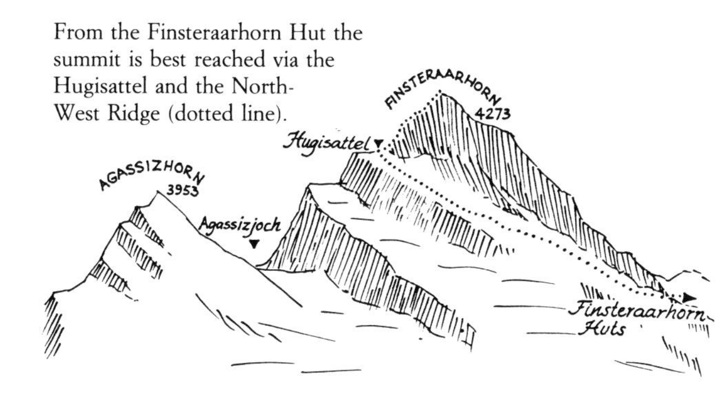

John Allen

(above) The Finsteraarhorn seen across the Fiescher Glacier from the summit of the Gross Fiescherhorn.

In heavy traffic it is worth considering making direct for the summit from the Breakfast Ledge, following the South-West Ridge. This can also be reached by a traverse from 3900m, a little higher on the route.

The Normal Route itself traces a path across the glacier to the north of the South-West Ridge and climbs to the Hugisattel (beware of lurking crevasses!). From the saddle there is a fine view across to the Schreckhorn and the Lauteraarhorn. The final two hundred metres of the North-West Ridge to the summit is airy in places and gives technical climbing (initially on the right) where, when the rocks are verglassed, parties are sometimes forced to retreat.

The North Face Era

The age of North Face climbing began in the Bernese Alps on 16 July 1904 when Gustav Hasler, from Berne, and his skilful guide Fritz Amatter made their ascent of the 1000m North-East Rib of the Finsteraarhorn to produce the most difficult route on the mountain. Accounts of this, earlier attempts and later ascents, reveal a route of great seriousness and difficulty and together they constitute a stirring (yet little known) saga, comparable to the annals of any of the great alpine north faces. The resulting notoriety of the face no doubt ensured unpopu-

John Allen

(left) The Finsteraarhorn towers above the Studerhorn when seen from the Oberaarhorn to the east. The South-East Ridge, originally tackled by the Meyer party, is on the left.

VALLEY BASES

Berghaus Oberaar and *Fiesch* see Fiescherhorn p46

HUTS AND OTHER BASES

Finsteraarhorn Hut see Fiescherhorn p46

Oberaarjoch Hut 3285m. SAC. Just above the Oberaarjoch. 45 places. Staffed at weekends in the summer *tel* 036/ 73 13 82. 5 hours from Berghaus Oberaar.

Aar Bivouac see Lauteraarhorn p39

NORMAL ROUTE

South-West Flank/North-West Ridge PD– II, I. 5 hours/1250mH from the Finsteraarhorn Hut. A glacier tour to the Hugisattel, then snow and rock. *As a ski tour:* Ignore the col at P.3231 and follow the arm of the glacier north of the hut to pick up the Normal Route and the ascent to the Hugisattel (ski depot).

RIDGES AND FACES

South-West Ridge PD II. 5 hours from the Finsteraarhorn Hut. 1250mH. Mixed climbing.

North-West (Agassiz) Ridge PD+ II. 7 hours/1250mH from the Finsteraarhorn Hut via the Agassizjoch at 3751m. 11 hours from Schreckhorn Hut. Glacier approaches, then mixed climbing.

South-East Ridge PD+ III. To 50°. Intégral – 11 hours from the Oberaarhorn Hut via the Gemslücke. 6 hours from Finsteraarhorn Hut by way of the notch after the third tower.

East Rib D+ IV+ (sections), IV and III. 10 hours/850mH from base of the route (2hrs from Oberaarjoch Hut). The finest rock climbing on the Finsteraarhorn.

North-East Rib TD+ V and VI– (on the Grey Tower), otherwise IV (on either by-pass) and III. 12 hours/1000mH from the bergschrund. Sustained mixed climbing on loose and frequently verglassed rock. One of the most difficult and dangerous routes in the Bernese Alps.

MAPS/GUIDEBOOKS

See Mönch p31

larity (with only eleven ascents recorded to 1977), but in those early years of the century it was one of the most coveted 'last great problems', of the Alps.

The first party to make a determined attempt was that of Gertrude Bell with Ulrich and Heinrich Führer. Bell, then aged thirty-four, was a noted Arabist and archaeologist of whom a sheikh remarked 'If this is one of their women? Allah, what must their men be like?' On the Finsteraarhorn their attempt ended at 4000m, high on the face at the Grey Tower, where bad weather forced a bivouac and then a dramatic retreat.

The Hasler and Amatter ascent two years later proved no less eventful.

'I don't know what Amatter felt like when [on reaching the Grey Tower] we first took stock of the situation, but I think we both made simultaneous use of the same word and then relapsed into silence. Perpendicular and monstrously smooth, there was no question of a frontal attack on that obstacle . . . I felt for a moment that there was nothing for it but inglorious retreat over the most repellent ground.'

Eventually they turned the obstacle on the left and fought their way to the top (Amatter making some heroic leads) over very tricky mixed ground. In 1906 the second ascent by H. Bruderlin and Valere A. Fynn, was even more dramatic as Hasler reported in the paper he read to the Alpine Club in 1922†:

'They seem to have heard and seen a good many serious stonefalls . . . a direct hit or two being registered.'

Stonefall was again a concern on the third ascent on 3 September 1930 by the charismatic American Miriam O'Brien, with her regular guide Adolf Rubi and his brother Fritz, an epic ascent described in a dramatic chapter in O'Brien's classic book *Give Me the Hills*§:

'Then down the gully came another fall of stones. Flattening myself against the slope I threw my rucksack and my arms above my head, and just waited . . . although a great many stones hit me, they all seemed to be small ones and they had not fallen very far. Then a shout came from Adolf above, Stones are falling! A keen fear swept over me, that now there were big ones coming too . . .'

In late season the ice conditions were very severe and at the Grey Tower Rubi was forced into a desperate outflanking manoeuvre to the right ('for over 100m . . . I was just flirting with death'), and as the others followed, Fritz (carrying two sacks) had a serious penduluming fall which Miriam held (unbelayed and with just a rope twist round her arm) precariously supported from above by Adolf. The Grey Tower was eventually climbed direct in 1967 by the Poles Kazimierz Glazek and Krystzof Zdzitowiecki and the route was climbed in winter in 1970 by the Swiss trio of Paul Etter, Ueli Gantenbein and E. Scherrer.

†*A.J.* XXXIV pp268-280 §Methuen, London, 1956

(right) An aerial view of the East and North-East Faces of the Finsteraarhorn.

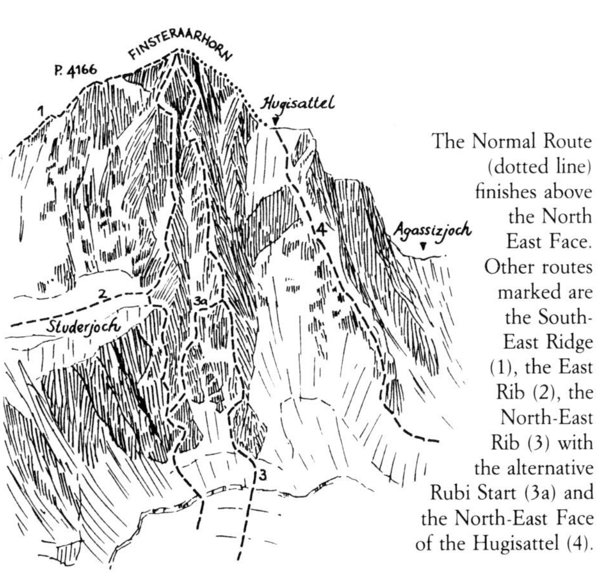

The Normal Route (dotted line) finishes above the North East Face. Other routes marked are the South-East Ridge (1), the East Rib (2), the North-East Rib (3) with the alternative Rubi Start (3a) and the North-East Face of the Hugisattel (4).

Willi Burkhardt

The Pennine Alps and

The Swiss Canton Valais with its regional capital, Sion, encompasses not only large sections of the Bernese Alps to the north-west of the Rhône Valley, but also the greater part of the Pennine Alps range (Les Alpes Valaisannes/ Die Wallisen Alpen), stretching south-east from the Rhône Valley to frontier crest and beyond well into Italy. The rock here is gneiss and mica-schist. In the north-east the range is split off from the Lepontine Alps by the great trench of the Simplon, and in the south the Aosta Valley in Italy separates it from the Graian Alps and the Gran Paradiso, while its south-western satellite peaks border on the Mont Blanc group.

The splendour of the ice-clad peaks of the Pennine Alps soon becomes apparent as one approaches from the long sweep of the Rhône Valley, on whose sun-pampered slopes the vineyards flourish and where the local people have retained much of their unaffected and candid manner, where taciturn and gnarled old farmers, their roots buried deep in their native soil, tend proud farmsteads perched high on the hillsides. From the Rhône Valley, several valleys branch off southwards to the mountaineers, resorts of Saas Fee, Zermatt, Zinal, Les Haudères and Arolla. It is a similar picture on the Italian side of the mountain chain, where the valley bases are Vaud, Lago di Place Moulin, Breuil, Saint Giacomo, Gressoney, Alagna and Macugnaga. Lying between the Mattertal and Zinaltal, the Weisshorn/ Dent Blanche group inspires one to great things, with the clean, keen lines of its high peaks and its forbiddingly steep face routes, while the Weissmies range soaring between the Simplon and Saastal makes a rather more easy-going and sociable impression. In between these

the Monte Rosa Group

two chains, sandwiched between the Mattertal and Saastal lies the Mischabel group, made up of sharp razor-edged peaks in the north and broad, bulky massifs further south, all defended by crevasse-pitted glaciers. But it is in the Matterhorn and Monte Rosa group that the Pennine Alps achieve their crowning glory – glittering diamonds in a diadem of precious stones. Compared to the Matterhorn with its inimitable contours, Monte Rosa dazzles and captivates by its sheer size and presence, surpassed in the Alps by Mont Blanc alone.

West of the Matterhorn, beyond its scarcely less imposing satellite, the Dent d'Hérens, stands the isolated mass of the Grand Combin, huge and white-cloaked, forming with its satellite peaks a constellation of its own. Beyond lies the Mont Blanc group, linked to the Pennine Alps in winter and summer by a chain of glacier highways that provide the spectacularly scenic Haute Route from Chamonix to Saas Fee.

The Valais people have laboured assiduously to open up their mountains for the pursuit of winter sports, with networks of ski-lifts, mountain railways and téléphériques. But the natural landscape has had to foot the bill with swathes of mountainside at the heads of Saastal and Mattertal criss-crossed with cableways. Artificial climbing aids have,thankfully, been only inconsistently used, restricted to difficult sections on the most popular peaks, notably the Matterhorn. The cableways and railways ease access to the mountains, removing the need for many a punishing hut walk, but it is nevertheless to be hoped that these dubious developments will soon end, for it would be a great pity if those remaining corners of Paradise were to fall victim to the interests of business and guiding.

(previous page) The Pennine Alps seen from the Eggishorn above Fiesch, with the Lagginhorn group (left), the Mischabel group (centre) and the Weisshorn (right). The Monte Rosa group and the Matterhorn are prominent beyond the nearer massifs. Photo: Willi Burkhardt

Lagginhorn *4010 m*

The Lagginhorn, in the middle of the Weissmies/ Fletschhorn chain, rises from the frozen breakers and icy trenches of four glaciers. Towards the Fletschhorn (3993m), which was shown on some maps as a four-thousander until 1951, the Fletschjoch marks the northern-most boundary while to the south the Lagginjoch divides the mountain from the Weissmies. The squat, thickset profile of this, the most northerly of the four-thousanders in the Pennine Alps, consists for the most part of rather unkempt rock, with a few nondescript snowfields clinging to its flanks.

As late as 1886 the peak was described as one of the 'Fletscherhorner' but eventually the southern 'horn' was acknowledged as the Lagginhorn. Confusion also reigned over the height of the peak which in the last century was given as 3917m until the map produced by the Swiss Alpine Club put it at 4016m.

The eastern side of the Lagginhorn facing Laggintal attracts little attention, but the western approach from the Weissmies Hut above the populous Saastal is more favoured and it is from here, along the West Ridge, that the summit is most frequently climbed. This is the easiest route to the top and it can also be comfortably reached from the top station of the Hohsaas cableway from Saas Grund. The strategic position of the Hohsaas cableway also means that a traverse of the mountain, starting with an ascent of the South Ridge, becomes a viable, and worthwhile, alternative.

The North-East Ridge, above the Fletschjoch which is guarded by ice cliffs on both sides, is only really worthwhile when climbed as part of the traverse from the Fletschhorn – a longer trip but still very worthwhile.

The Approach from the East

On the east side shelter is provided by the Laggin Bivouac Hut. The original refuge was a lightweight metal construction and stood about 300m higher than today's hut, at the lower end of the South-East Ridge (Hohsassgrat) of the Fletschhorn. The four-hour trek up to the hut has the advantage of providing views of a little-frequented corner of the alps. From Simplon Dorf an ancient bridle-path is followed, past the wayside shrine of Antonius and a cross above the slopes of the Goldwen and across the desolate high pastures of Hohsass to the south-east flanks of the Laggintal. Where the track is indistinct, cairns mark the route. The gaze wanders across a lonely and charismatic landscape: to the south-west, across the Simplon Pass, the icefields of Monte Leone and the Gondo Gorge.

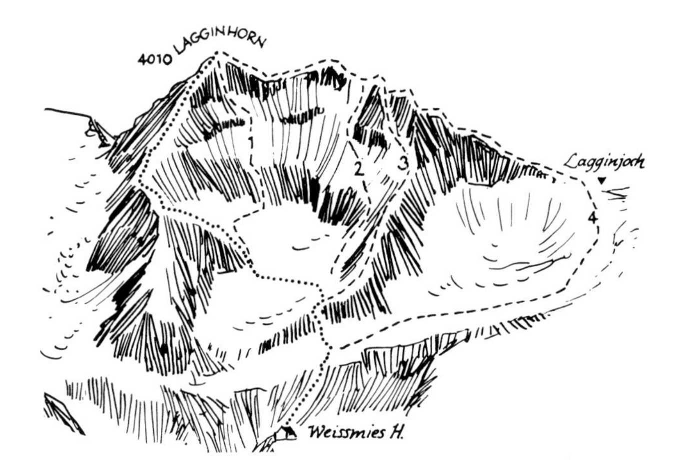

The Normal Route up the West Ridge (dotted line) with the West Face (1), West Face/South Ridge (2), South-West Rib (3) and South Ridge (4).

Willi Burkhardt

Willi Burkhardt

(above) A winter aerial view of the East Faces of the Lagginhorn and the Fletschhorn. The South-East Ridge of the Fletschhorn runs diagonally across the picture from the left.

Further to the right the Zwischenbergtal is one of the magical high mountain valleys of Switzerland, lost to the outside world.

Above the new Laggin Bivouac Hut it is possible to gain access to the East Spur of the Lagginhorn. Close to the site of the old hut cables safeguard a 100m down-climb to the moraines of the Hohlentrift Glacier. The spur itself is 400m high. It provides a quiet and peaceful ascent of the peak, though here and there the rock is a bit loose. An alternative might be an ascent of the more solid, and generally more worthwhile, South-East Ridge of the Fletschhorn (AD, II/III) and to continue via the Fletschjoch to gain the summit of the Lagginhorn by the North-East Ridge.

The West Ridge

On promising summer days, the custodian of the Weissmies Hut usually counts on up to fifty Lagginhorn aspirants, not including those who join them from Hohsaas. The West Ridge becomes defined at an altitude of 3420m

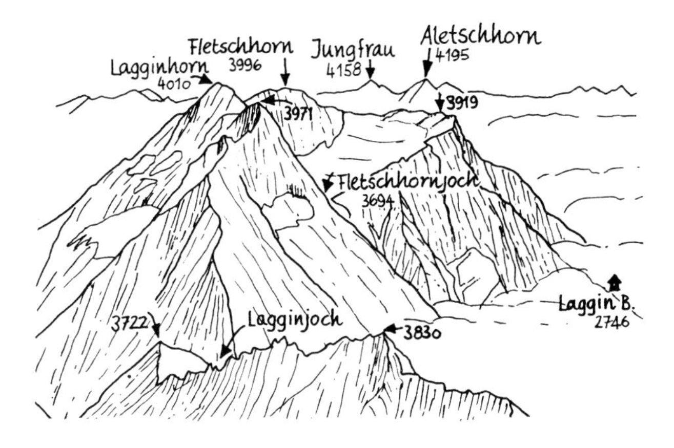

VALLEY BASES

Saas Grund 1559m. Formerly the major centre and parochial village of the valley. 21km from Visp (Rhône Valley), and 14km from Stalden (nearest railway station). Post Bus service. Hotels, inns, pensions.

Simplon Dorf 1472m. 10km south of the Simplon Pass, 32km from Brig (Rhône Valley) and Domodossola (Italy). Hotels, inns, pensions. Post Bus service.

HUTS/OTHER BASES

Weissmies Hut 2726m. SAC. On a terrace on the medial moraines of the Hohlaub Glacier. 124 places. Staffed from mid-June to end-September *tel* 028/ 57 25 54. ¾ hour from the Kreuzbodenalp station (2400m) of the Saas Grund/Hohsaas cableway. 3¼ hours from Saas Grund via Kreuzbodenalp.

Berghaus Hohsaas 3100m. Private. South-west of the Lagginhorn on Hohsaas. 36 places. Staffed from 20 June to 10 October *tel* 028/ 57 18 22. Near the top station of the Saas Grund/Hohsaas cableway (first lift 7 a.m.).

Laggin Bivouac Hut 2450m. SAC. On the moraines between the Hohlentrift and Sibilifluh Glaciers. 10 places. Open all year. 4 hours from Simplon Dorf.

NORMAL ROUTE

West Ridge PD II. 5 hours from the Weissmies Hut (slightly less from Hohsaas). 1280mH. Mixed climbing.

RIDGES/FACES

South Ridge AD III, II. 4 hours/500mH from the Lagginjoch (3495m) (1 hour from Hohsaas, 2¼ hours from the Weissmies Hut). Mixed ground with loose rock on the lower part, more solid higher up.
North Ridge AD– III, II. 1½ hours/300mH from the Fletschjoch.
South-West Rib AD II. 4 hours/800mH from start of route.
West Face D III, II. To 50°. 6 hours/550mH from the start of the route. Mixed climbing and ice work. Stonefall danger.
East Spur AD II. 7 hours from Laggin Bivouac Hut. 1700mH. Mixed climbing on friable rock.

MAPS/GUIDEBOOKS

Landeskarte der Schweiz 1:50,000 Sheet 5006 *Matterhorn – Mischabel. Pennine Alps East* by Robin Collomb (Alpine Club). *The Alpine 4000m Peaks by the Classic Routes* by Richard Goedeke (Diadem/Menasha).

above the basin of the Laggin Glacier. On the craggy terrain leading up to the ridge, stones dislodged by one of those in front occasionally come crashing down, but when the ridge itself is gained these dangers are removed and, in snow free conditions, one can enjoy entertaining climbing on its compact, blocky rock. Further up is the mixed ground of the blunt snowy arête (sometimes with patches of ice), which grows steadily steeper as one gains height. The final climb to the summit follows a giant's staircase of gneiss.

The Clergyman of Saas

Although the Lagginhorn is among the lowliest and easiest of the four-thousanders, it was climbed for the first time at a relatively late date, possibly as a result of the forbidding rocky appearance (at a time when snow was preferred) of the Saas flank. It was this, however, which evidently fascinated the Saas Grund clergyman, Johann Joseph Imseng. The Abbé had the reputation of being something of an eccentric and many considered it unseemly for a man of God to be running around the mountains clad in his cassock and armed with a long stick. Yet Imseng remained untroubled by the gossip-mongers, and nowadays, in the village square of Saas Fee, he is honoured by a statue, both as a mountaineer and, perhaps more important in local eyes, as a pioneer of tourism. For it was this man of the cloth who suggested the peak to the first tourists – chiefly Englishmen and Swiss-Germans from Zürich, Basle and Berne – and indeed conducted a tourist party on its first ascent.

Imseng enlisted the help of his manservant Franz Joseph Andenmatten, and three other guides, to assist the party of the barrister Edward Levi Ames and three other Englishmen. At 3 a.m. on 26 August 1856 this nine-strong team set out from Triftalp for the Lagginhorn. They followed the valley upwards to the plinth of the West Ridge. Here the climbing began. For a good four hours they scrambled up cliffs of gneiss, mixed with splinters of glistening slate towards the summit, until triumphantly they gained the top. Little did they realise that they had ascended a four-thousand metre peak. In those days the neighbouring Fletschhorn hogged the limelight as it was still a member of the hallowed circle of four-thousand-metre peaks, a situation which Saas Grund community would dearly like to re-establish. In 1988 it was decreed that: 'The rocks which are in such abundance on the summit are to be piled up gradually, over several years . . . until they reach a height of 4001 metres.'

(below) A view from the Weissmies to the Lagginhorn with the Fletschhorn and the peaks of the Bernese Alps beyond.

John Allen

Weissmies *4023m*

The finest and highest mountain east of the Saastal marks the culminating point of the north-south chain of gneiss peaks which stretches from the Fletschhorn across the Lagginhorn to the Portjengrat. Long, inclined ridges have moulded the summit region into a regular pyramidal shape – the ideal blueprint for a coveted four-thousander. The ascent is made easier because the approach from the Saas side has been markedly shortened by the Saas Grund cableway which reaches up to the 3100-metre level.

In contrast to the craggy eastern aspect above the upper reaches of the Laggintal, the Saastal flank is heavily glaciated with several ice-clad precipices and the whole massif is guarded by an armoury of three glaciers: the Trift Glacier to the west, the Rottal Glacier to the south and the Weissmies Glacier to the east. In addition to its other attractions, a widely-renowned panoramic view from the summit has contributed to the mountain's popularity. It is said that on clear days one can even make out the pinnacles of Milan Cathedral and some of the lakes of Northern Italy.

A Convenient Normal Route

Ascents of the Weissmies, making use of the Hohsaas station at the top of the cableway, are generally one-day excursions from the valley, and it is also a viable ski-mountaineering objective. With less than 1000m of climbing over about two kilometres from the Hohsaas station to the summit, it has statistics which could just as easily apply to some modest Eastern Alps two-thousander. On the Weissmies, however, one has to contend with glaciers above the 3300m mark.

The usual summer and winter route runs from the Trift Glacier, through an ice-fall, and on up to the South-West Ridge (Triftgrat). If the névé is well consolidated and the bergschrund easily negotiated those who enjoy cramponing might opt to bear half-left at the flat section of the Trift Glacier and tackle the summit up the 45-50° slopes of the 600-metre West Face. The easy way joins the South-West Ridge at a snow depression to the left of the snow dome of P.3816 after just two hours of climbing from Hohsaas. The continuation is along the Triftgrat. Crevasses are occasionally in evidence, with cornices to the right, but with care there are no real problems.

(left) The South Face of the Weissmies rises above Almagellertal. The Normal Route ascends the Trift Glacier on the left, its lower section a complicated ice-fall (right).

The North Ridge

The most exciting Weissmies route leads up the 2.5 kilometre North Ridge of the mountain, first climbed in 1884 by W.H. and Miss E. Paine with Theodor Andenmatten and the owner of the Monte Moro Hotel in Saas Grund, Johann Peter Zurbriggen.

If this is approached from the Weissmies Hut, very careful scrutiny is needed to pinpoint the line to the Lagginjoch (a caveat that equally applies when heading for the South Ridge of the Lagginhorn). The ridge provides a classic route, initially on a succession of small rock pitches of only an average solidity. The crux is the 15m Grande Dalle (Big Slab), which requires grade IV free-climbing with two pitons for protection. Once one has got used to the style of climbing, the North Ridge will provide an unforgettable experience. It is a long climb – four hours is a fast time from the Lagginjoch and an ascent in six is still very respectable. The top part of the ridge is on snow which is often spectacularly corniced over the East Face.

From the South

The network of lifts on the western side has pushed the formerly traditional and comparatively safe route from the south into relative obscurity. For this, a night is usually spent at the Almageller Hut. On the following morning the first stop is the Zwischbergen Pass (3267m),

Jim Teesdale

John Allen

(left) The view south-west to the Mischabel group from the summit of the Weissmies with climbers on the final part of the Normal Route.

from where there are fine views to the Monte Rosa massif. Tracks often point the way from the pass over the snow to the South-East Face, which is climbed via a steep (40°) gully to the rocky staircase of the South-East Ridge. After the snow shoulder of P.3961, a further half-hour's climb along the narrow snow arête leads to the enticing main objective.

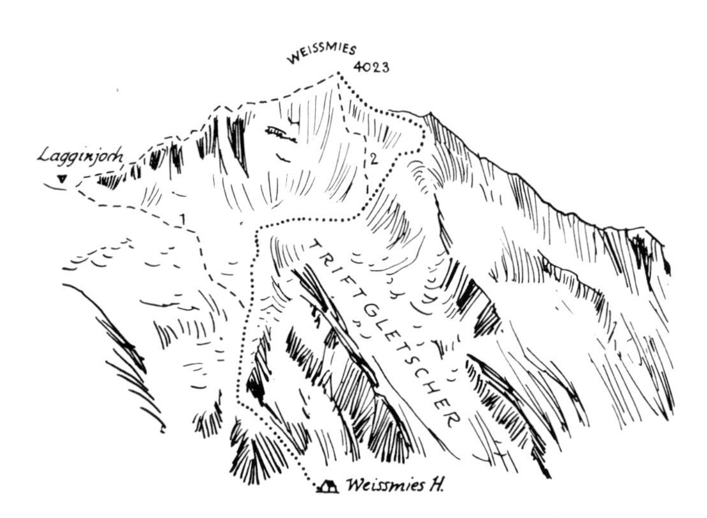

The Weissmies with the Normal Route (dotted line), West Face (2) and North Ridge (1).

The First Ascensionist – a Notary Public

The first ascent of the mountain was made from the Almageller side in 1855, but the climb was soon shrouded in controversy. The local guides were initially very sceptical, for it had been two 'foreigners' who had first set foot on the summit by way of the Triftgrat. True, Peter Joseph Zurbriggen did hail from the Valais but he was a solicitor by profession and, therefore, in the opinion of the guides who – even in those days – were a conceited bunch, was not equipped to climb such a mountain without having one of them along. The same applied to Zurbriggen's companion, the Zürich mountaineer Jakob Christian Häusser. Consumed with jealousy and suspicion, the sceptics went up to the Almageller Alp and retraced the footsteps of the two men, only to discover that they had indeed reached the highest point.

Other Climbs

Twenty-two years later the loose and dangerous East Face was climbed by Mr and Mrs E.P. Jackson and J.A. Peebles with guides Peter Schlegel, Ulrich Rubi and Jean Martin.

In the same idiom but even more unpleasant was the 1884 ascent of the 500m South Face. Amid the crashing and cracking of stonefall, Claude and Herbert Wilson, with the guides Aloys Burgener and Josef Furrer, fought their way up on to the upper part of the South-West Ridge. The ascent of the North Ridge two weeks later marked a much more worthwhile discovery – involving some difficult rock climbing led by the hotelier Zurbriggen in the days before pitons were available.

The most recent route is the Via Andrea, climbed on 10 August 1986 by the German team of Jürgen Straub and Hans Rotwangl who forced a direct line up the 680m North-West Face to the left of the 1971 Vanis route. Vertical in places, it contains pitches of III to IV and has considerable objective dangers.

VALLEY BASES

Saas Grund see Lagginhorn p59

Saas Almagell 1673m. In Saastal 4km south of Saas Grund on. Post Bus service. Hotels, inns, pensions.

HUTS/OTHER BASES

Berghaus Hohsaas/Weissmies Hut see Lagginhorn p59

Almageller Hut 2860m. SAC. South-west of the Weissmies below the rocky spur of the Dri Horlini. 100 places. Staffed from beginning July to end September *tel* 028/ 57 11 79. 4 hours from Saas Almagell via the Almagelleralp Hotel (overnight accommodation) at 2194 metres.

NORMAL ROUTE

Trift Glacier/South-West Ridge PD To 40°. 4 hours from Hohsaas. 1050mH. A glacier climb with some crevasse danger. *As a ski tour:* As for the normal route though the steep section is sometimes only possible on foot.

RIDGES/FACES

North Ridge AD IV (one pitch), III, II. 5 hours/530mH from the Lagginjoch (1 hour from Hohsaas, 2 hours from the Weissmies Hut). A rock and mixed ridge, followed by snow and ice. Cornice danger.

South-East Ridge F I+. To 40°. 4 hours from the Almageller Hut. 1170mH. A snow slope (some stonefall danger) then mixed climbing.

South Face D IV, III. 5 hours. 500mH from the foot of the face. Mixed climbing with vertical ice to finish.

MAPS/GUIDEBOOKS

See Lagginhorn p59

Lenzspitze *4294 m*

The five-kilometre chain of the Mischabel group of eight four-thousand metre peaks separates great valleys of Mattertal and Saastal. The chain stretches from the Alphubel in the south, across the Täschhorn, Dom, and then over the five summits of the Nadelgrat to the Galenjoch in the north.

The Lenzspitze, rising between the Dom and the Nadelhorn, is the most easterly peak of the chain. Opinions differ about whether the Lenzspitze, or 'Sudlenz' as it was formerly known, really belongs to the Nadelgrat or not. I prefer to treat the peak as an independent mountaineering objective and a four-thousander in its own right, less for geographical reasons than for the range of routes on offer. This in no way precludes it from being included as part of the Nadelgrat, of which more later.

As insignificant as the mountain may appear from the west, the view from the north-east is strikingly effective. From the Windjoch or from the Ulrichshorn, the 500-metre North-East Face hangs from the summit ridge like a colossal linen sheet. This side of the peak also offers the Normal Route by the East-North-East Ridge from the Mischabel Hut, one of the hardest of all the Normal Routes, first climbed on 3 August 1882 by the British climber William Woodman Graham (the first climber to reach the highest point of the Dent du Géant, an early Himalayan pioneer who later went to America to become a cowboy) with the guides Ambros Supersaxo and Theodor Andenmatten.

Dent and Burgener

The first ascent of the mountain had been made twelve years earlier by the English surgeon and experienced alpinist Clinton Thomas Dent, with his famous guide Alexander Burgener and a porter, Franz Burgener. They took a rather unpleasant (and obviously quite serious) route up the 400m North-East Face (rather to the right of the ice sheet) to the col of the Nadeljoch, and thence along the North-West Ridge to the summit. Dent's account of this climb* is laced with the self-deprecating humour so typical of Victorian mountaineers:

'The entire staff and personnel of the hotel would have turned out to wish us luck but did not actually do so as it was engaged on milking a cow . . . We had with us a porter [F. Burgener] of advanced years whose conversational powers were limited by an odd practice of carrying heavy parcels in his mouth . . . he assisted my upward progress with a stick after the fashion of an old Smithfield drover persuading a refractory beast to enter a pen . . . Probably my progress was about as graceful as a puppy on a frozen pond.' Dent later described Alexander Burgener as having 'a full share of the rashness of youth' and noted that together they made a number of 'naughty boys' choices, and lived to tell the tale.

Dent and Burgener went on to even greater things – their most notable achievement being the first ascent of the Grand Dru in 1878 after no fewer than eighteen previous attempts by Dent.

Dent became President of the Alpine Club, was a prolific writer and photographer, and played a part in the establishment of the alpine distress signal. Sadly, in 1912, this talented man was cut down at the zenith of a glittering professional career, when he succumbed to a sudden and mysterious attack of blood-poisoning.

Descent from the Lenzspitze

Once on the summit of the Lenzspitze, though there are

*A.J. XI, p389

(right) The East-North-East Ridge of the Lenzspitze (in profile) and the North-East Face seen from the Windjoch.

John Allen

Willi Burkhardt

(left) The North-East Face of the Lenzspitze.

(right) The Mischabel peaks seen from the north-east.

several options, the easiest route of descent is to climb on over the Nadelhorn, which brings us back to the subject of the Nadelgrat. The Lenzspitze/Nadelhorn connection (the Southern Nadelgrat) is without doubt the most handsome outing hereabouts and fits comfortably into one day (nine hours hut to hut). This ridge can be greatly extended by continuing to the Hohberghorn, and even the Dürrenhorn, but it makes for a very long day so this Northern Nadelgrat is best be left for a second expedition.

The Lenzspitze from the West

If one has chosen the Dom Hut as one's quarters for the night the first task is to cross the Festi Glacier and attain the Festijoch. High on the far side, on the uppermost reaches of the Hohberg Glacier, one can cross the bergschrund and climb the West Flank to gain the South-East Ridge above its main gendarme, or one can follow the whole ridge from the Lenzjoch.

The North-East Face

Regarding the North-East Face, thirty years after its first ascent on 7 July 1911 by Baron Dietrich von Bethmann-Hollweg with Oskar and Othmar Supersaxo, the face had seen only five repeats. Nowadays it is among the most popular ice faces of the Alps and, on fine days, it is not unusual to see roped teams arranged along the route like a string of beads. The deceptive foreshortening effect gives a view directly up the Face which is most stimulating – it seems to be totally blank and smooth – and when, on top of all this, an extreme skier is seen to shape up for the descent (a feat first accomplished by Heini Holzer on 22 July 1972), it is enough to make a simple climber's hair stand on end!

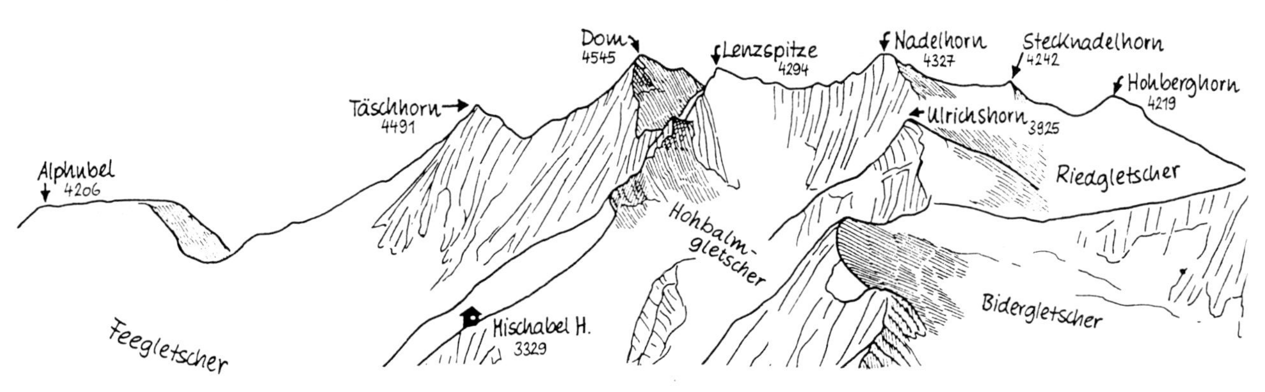

Dave Wynne-Jones

John Allen

(above left) On the slabs of the Grand Gendarme of the East-North-East Ridge of the Lenzspitze.

(above) The South Ridge of the Lenszpitze seen from the Dom.

The Intégral Traverse

When the rock is dry the difficulties on the East-North-East Ridge are nowhere greater than grade III, yet after fresh falls of snow or in icy conditions countless parties have been forced to retreat. Even the first tower can prove recalcitrant when the few footholds and handholds are slippery. The crux is on the Grand Gendarme, and the slab which is its crucial pitch will remain for ever in the memories of those who have climbed it. The *in-situ* iron bar is useful only as a running belay. From the tower, a crack leads down to a horizontal section of the ridge (five-metre abseil if necessary) which forms a convenient 'Breakfast Ledge' as the main difficulties are now below. The final upward sweep of the ridge should present no further problems and the traverse of the last snow arête with the abrupt drop of the North-East Face to the right is pure delight.

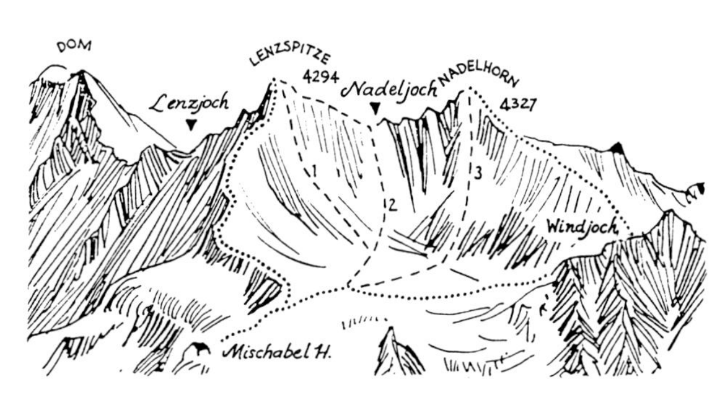

The Mischabel Hut is the starting-point for the normal routes of ascent (dotted lines) on the Nadelhorn (North-East Ridge) and the Lenzspitze (East-North-East Ridge) with the North-East Face of the Lenzspitze (1), the North-East Face/North-West Ridge (2), the East Face of the Nadelhorn (3).

The next stage to the Nadelhorn will take 2 to 2½ hours. An airy stripe of névé, with occasional detours right and left, leads gently down in about one hour to the Nadeljoch at 4213m. The climb out of the col on the opposite side, up the South Ridge of the Nadelhorn, is one of the finest parts of the Nadelgrat. The individual pinnacles of solid gneiss can either be taken direct or turned with equal interest. Between them lie jagged notches and fissures in the ridge. Face and slab climbing, alternating with exposed passages on the crest, leads up to the twin peaks of the Nadelhorn at a height of 4327m.

When measured against what has already been achieved, the descent of the North-East Ridge of the Nadelhorn is child's play. For the most part, a well-trodden trail points the way down to the Windjoch and across the Hohbalm Glacier to the Mischabel Hut.

The Mountain's Fair Countenance

The Lenzspitze inspired Karl Blodig to write one of the more effusive purple passages of alpine literature:

'In a land far away, yet not inaccessible since our footsteps will take us there, as headstrong and bewitching as the maiden of the mountains who refuses to surrender herself to the first available suitor and would be ardently courted and dauntlessly won over, there stands a fortress of rock. At her feet is spread the most sumptuous carpet of savagely riven glaciers, shimmering blue, while her elegantly slim body soars skywards, piercing the air. On the shining crown of her head she wears a circular diadem of snow. This is the Sudlenzspitze.

'In the great arc of mountains which rise above Zermatt's glorious meadows I know of no peak which could

(right) Solid gneiss makes the rock climbing on the gendarmes of the Nadelhorn's South Ridge a delightful experience in dry conditions, though rather more difficult under snow cover.

not be set at her side. One has to have seen her from the east – from the Ulrichshorn, perhaps, or from one of the summits on the Saasgrat – see how she stands, graceful and noble, between the solid mass of the Dom and the dark Nadelhorn. The breast of this seductive nymph is armoured in a cuirass of green plates, fashioned from ice. He who beholds her will for ever carry with him an unquenchable desire to conquer her.

'Not a single capricious stroke disturbs the balanced beauty of the complete canvas, as the snow and rock ridges thrust upwards towards the magnificent peaks in grand, truly classical lines.

'Arriving at Fee, it is the Sudlenzspitze which makes the greatest impression on us, sweeping up at the steepest angle, seemingly the loftiest of all the summits. Burgener shows us the narrow ridge by which we are to reduce her to submission on the following day.'

VALLEY BASES

Saas Fee 1792m. In a high side valley of the Saastal, 25km from Visp and 18km from Stalden (nearest railway station), 4km above Saas Grund. Post Bus service. Large car-park on the edge of the village, garage. Hotels, inns, pensions.

Randa 1439m. In the Mattertal, 23km from Visp (Rhône Valley). Post Bus and Railway Services. Car-park. Hotels, pensions, and camp site (half-way between Randa and Täsch).

HUTS/OTHER BASES

Mischabel Hut 3340m. Akademischer Alpenclub Zürich. Near the foot of the East-North-East Ridge of the Lenzspitze. Two huts, 120 places. Staffed in summer *tel* 028/ 57 13 17. 4 hours/1550mH from Saas Fee (a big walk – best in afternoon shade). 3 hours from Hannigalp (2349m) reached by a lift from Saas Fee.

Dom Hut 2940m. SAC. West of the Lenzspitze below the northern moraines of the Festi Glacier. Rebuilt in 1978. 75 places. Staffed from mid-July to the end of August *tel* 028/ 67 26 34 (self-catering room). 5 hours/1520mH from Randa – a notoriously steep hut walk.

NORMAL ROUTES

East-North-East Ridge AD III (several pitches), II, I. 5 hours from the Mischabel Hut. 960mH. Sustained mixed climbing.

South-West Ridge (West Flank) PD II+, II. One pitch of II on the approach to the Festijoch (3723m). 6 hours from the Dom Hut. 1360mH. Glacier climbing then mixed climbing. Mixed climbing on the West Flank approach (danger of stonefall, snow slides).

RIDGES/FACES

North-East Face D To 50°-55°. 4 hours/490mH on the face, start 1½ hours from the Mischabel Hut. An ice face.

North-West Ridge/South Ridge of Nadelhorn AD– II. 110mH from Nadeljoch. Mixed and rock climbing. The southern section of the Nadelgrat, Mainly rock climbing and scrambling (sometimes verglassed) with some mixed climbing.

MAPS/GUIDEBOOKS

See Lagginhorn p59

Dave Wynne-Jones

Jim Teesdale

Nadelgrat

Nadelhorn 4327m Stecknadelhorn 4242m Hohberghorn 4219m Dürrenhorn 4034m

The collective term 'Nadelgrat' is widely used to describe the ridge which drops north-west from the Nadelhorn to the Galenjoch, at the northern end of the lofty Mischabel chain. Of the four peaks above four thousand metres on this high mountain spine only the Nadelhorn is honoured with a certain independence – the other summits being only infrequently visited as separate entities. Nevertheless each peak has its own first ascent details which are summarised in the notes. The traverse from the Lenzspitze to the Nadelhorn was made in 1886 by Harold Ward Topham with Xaver Imseng and Aloys Supersaxo. The construction of the Dom Hut in 1890 allowed more ambitious expeditions to be entertained (the Mischabel Hut followed in 1903) and the traverse from Hohberghorn to Lenzspitze was done in 1892 by a team led by the Engadine guide Christian Klucker approaching from the Dom Hut. The Lenzjoch to Dürrenhorn traverse was made in 1896 by the Viennese brewer Moritz von Kuffner with Alexander Burgener. In 1916 this was extended to the Dürrenjoch and down the Galengrat by Adrian Mazlam with Josef Knubel.

Soon after the opening of the Bordier Hut in 1927 the whole ridge from Galenjoch to the Lenzjoch was climbed (uphill) by the famous Swiss cartographer Marcel Kurz with Josef Knubel. Thus the Nadelgrat, by one of these combinations, came to be regarded as one of the most prestigious outings of its type in the Western Alps.

(left) The Nadelgrat seen across the Ried Glacier from above the Bordier Hut. From right to left the peaks are Dürrenhorn, Hohberghorn, Stecknadelhorn, Nadelhorn and Lenzspitze.

(right) On the Nadelgrat: descending south-east from the Hohberghorn on the way to the Stecknadelhorn, the Nadelhorn and the Lenzspitze.

Certain standard ways have become established, such as the Lenzspitze/Nadelhorn/Hohberghorn tour (often with the short climb up the Dürrenhorn added), descending from the Hohbergjoch to the upper Ried Glacier. On this route the gully below the Hohbergjoch (tackled late in the day) can be the most difficult part of the whole expedition and in icy conditions a detour on to the rocks of the containing walls may be necessary. For this reason this itinerary is often done in the reverse direction with a direct descent to the Windjoch from the Nadelhorn. If you have chosen to use the Dom Hut as a base and incorporated the Lenzspitze in the route (be on the summit at ten o'clock in the morning at the latest), the traverse also leads across to the Hohbergjoch and on to the Dürrenhorn but in this case the return trip is made across the Hohberg Glacier and the Festijoch to the Dom Hut. Again, the itinerary in a reverse direction would avoid a late afternoon descent of the unpleasant western couloir of the Hohbergjoch. It is also best to avoid the seemingly inviting, but often stone-raked, gully which drops down between the Stecknadelhorn and the Hohberghorn to the Hohberg Glacier.

Approaching from the Bordier Hut the intégral traverse starting from the Galenjoch has much to recommend it, though bands of crevasses sometimes makes it inaccessible. But at such times the couloir leading up to the Hohbergjoch provides a useful alternative start. On this expedition, if the extended traverse to the Lenzspitze is thought too long, it is equally attractive to descend over the Ulrichshorn and return to the hut by the Ried Glacier.

Nadelhorn to Dürrenhorn

If the Lenzspitze is left to a separate expedition, the Nadelhorn will be the first summit of the day. From the Mischabel Hut, four hours should be allowed to cross the Hohbalm Glacier to the Windjoch and climb the North-East Ridge to the summit of the Nadelhorn at 4327m.

If one has already climbed the Nadelhorn as part of the Lenzspitze itinerary, it is possible to traverse directly across to the Stecknadelhorn from the upper part of the North-East Ridge, on a path which is usually well-defined. This saves about forty minutes, but detracts from the overall experience of the climb with its commanding

John Allen

Jim Teesdale

Jim Teesdale

(far left) The high line across the Ried Glacier from the Windjoch on the approach to the Dürrenjoch.

(near left) The North-East Ridge of the Nadelhorn.

views from the highest summit. At the top of the Nadelhorn, some three hours separate us from the Hohbergjoch, the next tolerable escape route for a descent from the ridge (the western descent from Stecknadeljoch being considered only in the direst circumstances). From the peak of the Nadelhorn we turn to face the North-West Ridge. In heavy snow the rock spikes (and therefore the belays) will be covered but it is possible to move on to the flank slightly to the right of the crest for the steep initial descent.

On ascending the South-East Ridge of the Stecknadelhorn things are a little easier. A tower is avoided on the left-hand (Mattertal) side and the line of névé then points straight to the summit. The route subsequently follows a slanting ledge system to the left of and below the spikes of the North-West Ridge of the Stecknadelhorn and, in perfect conditions, twenty minutes will see you down the 100m descent to the deeply indented notch of the Stecknadeljoch (4142m), and a similar time is required to progress to the summit of the Hohberghorn (4219m) by a steadily steepening snow ridge. Mixed terrain returns on the North-West Ridge of the Hohberghorn, with a short, steep little wall being turned on the right. A 300m height-loss is involved. Then there is a moment's reflection at the Hohbergjoch where one considers whether there is enough time to do the Dürrenhorn – about forty minutes of climbing time on blocky ground cemented together with snow. The Dürrenhorn can, of course, be traversed, although the descent of the South-West Ridge (Dürrengrat) to the two-man bivouac at the Hohenberghöhle and on down the Birbachtal to Randa has very complicated route-finding, particularly in descent. It is more practical to descend the Dürrenhorn's North Ridge to the Dürrenjoch at 3863m, go over the Chli-Dürrenhorn (3889m) to P.3816 on the North-West Ridge above the Galenjoch, and bear left at the fork in the ridge on to the flank between the ridges, dropping down to P.3188. The route then leads down the Steintalle (faint track) to the Geisstriftbach to pick up a faint path (faded paint marks) that leads down to Herbriggen in the Mattertal. This route should only be attempted in good visibility.

Jim Teesdale

(left) Icy conditions on the summit of the Nadelhorn. The Ulrichshorn is the peak in the background.

John Allen

(above) The southern precipices of the Hohberghorn, the Stecknadelhorn and the Nadelhorn seen from the Dom.

The Nadelgrat (showing the various options from the Festijoch approach) with the Normal Route on the Dürrenhorn, the approach to the Hohbergjoch (dotted line), the West Face of the Hohberghorn (1), the Stecknadeljoch Couloir (dotted line), the South-West Face of the Stecknadelhorn (2) and the South-West Flank of the Nadelhorn (3).

VALLEY BASES

Saas Fee / Randa see Lenzspitze p67

Gasenried 1659m. On a high alp above the village of St Nikolaus reached by a 9km approach road. Hotels, pensions.

HUTS/OTHER BASES

Mischabel Hut / Dom Hut see Lenzspitze p67

Pierre Bordier Hut 2886m. SAC. To the north of the Nadelgrat on the east side of the Ried Glacier. 43 places. Staffed in July and August *tel* 028/ 56 19 09. 4 hours from Gasenried. From Grachan take a cable-lift to the top station at Seetalhorn (2870m) and then a descending path via Farichfad, 2430m (3½ hours).

RIDGES

Nadelgrat AD II+ (sections), II and I. To 45° 9 hours from the Mischabel Hut to the Dürrenhorn. 1300mH. Mixed climbing, objective dangers on the ridge and some but cornice risk. An awkward mixed couloir descent (or ascent). Glacier approach and return work.

INDIVIDUAL PEAK DETAILS

Nadelhorn First climbed from the Windjoch by Joseph Zimmermann, Aloys Supersaxo, Baptiste Epiney and Franz Andenmatten, 16 September 1858 (for surveying purposes).

Stecknadelhorn First climbed by Oscar Eckenstein and Matthias Zurbriggen on 8 August 1887 by the stone-chute falling from the Stecknadeljoch to the Hohberg Glacier.

A worthwhile training route for the bigger ice faces is the 350m North Face, which reaches 50° in places.

Hohberghorn The only snow peak on the Nadelgrat. The first ascensionists were R.B. Heathcote, Franz Biner, Peter Perren and Peter Taugwalder jnr, who also used the west gully to the Stecknadeljoch.

The Hohberghorn also boasts the useful 320m North-East Face, set at an angle of 50° (maximum), which can be climbed in two hours, and would provide a good start to the Nadelgrat (*sans* Dürrenhorn).

Dürrenhorn A more complex mountain than the other satellites, comprising the 3889m Chli-Dürrenhorn and the main summit. It marks the start (or the finish) of the Nadelgrat. The easiest route of ascent is the South-East Ridge rising from the Hohbergjoch and this is the usual route taken on the final section of the Nadelgrat. The North Ridge, which starts from the Dürrenjoch, is rather more difficult and very much longer if one begins the climb at the Galenjoch, and includes a traverse of the Chli-Dürrenhorn. This was the way (from the Dürrenjoch) taken by the first ascensionists Albert Frederick Mummery and William Penhall with Alexander Burgener and Ferdinand Imseng on 7 September 1879.

MAPS/GUIDEBOOKS

See Lagginhorn p59

Dom *4545 m*

The Dom is the highest peak of the Mischabel chain and the highest mountain entirely in Switzerland. However, its name [*trans.* cathedral] has less to do with its commanding position or the fact that, seen from the north, it shines like some celestial temple of snow, but because it is said to be named after Canon Berchtold of the cathedral at Sitten, who was the first to survey the area.

Though high, by its Normal Route this is an easy four-thousander and thus a ski-mountaineers' peak. Its ascent from the north, up interminable snow slopes, is monotonous and many climbers will opt for the more varied North-West Ridge, or Festigrat. This was the route taken by the first ascent party (11 September 1858) led by the Welsh cleric and scholar Rev. John Llewellyn-Davies with his trio of Zermatt guides, Johann Zumtaugwald, Johann Krönig and Hieronymus Brantschen.

The steep North-East Ridge rising from the col of the Lenzjoch will probably appeal to rock climbers, though the route is, in places, loose and interfused with ice.

The South Ridge, which rises from the Domjoch is usually climbed as part of the traverse from the Täschhorn, either quickly or with some difficulty if the pinnacles are heavily iced, as they often are in such an exposed place.

The West Arête, rising above the Festi-Kin-Lücke, was first attempted in 1879 by two parties: Mrs E.P. Jackson with Aloys Pollinger, Peter Joseph Truffer and J. Biner; Percy Thomas with Josef Imboden and J. Langen. They avoided the upper section in favour of a traverse across the upper West Face to join the final part of the Festigrat. The ridge was completed in 1882 by Paul Güssfeldt with Alexander Burgener and Benedict Venetz. The West Face direct was not climbed until 1962 (Fons Driessen and Peter van Lookeren-Campaque) and is said to be a fine ice route, free from objective danger (50°, TD–).

The South Face was climbed in August 1906, two weeks after the ascent of the similar rock wall on the Täschhorn, by Geoffrey Winthrop Young and R.G. Major with Josef Knubel and Gabriel Lochmatter. Young reported that, once established on the face, it was rather more solid than the Täschhorn climb but his full account* puts that into context.

'There are good faces and bad faces, and nearly every face, however evil its reputation, will be found, if properly investigated, to have its sound points . . . The more pronounced the stonefall, the easier for the seeing eye to trace out the protruberant wrinkles . . .

'We collected our breath, and took the danger zone at a hand and foot gallop.'

**A.J.* XXIII p600

(left) The tracks of the Normal Route on the Dom can be seen in this view from the Nadelgrat. The more technical Festigrat (below) takes the edge on the right. Both are popular ascent routes from the Dom Hut (below left).

John Allen

John Allen

John Allen

The East Face of the mountain, that overlooking Saas, is hardly less daunting. The main line to the summit was climbed in 1875 – an ascent inspired and led by Johann Petrus with his clients Alfred and Walter Puckle with Lorenz Noti, a local chamois hunter. The climb was made at high speed and mainly during the night as 'the ice masses on the summit ridge . . . occasioned some misgivings [and] a large avalanche swept down fifty yards from us.' The more formidable section of the East Face, below P.4168, was climbed in August 1942 by Mme. Marguerite Deferr with Hans Tischhauser and Josef Imseng – this is graded D+ but is said to be very serious.

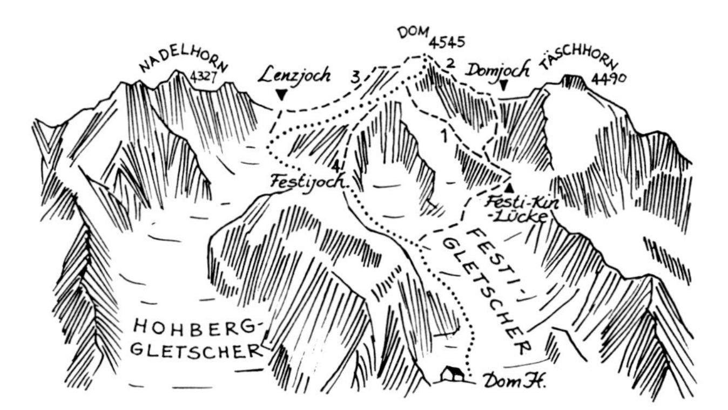

From the Dom Hut, the normal route (dotted) crosses the northern slopes to the summit. Other routes marked: West Ridge (1), South Ridge (2), North-East Ridge (3), Festigrat (4).

The Normal Route: Festigrat or North Flank?

The North Flank route, though there is an ice cliff to pass under and crevasses to negotiate, is thereafter a two-hour 'heads down' snow plod. From the Dom Hut a path leads to the crest of the northern lateral moraines of the Festi Glacier from where the Dom seems insignificant, the perspective disguising a height difference of 1000m.

The path works up cliffs above the northern edge of the glacier to gain the strategic notch of the Festijoch.

(above) The northern slopes of the Dom seen from the Festigrat with the Weissmies in the background.

The Normal Route now drops down to the Hohberg Glacier, but the Festigrat rises from the col, initially as a rock ridge – (belays advised) and, 200m higher, changing to névé and ice. Here one keeps to the left-hand flank, avoiding the sérac zones, to the turret-like false summit which is also turned on the left to reach the saddle (Gabel) where the Normal Route is rejoined for the final steep slope to the summit.

Arnold Lunn's Ski Ascent

The Dom presents no problems for the ski-mountaineer, though summit to valley runs are lacking as the slopes below the hut are too steep and broken. The first ski ascent was made on 18 June 1917 by Arnold Lunn and Josef Knubel. Lunn was a major pioneer of ski-mountaineering who made some thirty first ski (or ski-aided) ascents including those of Dom, Weisshorn and Eiger. He was also a seminal figure in the normal skiing world and was nicknamed the 'Ski Pope' and eventually knighted for his efforts.

Knubel was also famous for his many great alpine climbs and particularly for his celebrated 1911 lead of the Knubel Crack (V+) on the Grépon [at least 5a or 5.8 by today's standards. *Editor*].

On that June day in 1917, they skied up the Hohberg Glacier to the summit of the Dom. The final part of the ascent was described by Lunn in his book *The Mountains of Youth**:

'From the sattel . . . the slope steepens suddenly. Its average angle must be forty degrees and in parts it reaches forty-five degrees, which is as steep as snow will lie. On any other peak we should have removed our ski and proceeded on foot but we were anxious to cut a ski track to the actual roof of Switzerland and we eagerly canvassed the possibilities of doing so in safety. On hard snow the slope would have been far too steep. Had the snow been powdery the danger from avalanches would have been too great. Luckily it was ideal for our purposes. It was caked powder, that is powder snow that has achieved a certain consistency because of the wind . . . By half-past eleven we had cut the first ski track up the highest snowslope in Switzerland.

'We . . . started down with some trepidation. We had to ski . . . in our tracks and dared not risk a sudden swing lest the snow should slip. It was safe but sensational. From the sattel onwards all was pure joy.' They took just forty minutes to descend the 1600m to the Dom Hut.

*Eyre and Spottiswoode, London, 1925.

VALLEY BASES
Randa / Saas Fee see Lenzspitze p67
HUTS/OTHER BASES
Dom Hut see Lenzspitze p67
Mischabel Bivouac see Täschhorn p80
NORMAL ROUTES
North Flank PD II (one section below the Festijoch). 6 hours. 1600mH. A glacier tour. *As a ski tour:* Deposit skis at the saddle.
North-West Ridge (Festigrat) PD+ II sections). To 50°. 3 hours/820mH from the Festijoch. Mixed and ice climbing.
RIDGES/FACES
North-East Ridge TD– IU+ (sections), III and II. 4 hours/420mH from the Lenzjoch (4 hours from the Dom Hut).
South Ridge PD/AD+ III (sections). 3 hours/270mH from the Domjoch.
West Ridge D IV (sections), III and II, 8 hours. 1600mH. A major mixed climb – rarely repeated.
East Face D III 6 hours/1000mH from foot of the face. A serious mixed climb.
MAPS/GUIDEBOOKS
See Lagginhorn p59

(below) The fabulous view from the summit of the Dom to the Monte Rosa massif and the Liskamm. The Rimpfischhorn and the Strahlhorn are on the left and the Täschhorn the shadowy peak on the right.

Jim Teesdale

Täschhorn *4490 m*

The Täschhorn, a keen-edged pyramid with three precipitous faces and three ridges, is the most impressive and difficult peak of the Mischabel Group. However, from Saas Fee, optical distortion makes the mountain appear as merely a secondary top.

The North-West Face, really a steep glacier, was followed by the first ascent party in 1862. Four years after his Dom climb, the Rev. John Llewellyn-Davies returned to the scene of his triumph with Rev. J.W. Hayward, again guided by Johann Zumtaugwald with his relative Stephan. The ascent, by a route over the Festi-Kin-Lücke, would have been an obvious next project after the Dom climb and appears to have been done with little fuss, as reflected by the terse but appreciative entry in Zumtaugwald's *Führerbuch**. The glacier has undergone a slight change in the structure of its uppermost part, which in earlier days reached to the summit of the mountain, as it still does on the Dom.

This route has now been replaced by the South-East Ridge as the most popular line of ascent. In 1966 the SAC (Geneva Section) erected a bivouac box among the crags above the Mischabeljoch. Since then this ridge, first climbed in 1876 by the Rev. James Jackson, with Christian and Ulrich Almer, has captured the lion's share of the mountain's patronage, a popularity increased by the extension of the road from Täsch to the Upper Täschalp (2214m) and the train link to Mittel Allalin. Admittedly, even with the road it is still a good five hours to the Mischabeljoch from the Täsch side, but this is still the most convenient and the easiest approach from the Mattertal. The approach is slightly shorter from the Saas side but is in effect a climb in its own right.

1876 also saw the first ascent of the East Face (by the main summit rib) by the Rev. F.T. Wethered and P. Watson with Alexander Burgener and Benedict Venetz.

The 1.8km long Teufelsgrat (West-South-West Ridge) is among the most famous ridge routes in the Pennine Alps, though somewhat loose, but as its crest presents just two large gendarmes a steady ascent is possible. This great route was climbed first on 18 July 1887 by Albert Frederick Mummery accompanied by his wife and guided by that fiery spirit Alexander Burgener with Joseph Andenmatten. A particularly notable early repeat took place on 4 August 1922 when the ridge was soloed for the first time (in dense mist) by the Viennese mechanic Alfred Horeschovsky.

The North Ridge (first climbed in 1878) comes into context as part of the traverse to the Dom. The 600m leading down to the Domjoch is not excessively difficult but, in common with the South Ridge of the Dom, becomes extremely touch-and-go when icy, and then requires double or treble the normal guidebook time.

The Epic on the South-West Face

Anyone wishing to climb the South-West Face of the Täschhorn must be an old hand on rock and ice, indeed, in terms of seriousness and difficulty, it can be compared with the North Face of the Matterhorn. The English guidebook likens it to 'a near vertical slag-heap, held together well or badly, by variable amounts of snow or ice welding the joints', but this description may do the route a disservice. However, all authorities agree that the face is extremely serious. One of the very best climbers of the area, Franz Lochmatter from St Nikolaus, then just

**A.J.* XXX p328

Willi Burkhardt

(left) The Mischabel peaks seen from the slopes of the Weisshorn to the west with (left to right) Nadelgrat, Dom, Täschhorn and Alphubel.

(right) The full splendour of the icy North-West Faces of the Dom and the Täschhorn is revealed in an aerial view.

John Allen

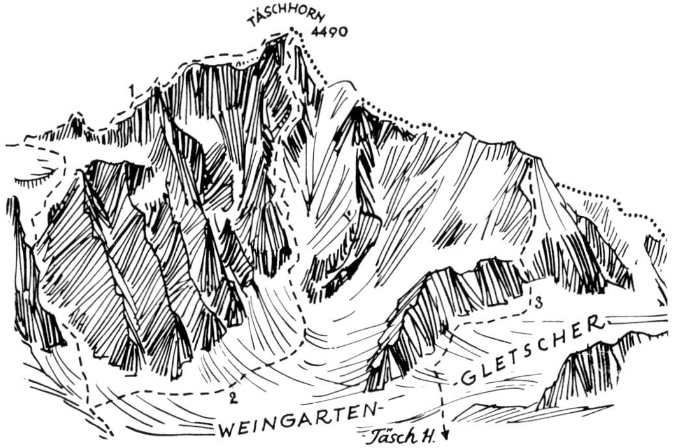

The Täschhorn with the South-East Ridge (dotted line), the direct approach (3), the South-West Face (2) and the Teufelsgrat (1).

nineteen years old, led the first ascent on 11 August 1906. This climb turned into one of the most epic adventures in Alpine history. It involved Franz's brother Josef and their regular client Valentine John Eustace Ryan – one of the most successful guide/client teams of all time. Also involved were the equally noted team of Geoffrey Winthrop Young, at thirty the oldest of the party, and Josef Knubel. It was Young who suggested the climb and he who wrote it up with typical erudition in a memorable chapter of his book *On High Hills*. The five climbers, all very fit and determined, soon found themselves totally committed on an unexpectedly serious route that offered hardly any secure belays:

'I looked down to see the deadly continuation of descending precipice, with its narrow snowy eavelets leaning out one above another . . . and I realized in a flash what a return down them must mean. For hours . . . we must have been climbing in reality of our several risks . . . the slip of any one of us imperilling the rest.'

They continued, becoming more and more committed on very fragile and unprotected mixed ground, until, close under the summit, as snow flurries began to dust the face, they were confronted by a major rock pitch. This was led (on joined ropes) by Franz with a superhuman effort, Josef followed and then both Ryan and Young had pendulum falls trying to follow and only with the most desperate manoeuvres did they manage to reach the two guides. Finally Knubel followed the pitch carry-

Willi Burkhardt

John Allen

(top left) Approaching the shoulder on the snow ridge halfway up the South-East Ridge of the Täschhorn.

(far left) The South-West Face of the Täschhorn.

(near left) Moving up to the final rocky section of the South-East Ridge from the snow arête and the view back down the ridge from the summit (right) with the Alphubel in the background.

ing three sacks and several axes. On the summit Young commented to Lochmatter, 'You will never do anything harder than that, Franz.' 'No,' he said reflectively, 'Man could not do much more.'

Thirty-seven years later the climb was repeated by the Swiss team of Georges de Rham, Alfred Tissieres, Gabriel Chevalley and André Roch. They enjoyed a little extra security from the use of pitons, yet they took a similar time to the first five. De Rham, who led the crucial pitch using four pitons, stated 'even with all the resources of modern technique, pitons, clasp rings and rubber shoes, I thought it was exceptionally severe'.

In the summer of 1956, on the sixth ascent, the Austrians Erich Vanis and Hans Chval, encountered ideal conditions and were able to climb the face as an out-and-out ice route and in only 5½ hours, though they took a line to the right of the original route.

The Ascent from the Mischabeljoch

The South-East Ridge can be started direct, missing out the Mischabeljoch and the bivouac box. This variation leaves the Weingarten Glacier at about 3700m, climbing a snow gully and a brittle rib to P.4175 on the ridge.

At first the rock above the bivouac box is not particularly solid, but neither is it too difficult and the route keeps right of the crest, with scrambling over several pinnacles beyond the initial rise. P.4175 is reached after two hours climbing. The terrain is now harmless for a little while. Care is needed where a steep snow couloir drops to the east and the snow ridge beyond this is often corniced and usually prompts a traverse across the steep and icy west flank.

The summit horn swings up from the indentation that

(below) The south side of the Dom from the Täschhorn's summit.

Wil Hurford

Dave Wynne-Jones

Wil Hurford

VALLEY BASES

Täsch 1449m. In the Mattertal at the end of the road from Visp (3km). Large car-park (toll). Station on the Zermatt Railway. Hotels, inns, pensions. Touristenlager (bunkhouse) Schulhaus *tel* 028/ 67 25 23. Campsite half-way between Täsch and Randa *tel* 028/ 67 25 55.
Randa/Saas Fee see Lenzspitze p67

HUTS/OTHER BASES

Dom Hut see Lenzspitze p67
Täschalp 2214m. Private. At the end of the narrow metalled road (2.3km) from Täsch. 15 places. Staffed from beginning June to end October *tel* 028/ 67 23 01.
Täsch Hut 2701m. SAC. At the foot of the Rotgrat, south-west of the Täschhorn. 60 places. Staffed from mid-July to end August and in the early months of the year if there is sufficient demand *tel* 028/ 67 39 13. 1¼ hours from Täschalp.
Mischabeljoch Bivouac 3861m. SAC. At the foot of the South-East Ridge of the Täschhorn, just above the Mischabeljoch. 8-10 places. 4 hours from the Täsch Hut (grade II– scrambling, avalanche danger). 5 hours from the Längflue (sections of II+, ice-falls).
Hotel Längflue 2870m. East of the Täschhorn near the top station of the Saas Fee – Chalbermatten lift, on the Längflue (Fee Glacier). 220 places. Open in winter and summer seasons *tel* 028/ 57 21 32. First lift 8 a.m. (closed 9-19 June). Valley station ¼ hour from the terminus of the Post Bus.

NORMAL ROUTES

South-East Ridge AD III(sections), II and I. 5 hours/630mH from the Mischabeljoch bivouac. Mixed climbing.
North-West (Kin) Face PD+ II+(sections). 6 hours from the Dom Hut. 1700mH. A complex glacier tour.

RIDGES/FACES

North Ridge AD II+. 1¾-2 hours/210mH from the Domjoch.
West-South-West Ridge (Teufelsgrat) AD+ IV (several pitches). 8 hours/700mH from the Kin-Lücke. Mixed climbing on generally loose terrain.
South-West Face TD+ V and IV. 11-16 hours/850mH from foot of the face. A serious and poorly protected mixed climb. Loose.
East Face AD+ III–. 8 hours from the Längflue, 1650mH. Mixed climbing. Loose and serious.

MAPS/GUIDEBOOKS

See Lagginhorn p59

marks the end of the snow arête. Under the most favourable conditions, the last bit can be dispensed with in half an hour and gives splendid climbing on predominantly good rock, poised high above the glistening blue sea of crevasses of the Fee Glacier. From the summit one can consider the options of retracing one's steps, descending the Kin Glacier, or continuing along the high linking ridge to the Dom to complete one of the finest high traverses in the Alps. This marvellous climb was first done (in the more difficult north-south direction) on 26 July 1894 by the ship-owner Robert Corry and Edmund Johnstone Garwood, guided by César Knubel and Roman Imboden, who took fifteen hours from the Dom Hut to Randa. The first traverse from south to north was made the following year by Owen Glynne Jones with Elias Furrer.

(left) Looking south from the Domjoch, the halfway point on classic ridge-traverse from the Täschhorn to the Dom.

Alphubel *4206 m*

Seen from the Saas side, the Alphubel, the most southerly peak of the Mischabel group, is a colossal glacier dome, lacking both clearly expressed ridge lines and a clearly definable summit. The latter is in fact an extensive snow plateau, exceeding 4100m in height, which, upon closer inspection, reveals several higher bumps and hummocks. The main summit curves up to the south, where the West Ridge ends at P.4164. About 300m to the north of the main summit one comes across P.4188. The main North Summit is, in turn, situated a further 300m away to the north-west and is a magnificent place from which to view the Täschhorn.

In thick mist it becomes difficult to locate the highest point, although one really ought not to be on such a route from the outset in unsettled weather as route-finding problems amidst the uniformity of the icefields have been the cause of the grim fate of many a mountaineer. Even though ski-lifts now make access to the Fee Glacier simple and the 'Metro-Alpin' runs up to 3500m on the Mittel-Allalin, the character (and seriousness in bad weather) of this featureless terrain remains basically unaltered.

From the Täsch side the mountain presents an entirely different aspect. Here there are no lifts and the mountain displays bands of cliffs that dominate the southern arm of the Weingarten Glacier.

In the earlier days the Alphubel attracted more attention in the Mattertal than it did in Saas Fee and the first ascent thus took place from that quarter. The popularity of this Täsch Hut/Alphubeljoch/South-East Ridge route is still maintained. It is quieter than the eastern approaches but an advantage is that the Täsch Hut is known to be a homely little refuge.

The alternative approaches from Saas Fee are now the established Normal Routes. You can be transported by ski-lift to the Längflue from where ski-mountaineers can skin right up to the summit of the Alphubel, providing the snow cover on the East Flank allows it. Otherwise they will go to the Alphubeljoch and finish the climb on foot. The approach from the Metro-Alpin is shorter but more difficult. It gains the Feejoch and then crosses the Feekopf to the Alphubeljoch and the South-East Ridge.

Apart from these various Normal Routes, the North

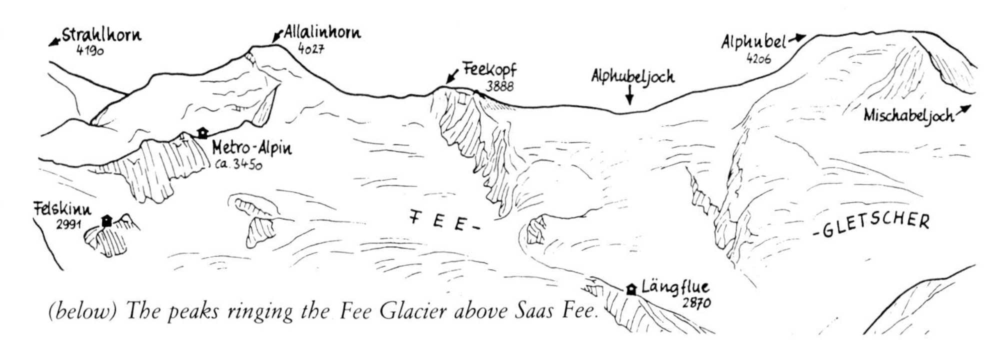

(below) The peaks ringing the Fee Glacier above Saas Fee.

Willi Burkhardt

Mike Pinney

Ridge has had more traffic (much of it in descent) since the construction of the bivouac box on the Mischabeljoch in 1966. The sharply-defined West Ridge or 'Rotgrat' is steeped in tradition. After its first ascent in 1889, by the Rev. George Broke with Adolf and Xavier Andenmatten, it remained unrepeated for half a century until the Täsch Hut was built in 1945. With generally stable rock it provides an interesting prelude to a traverse of the mountain possibly using the North Ridge for descent. The North Ridge also gives a fine outing when climbed in the opposite direction, in which case the descent might be made by way of the South-East Ridge.

A route of particular interest to rock climbers is the West Rib which provides a classic climb of about Grade III difficulty with a short harder section (IV+). This was first done, in the year of the opening of the Täsch Hut, by Edouard Wyss Dunant (later to lead the first Swiss Everest Expedition) with Alphons Lerjen and Pius Mooser.

(left) The steepest section of the Alphubel's Rotgrat.

The Normal Route by the Fee Glacier

In terms of pure technical difficulty, the climb from the Längflue presents no problems whatsoever, but on the middle section the route passes through a zone of crevasses and at the bergschrund a tortuous jumble of ice debris has to be negotiated. In suitable conditions the very roof of the mountain can be reached on skis. But be warned, there are cornices on the west side! A worthwhile variation leaves the Normal Route at roughly 3800m, and heads south to the Alphubeljoch, from where the delights of the South-East Ridge are yours for the taking. This is without question much finer than the usual route on the East Flank.

From the Täsch Hut

From the edelweiss paradise of the Täsch Hut, the first task is to attain the Alphubeljoch across the southern Alphubel Glacier. The climb to the tongue of the glacier leads past an idyllic little lake at 3000m, not marked on any of the maps. An early start will guarantee you the spectacle of sunrise at the col – the curtain rises towards 5 a.m. at the beginning of August. From the initially broad saddle of the Alphubeljoch, the South-East Ridge rises in a 200m sweep, usually as a snow climb, but occasionally hardened by water ice. About ninety minutes is usually required for the climb from the Joch to the summit, exactly 424m higher.

Willi Burkhardt

(left) The South-East Ridge of the Alphubel with the Rotgrat on the left and the East Face on the right.

(above left) *The West Face of the Alphubel in winter with the Mischabeljoch on the left and the Alphubeljoch on the right.*

(above right) *The summit plateau of the Alphubel. The South-East Ridge of the Täschhorn is prominent in the background.*

Willi Burkhardt

Willi Burkhardt

From the Metro-Alpin

This approach also makes use of the South-East Ridge. From the Metro-Alpin a well-trodden path leads at first to the Feejoch. Grade II scrambling up the subsequent rocky ridge lands you at the Feekopf, where the snow is again the determining factor.

Move right and climb the eastern slope of a snow dome to the lowest point of the Alphubeljoch and the final promenade along the South-East Ridge.

The Playground of Europe

This was the title of the book about the Alps by Leslie Stephen, first published in 1884. Stephen, who was born in 1832 and lectured in Theology at Cambridge University, aroused considerable unrest over the papers he wrote on the defence of disbelief and he was branded an apostate cleric. His countryman R. Mortimer wrote of Stephen that he '. . . preferred lengthy walks to lengthy prayer', indeed he was renowned for his walks from Cambridge or Brighton to attend Alpine Club meetings in London. Contemporaries accused him of mystification of the Alpine experience and of representing the sport of mountaineering as something which was intellectually incomprehensible and irrational. Nonetheless, in Britain, Stephen acquired a reputation for his scholarship and was eventually knighted for his years of work on *The Dictionary of National Biography*. I have already noted his 1861 Schreckhorn ascent but, on 9 August 1860, Stephen and his compatriot Thomas Hinchliff and their guides Melchior Anderegg and Peter Perren made the first ascent of the Alphubel from Täsch, by way of the South-East Ridge from the Alphubeljoch.

Ski-mountaineering in 1910

Nowadays, those whisked by ski-lift to the Längflue can barely imagine the rigours involved in ski-mountaineering at the turn of the century. On 29 March 1910, the first ski ascent of the Alphubel took place from the Saas Fee side. Alfred von Martin, and Oskar Supersaxo passed by the houses of the sleeping hamlet of Chalbermatten shortly after midnight. A ten-hour uphill march took them to the Alphubeljoch. Two-hundred metres above the col they left their skis and finished the climb on foot. Towards one o'clock in the afternoon they quit the summit and an hour later were back at the Alphubeljoch. They finished their day descending to Täsch with, as von Martin recalled:

'. . . an outstandingly fine ski descent of the Wandgletscher [Alphubel Glacier] to the floor of the Mellichental in forty minutes.'

VALLEY BASES

Saas Fee see Lenzspitze p67

Täsch see Täschhorn p80

HUTS/OTHER BASES

Hotel Längflue/Täschalp/Täsch Hut/Mischabel Bivouac see Täschhorn p80

Metro-Alpin 3456m. On the Mittel-Allalin north-east of the Allalinhorn. Top station of the metro that extends the ski-lift from Saas Fee to Felskinn. First lift from Saas Fee in August at 7.30 a.m.

NORMAL ROUTES

East Flank PD To 35°. 4½ hours from Längflue. 1350mH. A glacier tour. *As a ski tour:* The whole route is possible in suitable snow conditions.

Alphubel Glacier/South-East Ridge PD To 40°. 5 hours from the Täsch Hut. 1500mH. After a glacier approach, ridge climbing on névé and ice. *As a ski tour:* Leave skis at the Alphubeljoch.

Feejoch/Feekopf/South-East Ridge PD II (sections). To 40°. 4 hours from Metro-Alpin. 870mH. A glacier/ice route with rock climbing on the Feekopf.

RIDGES/FACES

North Ridge PD II– (short sections). 2 hours/360mH from the Mischabeljoch. Mixed climbing.

West Ridge (Rotgrat) PD IV (one pitch), III, II. 6 hours from Täsch Hut. 1500mH. Mainly rock with a névé ridge approach.

West Rib of North Summit AD+ IV+ (two pitches), III and II. 7 hours/880mH from the start of the route. A fine rock route.

South Face D III+. 6 hours/650mH from foot of face. Mixed climbing.

North-East Face D To 55°. 6 hours/600mH from foot of face. Mixed climbing with objective dangers.

MAPS/GUIDEBOOKS

See Lagginhorn p59

Allalinhorn *4027 m*

The Allalin group of three peaks at the head of Saastal forms the hinge between the Mischabel chain and the huge Monte Rosa Massif – delineated to the north by the Alphubeljoch and to the south by the Neues Weisstor, the lowest point on the linking ridge to Monte Rosa.

'Allalin' is said to derive from the Latin 'Aquilina', meaning 'little eagle'. The three main summits of the group – Strahlhorn, Rimpfischhorn and Allalinhorn – are separated by gently interspersed cols which enjoy great popularity amongst ski-mountaineers, and also have an historical importance in the history of alpine travel. The frozen waves of four great glaciers break on the slopes of the mountain – the Fee, Allalin, Mellich and Hohlaub – and from out of the ice four rocky ridges rise as stanchions forming a clear X configuration. Of these ridges, only the East reaches as far as the summit – the others being subsumed by the impressive summit ice-cap.

Due to its central location and widespread renown as a fine viewpoint, the Allalinhorn (together with the Strahlhorn) has always been the peak most frequently climbed from the Britannia Hut.

The Metro-Alpin tube-train extension of the Saas Fee – Felskinn cableway leads to Mittel-Allalin at almost 3500m where there is the highest revolving restaurant in Europe. This strategic point is just 570m below the summit of the Allalinhorn and, on fine days, hundreds of tourists reach the summit in about two hours – always presuming that they do not run out of steam first, as the necessary acclimatization is widely ignored.

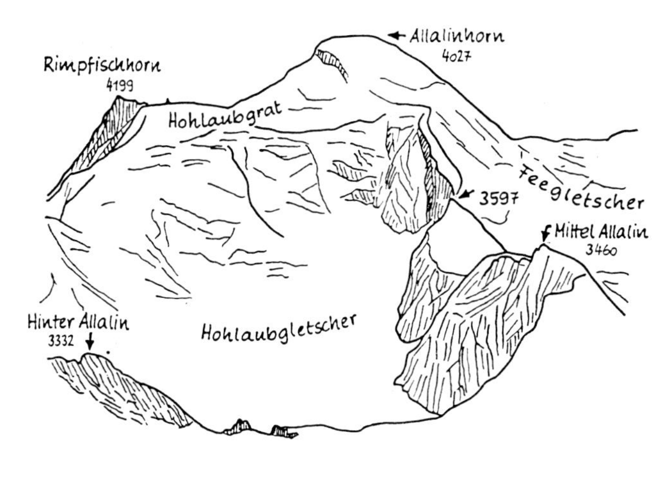

(left) The North-East Face of the Allalinhorn

In August, the first Felskinn cable-car leaves at 7.30 a.m. and you can be at Mittel-Allalin shortly before eight o'clock and, after a rapid ascent of the peak, you could be enjoying the alpine arena of Saas from the revolving restaurant by lunchtime. A four-thousander for breakfast! Times have changed, to be sure.

Another magic word is 'heli-skiing'. Helicopters fly well-to-do skiers up to the Allalin Pass at 3564m where mountain guides point out the various ski-runs on the glaciers.

The Metro-Alpin has halved the time required to climb the North-East Ridge, an expedition that originally started from the Britannia Hut. From the top station, the névé saddle beneath P.3597 on the upper quarter of the ridge can be reached in about thirty minutes across the Fee Glacier. But although the route is truncated there are still bergschrunds, and the steep summit slope which is often icy and certainly no pushover.

The South-West Ridge rises from the Allalin Pass. This was the scene of the first ascent, and it remained popular for many years. These days, with the convenience of the Metro-Alpin and the 'doctoring' of the Hohlaubgrat, it has become a lonelier place and this is without doubt a bonus.

The East Ridge (Hohlaubgrat) is the classic ridge route of the Allalinhorn, but sadly the crux, a 20-metre rock barrier on the upper part, has had much of its sting removed with the placement of three iron spikes.

The 'Last Great Problem' of the Allalinhorn was solved in 1976 by Guido and Hans-Jorg Bumann when they climbed the North-East Face. Their route went straight up the mighty ice-bulge on this partially overhanging wall which gives extreme rock and ice climbing throughout.

These, then, are the two extremes of the Allalinhorn – mass tourism and dangerous isolation.

A Mad Dash to the Top and Back

Allow just over an hour to reach the Feejoch. Three-quarters of an hour from there to the summit, and perhaps a little over an hour for the descent, to make a round trip of just over three hours. An elegant midday meal at the revolving restaurant followed by an afternoon stroll across the glacier (amid impressive scenery) to the Längflue, to aid the digestion, and then an airy trip down the cableway to return to Saas Fee to complete the most leisurely four-thousander expedition.

The situation is similar for ski-mountaineers, except that in June the first metro leaves the Felskinn at 8 a.m. Skis are usually deposited on the Feejoch before stamping up the final 200m of the summit slope. Crampons are often necessary, according to the conditions. There is really only one dangerous area, at the gaping diagonal crevasse on the climb up to the Feejoch where the broad path sweeps around this obstacle in a wide arc.

The South-West Ridge starts with the approach to the Allalin Pass and this requires about three hours from either the Britannia or the Täsch Hut, routes which are also very worthwhile on skis. A further two hours should be allowed to climb the ridge, which gives varied climbing on mixed ground, snow slopes and arêtes, rocky ledges and towers and is, overall, rather more difficult than the Feejoch Route.

The Desecration of a Landscape

The construction of the cableway from Saas Fee to the Felskinn at 2991m on the eastern Fee Glacier was the first drastic caesura in this region of the Pennine Alps. 'Snow Cats' then transported sun-hungry day-trippers ever higher up the mountain. Next, the network of lifts was to be extended to the Feekopf at 3888m, but the Federal Council refused the concession for this project. However, a loophole soon appeared and the underground railway of the Metro-Alpin was created, running 1473m from the Felskinn to the Mittel-Allalin, and gaining 465m in height.

From the top station, a twenty-minute stroll along a

VALLEY BASES
Saas Fee see Lenzspitze p67
Täsch see Täschhorn p80
HUTS/OTHER BASES
Metro-Alpin see Alphubel p83
Täschalp, Täsch Hut see Täschhorn p80
Britannia Hut 3029m. SAC. North-east of the Allalinhorn on the eastern lower slopes of the Hinter-Allalin. 113 places. Staffed from end February to 1st October *tel* 028/ 57 22 88. Approx 40 minutes from the top station of the Felskinn cableway (first lift from Saas Fee at 7.30 a.m. in August) across the Egginerjoch (ski-lift).
NORMAL ROUTE
North-West Ridge F To 40°. 2 hours/570mH from the Metro-Alpin. A glacier tour suitable for a ski ascent to the Feejoch.
RIDGES/FACES
South-West Ridge F+ II. 2 hours/470mH from the Allalin Pass. Mixed climbing.
East Ridge (Hohlaubgrat) PD II(sections). To 40°. 5 hours from the Britannia Hut. 1050mH. Mainly a snow climb with a 30m rock barrier.
North-East Ridge AD+ To 50°. 3 hours/580mH from the Metro-Alpin. A snow and ice climb.
North-East Face TD IV, V. Ice to 65° with some vertical sections. 8 hours/570m from foot of the face. A hard ice route.
South Face AD+ IV, III. 4 hours/600mH from foot of the face. A mixed climb.
MAPS/GUIDEBOOKS
See Lagginhorn p59

path leads to the monument raised in the honour of the guides who have died in the execution of their profession. Many of those Grand Old Men would have turned in their graves, or maybe turned admiringly, at the sight of bikini-clad young women sunbathing where they once toiled with their clients.

To the Memory of the Guides

As early as 1828, Heinrich Michaelis and his guide crossed the Allalin Pass, thereby opening up the approach route to the South-West Ridge. A further twenty-eight years were to pass before the ridge itself was conquered, by the clergyman Johann Joseph Imseng from Saas Grund, with his manservant Franz Joseph Andenmatten, another member of the Imseng family and the English barrister Edward Levi Ames, two days after their first ascent of the Lagginhorn. The North-West Ridge was climbed in August 1860 by a large caravan comprising Leslie Stephen, W.F. Short, F.W. Jacomb, C. Fisher, Franz Joseph Andenmatten, Moritz Anthamatten, Peter Taugwalder and Johann Kronig. The Bernese teacher and historian Heinrich Dubi, who for many years edited the yearbook of the Swiss Alpine Club, succeeded in a remarkable undertaking when he climbed the North-East Ridge and descended the East Ridge on 27 July 1882, accompanied by his guides Alphons and Peter Supersaxo. The East (Hohlaub) Ridge had to wait five years for its first *ascent*, made by the Englishmen Harold Ward Topham and G.H. Rendall guided by Aloys Supersaxo. They turned the difficult rock band by a ledge and couloir on the right. Four years later, the South Face fell to a brilliant performance by C.A.C. Bowkler with one of the Supersaxos, a rock climb with pitches of IV whose first winter ascent was made in 1970 by the Swiss soloist R. Bracken.

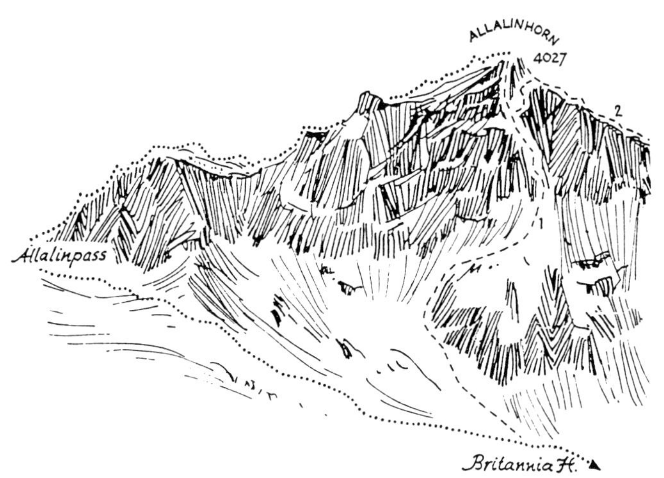

The original Normal Route by South-West Ridge starts at the Allalin Pass (dotted line). Also marked are the South Face (1) and the East-North-East Ridge (Hohlaubgrat) (2).

(below left) The rock barrier on the Hohlaubgrat.

(below right) Approaching the icy summit slopes of the Allalinhorn from the Feejoch.

Richard Goedeke

Dave Wynne-Jones

Willi Burkhardt

Rimpfischhorn *4199 m*

Just south of the Allalinhorn, beyond the important and historical thoroughfare of the Allalin Pass, stands the Rimpfischhorn – isolated and arrogant with a summit ridge of proud gendarmes. The mountain is a focal point at the end of long lonely glacier systems with none of the hustle and bustle of the ski-exploited slopes above Saas Fee. It *can* be approached from Saas Fee, indeed countless ascents, some of them on skis, are made from the Britannia Hut using the Felskinn lift. Yet the Rimpfischhorn is really a Zermatt mountain, from where it appears both commanding and difficult, its characteristic rock ridges dropping steeply to the Allalin and Adler passes. It is the highest and most difficult summit of the Allalin Group and the four-thousander with the longest ski-route, more highly-rated than the runs from the Allalinhorn or Strahlhorn and even that from the nearby Alphubel.

The mountain was first climbed from Zermatt on 9 September 1859, from Fluh Alp [Fluealp on the latest maps] via the Rimpfischwänge, by Leslie Stephen and Robert Liveing with their guides Melchior Anderegg and Johann Zumtaugwald. It was soon discovered that the final difficult section of this route, up the South-West Ridge, could be easily reached by a traverse across the Mellich Glacier from the Allalin Pass, thus allowing normal routes from either the Britannia or Täsch Huts. Both of these approaches, though longer than the Rimpfischwänge route, are more amenable for ski-mountaineers.

Those capable of mastering the grade III difficulties of the North Ridge, which rises from the Allalin Pass, will find it the finest route on the Rimpfischhorn. The 45m Grand Gendarme at 4104m can either be climbed by its exposed edge (IV) or turned on the left. Strong parties heading for the Allalin Pass might well use this route for the descent. The climb was first made in 1878

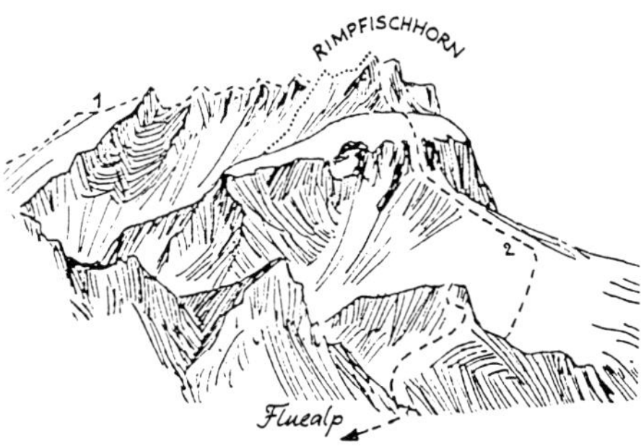

The Rimpfischhorn is most often climbed by its South-West Ridge (2). Other routes marked are the North Ridge (1) and the North-West Face (dotted line).

(above) The western slopes of the Rimpfischhorn above Fluealp.

Willi Burkhardt

by George Augustus Passingham with Ferdinand Imseng and Ludwig Zurbriggen.

In reliable snow conditions the North-West Face offers a difficult but entertaining alternative finish to the Normal Routes that cross the Mellich Glacier. As with so many Swiss ice faces, this was first climbed by the Geneva pianist Emile Robert Blanchet (13 July 1923), on this occasion guided by Heinrich Imseng (he was usually partnered by Kaspar Mooser). Leaving the tracks of the Normal Route at a depression in the glacier before the steepening snow slope you swing up to the left and on to the uniformly high-angled flank which is climbed to join the North Ridge not far from the summit.

From the Haute Route

Those doing one of the longest stages of the celebrated Chamonix to Saas Fee Haute Route pass below the South-East Ridge as they cross the Adler Pass. This, too, was climbed in 1878, by a party led by A. Slee, and it offers quite a hard climb with some delicate rock pitches. But as this stage of the Haute Route (Monte-Rosa Hut/Adler Pass/Britannia Hut) measures seventeen kilometres and takes at least seven hours, the easier Strahlhorn, to the east of the pass, is probably the more suitable summit to include.

A Common Route to the Summit

All the Normal Routes meet at the Rimpfischsattel at the four-thousand-metre mark – four hours from Flue, five hours from the Britannia Hut, slightly longer from the Täsch Hut. Above, the South-West Ridge presents just 200m of climbing to the summit, but those 200m certainly have something about them! In perfect conditions the passage can be completed in less than an hour, but care

(above) The Rimpfischhorn and Strahlhorn from the summit of the Klein Matterhorn to the south-west. The ordinary route up the Strahlhorn follows the skyline ridge from the Adler Pass.

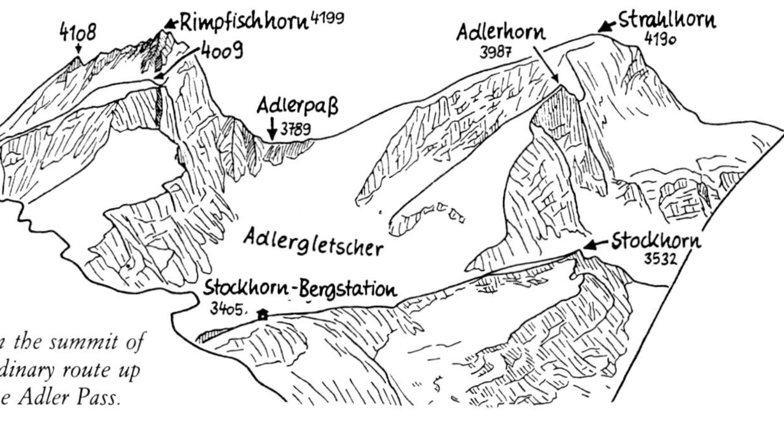

is needed and it is far from easy in cumbersome ski-boots.

Sandwiched between two rock ribs, a couloir shoots upwards at an angle of about 50°. The conditions here – snow or ice – determine the degree of commitment required. Keeping to the rocks which bound the couloir on the right, the lower third is climbed to a point where, despite the apparently tempting nature of a direct continuation (it actually finishes with difficult climbing), a move out left has to be made. This leftwards traverse is no fun at all, with off-balance moves on ledges which only appear to be solid and have an awkwardly tilted rock strata. The traverse leads across to a little notch on a lateral ridge to the west where, happily, the rock turns out to be absolutely bomb-proof. The crux follows, an exposed twenty-metre slab (III) which is tackled on the right, and beyond this the first summit is gained in a few minutes. From the saddle between the two peaks the route goes up a snow arête and easy rocks to the highest point.

John Allen

(above) The Rimpfischhorn from the upper Mellich Glacier near the Allalin Pass.

The Traverse – Adler Pass to Allalin Pass

As night fell on 12 August 1906, Henry Hoek and Franz Kostner arrived at the inn on the Fluealp. Hoek (1878-1951) was born in Davos but later moved to Freiburg, near the Black Forest, where, in 1901, he won the German Cross-Country Ski Championship. Later he was to play a leading part in exploring the Dolomites on skis. His books are considered by experts as being among the best of Alpine literature. Kostner was a carpenter from the Romansch-speaking south-east Switzerland. In 1897 he had qualified as a mountain guide and had gathered considerable experience during the early explorations of the Tien Shan mountains of Turkestan.

Hoek and Kostner planned to traverse the Rimpfischhorn by climbing the south-east side of the mountain and descending the North Ridge. At three in the morning the glow of their lanterns could be seen flitting across the lateral moraines of the Findelen Glacier. After a while, they stepped on to the glacier and, a little higher, continued their climb across the Adler Glacier and up to the Adler Pass (nowadays the route-finding hereabouts is very complicated due to ice-falls). Beneath the cliffs of the South-East Flank the two men paused for half an hour to eat.

John Allen

(left) Starting up the North Ridge of the Rimpfischhorn.

Henry Hoek described the climb:

'At first one could hardly call them cliffs. It was all really just rubble broken up by isolated steps. Shortly we could clearly see that the ridge running up from the Adler Pass did not lead to the summit of the Rimpfischhorn itself but to a false summit which lay in front of it and to the west.

'From the main peak an indistinct rib dropped down, dividing the upper part of the summit wall into a south-eastern and an eastern section and disappearing completely in the lower half.'

Kostner and Hoek now made a rising traverse to the South-East Ridge and soon reached the summit, exactly an hour and three-quarters after setting off from above the bergschrund. The descent of the North Ridge lay ahead. On the first section, to the Grand Gendarme they encountered few difficulties.

'The climbing was, to be sure, very airy in places and one or two passages were certainly rather delicate, but all in all it was highly enjoyable work. From the indentation in the ridge before the tower we climbed down slabs [on the west side] below its steep face for about fifty metres. There followed a horizontal traverse of maybe thirty metres on tiny footholds. There was no feeling of exposure, although a fall on the steep slabs would have ended several hundred metres further down.

About twenty-five metres of steep face climbing on very loose rock followed to gain the rib which rises from the Hubel [Mellich] Glacier to P.4119. Once we were on

Jim Teesdale

Dave Wynne-Jones

(above) The summit of the Rimpfischhorn.

this rib we had won the game. We traversed a further forty metres or so, mostly on hands and knees, across smooth slabs and then the first pieces of ice broke under Kostner's axe blows and went whistling and clattering down to the glacier.

After about eighty steps horizontally across to the main ridge the snow became softer. The steep, sharp snow ridge which runs up from the Allalin Pass to the tower at 4119m turned out to be hardly corniced at all – indeed, in those excellent snow conditions it was really harmless. At 1.15 p.m., that is to say 2¼ hours after leaving the summit, we stood in the hollow of the Allalin Pass.'

(left) The view south from the summit of the Rimpfischhorn across the Gorner Glacier basin to the Liskamm.

Rimpfischhorn Notes

VALLEY BASES

Zermatt 1616m. A car-free village at the head of Mattertal. Narrow gauge railway from Visp. Nearest car park (2000 places) at Täsch, 5km from Zermatt. Hotels, inns, pensions. Camping Spiss. Youth Hostel *tel* 028/67 23 20, Naturfreundhaus *tel* 028/ 67 27 68. Stafelalp Hotel *tel* 028/67 30 62. Alpine Museum – open daily in summer (10 a.m. to noon, 4 p.m. to 6 p.m.).
Täsch see Täschhorn p80
Saas Fee see Lenzspitze p67

HUTS AND OTHER BASES

Fluh Alp Hotel 2612m. Private. On the Fluealp, west of the Rimpfischhorn. 50 places. Staffed in the summer and winter seasons *tel* 028/ 67 25 51. 3 hours from Zermatt, ¾ hour from Blauherd (2601m), reach by cablelift from Zermatt via Sunnegga.
Täsch Hut see Täschhorn p80
Britannia Hut see Allalinhorn p86

NORMAL ROUTES

West-South-West Ridge (Rimpfischwänge) PD+ III– (one pitch), II, I. To 50° above Rimpfischsattel. 5 hours from the Fluealp. 1600mH. A glacier tour, then mixed ground above the Rimpfischsattel. *As a ski tour:* As for the normal route. Leave skis at the Rimpfischsattel.
South-West Ridge from the Allalin Pass PD+ To 50°. 5 hours from the Britannia Hut, slightly longer from the Täsch Hut. 1220mH. A glacier tour then mixed ground.

RIDGES AND FACES

North Ridge AD III (sections). 4 hours/650mH from the Allalin Pass.
South-East Flank/Ridge AD/D IV– (one section). 4 hours/410mH from the Adler Pass. Loose, mixed climbing.
North-West Face D To 55°. 3 hours/300mH from the foot of the face.

MAPS/GUIDEBOOKS

See Lagginhorn p59

Strahlhorn Notes

VALLEY BASES

Saas Fee see Lenzspitze p67
Zermatt see Rimpfischhorn p91
Macugnaga 1378m. The last village in the Valle Anzasca, 43km from Domodossola, 140km from Milan; bus service. Hotels, inns, pensions. Campsite *tel* 0324/ 6 54 89.

HUTS AND OTHER BASES

Britannia Hut see Allalinhorn p86
Fluh Alp Hotel see Rimpfischhorn p91
Rifugio Eugenio Sella 3029m. CAI South of the Rimpfischhorn on a rocky spur on the Roffel Glacier. 35 places. Staffed at weekends from 1 June to 30 September and all week in July and August *tel* 0324/ 6 54 91. 3½ hours from Belvedere (1932m) reached by lift from Macugnaga-Pecetto (an additional 2 hours without the lift).
Rifugio Saronno, CAI, *tel* 0324/ 6 53 22.

NORMAL ROUTE

Allalin Glacier / North-West Ridge PD 5 hours from the Britannia Hut. 1250mH. A glacier tour, technically easy but with route-finding complexities in misty conditions.

RIDGES AND FACES

North-East Ridge AD II–. 5 hours from the Britannia Hut, 1250mH. A glacier and snow climb with rock difficulties on the summit block. The Fluchthorn can be conveniently included.
West-South-West-Ridge (over Adlerhorn) AD– 6 hours from Fluealp. 1600mH. A glacier and snow climb usually with crevasse complexities.
South-South-East Ridge AD+ II. To 45°. 6 hours from the Rifugio Eugenio Sella. 1200mH. Mixed climbing and snow and ice.
East Face Direct TD V, VI and III. 10 hours/900mH from the foot of the face. A remote rock climb.

MAPS/GUIDEBOOKS

See Lagginhorn p59

Strahlhorn *4190 m*

The Strahlhorn is the most southerly of the Allalin trio of four-thousanders. Although relatively easy it is remote, situated at the top end of three major glaciers just north of Scharzberg-Weisstor on the Swiss/Italian frontier.

The north side of the mountain does full justice to its name: a gleaming white horn of a peak, especially when viewed from the Rimpfischhorn. On this flank the seven-kilometre Allalin Glacier extends its icy embrace to the summit, broken only by the graceful sweep of the North-North-West Ridge. The Normal Route approaches from this quadrant, starting at the Britannia Hut and making a rising ascent across the glacier to the Adler Pass. The first visitors to this ancient link between Saas Fee and Zermatt found the feather of a golden eagle on the crest, which explains its name, 'Eagle Pass'. Nowadays the Adler Pass is a whistle-stop on the seventeen-kilometre stage of the Haute-Route between the Monte Rosa and Britannia Huts, during which it is both easy and logical to break off and climb the Strahlhorn.

For a normal ascent of the mountain most climbers choose the Britannia Hut as a base because it is close to the Felskinn lift yet high enough to make the summit climb relatively simple, albeit with some crevasse problems. This way is particularly valuable for ski-mountaineers and in the early months of the year hardly any crevasses will be encountered. The Adler Pass can also be reached from the Zermatt side via the Fluealp and the Adler Glacier, but it should be borne in mind that, in summers of little snow cover, the junction of the Findelen and the Adler Glaciers can be very broken and problematic. This was the approach of the first ascent party of the three intrepid Smyth brothers – the clerics James Grenville and Christopher and the Indian Army officer Edmund – with Franz Joseph Andenmatten and Ulrich Lauener, on 15 August 1854. From the pass they continued up the blunt backbone of snow that forms the North-West Ridge. An alternative approach from Fluealp is to head for the West-South-West Ridge by a route that traverses the Adlerhorn from higher up the Findelen Glacier, though this approach can also be plagued with glacial complexities.

Routes from Italy

On the Italian side, the Rifugio Eugenio Sella serves as a shelter from the elements and is a splendid balcony from which to view the titanic East Face of Monte Rosa at the

Alan O'Brien

(right) A view from the Adler Pass to the Allalin Glacier and the South Face of the Allalinhorn.

top end of the Macugnaga Valley. From the hut, a three-hour climb will take you over the col of Neues Weisstor (3499m, the lowest point on the linking ridge between the Allalin and Monte Rosa groups) to the Schwarzberg-Weisstor (3577m). Above this higher col the South-South-East Ridge provides an interesting and quite taxing mixed climb to the summit, which is said to compare favourably with the Triftjigrat on the Breithorn. This was first climbed in September 1925 by Augusto Dagglio and Attilio Sabbadini, but for many years was credited in the Swiss guidebooks to the Kenner/Imseng/Supersaxo party who actually *descended* the ridge in 1926.

A rarely repeated hard rock climb takes a direct line up the East Face which soars 750m above the Schwarzberg Glacier. The difficult lower section (V) was climbed as far as the obvious snow ledge on 3 August 1951 by the Geneva men Victor Russenberger and Lucien George. Three days later the same pair, accompanied by Miss Gwen Goddard, completed the slightly easier upper section of the face.

The Normal Route from the Britannia Hut

This hut was originally financed by a subscription from the British members of the Swiss Alpine Club, and is now run by its Geneva Section. It was conceived as a strategic high mountain refuge, reached by an arduous four-hour climb from Saas Fee. Then, in 1963, the cableway to Plattje (2570m) was erected, which cut the approach walk to two hours. The subsequent construction of the lift to Felskinn (2991m) left an approach of just forty minutes across the Egginerjoch and the receding Chesslen

(below) The Brittania Hut

Willi Burkhardt

Glacier, a traverse periodically strafed by rock fragments from Hinter-Allalin but assisted by wooden planks bridging troublesome crevasses. The Britannia Hut has thus become a tourist attraction but in the afternoon the tourists return to the lift, while the climbers remain to be woken the following morning by lively radio music to inspire them for their ascents of the Rimpfischhorn or the Strahlhorn.

At first the routes to the summits are identical, descending a pile of rubble to the Hohlaub Glacier which provides the key to the way on to the Allalin Glacier. Here the way goes parallel to the Hohlaubgrat and then runs roughly to the south-west, close under the North-East Ridge of the Rimpfischhorn, and increases in steepness. During a ski ascent in good conditions it is possible to head for the summit direct by bearing left about 100m below the Adler Pass and working through a zone of crevasses.

The summit climb generally begins from the Adler Pass where, on early summer days, dozens of sets of skis are stuck in the snow under a cloudless blue sky. Although one could get a little further on skis, the route from here is customarily done on foot – east of the crest of the North-West Ridge on 'vaporous' snow to P.3954 in about thirty minutes to a junction with the North-West Ridge proper. At the dome of the first summit (P.4128) the snow arête of the West-South-West Ridge merges from the right and from this point a twenty-minute snow plod leads to the summit.

A Brilliant Panorama

Karl Blodig described the view from the summit in characteristically evocative terms:

'We required a good half-hour from the moment we first set foot on the rocks until we stood atop the long summit ridge of the Strahlhorn. We cast only a cursory glance northwards to the Rimpfischhorn, which swung upwards from the Adler Pass in a 400m wall of rock and seemed to surpass in height the point at which we stood not by twelve but by at least fifty metres. Almost tossed away down the mountain by a hurricane-like wind, we faced about, climbed back for about half a dozen moves and with the axes fashioned seats in the snow of the South slope for ourselves with the axes. I had expected much of the view from the Strahlhorn, yet it offered infinitely more, above all the simply overwhelming sight of the eastern precipices of the Monte Rosa massif. One holds one's breath involuntarily when, with an armed eye, one examines those slopes and considers that dear friends are perhaps just at that moment gambling with their lives on the gigantic scoured slabs and in the smooth-swept gullies. The Liskamm, the Zwillinge and the Breithorn are, in the shadow of this massif, not really shown to best advantage but we were agreed that we had never before seen the Matterhorn looking so slender, so ethereal, and in the evening, as we were walking out through the Findelental, I admitted to Compton* that I had come round completely to his opinion and that the view of the Matterhorn from Stellisee and from the path down to Findelen was preferable to that offered from any other vantage point. On each side of the Matterhorn there appears the sea of peaks which rise between Zermatt, Chamonix and the Dauphiné; Mont Blanc itself, the final and culminating peak of the whole range, shines with a phosphorescent yellow glow in a strange and marked contrast to the violet haze hanging over the rest of the group. It is joined by peaks which, after the Matterhorn, are the most beautiful in Europe: Dent Blanche, Gabelhorn, Rothorn and Weisshorn. The chain of the Mischabel Horns, thrusting upwards to the north of the Rimpfischhorn, is unfortunately foreshortened, while above the deep trench of the Saastal the Bernese Alps make their appearance and, further east, the Uri range with the Dammastock, the broad mass of the Todi, the slim figure of the Brigelserhorner and their neighbour, Churss Ringelspitze. The mountains of the Grisons merge with the Bernina, with the Disgrazia and the sharply defined peaks of the Albigna Group.

'From the sea of cloud which covers the plains of upper Italy, single peaks protrude; the triangle of the Monte Legnone at Lake Como is particularly clear. And down below, at the end of the Schwarzenberg Glacier, the little whitewashed house at Mattmark calls a greeting while at the edge of the Findelen Glacier, which pours its thin brew of snows off to the west, one can just catch sight of the Fluh Inn.'

*Edward Theodore Compton, a prolific climber and Blodig's regular companion. An English artist resident in Austria.

The Normal Route runs along the North-West Ridge (dotted line) to the summit. Other routes are the North-East Ridge (1) and the North-North-West Ridge (2).

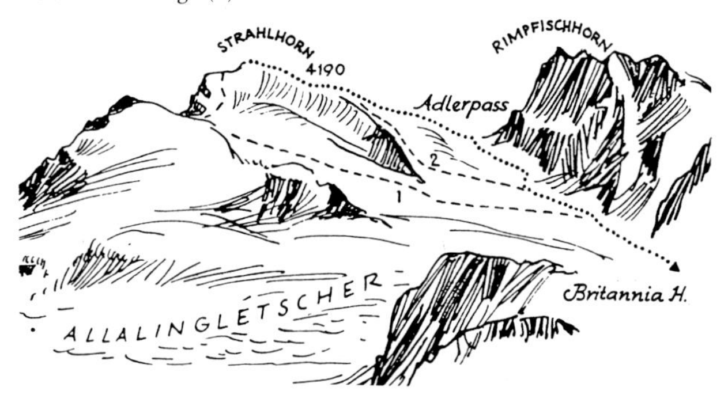

(right) A long-focus view of the Strahlhorn from the north-east.

Monte Rosa: Dufourspitze *4634 m*

'No other mountain lies at such a height' noted Leonardo da Vinci, who would have studied it when he climbed Monte Boso above Valsesia at the end of the fifteenth century.*

No wonder Leonardo was impressed. This is the mightiest massif of the Alps. Though Mont Blanc exceeds it in height, Monte Rosa has a much larger area and is thus the highest *massif* in Western Europe. On the Swiss side it is festively clad in the swelling waves of ice of glaciers which begin just below the summit ridge. In contrast, the Italian side to the east and south presents a façade of sinister precipices which seems to shatter the bounds of human comprehension. Thus the easier Swiss slopes ensure that the majority of ascents of the highest summit, the Dufourspitze, are made from Switzerland.

Ten Four-Thousand-Metre Peaks

The massif boasts ten four-thousand-metre summits with an average height of 4389m. One can climb them all in a two-day expedition. Alternatively, they can be viewed as individual objectives in their own right. The intégral traverse, of international renown, is possible because of the unique position of the Margherita Hut on the summit of the Signalkuppe, which enables the Nordend, Dufourspitze and Zumsteinspitze to be traversed on the first day (thirteen hours, sections of III and II– predominantly ice and snow) and the remaining peaks taken in on the second day during a five-hour expedition that ends at the Gnifetti Hut.

*Douglas Freshfield discusses this in his paper "Mountains and Mankind" *A.J.* XXII, p276. The exact location of the mountain that Leonardo climbed is unclear, this being Freshfield's best judgement based on available evidence.

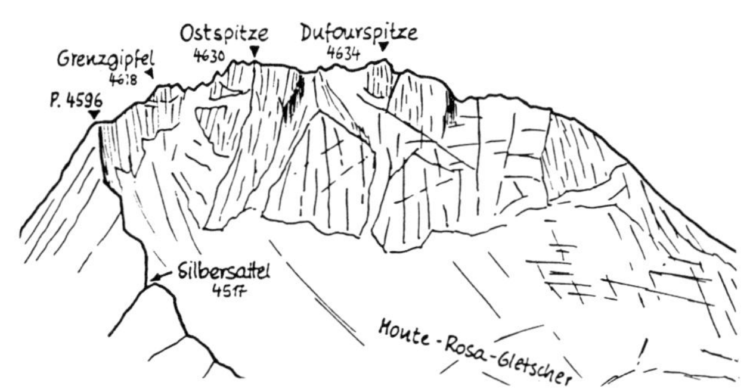

(left) The Monte Rosa massif from the Gornergrat with Nordend and Dufourspitze the prominent summits. The Cresta di Santa Caterina is profiled on the left.

The Peaks as Single Objectives

If this energetic traverse does not appeal, a week's holiday based on the Gnifetti Hut will allow sufficient time to acclimatise on the minor ascents after which the main summits can be combined into suitable expeditions. Unfortunately this strategy leaves the Nordend inconveniently placed unless one plans to descend to the Monte Rosa Hut. These comments apply to climbers on foot but obvious attractions are offered by ski-mountaineering tours across terrain largely free of avalanche danger. The individual peak-bagging strategy works less well from the Monte Rosa Hut, though from here Nordend and Dufourspitze may be most conveniently climbed. In the following chapters the main peaks are described separately and the lesser ones in convenient groups, in each case stressing the least arduous route of ascent.

The Highest Monte Rosa Peak

The summit of the Dufourspitze is 180m west of the Italian border and is, therefore, claimed by Switzerland. The summit ridge has a number of satellite tops, the most important being the Ostspitze (4630m) and the Grenzgipfel (4618m) – the frontier peak. The summit was originally called the Höchspitze but was renamed in 1863 after the Swiss general, Guillaume Henri Dufour (1787-1875), who abolished the separatist league of the seven ultramontane cantons in the war of 1847. He also published the first topographical atlas of Switzerland (the Dufourkarte), of twenty-five 1:100,000 sheets.

The first ascent is formally credited to the large party that reached the Dufourspitze on 1 August 1855, but considerable prestige should be accorded to earlier pioneers. The Silbersattel (4517m) was reached in 1847 by the French climbers M. Victor Puiseux and Dr Edouard Ordinaire with the guides Johann Brantschen, Johann and Matthias Zumtaugwald and Josef Moser. A year later Professor Melchior Ulrich from Zürich watched from the Silbersattel as his guides, Johann Madutz and Matthias Zumtaugwald climbed a couloir on the North Face to gain the summit ridge between the summit and the Ostspitze. In view of the small additional height involved,

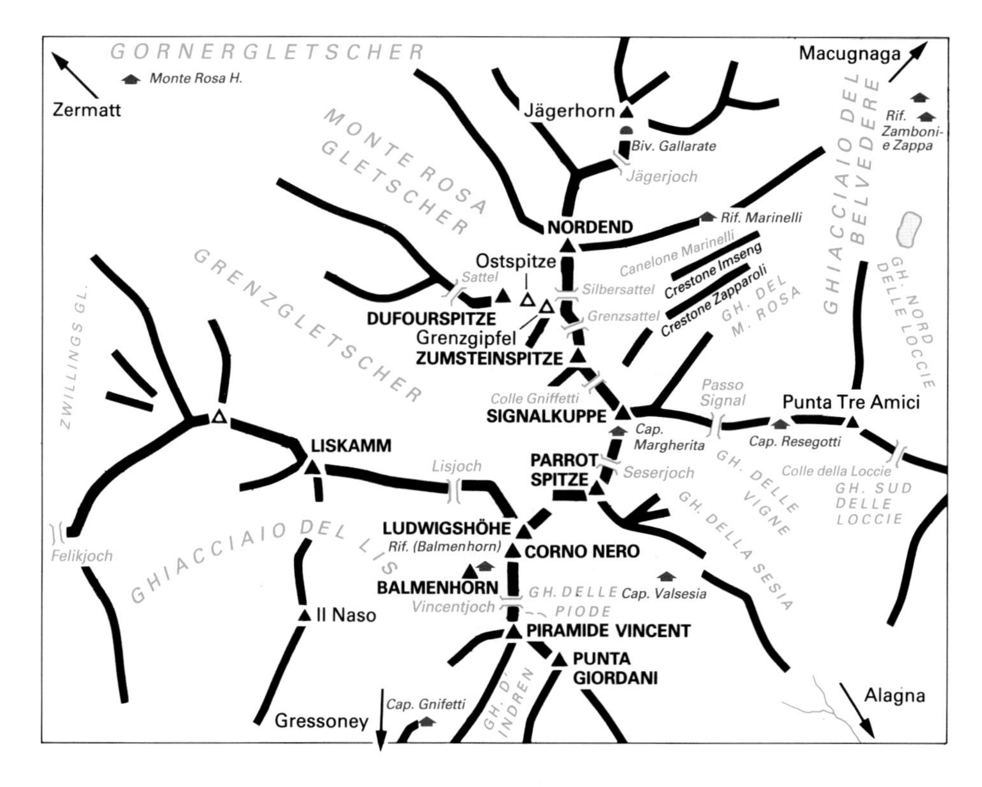

Richard Goedeke

Bill O'Connor

Bill O'Connor

and the difficulty (AD) of their route, many will regard this as the 'moral' first ascent. William Longman records that:

'At this point Zumtaugwalder [*sic*] declared that he would rather die than descend by the route they had ascended. But Madutz attached him to the rope and let him down by degrees from point to point.'†

There followed four further ascents from the Silbersattel, all to the Ostspitze: in 1851 by the brothers Adolf and Hermann von Schlagintweit with Peter Taugwalder, Johann Zumtaugwald and Peter Inderbinen, and in 1854: the three Smyth brothers with their guides Ulrich Lauener and Johann and Matthias Zumtaugwald; Edward Shirley Kennedy with the aforementioned Zumtaugwalds plus Benedict Leir; Edward Levi Ames with Matthias and Stephan Zumtaugwald.

None of these parties attempted to cross the linking ridge to the Dufourspitze, indeed at that time it was unclear which of the two tops was the highest.

In 1855 the Dufourspitze was the target for a large party comprising the very experienced Rev. Charles Hudson, the brothers James Grenville and Christopher Smyth, John Birkbeck and Edward John Stevenson with the guides Ulrich Lauener and the Zumtaugwalds – Johann and Matthias (though their *Führerbuch* is vague on this point). It seems that high on the mountain the guides wished to continue by the established route whereas Christopher Smyth and Hudson were determined to go by the Sattel and the West Ridge. The clients' will prevailed and they led, leaving the guides to follow, though Lauener was in the party that reached the top and one of the Zumtaugwalds (probably Matthias) arrived somewhat later.

Also of note in this early period is the solo ascent by the Irish glaciologist John Tyndall in 1858. Having climbed the peak with Ulrich Lauener, he soloed it the following day, lightly clad and with just a sandwich and a bottle of tea for sustenance.

The Ascent via the Grenzsattel

The mountain can also be climbed by the South-East Ridge from the Grenzsattel. This was first climbed in 1874 by F.P. Barlow and G.W. Prothero with Jean Anthoine Carrel and Peter Taugwalder. It adds two hours to the ascent time from the Monte Rosa Hut and is perhaps more useful as part of the intégral traverse or in an ascent from the Margherita Hut.

†*A.J.* VIII, Appendix pp31-32

(top left) Crossing the Satteltole heading towards Sattel during an ascent of the Dufourspitze.

(far left) On the steep snow slopes of the West Ridge of the Dufourspitze with the same section viewed from the col below (near left).

Wil Hurford

(above) On the Monte Rosa traverse – descending the rocks of the Grenzgipfel to the Grenzsattel.

Nordend – Dufourspitze Combination

These two mountains can be climbed in a single day from the Monte Rosa Hut. The ascent options on Nordend are described in the following chapter and, from the Silbersattel, the North Flank and the North Ridge of the Dufourspitze both rise to gain the Grenzgrat. A chimney pitch provides both the key and the first real obstacle. From the Grenzgrat to the Grenzgipfel slightly more than an hour is needed. The traverse beyond over the Ostspitze and other minor tops is impressive but not hard, with two further chimneys (one climbed, the other descended) before the summit is gained.

The Cresta Rey

One further route is worthy of note on the Swiss side. This is the South-South-West Rib or 'Cresta Rey' named in memory of Guido Rey (1861-1935), the distinguished Turin mountaineer and author who, apart from numerous new routes, also made the third ascent of this ridge. It was first climbed by Eustace Hulton with Peter Rubi and Josef Moser on 20 August 1874 but for some reason is not called the 'Cresta Hulton'. The route is very direct; a pronounced rib leads straight to the summit from the Grenz Glacier and offers reliable rock and, usually, good conditions (due to the southern aspect). The short crux pitch calls either for combined tactics or an outflanking manoeuvre on the left.

The Normal Route from the Monte Rosa Hut

The Monte Rosa Hut stands on the Plattje, a island of rock in the sea of ice of the Gorner, Grenz and Monte Rosa Glaciers. The first building on this site was known as the Bétemps Hut, in honour of François Bétemps who made a generous donation to the SAC for its construction. For those heading for Monte Rosa (and indeed for most other expeditions) the alarm call at three in the morning is followed by a bustle of ant-like activity and the refreshing chill outside. It is wise to take things slowly on the medial moraines of the Grenz Glacier beyond the hut, for to stray off-route at night amid this jumble of rocky monoliths would cost dearly in terms of time. The Monte Rosa Glacier is reached in little more than an hour, the tracks skirting its crevasses, and soon the first light of day colours the tips of the Matterhorn, Weisshorn, Breithorn and Dent Blanche a vivid red.

At the glacier cwm of Satteltole at 4200m the path splits, the route to Nordend heading east and that to the

Wil Hurford

(left) The slabby rocks of the Cresta Rey – one of the best routes on the Dufourspitze.

(right) The southern cliffs of the Dufourspitze from the Zumsteinspitze. The Ostspitze and the Grenzgipfel are the two tops on the right. The sunlit buttress of the Cresta Rey leads to the summit on the left.

Dufourspitze going to the right. Some steep climbing leads to the Sattel at an altitude of 4359m. The West Ridge rises from here with still 300m of ascent, rather longer than appearances would suggest. A steep ridge of névé, in places ice-smooth, is followed by a horizontal rock passage. Beyond a little notch more snow, slabby boulders and an iced-up chimney provide a finale, with fresh snow making the last climb to the summit additionally troublesome and the exposure keeping the nerve-ends tingling.

The Macugnaga Face

With a height of more than two thousand metres the East Wall of Monte Rosa is the greatest sheer face in the Alps, and a full ten kilometres wide. The impression is one of infinite size and might, particularly when seen from the Monte Moro Pass. The face had been studied for many years; as early as 1787 the Italian Count Morozzo had been met with a stern rebuff. In the days before the ascent, famous guides including Christian Almer, Alexander Burgener, the Lauener bothers and Josef-Marie Lochmatter had all considered the problem but judged the face too dangerous. One man thought it possible – the twenty-seven year old hunter from Saas, Ferdinand Imseng, who in 1873 persuaded Richard Pendlebury to hire him to lead an attempt. The party was a truly European one, made up of the Englishmen Richard and William Pendlebury with the Rev. Charles Taylor, Imseng (Swiss), Gabriel Spechtenhauser (Austrian) and Giovanni Oberto (Italian). Imseng had studied the face and believed he had spotted a comparatively safe line of ascent, crossing the great central couloir and then moving up its left side and the snow and ice slopes above to reach the Grenzsattel. His confidence inspired the amateurs, though their experienced guide, Spechtenhauser, remained decidedly sceptical about the whole venture (particularly when an avalanche was heard at 2 a.m. just before they set off). The ascent was made, not without incident as later described by Taylor to members of The Alpine Club§, many of whom, in common with the guides, considered the face to be unacceptably risky. Taylor's account of what became a desperate venture, is laced with self-justification and brittle with tension:

'. . . in spite of all whispered doubts [about] progress we remained steadily in the ascendant, and we determined, without too closely defining the meaning of our sage resolve, that we would go as far as we could with safety go . . . Our way was, for a time safe and plain . . . and we grew more and more convinced at every step that Imseng was a true prophet.'

After crossing the great couloir they moved steadily up the face until, in the early morning, a huge bergschrund barred the way with the only crossing point being a pile of avalanche debris on the extreme left, below the Zumsteinspitze.

'. . . Gaber [Spectenhauser], though by nature a man of the rocks, is fast developing a taste for crevasses, and it was no ordinary pleasure for him to lead us over the most voracious-looking "schrund" that it had ever been his happiness to cross.'

By 10 a.m. they were on the slopes below the Grenzsattel but here the snow began to deteriorate:

'. . . everything was going well, and the idea of failure had vanished from our minds, at a moment when we were on the verge of the most alarming situation of the day. A sudden sliding of the surface . . . brought the whole party to an instantaneous halt . . . no sound could be heard but the hiss of snow as it skimmed down the steep slopes on every side. Perhaps an avalanche was coming, perhaps not . . . nothing could now be more self-evident than that we must abandon the Sattel. The sliding went on without diminution . . . The snow was in motion left and right and some distance in front.'

In a situation of extreme tension they began to work up and across to gain the safety of the lowest rocks of the Grenzgipfel.

'The simple fact was that six men, joined by some fifty yards of cord, were nearing the end of a short, steep snow slope. A few steps and the head of the column was hopefully near the goal, a few more, with growing confidence but undiminished care, and the last film of doubt was scattered by a subdued jodel from Imseng, which announced that the rocks were reached and the day was won.'

They pressed on directly up the rocks to the Grenzgipfel and then made the first traverse of the entire summit ridge to link the Ostspitze with the Dufourspitze before descending to Riffel to complete an historic eighteen-hour expedition. Imseng became famous because of this ascent and was soon much sought as a guide. In the sub-

§*A.J.* VI, p232

Jim Teesdale

sequent years he made a number of major ascents, but the success was not to last. In 1881 he went to attempt the third ascent of the route with Damiano Marinelli and the Bormio guide Battista Pedranzini and an unnamed porter. In the late afternoon of 8 August they were trying to reach a high bivouac site on the exposed rocks to the left of the couloir when they were surprised by an avalanche at 3400m and swept off into the abyss, falling 1200m. The porter, who was a little behind the others, survived to tell the tale. The Marinelli Hut and Marinelli Couloir were named in memoriam, as was the Imsengrücken (rock spur), which bounds the Marinelli Couloir to the south. Nowadays, the stone-built Marinelli Hut serves as a high-altitude point of departure. There have been many varied ascents of this face, yet nothing can disguise the sobering fact that the ice avalanches still thunder down the couloir and that there are only very few places on the wall where one is safe from falling debris. Technical difficulties are always over-shadowed by these ever-present dangers. In optimum conditions, ascents take up to ten hours. It is best to start from the hut at midnight. The traverse of the feared Marinelli Couloir demands haste, an attribute which might well be applied to the entire face. The prime requirement for a successful ascent is a cold night, with temperatures below –10°C, and a well-consolidated covering of névé. Warm weather brings the East Face to life, and this can prove fatal!

Ski Extreme

The face has been climbed solo, descended and climbed in winter but perhaps the most amazing feat took place on 7 October 1969 when Sylvain Saudan from Geneva made a ski descent from the Silbersattel.

'I couldn't even see the Marinelli Couloir from the Silbersattel; the start was hidden by the cornices on the ridge. So I was forced to smash through the cornices. I then had to pass through the gap created and, groping blindly at first, find the best part of the couloir to start the descent.

To do so I had to move along below the lower edge of the cliffs, beneath the Dufourspitze, and negotiate a really ticklish traverse above a 2500m drop . . .

'Mistakes are out of the question. Up there, you have to ski without any exaggerated movements. The dynamics come from the feet, with the whole body joining in the movements. If more power is needed, it comes from the hips, but this is held in reserve. The whole thing has to be perfectly synchronised, including of course the placing of the ski sticks; this must be calculated precisely, for if you plant them too far away this will knock all your turns off-balance.'

VALLEY BASES

Zermatt see Rimpfischhorn p91
Macugnaga see Strahlhorn p92

HUTS/OTHER BASES

Monte Rosa Hut 2795m. SAC. Situated on the western edge of the Plattje above the Grenz Glacier. 128 places. Staffed from 15 March to 15 September *tel* 028/ 67 21 15. 2¼ hours from the Rotenboden station of the Gornergrat Railway, first across the slopes of the Gornerli to P.2657 and then across the Gorner Glacier (waymarked with snow stakes, crevassed before the Plattje moraines). In winter descend directly to the Gorner Glacier at the steep hollow of the Moritzloch, approx 400m beyond P.2775.
Kulmhotel Gornergrat 3100m. At top station of the Gornergrat Railway. 80 places. Open during the summer and winter seasons *tel* 028/ 67 22 19.
Rifugio Damiano Marinelli 3036m. CAI. Small stone-built hut below a rock spur on the East Face of Monte Rosa. 12 places. Stove (no wood), unstaffed (ask for the key from Costantino Pala, Macugnaga-Staffa) *tel* 0324/ 6 51 27. 5 hours from Macugnaga-Pecetto, or 3 hours from Belvedere (1932m) reached by lift from Macugnaga-Pecetto (where there is also *Rifugio Saronno tel* 0324/ 6 53 22) via the *Rifugio Zamboni Zappa* 2070m. CAI. 52 places *tel* 0324/ 6 53 13; 45 min. from Belvedere. Track marked on upper section.
Capanna Regina Margherita see Signalkuppe p106

NORMAL ROUTE

North-West Flank/West Ridge PD II+ (sections on the summit ridge), to 40°. 7 hours from the Monte Rosa Hut. 1850mH. A glacier tour and steep névé to the Sattel then rock and mixed ground on the West Ridge. *As a ski tour:* Follow the Normal Route to the Satteltole or even the Sattel, then continue on foot.

RIDGES/FACES

North-West Flank/North Ridge AD III (sections), II. 2 hours/ 120mH from the Silbersattel. 7 hours/1850mH from the Monte Rosa Hut. A glacier tour with mixed climbing then rock climbing (often ice encrusted).
South-East Ridge AD III, II. 2 hours/185mH from the Grenzsattel. 7½ hours/1850mH from the Monte Rosa Hut. 3 hours from the Capanna Margherita. Glacier tour then mixed climbing.
South-South-West Rib (Cresta Rey) AD III+ (one section), II. 3 hours/440mH from foot of rib. Rock and mixed climbing.
South-West Ridge/West Ridge D– IV and III. 6 hours/700mH from the foot of the route (2½ hours from the Monte Rosa Hut). Rock and mixed climbing. Joins the Normal Route at the Sattel.
East Face (Marinelli Couloir) D+ To 55°, III+ (sections) on the direct finish. 8-10 hours from the Marinelli Hut, 1600mH. A snow and ice climb with rock on the direct finish. Serious – threatened throughout by stone and ice fall.

MAPS/GUIDEBOOKS

Landeskarte der Schweiz 1:50,000 Sheet 5006 *Matterhorn – Mischabel. Pennine Alps Central* by Robin Collomb (Alpine Club). *The Alpine 4000m Peaks by the Classic Routes* by Richard Goedeke (Diadem/ Menasha).

Monte Rosa: Nordend *4609 m*

Nordend's isolated position at the northern end of the massif, upstaged by the Dufourspitze, ensures it sees fewer ascents than any of the Monte Rosa summits, yet it is a high and important peak with several major routes. It is perfectly feasible to climb both the Nordend and the Dufourspitze in a day, usually by an itinerary based on the Silbersattel. The South-West Ridge, that links the saddle to the summit, was first climbed 26 August 1861 by the Chamoniard Michel Payot with his Swiss colleague Binder* as guides for the English brothers Edward and T.F. Buxton and John Jermyn Cowell.

The North-West Buttress has much to recommend it as a more difficult alternative to the Normal Route and as part of the intégral traverse, and is done from the Monte Rosa Hut with a rather long approach.

*The Swiss and British guidebooks omit this name.

Of the other routes on the mountain the North-East Ridge (really more of a face), better known as the 'Cresta di Santa Caterina', is considered by many as one of Monte Rosa's finest climbs. It was first *descended* on 5 September 1899 by Walter Flender, Heinrich Burgener and Ferdinand Furrer. With a start from the remote Gallarate Bivouac Hut on the Jägerjoch it provides a challenging climb in a wonderfully remote setting. The first ascent in 1906 put another feather in the cap of that redoubtable rock climber Franz Lochmatter who, with brother Josef and their regular employer Valentine Ryan, led the climb (V, IV) without the assistance of pitons (though several have appeared since).

Quite different behaviour took place on the heavily aided first ascent of the North Pillar in August 1944 by Swiss climbers Vogt, Perren and Petrig. In 1969 this was straightened out and climbed in a freer form by the Polish trio of Furmanik, Tarnawski and Tysak. The route has pitches of V+ and A1 and is technically the most difficult line on the Nordend.

The East Face of Nordend

The section of the East Face below the summit of the Nordend boasts the classic Brioschi Route, which was first climbed in July 1876. This climb was another result of the restless ambition of Ferdinand Imseng who with Abraham Imseng guided Luigi Brioschi on a twenty-one hour climb up intricately linked arêtes. It is said to be less dangerous than the Marinelli Couloir, though still very serious, the more so in these days of retreating snow. Stonefall is now a major factor, the ribs having insufficient profile to adequately funnel projectiles into the dividing couloirs. To the right of the Brioschi are the 'Cresta del Poeta' (1937) and the 'Canale della Solitudine' (1948), both established by the Italian musician, artist and solo-climber Ettore Zapparoli. To its left, on the face below the South-West Ridge, are the 'Via Restelli' (Carlo

Jim Teesdale

(left) Nordend from the Dufourspitze.

(right) An aerial view of Monte Rosa's 2000m East Face in spring snow conditions.

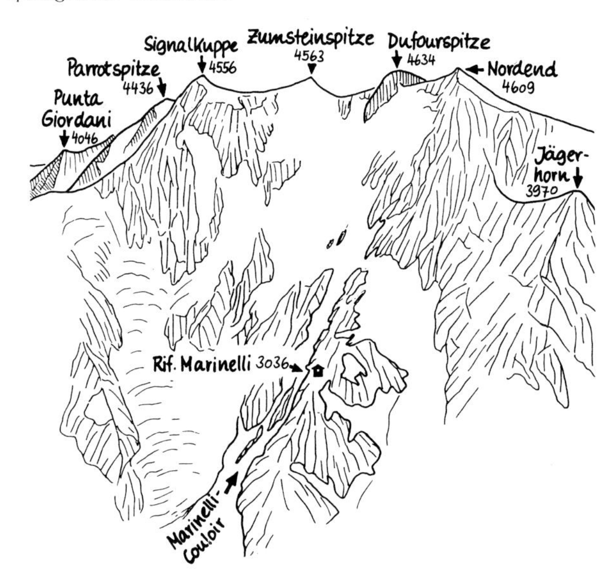

John Allen

(above) The Dufourspitze seen from the summit of Nordend with figures ascending the final part of the West Ridge (Normal Route) on the right.

Restelli, Matthias Zurbriggen and Louis Burgener, 1893) and the 'Voie Directe' (Erminio Ranzoni and Felice and Clementino Jacchini, 1949). All these climbs are very serious and rarely repeated.

By way of the Silbersattel

The normal routes to the top of the Nordend and the Dufourspitze are identical as far as the Satteltole at 4200m. Here the Nordend route veers off to the east below the northern precipices of the Dufourspitze. Crevasses and ice cliffs in the jumble of the upper Monte Rosa Glacier are given a wide berth, and the bergschrund sometimes calls for evading action. If the slope leading up to the Silbersattel is icy, steps may have to be cut. The South-West Ridge beyond can also be icy and usually has large cornices.

Ski-mountaineers will advance as far as conditions allow but will certainly have to exchange skis for crampons at the Silbersattel, and possibly a good deal lower.

On the North-West Buttress the conditions again determine the route taken. If corniced, one keeps to the left, otherwise the crest direct provides a splendid trip, with the last thirty metres on rock.

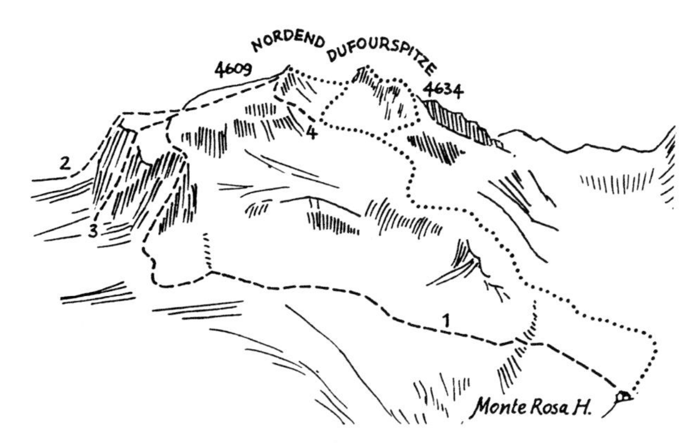

The Normal Routes on the Dufourspitze and the Nordend are marked with dotted lines. Other routes are the North-West Buttress (1), the North-East Ridge (2), the North Pillar (3) and the Morshead Spur (4).

VALLEY BASES

Zermatt see Rimpfischhorn p91
Macugnaga see Strahlhorn p92

HUTS AND OTHER BASES

Monte Rosa Hut, Marinelli Hut see Dufourspitze p99
Gallarate Bivouac Hut 3969m. CAI. Below the summit of the Jägerhorn above the Jägerjoch. 9 places. Always open. 6 hours from the Monte Rosa Hut. 1118mH.

NORMAL ROUTES

South-West Ridge PD II– (on summit cliffs). To 40°. 7 hours from the Monte Rosa Hut. 1820mH. Glacier and snow and ice climbing.
As a ski tour: In favourable conditions skis can be left as high as the Silbersattel.

RIDGES/FACES

North-West Buttress AD II(sections). 8 hours from the Monte Rosa Hut. 1820mH. A mixed climb with stonefall danger at the foot of the buttress.
North-West Spur (Morshead Spur) AD IV(sections), II. 3 hours/400mH from foot of the spur. Rock and mixed climbing.
West Face D To 48°. 3 hours/400mH from the foot of the face. Ice and mixed climbing.
North-East Ridge (Cresta di Santa Caterina) TD– V (one section) and IV (sustained). 8 hours/700mH from the Jägerjoch. Mixed and rock climbing on the lower 450m, then névé to the summit.
East Face (Brioschi Route) D+ IV, III. To 60°. 12 hours/1500mH from the Marinelli Hut. Serious mixed climbing.

MAPS/GUIDEBOOKS%

See Dufourspitze p99

Monte Rosa

Zumsteinspitze 4563m Signalkuppe 4556m

ZUMSTEINSPITZE
Although this unassuming peak falls naturally into the intégral traverse and can also be climbed in conjunction with the Dufourspitze, it is most conveniently reached in a short excursion from the Signalkuppe via the Colle Gnifetti. Joseph Zumstein took the South-East Ridge from the col with companions, guides and porters, to make the first ascent on 1 August 1820 – the first of Monte Rosa's highest tops to be climbed.

On the other side of the summit dome the North Ridge rises from the Grenzsattel, or Colle Zumstein, and this was first negotiated (in descent) in 1882 by Karl Blodig and Christian Ranggetiner. Also of interest on the Swiss side is the South-West Arête which provides a more direct way up the mountain on ascents from the Monte Rosa or Gnifetti Huts.

The East Face, though very dangerous, has a network of routes. The Grenzsattel, the original target of the Pendlebury/Imseng party, was reached in 1889 by Achille Ratti (later to become Pope Pius XI), guided by Luigi Grasselli, Joseph Gradin and A. Proment. Guido Rey's attempt to repeat this route in 1893 led to an extreme diversion from below the bergschrund, with a long traverse to the left to gain an icy ramp that led across the upper face of the Zumsteinspitze to the Colle Gnifetti.

Low on the East Face a rock spur (originally known as the Crestone Innominato but later renamed Crestone Zapparoli), somewhat south of the Marinelli Couloir, was used to start routes to the Grenzsattel (1925), Zumsteinspitze (1930) and Colle Gnifetti (Zapparoli, solo, 1934). All are described in the Swiss guidebook as extremely dangerous, a fact reinforced by the disappearance of Ettore Zapparoli while attempting yet another solo climb on the face in 1951.

Willi Burkhardt

(right) An aerial view of the East Ridge (Cresta Signal/Topham Ridge) of the Signalkuppe with the Zumsteinspitze, the Dufourspitze (Grenzgipfel) and Nordend on the right standing above the sweep of East Face.

Willi Burkhardt

Wil Hurford

SIGNALKUPPE (PUNTA GNIFETTI)

This is, orographically, the most important point of the entire Monte Rosa range after the Dufourpitze and, from a mountaineering point of view, the absolute focal point of the area. The names derive from the prominent gendarme (the Signal) at the top of the East Ridge and the man who made the first ascent in 9 August 1842, Giovanni Gnifetti, a clergyman from Alagna. Gnifetti and his seven companions laid down the route most often climbed these days; starting from Italy, crossing the Lisjoch and ascending the West Flank to the summit.

(left) The Margherita Hut on the summit of the Signalkuppe.

Capanna Regina Margherita

The first hut on the Signalkuppe, erected primarily for scientific purposes, provided mountaineers with the highest accommodation in Europe. Building work began in 1890, with the financial support of the Italian Crown, and the hut was inaugurated in 1893 under the personal supervision of Queen Margherita.

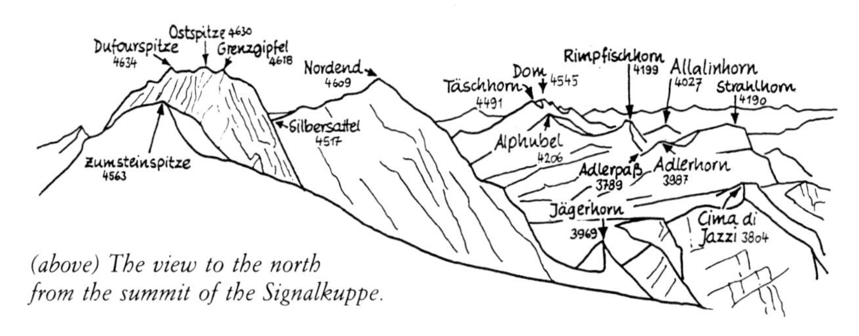

(above) The view to the north from the summit of the Signalkuppe.

(above) The Signalkuppe and the Zumsteinspitze (foreground) from the summit of the Dufourspitze.

The modern refuge has existed since August 1980. It is a double-walled wooden building clad in sheet copper and designed in accordance with the principles of the 'Faraday Cage' to provide a screen against extraneous electrical fields. Comfortably appointed, it boasts a snow-melting machine and offers gastronomic delights of a high standard at correspondingly high prices!

The Topham Ridge

Whereas the North Ridge and the South-West Ridge are more or less simple snow plods, the East Ridge is a classic expedition and in every respect an objective to be taken seriously. It is seven hours' walk from the valley to the hut and six to eight hours have to be set aside for the mixed ground of the ridge itself, which gives exciting climbing with no hint of the objective dangers that threaten the faces on either side. The climb is known as the 'Cresta Signal' or 'Topham Ridge', after Harold Ward Topham (polyglot sportsman and later an assiduous guideless climber) who did the first ascent on 28 July 1887 with Aloys Supersaxo and a porter.

The Normal Route from Italy

Those wishing to climb the Signalkuppe start from the Gnifetti Hut and climb first to the Lisjoch, passing close to the Piramide Vincent and the Balmenhorn *en route*. From the pass a right-hand sweep leads to the upper depression of the Grenz Glacier and, at about 4200m, a

(below) The West Flank of the Signalkuppe.

traverse of the northern slopes of the Parrotspitze and the Seserjoch brings you to the cwm below the Colle Gnifetti. Hereabouts, the route converges with that from the Monte Rosa Hut and, ignoring the route directly to the col, it is more interesting to break off to the right and climb the West Flank of the Signalkuppe to gain its West Ridge. Easy rocky scrambling then leads along the ridge to the final summit rise.

Ski-mountaineers should bear in mind that in May it is usually possible to descend right down to the Bocchetta delle Pisse station (2396m) of the 'Funivia Monrosa'.

The Swiss Route

From the Monte Rosa Hut the path keeps to the true right-hand side of the Grenz Glacier. Between P.3472 and P.3699 an ice cliff towers overhead, with bizarre séracs stretching up out of the jumbled maze. This threatening area is best negotiated by slinking off to the left of the clefts and crevices (to the right of a rock rib). After an easier section, the lower rocks of the South-West Ridge of the Dufourspitze and a zone of broken ice higher up force a move away to the south-east. The small, flat parts of the trail allow respite between the steep rises which, for many, induce the feeling of having lead in the legs.

Above the high scooped plateau at about 4200m the Italian route is joined and to the right the last strenuous traverse leads across to the West Ridge and the final climb to the coveted summit.

Stonefalls and Salvos of Ice

Although little frequented, the big faces of the mountain should be discussed here for the sake of completeness. They are the North-East (Macugnaga) Face and the South-East (Valsesia) Face, two great precipices guarded by hanging glaciers. A total of seven routes trace a way up these formidable walls which not infrequently resound to the crashing and tearing of stonefalls and salvos of ice.

The 900m South-East Face was first climbed in 1906 by A. Orio, F. de Zinis with G. Guglielminetti and G. Chiara. They ascended the face but finished the last steep section with the assistance of a rope let down from above, a pitch subsequently free-climbed in 1923.

French alpinism was worthily represented by Lucien Devies and Jacques Lagarde, with their first ascent of the North-East Face at the head of the Macugnaga cirque, on 17 July 1931, one of the most serious yet prestigious

(left) A view across the East Face of Monte Rosa with the Signalkuppe on the left. The Lagarde/Devies Route ascends the ice slopes below its summit. The Jägerjoch and the ribs of the Brioschi Route are prominent features on the right.

(right) The highest summits of Monte Rosa cloaked in winter snow in an aerial view from the south-west.

mixed routes in the Alps. Lagarde's account of this makes sobering reading*:

'Mountain in bad condition . . . The ice slopes were covered with snow except in the uppermost part. There the ice lay quite bare and the pick would not bite. The deep snow prevented any stonefall – nevertheless there must be great risk. Near the base of the great slope, some 100m below the upper bergschrund, the lower portion of the sérac bastion collapsed. The party had just time to shelter under an overhanging boulder; the avalanche swept right over us, raked the route followed for over an hour, then plunged down over 900m completely covering the bivouac islet which had appeared quite out of range the night before.

'All the lower part of the route down to about 3400m is exposed to sérac avalanches, fortunately these appear to be rare. [On the approach] At about 2400m there is risk from the Marinelli Couloir, while higher up the Signaljoch, Signalkuppe and Monte Rosa Glacier are all threatening. Hence a bivouac on the Signal Glacier is not to be recommended . . .'

Lagarde's advice on subtle variations to avoid some of the objective dangers of the route was taken seriously, so much so that the ascent in 1959 by the British climbers Colin Mortlock and Wilfrid Noyce with the American Jack Sadler deviated to such an extent at mid-height that they established a new line, taking a series of rising traverses to the right to finally break through a sérac barrier to gain the Colle Gnifetti. This steep mixed face below the col had already been climbed in a counter diagonal in 1933 by Maglioli, Mosca, Zurbriggen and Pironi who reached it by a long traverse across the East Face from the top of the Imsengrücken.

At the start of the summer in 1969, the Lagarde/Devies route had only seen six repeat ascents (including the first winter ascent in 1965) when Alessandro Gogna decided to attempt a solo ascent. During the night of 17 July, Gogna left Rifugio Zamboni-Zappa and at 3 p.m. the following afternoon reached the Margherita Hut in a raging snowstorm. He later described the route as having ice sections of 60° and very daunting objective dangers.

*A.J. 43, p37

VALLEY BASES

Zermatt see Rimpfischhorn p91
Macugnaga see Strahlhorn p92
Alagna see Liskamm p115

HUTS/OTHER BASES

Monte Rosa Hut, Marinelli Hut see Dufourspitze p99
Capanna Regina Margherita 4554m. CAI. on the summit of the Signalkuppe (Punta Gnifetti). 80 places. Staffed from 10 June to 10 September *tel* 0163/ 9 10 39. 4 hours from the Gnifetti Hut. 907mH. 7 hours from the Monte Rosa Hut. 1761mH
Rifugio Luigina Resegotti 3624m. CAI. 800m east of the Colle Signal. 20 places. Gas oven, kitchen utensils. Open all year. Gear dump for the Mountain Rescue. Approach from Acqua Bianca, 1600m, at the end of the little road beyond Alagna, passing the Chapel of St Anthony and via Vignealp to the Rifugio Barba-Ferrero (2 hours). From here 3½ hours to the hut. 6 hours from roadhead. 6½ hours from Rifugio Zamboni-Zappa via the Colle delle Locie.
Rifugio Citta di Mantova 3498m. Gressoney Guides' Association. On a rocky spur on the Garstelet Glacier on the Punta Indren – Gnifetti Hut trail. Built 1984. 112 places. Staffed 20 March to 14 April and 14 June to 25 September *tel* 0163/ 7 81 50. 1 hour from Punta Indren (lift from Alagna).
Rifugio Giovanni Gnifetti 3647m. CAI. On a rocky spur between the Lis and Garstelet Glaciers. 277 places. Staffed 14 April to 25 September *tel* 0163/ 7 80 15. Winter room (15 places) always open with gas stove. 1½ hours from Punta Indren (lift from Alagna) via the Mantua Hut.

NORMAL ROUTES

Zumsteinspitze: North Ridge from Monte Rosa Hut F+ I+ (summit ridge). 7 hours. 1780mH, A glacier tour to the Grenzjoch, thereafter mixed climbing.
Zumsteinspitze: South-East Ridge from Margherita Hut PD– To 40°. 1¼ hours from the Capanna Regina Margherita. 115mH from Colle Gnifetti.
Signalkuppe: West Flank/South-West Ridge F I (sections). 4 hours from Gnifetti Hut. 900mH. 7 hours from the Monte Rosa Hut. 1770mH. A glacier tour. *As a ski tour*: As normal route to P.4554 at the foot of the West Ridge. Deposit skis here. On the return to the Monte Rosa Hut rope up for the descent through the crevasse zone!

RIDGES/FACES

North-West Ridge F 30 minutes/110mH from the Colle Gnifetti.
South-West Ridge PD I– (section). 1 hour/260mH from the Seserjoch.
East Ridge (Cresta Signal) AD III, II. 7 hours from the Rifugio Resegotti, 940mH. A mixed climb on reasonably firm rock.
North-East Face TD+ VI, III. To 60°. 10-15 hours/1250mH from foot of the face. A very serious ice route with sections of sustained mixed climbing.

MAPS/GUIDEBOOKS

See Dufourspitze p99

Monte Rosa

Parrotspitze 4436m Ludwigshöhe 4341m Corno Nero (Schwarzhorn) 4322m

PARROTSPITZE

The Parrotspitze is perched directly on the frontier ridge with snowfields on the Swiss side, and a steep mixed face overlooking Valsesia in Italy. The mountain owes its name to the German doctor and physicist Friedrich Wilhelm Parrot who, with Joseph Zumstein, made the first attempt on Piramide Vincent in 1816.

The peak is almost exclusively visited as part of a high-level traverse either in ascent from the Lisjoch (usually taking in the Ludwigshöhe), or in descent from the Signalkuppe. The West Ridge provides a direct approach from the Lisjoch – the way chosen on the first ascent in 1863 (this being something of a formality as passing parties could easily have climbed the peak). The guides Melchior Anderegg and Peter Perren conducted their clients Reginald Macdonald, Florence Craufurd Grove, Montagu Woodmass and William Edward Hall* to the summit four days after their Dent d'Hérens success.

The 'moral conquest' of the Parrotspitze might well be accorded to the Rev. Hereford Brooke George and Adolphus Warburton Moore with their guides Christian Almer and Matthias Zumtaugwald, who forced a very difficult route up the East Face on 8 July 1862, reaching the frontier ridge above the Seserjoch, just one hundred feet below the summit – a climb later described by John Ball as 'amongst the most daring of alpine exploits'. Two years later Moore repeated the crossing finding it just as difficult, and it still retains a *Difficile* grading.

It was thus that in 1869, members of the Alpine Club learned with consternation that the Seserjoch had been crossed from west to east by the London sisters Anna and Ellen Pigeon, with the guide Jean Martin and a porter who 'professed to know the way' (the Lisjoch having been their real objective). In the morning mists, conscious of the need to stay clear of the North Face of the Liskamm, they missed the turn to the Lisjoch and found instead the Seserjoch with its steep eastern face. Climbing the ridge of the Parrotspitze for a short distance they soon located the exit of the Almer route but could find no easier line of descent, so at noon they began to climb down the mixed face previously ascended with such difficulty. Martin led, carefully locating the best way, and Anna Pigeon brought up the rear 'preferring to see the awkward porter in front of her rather than behind'. After a painstaking seven-hour descent they reached the glacier and 'crossed it at a running pace to avoid being benighted', reaching the chalets at Vigne at 9 p.m.† In their account the sisters, though noting Martin's skill in conducting the descent, are scathing in their general criticism of guide, porter and hotel. Their modest explanation of the 'feat' noted that snow conditions were particularly favourable, but this would still have been a very serious descent, such that the title 'Pigeonspitze' might well be considered a more suitable name for the peak!

(left) An aerial view of the eastern wall of the Parrotspitze, the Seserjoch and the Signalkuppe with the Liskamm and the Matterhorn in the background. The line taken by the 1862 party finished up the obvious sunlit snow ridge on the lower left.

(right) The Parrotspitze from the Zumsteinspitze with Ludwigshöhe and Corno Nero on the right.

The Climbs

The normal route of ascent requires no special description as the well-beaten tracks that are usually to be found in this area give quite adequate guidance. A hot tip for budding ice specialists is the North-West Face, set at an angle of about 50°. When the snow is consolidated this is a tasty little morsel to be devoured almost in passing but, when icy, it can require front-pointing and even step-cutting.

The 800m Canzio/Guglermina/Lampugnani route on the South-East Flank offers altogether sterner fare (AD) and can take as long as seven hours from the Valsesia Hut. It is best done in early season when the snow and ice cover is still deep. Harder still is the 1985 route of the Italian pair D. Deiana and M. Moretti up a reddish pillar to the left of the central zone of slabs. This has pitches V and V+ on good rock.

Jim Teesdale

LUDWIGSHÖHE

Ludwig von Welden was the man who, on 25 August 1822, with several others, first set foot on the peak in pursuit of topographical information. Such an insignificant lump had little importance in those days and only merits attention now because of its four-thousander status.

The peak is conveniently situated for an ascent from

*Hall was not mentioned in Macdonald's *A.J.* report of the climb. This may have been an oversight as his name is recorded in the Monte Rosa Hotel register and the A.C. register, Vol. I, p130.

†The Pigeons' *A.J.* report on the climb states that the elder sister came last. Records at West Norwood Cemetery (London) show that Anna died in 1917 aged 84 and Ellen in 1902 aged 66.

the Lisjoch. On the frontier ridge it is defined to the north-east by the Piodejoch, which is not mentioned on the Swiss maps and on the Italian maps is called the 'Colle Ippolita o delle Piode'. To the south the diminutive Zurbriggenjoch divides it from the Schwarzhorn.

From the summit a broad snow ridge runs down to the north-west to the Lisjoch via P.4260. The Ludwigshöhe can be reached without difficulty by short snow ascents from all sides except the south-east, where a steep precipice was first mastered on 24 June 1949 by Adolpho Vecchietti and Ovidio Raiteri with their 'Via degli Alpini', an AD climb.

Willi Burkhardt

CORNO NERO

The Corno Nero (or Schwarzhorn) is just 215m south-west of the Ludwigshöhe across the Zurbriggenjoch. To its south the Vincentjoch is the low point before the Piramide Vincent. The standard routes of ascent are the North-West Flank from the Zurbriggenjoch and the South-West Flank from the Vincentjoch, both of which are crossed during the Monte Rosa traverse. It was in such circumstances that Marco Maglionini and Albert de Rothschild, with the guides Edouard Cupelin, Peter and Niklaus Knubel and three porters, made the first ascent on 18 August 1873.

On an expedition from the Gnifetti Hut one could include Corno Nero with ascents of the Piramide Vincent, the Balmenhorn and the Ludwigshöhe though it is better taken in during a descent from the Signalkuppe where one can constantly enjoy the unfolding views on the southerly flank of the massif. There are several possible combinations and those with plenty of energy will doubtless wish to link all the minor summits into one glorious peak-bagging descent.

(above) A view up the Grenz Glacier to Monte Rosa.

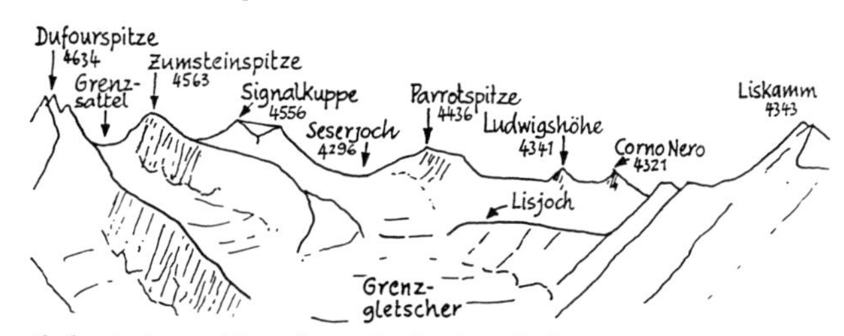

(below) Corno Nero from the Ludwigshöhe.

VALLEY BASE
Alagna see Liskamm p115
Zermatt see Rimfischhorn p91
HUTS/OTHER BASES
Rifugio Citta di Mantova, Rifugio Giovanni Gnifetti see Signalkuppe p106.
Capanna Valsesia (Gugliermina) 3312m. CAI. Situated on the large island of rock between the Sesia and the Piode Glaciers, south of the Parrotspitze. 12 places. Gas stove and cooker, dishes. Open all year. 5 hours from Acqua Bianca, at the head of the little road beyond Alagna, passing the Chapel of St Anthony.
NORMAL ROUTES
Parrotspitze – West Ridge To 40° 3 hours from the Gnifetti Hut. 790mH. A glacier tour.
Ludwigshöhe – North-West Ridge To 40°. 2½ hours from the Gnifetti Hut. A glacier tour.
Corno Nero – South-West Flank I+ To 40°. 2½ hours from the Gnifetti Hut. 720mH. Glacier approach, rocky finish.
Corno Nero – North-West Flank I (sections). To 43°. 2½ hours from the Gnifetti Hut. 720mH. Glacier approach, rocky finish.
Balmenhorn 1½ hours from the Gnifetti Hut. 560mH.
Piramide Vincent – South-West Ridge PD– I. To 35°. 2 hours from the Gnifetti Hut. 605mH. Glacier then mixed. *As a ski tour:* From the hut go north, past the western slopes, to flat glacier fields at 4000m. Bear right, heading for the Colle Vincent, but slightly below this move right and climb the snow of the North-West Flank to the summit.
RIDGES/FACES
Parrotspitze: North-West Face To 50°. 1 hour/200mH from foot of face. A snow and ice face.
Parrotspitze – South-East Flank AD III and II+. 7 hours from the Valsesia Hut. 1050mH.
Corno Nero – South-East Face AD 7 hours from the Valsesia Hut. 1029mH. A rock (reputedly solid) and mixed climb.
Piramide Vincent – South-West Face AD+ Three varied lines. 3 hours/350mH from foot of the face. Mixed and rock routes (reputedly worthwhile).
Punta Giordani – North-East Arête AD 5 hours from the Valsesia Hut. 734mH. A mixed climb.
MAPS/GUIDEBOOKS
See Dufourspitze p99

John Allen

Monte Rosa

Balmenhorn 4167m   Piramide Vincent 4215m   Punta Giordani 4046m

BALMENHORN
The Balmenhorn is higher, for example, than the Aiguille Verte, the Jungfrau and the Breithorn. Yet can it really be regarded as a four-thousander? It is little more than an awkward protuberance breaking the surface on the northern edge of the Lis Glacier – yet punctilious collectors of four-thousand metre peaks use it to add to their tick-list. It is conveniently situated on the route to more important peaks, but no doubt it would soon be relegated to 'top' status if it were less easily accessible.

Hidden away in the summit cliffs, the little Capanna Balmenhorn, originating from the First World War, is a rather squalid hovel to be used only in the direst emergency! A few metres higher an over-sized statue of Christ 'Christo delle Vette' was erected in 1955 and protected by a lightning conductor. The sculptor was Alfredo Dai.

PIRAMIDE VINCENT
The Piramide Vincent is the southernmost four-thousand metre *peak* of the Monte Rosa Group if Punta Giordani is considered to be merely a shoulder on the South-East Ridge of the mountain.

The Alpine history books name Johann Nikolaus Vincent as the first ascentionist. Owner of the gold mines around Alagna, he made the ascent on 5 August 1819 with two miners and a chamois-hunter. In 1851 the widely-travelled von Schlagintweit brothers, guided by Peter Beck, decided on the North Ridge from the Colle Vincent, a route which is also valuable as a ski-mountaineering outing.

Generally, however, the col is avoided in favour of the somewhat shorter North-West Flank and, for a summer ascent, the South-West Ridge, though slightly harder, has proved its worth.

There are two routes (V) on the 500m South Face but these are loose and dangerous and not recommended. Conversely the 350m South-West Face has three quite interesting mixed routes (all AD+).

The Piramide Vincent can be climbed in about two hours from the Gnifetti Hut via the South-West Ridge, and its status as a valuable training and acclimatization peak is therefore secure.

PUNTA GIORDANI
Apart from its respectable height, the Punta Giordani lacks all the features of a mountain in the conventional sense of the term. Were this lump on the South-East Ridge to lie below the four-thousand-metre mark, no one would have ever consciously cast a glance in its direction. The fact that on 23 July 1801 the physician Dr Pietro Giordani climbed the secondary peak from the south-east has been variously disputed. Hard evidence suggests that the first people on the true summit were two Italians in 1871. The time gap between the probable and the definite first ascent shows that, even in an era when the emphasis was on seeking out new routes, the Punta Giordani enjoyed little respect.

Ludwig Reh noted that the northern approach from the Valsesia Hut is 'the most interesting and impressive of all', but such advice is likely to be heeded only by the true connoisseur since the Valsesia Hut takes at least five hours to reach, followed by a 700m climb. The contrast between this approach and that from the west could not be greater: it takes a mere forty minutes (downhill) to reach Punta Giordani from Piramide Vincent. Ski-mountaineers have it even easier. They ski down from the Gnifetti Hut path to the Indren Glacier, reaching the summit over the snow slopes from the south-west – about three hours, there and back.

(below) Signalkuppe (top left), Parrotspitze, Ludwigshöhe, Corno Nero, Balmenhorn, Piramide Vincent and Punta Giordani in an aerial view across the Lis Glacier from the south-west.

Willi Burkhardt

Liskamm *4527 m*

Few mountains in the Alps are as feared as the Liskamm, which exudes an aura of horror aptly caught by Oscar Erich Meyer: 'There is something strange about the Liskamm, something which sets it apart from all the others. . . . [its] two ridges, far removed from each other, do not converge on a single summit, but hang suspended in space as the apex of a roof, as if they did not wish to bring their dizzy heights to a culminating point, only to sink again. . . . there is no mountain in the Alps upon which the vertical upthrust of Gothic architecture and, at the same time, the decorative frieze of the Greek temple dwell more conspicuously.

'Then, there is the Wall . . . where flat ribbons of rock peek tentatively through the ice. A compact entity, it stretches out its monstrous shape, cranes its neck in vertiginous steepness, whether viewed from the side or head-on . . . the beauty of the mountain is celestial, as no other in the Zermatt area.

'Yet quite apart from the beauty . . ., a horror dwells in the soul of the onlooker. It is the memory of those whom the mountain has struck down . . . They did not die at its foot, on its walls or on its ridges, but were cast from the crest into the depths. All at once, all whom the rope had bound together. For thus are its cornices.

'Day after day, the wind kneads and shapes them, sticking one crystal after another to the narrow roof-ridge; a white balcony built far out over the void, suspended above the drop. And . . . it is man who, in a deadly bond with his companions, added the last gram to the balance, tipping the scales. And an avalanche of ice is swept down to the valley with the corpses. Thus the Liskamm kills. It gives no warnings. It strikes like lightning.'

Accidents

The Liskamm became associated with tragedy early in its mountaineering history when, on 6 September 1877, the English alpinists William Arnold Lewis and Noel Paterson and the brothers Niklaus, Johann and Peter-Joseph Knubel fell to their deaths from high on the ridge leading from the Lisjoch to the East Summit, the whole party being caught by a breaking cornice and falling over 500m to the Grenz Glacier. In 1896 there was an almost identical accident at virtually the same spot, the casualties on that occasion being Dr Max Günther with his guides Roman Imboden and Peter Ruppen. Since then periodic tragedies have served only to increase the mountain's grizzly notoriety.

(left) The 1100m North Face of the Liskamm with the North-East Face on the left and the North-West Face and the Zwillings Glacier on the right.

(right) Heading east along Liskamm's summit ridge.

A Barrel-Chested Massif

The huge massif of the Liskamm, with its barrel-chested northern aspect, measures approximately five kilometres in length and extends from the Lisjoch in the east to the western col of the Felikjoch. It is remote, high and savage and its ascent is therefore a prized target for every serious alpine mountaineer.

Viewed head-on from Monte Rosa, the three-kilometre-long wall of the North Face appears to be steeper than it actually is. Here lie the most difficult routes to the culminating points of the Liskamm, the 4481m West Summit and the East (Main) Summit, whose domes are linked by the Grenzgrat.

The mountain which has been nicknamed 'Man-Eater' because of its hair-raising crest of cornices. Unusually large and often complex, they are formed by the interplay of the south and north winds, their peaked caps jutting out from the ridge on both sides, dangerous and often unpredictable. In spite of this, hardly a summer's day goes by when parties are not seen traversing the Grenzgrat.

Richard Carter

The First Ascent

The Main Summit was first reached in 1861 from the Lisjoch by a party of eight Englishmen and six Swiss guides (J.F. Hardy, Prof. A.C. Ramsay, Dr F. Sibson, T. Rennison, J.A. Hudson, W.E. Hall, C.H. Pilkington and R.M. Stephenson with J.P. Cachet, F. Lochmatter, K. Herr, S. Zumtaugwald and P. and J. Perren). On this East Ridge, today's Normal Route, cornices overhang the South Flank, but they are easier to get the measure of than those on the Grenzgrat. The first traverse, made on 16 August 1864 in a west-east direction, started from the Felikjoch, and also marked the first ascent of the West Summit. This was achieved by Leslie Stephen and Edward

Willi Burkhardt

(above) Liskamm's East Ridge and South Arête (left) can be seen clearly in this aerial view from the east.

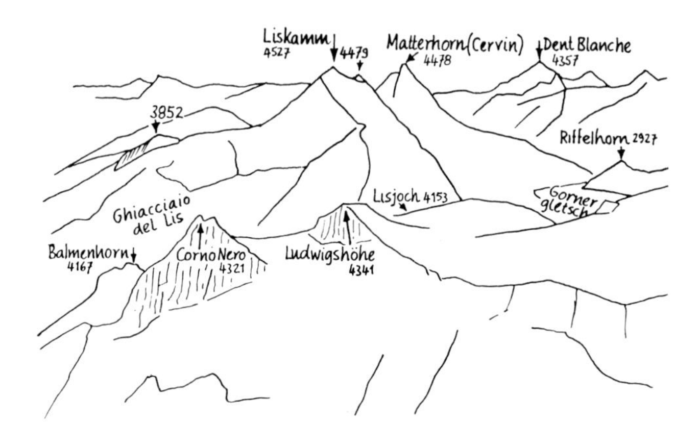

N. Buxton with their guides Jakob Anderegg and Franz Biner.

Despite its dangers the traverse soon became popular, and just two years later there were simultaneous ascents from the west and east with the parties (one led by Frederick Morshead and including Jakob Anderegg, the other by John Hawthorn Kitson guided by Christian Almer) traversing the mountain and descending by each other's ascent routes.

The North Face

For ice experts, the 700-1100m North, North-East and North-West precipices are coveted objectives, though the face is guarded by hanging glaciers and continuously rumbles to the sound of avalanches. Indeed, on an early attempt in the centre of the face (c.1880s) the two Kalbermatten brothers were avalanched back to the glacier, luckily without injury.

The first breach of this formidable barrier was made on the north-east side in 1890 by Christian Klucker and his regular employer Ludwig Norman-Neruda with the Austrian guide Josef Reinstadler. After ascending the initial ice slopes they followed a low relief rock rib directly to the Main Summit, which Klucker, who was expert on mixed ground, had judged to be the safest line, despite objections from Reinstadler. Their route is now regarded as a classic expedition. Willi Welzenbach and Rudolf Wolter added a left-hand variant to this in 1925 (subsequently criticised by Klucker as unjustifiable), and in 1967 an even steeper route was made through the ice cliffs further to the left by Max Fischer and Franz Wilde.

The avalanche-raked central section of the North-East Face to the right (that tried by the Kalbermattens) is breached only by the manifestly risky Blanchet/Mooser/Aufdenblatten route (1927).

Further right at the end of the North-East Face, below the West Summit, the wall is much higher. Here, on a section that is steeper but comparatively less threatened by avalanche, there are two major routes, each with an important variant. The least-threatened snow and ice line was climbed by Kurt Diemberger and Wolfgang Stefan in 1956 to which the mixed, and probably more serious, Gross/Hiebeler Variant was added in 1960. Further right, where the wall is actually north-facing, the second major line was climbed in July 1961 by Toni Hiebeler (the influential editor of *Alpinismus* during the sixties) and Heinz Pokorski, by a devious route (average angle 59°) threatened in its middle section by the summit ice cliffs. A week later the Italians Piero Nessi and Giuseppe Andreani added a safer but harder direct start up the mixed buttress of the summit fall-line, and in 1981 Patrick Gabarrou, GianCarlo Grassi and Carlo Stratta forced an even more direct line up steep couloirs to the left.

The 1150m North-West Spur (AD+ – reportedly a fine climb) was first climbed in 1902 by Mrs Roberts-Thomson with the guides Christian Klucker and Christian Zippert, but here a steeper and more direct alternative (B. Lendorff and M.C. Teves, 1925) is said to be more serious. The face between this and the Hiebeler/Pokorski line had ice-threatened routes added to it in 1963 and 1972.

A variety of less important routes have been established on the easier-angled southern and eastern slopes of which the South Ridge (Cresta Sella), climbed by Percy Thomas with Josef Imboden and L. Langen on 1 September 1878, is the most noteworthy.

The Normal Route from the Gnifetti Hut

The track from the Gnifetti Hut (or the lower but more comfortable Mantua Hut) to the Lisjoch is usually well-trodden. Above the Lisjoch, the East Ridge is often scored by a well-marked track. After an initial steep rise, the snow ridge lies back, becoming almost flat for a while. From P.4343 the ground again steepens and when the ice shines it is advisable to place screws for protection. Continue, keeping to the northern flank close to the crest, to a junction with the South Ridge. From here, twenty minutes along a very exposed snow and ice arête will take you to the top.

The Traverse

The traverse of the Grenzgrat from the Main Summit to the West Summit takes about two hours and is more exacting than ground already climbed, particularly beyond the lowest point (4418m) where two rocky rises (II) must be overcome. Throughout its whole length the danger from cornices must always be taken into consideration.

The West Summit from the Felikjoch

This is really only worthwhile either when done from the Sella Hut or as a ski-mountaineering trip starting at the Monte Rosa Hut. In my experience, the West Flank is often icy and can require time-consuming step-cutting. As a warm-up there is a sharp snow/ice ridge. Further up the route it is often better to move across to the rocky terrain on the right of the ridge; three to four pitches then land you at the false summit at 4447m, a short distance below the West Summit.

The Traverse, Twice in a Day

A particularly notable feat of mountaineering endurance was made c.1907 by Geoffrey Winthrop Young and 'a young guide of promising record'. Young's plan was to traverse all the frontier peaks between Nordend and Breithorn in a day. They set out from Riffelberg at midnight and by mid-morning had reached the Lisjoch, having crossed all the Monte Rosa summits down to the Ludwigshöhe. After traversing the Liskamm, and on the steep descent to the Felikjoch, Young noted (*On High Hills* pp114/115) that the guide began to register signals of stress. 'It was not long before I knew what the jockey must feel like when the favourite begins to falter under him . . .

'The cumbrous head of Castor, bulking over us discouragingly, condensed the vapour of funk into concrete symptom. It took the form of a sprained wrist. The consequences of further step-cutting or even rope-holding were declaimed in tones of disaster.'

They crossed Castor but to Young's disgust his plans for Pollux and the entire ridge of the Breithorn were vetoed. They returned to the Felikjoch where, to extend his expedition, Young persuaded his reluctant companion to re-traverse the Liskamm in preference to a descent of the crevassed Zwillings Glacier. He fully intended to traverse back over Monte Rosa as well, but at the Lisjoch his powers of persuasion ran out and in late afternoon they descended.

'. . . the cauldron of the Grenz Glacier bubbled and treacled bluish white in the heat. Crevasses steaming open at our feet . . . the wider its cracks gaped, the higher and longer we hopped and skimmed, like heated rubber balls . . . I noticed, too, with dark satisfaction, many envious glances at the far convex solidarities of the Breithorn, up which we might at that hour have been safely speeding.' Young's sarcasm for a luckless guide who failed to match his own limitless energy is mitigated by his elaborate account of an otherwise marvellous expedition.

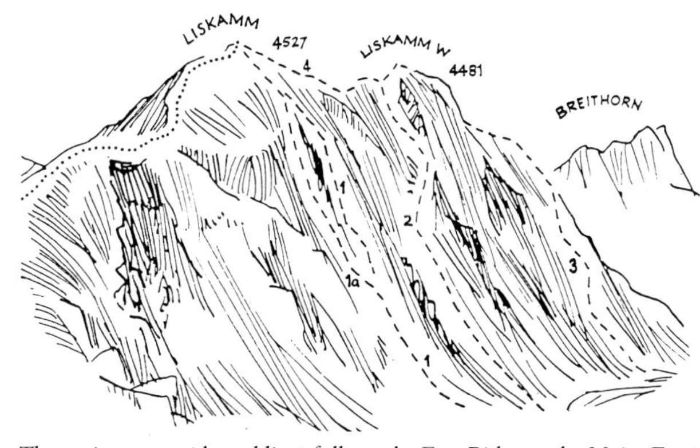

The easiest route (dotted line) follows the East Ridge to the Main (East) Summit. Also marked are the North-East Face – Klucker/Neruda Route (1) with the Welzenbach variation, the Blanchet/Mooser/Aufdenblatten Route (2), North-West Face – Lendorff/Teves Route (3). Grenzgrat or Frontier Ridge (4).

VALLEY BASES

Alagna 1180m. South-east of the Liskamm in the Val Sesia, 35km from Varallo (nearest railway station), bus service. Hotels, inns, pensions. Campsite *tel* 0163/ 9 11 51. Museum.

Zermatt see Rimpfischhorn p91

Staval see Castor p120

HUTS/OTHER BASES

Rifugio Citta di Mantova, Rifugio Giovanni Gnifetti see Signalkuppe p115.

Capanna Quintino Sella see Castor p120.

Monte Rosa Hut see Dufourspitze p99.

NORMAL ROUTE

East Ridge PD II, I, to 40°. 5 hours from the Gnifetti Hut. 890mH. A glacier tour then a snow and ice climb. *As a ski tour:* Leave skis at the Lisjoch.

West Summit – South-West Ridge PD II (sections), to 40°. 3 hours/390mH from the Felikjoch. Mixed climbing. *As a ski tour:* Leave skis at the Felikjoch.

RIDGES/FACES

South Ridge (Cresta Sella) PD II. 5 hours from the Gnifetti Hut. 890mH. A mixed climb.

South-East Face AD+ III+, 7 hours from the Gnifetti Hut, 890mH. Various mixed lines, the best and safest being the central buttress.

North Face Direct of East Summit D To 55°. 7 hours/700mH from the foot of the face. Sustained mixed and ice climbing. Classic and with mimimal objective danger.

Other North-East and North Face Routes All difficult and dangerous in varying degrees. One of the most serious ice faces in the Alps.

MAPS/GUIDEBOOKS

See Dufourspitze p99.

Willi Burkhardt

(right) The 700m North-East Face of the Liskamm. The Normal Route follows the prominent ridge on the left.

Castor *4226 m* Pollux *4091 m*

Perched between the immense edifices of the mighty Breithorn and Liskamm are the Dioscuri, Castor and Pollux – in Greek mythology the sons of the Goddess Leda – shapely but diminutive peaks that present a distinctly lesser status than their massive neighbours. In terms of access, however, both are well defended to the north by heavily crevassed glaciers that compel climbers to seek easier ways from the southern and western sides.

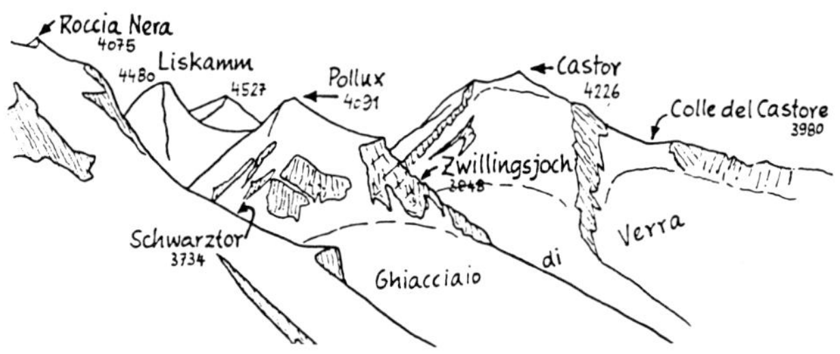

(below) The view east from the Breithorn Pass over the Verra Glacier to Pollux and Castor.

CASTOR

Castor, 950m south-east of Pollux and separated from it by the col of the Zwillingsjoch, is the higher and more elegantly shaped of the 'Snow Twins' and the peak more often climbed. Its summit, a craggy rise when swept clean of snow, sits just on the Italian side of the frontier and is, therefore, more correctly called Punta Castore. The South-East Ridge is the frontier – another Grenzgrat – and boasts a further four-thousand metre top: the Punta Felik or South-East Summit (4174m). If one adds the 4205m North-West Summit which lies on the Swiss side there are, technically, three four-thousanders to collect on Castor. In summer, a direct approach to Castor from the Monte Rosa Hut up the heavily crevassed Zwillings Glacier is often impractical, though it is usually a feasible route for ski ascents earlier in the year. The best way is from Italy, particularly since the rebuilding (1980) of the Sella Hut from where the Felikjoch is easily reached.

John Allen

Castor: The Normal Route

The South-East Ridge, which rises from the Felikjoch, was taken in 1861 by the first ascent party of William Mathews, one of the founders of the Alpine Club, and F.W. Jacomb. They were led by the Chamonix guide Michel Croz, who was to fall to his death four years later during the first ascent of the Matterhorn.

From the Sella Hut the route up the Felik Glacier is usually well-trodden by previous parties. It is best to avoid the temptation of making directly for the ridge up the South Flank, as experience has shown that the slopes are often icy. Instead, keep to the right below the steeper section and follow a blunt rib to the Felikjoch, from where the South-East Ridge – rocky in places – leads to the top. A steep descent down the North-West Ridge (Grenzkamm) to the Zwillingsjoch places Pollux in easy reach, but if a round of both peaks is planned the Klein Matterhorn is a more logical base than the Sella Hut.

Other routes on Castor

The Zwillingsjoch lies within the sphere of influence of the Klein Matterhorn cableway which provides the best approach from Zermatt. Large groups reach the peak from there, by a route that crosses the Breithorn Pass and the upper reaches of the Verra Glacier. Queuing for a place, they then proceed to the summit, either by following the North-West Ridge (Felix Schuster, Peter Baumann and Peter Mooser, 1878) or by climbing the fine, consolidated snow of the West Flank, slightly to the right.

Ice climbers will find the North Face (Miss Katherine Richardson, Emile Rey and Jean-Baptiste Bich, 1890 – in descent) or the North-East Rib (George Ingle Finch, Guy Forster, Raymond Peto and George Francis Travers-Jackson, 1924) offer some tasty morsels, with varied and interesting climbs over terrain which is not excessively steep and is free from objective dangers.

The South-West Ridge (above the Mezzalama Hut), first climbed in 1911 by Carlo Fortina and Anthoine Welf, gives an interesting rock climb (IV) to the Colle del Castore and mixed climbing thereafter. It is favoured by

Willi Burkhardt

(above) A long-focus view of Castor and Pollux from the Gornergrat.

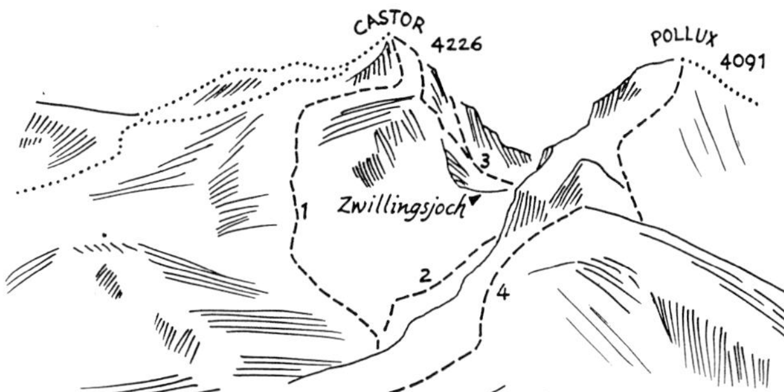

Castor and Pollux from the north, with the South-East of Castor and the West Face of Pollux marked with the dotted lines. Other routes are the North Face of Castor (1), the approach to the Zwillingsjoch (2), the North-West Ridge (3), and the North Ridge of Pollux (4).

the Italian guides, being well-protected and enjoyable. The Colle del Castore can easily be reached from either the Klein Matterhorn approach or the Sella Hut, so the upper part of the ridge is also a feasible Normal Route.

POLLUX

Pollux, or Monte Polluce, seems almost impudently out of place in the constellation of four-thousanders hereabouts, but it has a distinctive shape and, though its summit mass is small, it is far from easy, indeed it is a peak on which many noteworthy men have measured their skills.

On 1 August 1864 the first men to stand on the summit were the Genevan Jules Jacot, the Matterhorn conqueror-to-be Peter Taugwalder Snr and Joseph-Maria Perren. They climbed Pollux from the Schwarztor, a col originally traversed in 1845 by the Irishman John Ball and Gabriel Zumtaugwald. Ball is a noted figure in alpine history having been the first President of the Alpine Club (1857) and author of the first mountaineering guides to the Western Alps.

The most handsome route to the summit of Pollux, the North Ridge, fell to Captain John Percy Farrar and Robert

Bill O'Connor

(above) On the summit ridge of Castor with Pollux on left. Access to the ridge is gained on the left by a steep slope above the bergschrund (below).

John Allen

Wylie Lloyd, guided by Josef Pollinger, on 18 August 1910. Farrar, who had made the second ascent of the Peuterey Ridge in 1893 and, among others, the first ascents of the North Ridge of the Wetterhorn and North Ridge of the Ebnefluh, was one of the great personalities of British mountaineering. He too served as President of the Alpine Club and was also elected an honorary member of most of the other main Alpine Clubs. He was editor of the *Alpine Journal* and an assiduous researcher (his detective work on the Finsteraarhorn controversy having already been noted).

The Best Approaches to Pollux

The Rifugio Mezzalama is the nearest main hut to the peak, situated three kilometres to the south-west at the side of the Verra Glacier. Even more convenient is the tiny Cesare Volante e Giorgio Rossi Bivouac Hut on the lower rocks of the Roccia Nera above the Schwarztor.

The approach from the Gorner Glacier by the Schwärze Glacier is heavily crevassed, and only worthy of consideration as a ski route. The North Ridge by an approach along the Schwärze ridge above the cliffs of the Schalbetterfluh, although long, is a logical and elegant route if traversing the peaks from the Monte Rosa Hut.

However, the majority opt for the Klein Matterhorn approach to the mountain as it involves little loss of height. Now and then, mountaineers complain bitterly about the construction of ski-lifts, yet when it comes to the acid test they are quite pleased to have themselves transported on to the tops without any effort at all.

Pollux: the Normal Routes

From the Zwillingsjoch, the ill-defined and mixed South-East Ridge appears the logical way but is not particularly attractive. The slopes to its left are often favoured, picking the best line of snow, to gain the ridge higher up.

From the vicinity of the Schwarztor the North-West Ridge is equally unappealing but if the West Flank obliges with acceptable conditions (in the early months of the year), one can make tracks up the steep slopes to gain the top of the obvious rocky shoulder on the right.

A more entertaining line of ascent than any of these routes is provided by the West-South-West Ridge, either from its foot or by joining it at an obvious brèche by starts up the South or West Faces. Two-thirds of the ridge is rocky, the upper part having some steep pitches equipped with fixed ropes, and is reminiscent of sections of the Hörnli Ridge of the Matterhorn. The rock-climbing ends at the top of the aforementioned shoulder where there is a statue of the Virgin Mary. A snow ridge leads to the summit.

If one has already climbed Castor, steep cramponing down the upper part of the North Ridge provides an airy but attractive descent before traversing the north-west flank to the Schwarztor for a return to Klein Matterhorn. Those proceeding to Castor can either return by the same route or take the South-East Ridge (with its recommended variation) directly down to the Zwillingsjoch.

Ski Ascents of the Twins

For ski-mountaineers, the Twins offer an exceptional range of activities. Both mountains were first climbed on skis in March 1913. Pollux on the 7th by Dr Alfred von Martin and his trusty friend Karl Planck; Castor on the 5th by von Martin and Planck, with Hans Kammerer and Heinz von Roncador. On this ascent skis were left above the Felikjoch and the climbers proceeded on foot up the South-East Ridge.

For Castor one can use either the Sella Hut or Klein Matterhorn approach, but the northern approach from the Monte Rosa Hut should also be considered in winter. On this route the first rule is to keep a cool head in the unpleasant labyrinth of crevasses and séracs of the lower Zwillings Glacier. Two nasty slanting crevasses then have to be avoided, and the ice-falls on Castor kept at a respectable distance.

Bill O'Connor

Bill O'Connor

(above) *The Cesare Volante e Giorgio Rossi Bivouac Hut – a possible base for climbs on Pollux and the Breithorn.*

And that, basically, is that, at least as far as the Felikjoch, and thence to the summit of Castor. The ski descent down the northern slopes provides sport, and fun, of the highest order. If the weather is good the rope can be dispensed with at first, but in the jumbled ice blocks lower down it is absolutely vital. After a short climb back to the Monte Rosa Hut one can breathe a sigh of relief and relax. The complete Grenz/Gorner Glacier run down to Zermatt requires considerable mountaineering experience – where possible keep to the right (northern) edge of the glacier.

In addition to this classic ski tour of the past, there is also 'the route of the future' which begins at Klein Matterhorn and takes in the Breithorn Pass, Verra Glacier, Zwillingsjoch and Castor and Pollux.

Jim Teesdale

VALLEY BASES

Zermatt see Rimpfischhorn p91
St Giacomo (St Jacques) 1670m. A little mountain village in the upper Valle d'Ayas south of Pollux. 31km from Verres in the Aosta Valley (nearest station, bus service). Hotels, inns.
Staval 1823m. Part of Gressoney in the nethermost Valle di Gressoney, 4km from Gressoney-la-Trinité, 37km from Pont-St Martin in the Aosta valley (nearest station, bus service), 164km from Milan. Hotel Adler *tel* 0125/ 36 61 59/ 2 62. Small campsite.

HUTS/OTHER BASES

Monte Rosa Hut, Kulmhotel Gornergrat see Dufourspitze p99.
Capanna Quintino Sella 3585m. CAI. South of Castor on a rocky spur between the Vera and Felik Glaciers. Two buildings with a total of 200 places. Staffed from 20 June to 15 September *tel* 0125/ 36 61 13. From Valle di Gressoney take the chair lift from Staval to Colle di Bettaforca (2672m). Walk north for one hour to the Passo della Bettolina (2905m) passing this on the right. Finally, a *via ferrata* leads up to the hut. 4 hours from the chair lift. From the Valle d'Ayas: 6 hours from St Giacomo via Resy (2072m, the highest mountain village in Italy), the Colle di Bettaforca and then as above to the hut.
Rifugio Ottorino Mezzalama 3036m. CAI. South-west of Pollux on the Lambronecca moraines of the Verra Glacier. 34 places. Staffed at weekends (on request during the week) from Easter to end May and from 20 June to mid-September *tel* 0125/ 30 72 26 or 30 71 04. 4 hours from St Giacomo. A rutted track (possibly driveable) goes to Alm Pian di Verra Superiore (2387m), from where the hut is reached in 2 hours. Check the state of the road!
Bivacco Cesare Volante e Giorgio Rossi / Klein Matterhorn see Breithorn p125

CASTOR: NORMAL ROUTES

South-East Ridge From the Sella Hut: PD– To 35°. 2½ hours from the hut. 650mH. A glacier route. From the Monte Rosa Hut. PD To 35°. 6 hours from the hut. 1433mH. A complicated glacier tour. *As a ski tour:* Follow the Monte Rosa Hut route to a ski depot at the Felikjoch.
North-West Ridge PD+ To 40°. 1½ hours/ 390mH of ascent from the Zwillingsjoch (2½ hours from Klein Matterhorn). A snow and ice route.

CASTOR: RIDGES/FACES

South-West Ridge D– IV+ and IV(sections), III, II. 8 hours from the Mezzalama Hut. 1250mH. Rock to P.3992m, then mixed. Entertaining and quite hard.
North Face AD+ To 50°. 4 hours/600mh from the foot of the face.
North-East Rib AD+ To 45°. 2½ hours/350mH from the start of the route. At 3850m on the Felikjoch route up the Zwillings Glacier a rightwards traverse is made to the foot of the rib leading to the North-West Summit.

POLLUX: NORMAL ROUTES

South-East Ridge PD I+ (short section). To 45°. 50 minutes/ 250mH from the Zwillingsjoch. Snow and ice, with some short, loose, rock passages.
West-South-West Ridge PD II, I. Sections on the ridge are equipped with a cable. 2 hours/360mH from the foot of the ridge. Rock then snow.
West Face PD To 45° 1½ hours/360mH for the Schwarztor. A snow and ice route. *As a ski tour:* Leave the skis at Schwarztor.
North Ridge PD+ To 50°. 6 hours from the Monte Rosa Hut, 1350mH. A snow and ice ridge.

MAPS/GUIDEBOOKS

See Dufourspitze p99

(top left and left) *Two views of the steep section of the West-South-West Ridge of Pollux where it is equipped with fixed ropes.*

Breithorn *4165 m*

The Breithorn is the most westerly peak of the giants surrounding the Gorner Glacier basin above Zermatt. It is often called the Zermatt Breithorn to differentiate from the other notable Breithorns above Lauterbrunnen and Lötschental. To the north and north-east it takes the form of an extensive mountain rampart. The highest point is at the western end above the dangerous North Face – ice threatened and frequently avalanching. The Central Summit (4160m) and the Eastern Summit (4141m) stand above the North-East Face and, defending the eastern end, the proud turret of the Roccia Nera (4075m) dominates the snow col of the Schwarztor. The sharp, corniced and pinnacled East or Frontier Ridge links these points to form a high battlement towering above the Triftji and Breithorn Glaciers that grind and crunch northwards, completing its defences. In total contrast to this aggressive northern aspect, the southern flank is a concave snow slope a mere 200m above the innocuous undulations of the upper basin of the Verra Glacier. Benign in the morning, it becomes quite serious in the afternoon when snow slides and mini avalanches continually strip off the face to fill the yawning bergschunds below, leaving the snowy crest as a tottering pile of rotting slush to confound late finishers of the Younggrat.

A History of Breithorn Ascents

The peak was first climbed from the south-west (today's Normal Route) by Henri Maynard, Joseph-Marie Couttet, Jean-Baptiste and Jean-Jacques Erin, and Jean Gras in August 1813.

The next notable new route on the mountain, the North Ridge or Triftjigrat, was climbed on 15 September 1869 by Robert Fowler, with Peter Knubel and Gregor Ruppen. Leaving the Riffelalp at 4.30 a.m. they were on the summit by noon after a rapid and uneventful climb of what was to become a classic route.

In 1884 John Stafford Anderson, with his guides Ulrich Almer and Aloys Pollinger, took ten hours to traverse the complete Frontier Ridge from Roccia Nera to the main summit. With the ridge explored the way was clear for further forays up the northern flank. The first expedition took place in 1897 when H.J. Mothersill and C.S. Acherson with Ulrich Almer, Christian Kaufmann and Christian Jossi made what must have been quite a hard route directly up the headwall of the Breithorn Glacier to gain the summit ridge just to the west of East Peak. They reported that the wall 'consists of steep, firm, rock mixed with short slopes of ice and snow and was climbed in three hours . . . quite free from falling stones or ice, and though not easy . . . makes for an enjoyable expedition'.

This climb was comprehensively upstaged by the ascent of the adjoining Younggrat (the North Ridge of East Peak) in 1906. Geoffrey Winthrop Young was accompanied by C.D. Robertson, R.J. Mayor and guided by Josef Knubel and Moritz Ruppen on this important ascent, later described by Michel Vaucher as 'one of the finest ridges in the Alps'. Young's typically convoluted yet brilliant account of the climb in *On High Hills* (p196) ensured its subsequent fame, the final pitches causing them considerable anxiety until the crest was won. The implication is that the 1897 ascent, which involved a much longer passage of similar ground, just to the right of the Younggrat, must have been a tremendous lead by Ulrich Almer, at that time at the peak of his powers.

Another important route was added to the Breithorn Glacier headwall in August 1953, when Franco Cetti Serbelloni and the brothers Ernesto and Oliviero Frachey climbed the central rib of Central Peak (TD). First an ice face, then with mixed climbing, this is clearly a major undertaking, especially as the summit ridge above the route is fringed with sizeable cornices.

The first ascent of the serious and difficult 1100m North-West Face was made on 3 September 1919 by Baron Dietrich von Bethmann-Hollweg, partnered by the guides Othmar and Oskar Supersaxo. This climb was repeated in 1926 by a party led by Willi Welzenbach, in the belief that it was a new route. In June 1964, the Swiss guides Paul Etter and Réné Arnold with Herbert Maeder, forced an even more direct route up the face to the rib of rock which drops straight from the summit and nine years later this was climbed solo by that flagbearer of seventh grade climbing, the German ace Helmut Kiene.

Two hard (TD) climbs have been made to the left of the Younggrat: the 60° North-East Couloir (Erich Vanis, Leo Graf and Klaus Kubiena, 1954) and the rather ominous-looking North-East Spur of East Peak (Enrico Cavalieri and P. Villagio, 1961) which has two pitches of V. The many new rock and mixed climbs on the walls of P.4105.8 and Roccia Nera, as well as major mixed climbs added to the central section of the Breithorn Glacier headwall in 1979, 1980 and 1985, all attest to the growing popularity of these remote cliffs.

The Cableways

The cableway from the Italian village of Breuil to the Testa Grigia at 3480m, had already cut the trip to the top of the Breithorn to the scale of a half-day's outing when, in 1979, the completion of another cableway from Zermatt to Klein Matterhorn made it possible to start the climb at 3820m, knocked a further hour off the ascent time, and cut the distance to a mere three kilometres.

Environment protection groups managed to ensure that the lift did not terminate on the summit of the Klein Matterhorn, but at a point some sixty metres lower, from where a tunnel leads through to the Breithorn Plateau where the climbing begins. Skiers can go even higher as drag-lifts continue to the summit of Gobba di Rollin (3899m). Thus the whole Theodul Glacier basin has

The Italian side of the Breithorn with the normal route (dotted line) and the best descent from the Younggrat (1) and the best approach to the frontier ridge (2).

been developed for winter sports and tourism, but this has benefits for the summer mountaineer in terms of time saved and otherwise remote climbs made accessible.

The Best Approaches

From Breuil, aided by the Testa Grigia lift, the ascent can be made in under three hours. The main Italian approach used to be from the Mezzalama Hut – south of the Breithorn and 1100m lower – but this has now decreased in importance as a base, a decline matched by a growing concern about the slovenly conditions in the hut.

On the Swiss side, the classic route of ascent from the Gandegg Hut up the Theodul Glacier past the Theodulpass (where the Theodul Hut is located) is now rendered pointless by the Klein Matterhorn lift. Nevertheless, the comfortable Gandegg Hut remains the base for all main routes on the northern faces.

From the Schwarztor, the expedition along the 2.5km Frontier Ridge passes over five four-thousand-metre tops and normally takes a minimum of eight hours. It is best done in this direction, either by making an early start from the Theodul Hut or the new hut at Testa Grigia, or by using the Volante e Rossi Bivouac Hut at the Schwarztor as a base, as this allows most of the corniced sections to be dispensed with before the snow becomes soft.

The Normal Route

From the Klein Matterhorn, the South-West Flank of the Breithorn over to the left appears to be a route of moderate temperament. A wide, beaten track leads slightly downhill to a flat saddle where the trail strikes off left, flat at first and then steepening as it heads towards the Breithorn. In ideal snow conditions ski-mountaineers can reach the summit itself without removing their skis, but it can be icy when crampons become essential.

The Breithorn's reputation as 'the four-thousander which sees the most ascents', glosses over the ever present crevasse danger and the difficult route-finding when the weather is bad. In certain conditions it can become a deadly mantrap: in April 1977 it snapped shut on five German climbers. After a ski ascent of the Breithorn the mist came down and a storm blew up and, despite map, compass and altimeter, they were unable to find their way down. Rescue teams located them, frozen to death, not far from the Gobba di Rollin!

Bill O'Connor

Willi Burkhardt

(top right) The Breithorn massif seen from the summit of Pollux with the Roccia Nera in the foreground and the Schwarztor the snow pass running along the base of the photograph.

(right) The south-western slopes of the Breithorn from the Klein Matterhorn.

Willi Burkhardt

Bill O'Connor

(above) The North Face of the Breithorn from the Gandegg Hut with the sunlit ridges of the Triftjigrat and the Younggrat on the left.

(top right) Half-way up the Triftjigrat.

(right) Moving west along the Summit Ridge of the Breithorn.

(previous page) The late evening sun dramatises the North Face of the Breithorn seen from Gornergrat.

Bill O'Connor

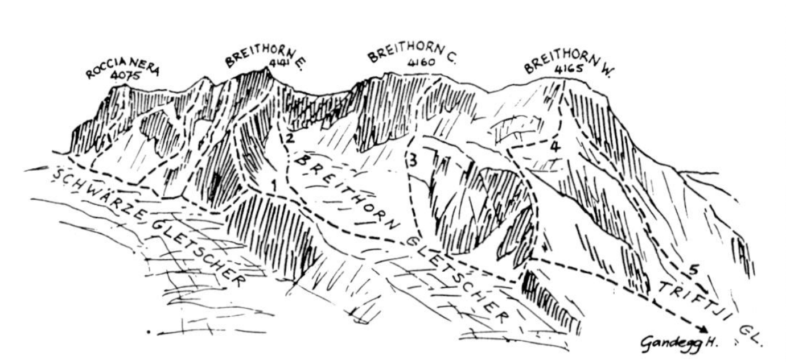

The northern precipices of the Breithorn showing routes to the Roccia Nera, P.4105.8 and East Peak, the Younggrat (1), the Mothersill/Acherson/Almer/Kaufmann/Jossi route (2), the Serbelloni/Frachey Route (3), the Triftjigrat (4), the North Face – Bethmann-Hollweg/Supersaxo Route (5).

A Political Crevasse Rescue

One celebrated crevasse incident was recorded in *Zwischen Himmel und Erde* by Walter Schmidkunz:

'During an ascent . . . by Quintino Sella, the famous Italian statesman . . . and founder of the Italian Alpine Club, his companion was Count Paar, who was then the Austrian envoy to the Sardinian government. [At that time] relations between the two states had become more and more strained and at risk yet Sella and Paar were bound by a . . . [mutual] love of the mountains [that] transcended mere politics.

'Count Paar and his guide had the misfortune to fall into a deep crevasse on the glacier. Sella had the presence of mind to ram his alpenstock . . . into the snow, and was thus able to hold the stricken pair on a tight rope, thereby saving their lives . . . After the greatest of exertions, they succeeded in dragging the two men from the abyss and after Paar had thanked Sella with warm-hearted words for saving his life, the latter [an energetic nationalist] . . . replied with a meaningful smile that it had been the alpenstock which had saved him . . ., adding that "had it not been there, the German Fatherland would, perchance, have raised a hue and cry at the treacherous foul-play of the Italians".'

The Younggrat and the Triftjigrat

Both these routes are normally approached from the Gandegg Hut by way of the Triftjisattel below P.3250.6. The Triftjigrat leads directly towards the summit from here, but higher up various icefalls compel a devious approach and the route as a whole is not without avalanche danger. For this reason it is best tackled early in the season.

Those heading for the Younggrat will have made an early start to reach the ridge at daybreak and will thus have to descend the shale couloir below the Triftjisattel in the dark. At its foot they must work through the maze of creaking séracs of the Breithorn Glacier which gradually take shape in the dim light of dawn. High on the left of the glacier, the foot of the ridge beckons invitingly. (N.B. This point can also be reached by a ramp leading up from the Schwärze Glacier.) The ridge is at once well-defined and often icy, with ice-encrusted gendarmes, and finally a Grand Gendarme barring the way to the prominent upper snow and ice ridge. This rears alarmingly, and by mid-morning may already be unstable, its thin snow cover sliding silently down into the Vanis Couloir on the left. At the top of the ridge solidarity returns in the icy shadow of the rocks of the North-East Spur and there are welcome piton belays below a final headwall. The steep final pitches, either directly up the rock or with an exposed traverse across the ice to a couloir/chimney, could not be better positioned for bringing the climb to a rousing finale. But this is a serious spot from where four French climbers* fell to their deaths in 1928. The exact cause of the accident was not clear; they appeared to have tried the couloir/chimney finish and were probably swept away by a cornice collapse from the ridge above – a factor that points to the rock headwall as being the safer finish as it is not overhung by cornices. The climb finishes near the East Summit and then there is merely the worrying aftermath of the sun-softened Frontier Ridge to contend with.

*Pierre Le Bec, Edouard de Gigord, Pierre Langlois and Yves Guibert.

John Allen

(above) On the traverse of the Breithorn – the steep descent from the Central Summit to the col at P.4076.

VALLEY BASES

Zermatt see Rimpfischhorn p91
St Giacomo (St Jacques) see Castor/Pollux p120
Cervinia (Breuil) 2006m. At the head of the Valtournanche. Access from Chatillon (24km, nearest railway station, 24km from Aosta). Bus service. Hotels, inns, pensions.

HUTS/OTHER BASES

Gandegg Hut 3029m. Privately owned, on a rocky outcrop (Lichenbretter) between the Lower and Upper Theodul Glacier. 30 places. Staffed from 22 June to 21 September *tel* 028/ 67 21 96 (in Zermatt). 4 hours from Zermatt or ½ hour from the Trockener Steg stop on the cableway (2939m).
Rifugio del Teodulo 3327m. CAI. Just above the Theodul Pass. 86 places. Staffed from beginning April to third week in September, winter room, *tel* 0166/ 94 94 00. ½ hour from Testa Grigia. Ski-lifts from the Trockener Steg cableway station.
Testa Grigia 3480m. Terminus of cableway from Breuil (Restaurant). New hut recently opened nearby by Breuil Guides.
Klein Matterhorn 3820m. Cableway terminus. First lift leaves Zermatt at 6 a.m. *tel* 028/ 67 13 16 or 67 12 52.
Rifugio Ottorino Mezzalama see Castor/Pollux p120.
Bivacco Cesare Volante e Giorgio Rossi 3850m. CAI. West of the Schwarztor (climb snow and rocks) on a rock rib of the Roccia Nera. 6 places. Open all year. 2 hours from the Klein Matterhorn, 2½ hours from the Mezzalama Hut.

NORMAL ROUTE

South-West Flank PD– To 45°. 1½ hours from Klein Matterhorn. 360mH. A glacier and snow and ice climb. *As a ski tour:* As above, or take in the Gobba di Rollin.

RIDGES AND FACES

East Ridge (Frontier Ridge) AD III (sections). 9 hours from Schwarztor. Alternating mixed, snow and ice and rock passages.
Triftjigrat AD III, II. To 50-55° (several pitches). 7 hours from the Gandegg Hut. 1150mH. A snow and ice climb.
North Ridge of East Peak (Younggrat) D VI (section), III. To 55° (on penultimate pitch). 10 hours from the Gandegg Hut. 1250mH. Snow and ice, with some mixed pitches.

MAPS/GUIDEBOOKS

See Dufourspitze p99

Bishorn *4159 m*

This is the most northerly four-thousander on the chain west of the Mattertal. Strictly speaking, it is merely the northern spur of the Weisshorn ridge system, a cornerstone of the massif, high above the Turtmann, Brunegg and Bis Glaciers that flow down to the Mattertal or Zinaltal. Yet the twin peaks of the Bishorn – the main summit and East Peak or Pointe Burnaby (4134m) – can lay just claim to independence, obvious when viewed from the Dom Hut or from distant views from the north. In view of its strategic position for examining the incomparable Weisshorn, no one will ever regret making the ascent. This is best begun from the Zinaltal – a valley which has retained much of its original character – from where a long hut approach leads up the mountain pastures of Combautanna to the Col de Tracuit where the hut is situated, its red roof visible from miles around.

From the hut one can view the Bishorn for the first time, wrapped in the cloak of névé which provided the route of the first ascent on 18 August 1884. The pioneers were G.S. Barnes, Rev. R. Chessyre-Walker, Josef Imboden and J.M. Chanton, though much of the credit might more rationally be accorded to Mrs Burnaby's party of two weeks earlier, about which, more later.

The Tracuit Hut Approach

The Normal Route from the Tracuit Hut dispenses with all the usual toil and has no hidden technical difficulties; the only possible inconvenience is posed by the occasional cornices hanging over the North Face on the steep ridge leading from the saddle to the gently sloping summit plateau. Rope up to be on the safe side.

The views from the summit repay the effort in full. Close at hand is the Weisshorn's mighty 1000m North-East Face, decorated with its panoply of hanging glaciers. Further south is the surge of the Zinalrothorn and the Ober Gabelhorn. Eastwards, beyond the shapely Brunegghorn, the serried peaks of the Mischabel dominate the far skyline of the Mattertal, while the northern view through the trough of the Turtmanntal is of the Rinderhorn, Altels, Balmhorn, Doldenhorn and the Blumlisalp group of the Bernese Alps.

Ski Possibilities

The easy-angled slopes of the Tracuit route make the Bishorn one of the best four-thousanders for ski-mountaineering and because of this it actually enjoys two seasons. In the spring one should take into account the fact that the lower slopes are mostly snow-free by Whitsuntide. Despite this, the run from the summit is very worthwhile, with a height loss of 800m to the upper reaches of the Turtmann Glacier and a further 800m down to the Roc de la Vache where, if conditions are as described, the skis have to come off.

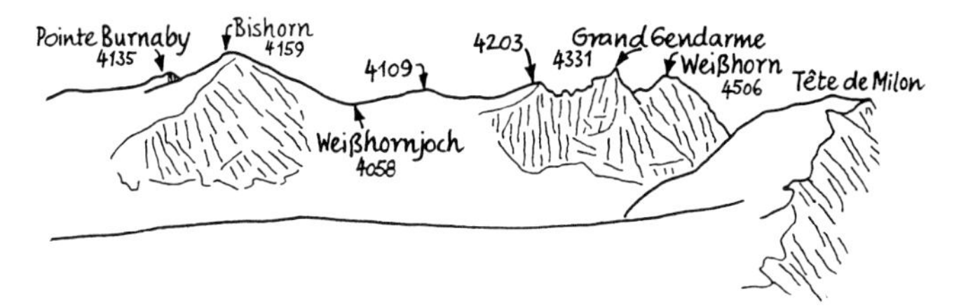

(below) The Tracuit Hut – base for the Normal Route on the Bishorn which takes the left-hand skyline.

Willi Burkhardt

(left) A long-focus view of the Weisshorn and the Bishorn from the north-east.

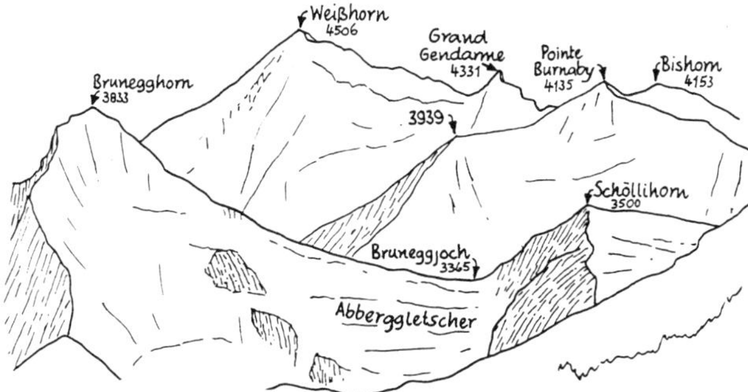

Willi Burkhardt

Willi Burkhardt

From the Turtmann Hut

Since the road up the Turtmanntal was lengthened, the walk up to the Turtmann Hut (2519m) now only takes about an hour and as a result there are more Bishorn-bound parties. The approach to the ordinary route, though technically easy, involves 1700m of ascent and almost six kilometres of the crevassed Turtmann Glacier to negotiate and thus has limited appeal. The Turtmann Hut is the base for parties heading for the North Face and the East Ridge, routes that deserve attention. The East Ridge, which begins at the Bisjoch, is of comparable quality to the more famous East Ridge of the Weisshorn. The adjoining North-East Face (Blanchet/Mooser/Lochmatter, 1924) provides a steep and elegant ice excursion with minimal objective danger above the preliminary sérac barrier.

The Bishorn-Weisshorn Traverse

This ten-hour expedition, with the descent of the East Ridge of the Weisshorn, is one of the most handsome excursions in the Pennine Alps. Many climbers use the easy ascent of the Bishorn as a preliminary for this infinitely more ambitious expedition, described and illustrated in the next chapter.

The Lady First Ascensionist?

The Bishorn will always be associated with that redoubtable Irish-born lady alpinist Mrs Aubrey Le Blond (1861-1934). As Mrs Fred Burnaby (*née* Elizabeth (Lizzie) Hawkins-Whitshed), with guides Josef Imboden and Peter Sarbach, she was the first to climb the East Ridge to gain the East Peak of the Bishorn (4134m) on 6 August 1884. This top was later named Pointe Burnaby in her honour. For some reason they failed to continue along the 600m of easy-angled ridge to the summit although the *A.J.* entry about the climb* says nothing of two peaks, and notes only a height of 4161 metres. Yet as Imboden was in the first ascent party, and as he and Mrs Burnaby subsequently completed fifteen seasons together, becoming close friends, it seems unlikely that the official record is incorrect. Whatever the circumstances, Mrs Burnaby and her guides, rather like Madutz and Zumtaugwald on Monte Rosa, could reasonably claim a degree of the credit for the first ascent of the mountain – an important

**A.J.* XII, p122

(top left) The Brunegg Glacier and the Bishorn from above the Turtmanntal to the north-west. The way to the Tracuit Route traverses below the Stierberg on the right.

(left) On the summit slopes of the Bishorn.

detail as this is one of the few four-thousanders where a woman was involved in the initial exploration (others being Pointe Éveline on the Aiguille du Jardin and Pointe Croz on the Grandes Jorasses).

Her private life, too, was characteristically active: three times married, her climbs are recorded under the names of her husbands, Colonel Fred Burnaby (who died on active service in 1885), D.F. Main (who died naturally in 1892) and the married name by which she is most commonly known, Aubrey Le Blond.

She was a skilful climber. 'I had to fight hard for my freedom,' she reveals, 'and my mother alone bore the consequences on my behalf when my Great Aunt [Lady Bentinck] sent out an agitated SOS. "For God's sake stop her from climbing these mountains! She brings scandal on the entire country."'

A passionate advocate of women's mountaineering, she founded the Ladies' Alpine Club in London in 1907 and served as its first President. She also wrote the first book on winter Alpine mountaineering, *The High Alps in Winter* which records her last major climbs – winter ascents of Monte Disgrazia and Piz Zupo in 1896. The death of Imboden's son, Roman, on the Liskamm, devastated his father and after this Mrs Le Blond virtually gave up alpine climbing.

With other members of the Ladies' Alpine Club, she was involved in supporting the wounded of the French Alpine Troops on the Western Front in the years 1914-16 and later played a major role in the restoration of Reims Cathedral and the erection of a statue of Marshal Foch in London. For these activities she was created an officer of the *Légion d'Honneur* in 1933. She died suddenly a year later. In her *A.J.* obituary that ever stern critic, Colonel Edward Strutt, made the following fulsome tribute: 'Her chief [mountaineering] characteristic was her extraordinary judgement . . . this has never been surpassed in any mountaineer, professional or amateur, of the so-called stronger sex. Her staying powers were quite outstanding; she was slight but very strongly built with the finished stride of a first class guide (she was a magnificent skater). [She] was certainly the first lady to make 'manless' ascents [which] were considered extraordinary – if slightly improper – in the Victorian era.'

Dave Wynne-Jones

(above) The North Ridge of the Weisshorn, with the Grand Gendarme in the centre, in a dawn view from the summit of the Bishorn.

VALLEY BASES

Zinal 1678m. In the Val d'Anniviers, which runs into the Rhône Valley south of Sierre. 28km from Sierre, bus service. Hotels, inns, pensions, campsite, Youth Hostel *tel* 027/ 65 18 14 or 65 14 08. Auberge Alpina Bunkhouse *tel* 027/ 65 21 24.
Gruben-Meiden 1828m. A cluster of hotels in the Turtmanntal. 17km from Turtmann in the Rhône Valley (nearest railway station), Post Bus service in the summer.

HUTS AND OTHER BASES

Cabane de Tracuit 3256m. SAC. 300m south-east of the Col de Tracuit on the edge of the Turtmann Glacier. 112 places. Staffed from 15 June to 15 September, open for the remainder of the year *tel* 027/ 65 15 00. About 4½ hours from Zinal via Roc de la Vache. The winter path marked on the maps across the Alpe L'Ar Pitetta involves a detour but is the route safest from avalanches.
Cabane Tourtemagne 2520m. SAC. On a rock spur above the snout of the Turtmann Glacier. 50 places. Staffed from July to mid-September *tel* 028/ 42 14 55. Minor road from Gruben to the bridge over the Turtmannbach (1901m). 1½ hours from there.

NORMAL ROUTE

North-West Flank F I (on the summit ridge). 2½ hours from the Tracuit Hut. 900mH. A glacier tour. *As a ski tour:* As for the normal route. Deposit skis below the rocks of the summit section.

RIDGES AND FACES

South-West Ridge PD I+. 3 hours from the Tracuit Hut, 900mH. A glacier tour.
East Ridge AD– II, I. 7 hours from the Turtmann Hut via the Bisjoch. 1700mH. It can also be climbed from the Topali Hut (2674m) above St Niklaus in Mattertal.
North-East Face TD– To 60° and more (crux pitch vertical), otherwise to 50°. 5 hours/650mH from the foot of the face.

MAPS AND GUIDEBOOKS

See Dufourspitze p99.

Weisshorn *4505m*

The sharp silhouettes of the three ridges, each strikingly symmetrical in shape, slant upwards to the highest point of the Weisshorn, the second highest peak solely on Swiss ground. Between the ridges, sheer faces of congealed ice snap to attention: the North-East Face above the Bis Glacier, pregnant with avalanches; above the Schali Glacier, the South-East Face, seamed with the ice and rock couloirs; and above the Weisshorn Glacier, the complex West Face, 1300m high in places, fearsomely loose and devoid of hiding places.

The beauty of its clean pyramidal form has made the Weisshorn one of the most sought-after four-thousand-metre peaks in the Alps. From the Dom Hut it looks particularly fine – the South-West Ridge (or Schaligrat) on the left, the North Ridge on the right and the East Ridge in the middle. It was by way of the latter that the mountain was first conquered on 19 August 1861, by the Irish physicist John Tyndall, accompanied by his mercurial guide Johann Josef Bennen with Ulrich Wenger. Their route is today's Normal Route which starts from the small but efficiently-run Weisshorn Hut.

The Normal Route

From the hut the climb to the shoulder at the start of the difficulties takes about three hours. Above this there is stonefall danger but at dawn the stones are silent, though it can be unpleasantly loud on the return trip. A tedious and quite hazardous scramble up loose craglets leads to the 'Breakfast Ledge' at P.3916, where the actual East Ridge begins. Once started this immediately steepens, and verglassed slabs often provide a surprise or two. Under the soles of your boots are the yawning depths of the North Flank, as one pinnacle follows another. Beyond P.4178 crampons must be donned for the 400m blade of névé that slices upwards, in places wickedly corniced, to the summit with Theo Imboden's wrought-iron cross. The sun will by now have softened the snow and the long descent can be very nerve-wracking. Many a tried and tested alpinist has paused at the shoulder and made the sign of the cross in gratitude for his safe return.

The Normal Route (dotted line) up the East Ridge with the South-West Ridge or Schaligrat (1) and the South-East Face (2).

Early Ascents

The first deviation from the original line was made in 1869 by Horace Walker's party when they descended from P.4178 on the East Ridge to gain the upper part of the Schali Glacier. Attention then moved to the South-West Ridge or Schaligrat. In 1877, William Edward Davidson, James Walker Hartley and Henry Seymour Hoare with their guides Peter Rubi, Johann Jaun and Aloys Pollinger, studied the ridge from the Schali Glacier but judged its lower towers too difficult. They therefore climbed directly up the South-East Face, braving volleys of stones, to gain the ridge above the main difficulties. Relieved and elated they crossed the summit and descended the East Ridge, reaching the inn at Randa just after 9 p.m. where, as Hartley described: 'we found a hot dinner, coffee and liqueurs, awaiting us. The inestimable [landlord] had seen our lantern in the wood and prepared a *table d'hôte* rivalling the luxuries of the Monte Rosa'.

The main line on the South-East Face (directly to the summit) was added on a cold and blustery day in 1906 by the Täschhorn South Face team of Young, Ryan, the two Lochmatters and Knubel, a route which, under normal

(right) The South-East Face of the Weisshorn seen from the Unterrothorn above Zermatt.

Willi Burkhardt

Willi Burkhardt

(above) The West Face of the Weisshorn above the Weisshorn Glacier with the Schalijoch on the right.

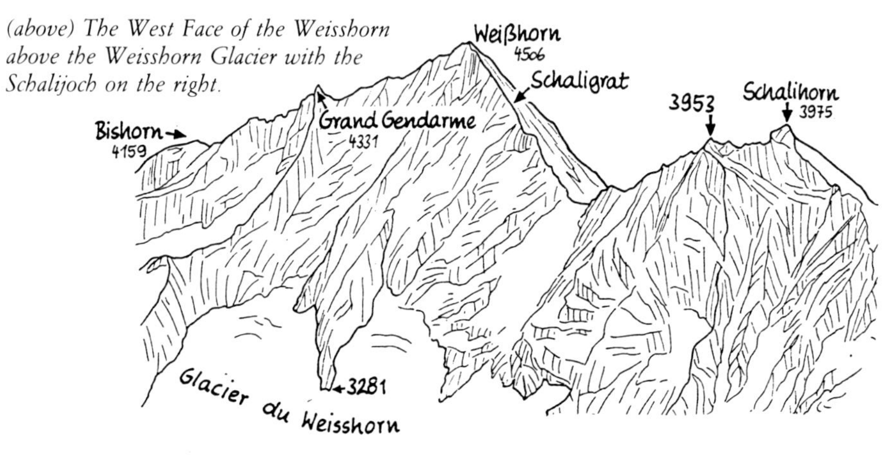

conditions, would probably be unjustifiably dangerous.* The Schaligrat was eventually climbed in 1895 by Edward Broome, Josef Biener and Ambros Imboden. Finding excellent conditions, they crossed many of the gendarmes with climbing up to Grade IV, and the route is still highly regarded for its quality and difficulty.

The West Face

In the 1880s attention had moved to the Zinal flank. On the direct fall-line from the summit the face is slabby, icy and serious, with rockfall in the couloirs and sustained difficulties on the ribs. It was here that three notable ascents took place, in 1879, 1883 and 1889. The first was made by George Augustus Passingham with Ferdinand Imseng and Louis Zurbrucken (called Aloys Zurbriggen in the SAC Guidebook) who encountered great danger from falling stones ('they hummed and howled in the air in a very disagreeable manner'). In 1883 Percy Farrar with the Bavarian guide Johann Kederbacher from Ramsau took a different line, avoiding the stonefall but were slowed by the difficult slabs below the summit, and were forced into an involuntary bivouac. Finally, in 1889, Theodore Cornish with Ulrich and Hans Almer, not knowing the line of the earlier ascents, elected for the West Face in favour of the Schaligrat and was impressed by both the danger (on the lower section) and the difficult slabs climbed in 1883. The face is graded TD, the only improvement on the line being the rather more direct ascent (also TD) in 1945 by Swiss Everesters René Dittert and Léon Flory with Francis Marullaz.

But yet again, as on the Breithorn, all these efforts were to be eclipsed by another Younggrat (AD+) which takes an easier, safer, more solid (though less direct) route up the West Rib of the Grand Gendarme (P.4331) of the North Ridge. This was climbed in 1900 by Geoffrey Winthrop Young with the Zinal guides Louis and Benoit Theytaz who subsequently rigged it with iron rungs and fixed ropes. Most of this paraphernalia was removed in 1965, and only a few iron rungs remain as welcome running belays, for either ascent or descent.

The North Ridge

The rib of the Younggrat had been noted as a possible descent route in 1898 by A.G. Cooke and his guides during the first ascent of the Grand Gendarme along the lower part of the North Ridge. A month later, on 21 September, Hans Biehly and Heinrich Burgener took advantage of this pioneering effort and crossed the Bishorn and the Grand Gendarme to make the first complete ascent of the North Ridge – now one of the most prized routes on the mountain. Keen blades of new snow and pinnacled rock arêtes alternate along its crest, with the prominent

*Geoffrey Winthrop Young gave a full analysis of this and the West Face climb in a talk to the Alpine Club in 1906 *A.J.* XXIII, p256.

Grand Gendarme as the main attraction for climbers who will have set out from the Tracuit Hut at midnight to be on the ridge by early morning.

The White Horn

'A ruffle of wind blew a window in the clouds overhead, a lucent oval in the darkness, ravelled into smoked silver round its edges by the hidden moon behind. And through the oval I was looking suddenly at the dream-white peak of the Weisshorn, impossibly remote, unearthly in its concealed illumination, unreal in its frosted loveliness.' Thus enthused Geoffrey Winthrop Young before his 1909 ascent of the North-East Face. This face was first climbed in 1871 by the engineer and locomotive designer John Hawthorn Kitson with Christian Almer and his son Ulrich, and repeated soon afterwards by W.A.B. Coolidge and Miss Meta Brevoort with the same two guides. The first ascent was a very rapid affair, Ulrich Almer cutting eight hundred steps at great speed in an attempt to reach the summit at a pre-arranged time for Kitson's wife to observe them from the Gornergrat: '. . . when he [Almer] was apparently working as hard as a man could work, he turned and asked, "Could you go a little faster if I cut steps faster, as I want to keep my word and be up by nine?" I, however, found quite enough employment in going his pace . . .'. But high on the mountain the difficulties accumulated and they actually reached the summit at noon. It was later established† that both the Kitson and Coolidge parties had climbed the face below the Grand Gendarme and then followed a hybrid of the North Ridge and North Face to the summit. In 1909 Geoffrey Winthrop Young and Josef Knubel, accompanied by the American rock-climber Oliver Perry Smith, who they had met on the Grépon, climbed the face by the main central rib. Young's long and haunting account in *On High Hills* takes us back to a wonderful climb. On a warm night they undertook a *reconnaissance* up the heavily riven Bishorn Glacier where 'occasionally the wet muffled echo of snow slipping from some ledge into further depth, betrayed its treacherous activity. . . . Josef mourned with reason "the Föhn is in the glacier".' Despite these bad omens Young nudged the party forward and on to the face and, by subterfuge and blandishment, ensured that height was steadily gained so that by sun-up they were fully committed.

'Climbing with a man of moods on a misty-moisty morning is like striking a damp safety match. Pressed too hard or too quick he loses his head and may sputter out. He has to be urged, lightly and tentatively, until – somehow – somewhere he kindles into flame. . . . Josef at this point dashed ahead, struck an attitude, and exclaimed: "Who follows me this day will reach the summit!". It was indeed sometime since we had remembered to remember that we were only *reconnoitring*.'

Their route was free from objective dangers. With an average angle of 48°, in good snow conditions it provides a splendid excursion, one of the least-frequented but most elegant expeditions of its type in the Alps. With it Young completed his third major face climb on a mountain with which he will always be associated.

†*A.J.* XXV, p165.

(below) The Grand Gendarme on the North Ridge.

Dave Wynne-Jones

Richard Goedeke

(above) Descending the East Ridge of the Weisshorn.

Wil Hurford

Richard Goedeke

A Mountain of Tragedy

On 22 August 1888 news reached Zermatt that the brilliant Munich rock climber Georg Winkler had died on the West Face of the Weisshorn. He had set out on 17 August but it was not clear whether he opted for the Passingham Route or for Farrar's less dangerous but harder line. A search party found only a photograph and his woollen hat at the edge of the avalanche debris.

The accident once again caused voices to be raised against solo-climbing, though a letter written shortly before his death showed that Winkler had no intention of climbing alone: 'Climbing is so much more entertaining with one or two companions and this year I will probably not do any climbs alone . . .' Yet Winkler had arrived at Zinal without his friends. In 1956 his body was found at the foot of the Weisshorn Glacier and buried at Ayer cemetery.

Another noted climber who died on the Weisshorn was the Halifax solicitor John Garforth Cockin, who was making his outstanding series of first ascents in the Caucasus (in the company of Ulrich Almer) in the same summer that Winkler perished. Twelve years later Cockin fell while soloing down a couloir at the foot of the South-East Face at the end of a long and difficult descent forced by poor conditions on the East Ridge.

Frau Eleonore Noll-Hasenclever, the popular and prolific alpinist from Duisberg, died on the Weisshorn's treacherous slopes in 1925. With her companions Hans Pfann and Herr Trier, she was approaching a low col on the East Ridge while crossing to the Weisshorn Hut after being forced off the North Ridge by bad weather. Just below the col (at 4 p.m.) the slope, which Pfann had suspected but judged safe, avalanched and swept all three into the bergschrund. Pfann and Trier survived but Frau Noll was buried and suffocated. The accident had a poignant aftermath. Frau Noll had been staying in Zermatt with her husband and two children, who decided that she should be buried among her beloved mountains. She was a Protestant so the service could not take place in the local church but the British mountaineers made their chapel available for the sad ceremony, thus ending the icy reserve which they had maintained towards German mountaineers in the years following the Great War.

(top left) On the upper section of the North Ridge of the Weisshorn with the West Face on the right.

(left) Traversing the main tower on the East Ridge of the Weisshorn. The Nadelgrat, the Dom and the Täschhorn are the principal peaks in the background.

(above) A view north-west from the Matterhorn to the Ober Gabelhorn, the Zinalrothorn and the Weisshorn.

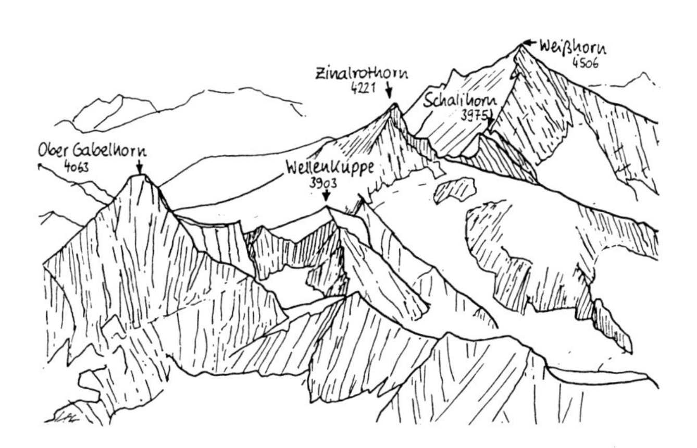

VALLEY BASES

Randa see Lenzspitze p67
Zinal see Bishorn p129

HUTS/OTHER BASES

Weisshorn Hut 2932m. SAC. On the slopes of the Hohlicht south-east of the Weisshorn. 36 places. Staffed from mid-July to mid-September *tel* 028/ 67 12 62. 5 hours from Randa.
Schalijoch Bivouac 3750m. SAC. On the Schalijoch below the initial rocks of the Schaligrat. 8 places. Always open. Metagas stoves (bring gas cylinders). 10 hours approach from either of the flanking valleys. From Zinaltal via the Cabane d'Ar Pitetta the approach is more difficult but not as prone to stonefall.
Cabane d'Ar Pitetta 2786m. SAC. On the slopes below the western flank of the Weisshorn, surrounded by glacial moraines. 20 places. Unstaffed and always open *tel* (guardian) 002/ 76 15 02. 5 hours from Zinal via the Alp Le Vicchiesso (1862m), and L'Ar Pitetta. Difficult to locate in mist.

NORMAL ROUTE

East Ridge AD III– (sections), II, I. To 45°. 7 hours from the Weisshorn Hut. 1600mH Rock scrambling and névé.

RIDGES/FACES

South-West Ridge (Schaligrat) D IV (several pitches), III, II. 6 hours/750mH from the Schalijoch. Rock climbing but with complicated glacier approaches to the Schalijoch.
North Ridge AD+ III (sections). 6 hours/450mH from the Weisshornjoch. About 8 hours from the Tracuit Hut. Some rock but mainly mixed climbing.
West Face Rib (Younggrat) D– IV–(sections), II, II. 8 hours from the Cabane d'Ar Pitetta to the 'Grande Gendarme'. 1550mH. Elegant rock climbing. Useful as a descent route.
North-East Rib D+ To 55°. 6 hours/1100mH from the foot of the face. An ice and snow route with complicated glacier approaches.

MAPS/GUIDEBOOKS

See Dufourspitze p99. The definitive SAC guidebook will be required for the North-East Rib or refer to the *Alpine Journal.*

Zinalrothorn *4221 m*

The Zinalrothorn (originally known in the local patois as Moming), like the Weisshorn, offers no easy route. It is a distinctive pinnacle of rough, solid gneiss that commands profound respect. Seen from the crest of the Ober Gabelhorn, the sharp sweep of the South-West Ridge forms with the summit structure an elegantly shaped horn, and from the Weisshorn it appears as a sharp aiguille perched above its formidable icy North Face. Thus it was obvious from early days that here was a mountain destined to be a real climbers' Mecca. And so it has proved as it offers three classic ridge routes on consistently good rock. The two main ridges, the North and South-West, are narrow and furnished with countless small pinnacles, while the South-East Ridge (the standard route from Zermatt) is somewhat broader in its lower section.

The First Ascent

Along with the Schreckhorn, the first ascent of the Zinalrothorn on 20 August 1864 was perhaps Leslie Stephen's greatest triumph, which he shared with Florence Craufurd Grove and the guides Melchior and Jakob Anderegg. The ascent is amusingly described in Stephen's *A.J.* account*, a shortened version of which subsequently appeared in his classic *The Playground of Europe*. They left Zinal at 1 a.m., ascended by the Zinal and Mountet Glaciers to reach to the upper end of the Arête du Blanc which led them to the shoulder below the difficult North Arête by 9 a.m.:

'. . . which here strikes up through the snow like the fin from a fish's back and guarded us from the assaults of a fierce southern gale. All along the arête to this point I had distinctly felt a keen, icy blast penetrate my coat as if it had been made from gossamer, pierce my skin, whistle merrily through my ribs, and, after chilling my internal organs, pass out the other side with unabated vigour. My hands were numb, my nose doubtless purple, and my teeth played involuntary airs like the bones of a negro minstrel.'

Nevertheless, with Melchior Anderegg leading, they set to work on the upper arête, which proved a stubborn test of ice-glazed rock climbing over sharp pinnacles and exposed edges. Steadily they rose: 'I was utterly insensible to the promptings of self-esteem which would generally induce me to refuse assistance . . . I found myself fumbling vaguely with my fingers for imaginary excrescences, my feet resting on rotten projections of crumbling stone, whilst a large pointed slab of rock pressed against my stomach . . .

'We seemed to be condemned to a fate which Dante might have reserved for faithless guides – to be everlastingly climbing a hopeless arête, in a high wind, and never getting anywhere near the summit.'

Nonetheless, in just over two hours all obstacles were overcome and they reached the top and two hours later had regained the snow arête where Stephen 'looked back triumphantly at the nastiest piece of climbing I have ever accomplished'. Modern climbers can tackle the climb from the conveniently positioned Mountet Hut and, in the conditions encountered on the first ascent, it can be quite hard (AD+).

The Classic

These days the North Ridge is neglected in favour of the Normal Route from the South-East but it deserves greater popularity as it can genuinely be described as a classic. Below the shoulder the elegant Arête de Blanc links the mountain with Blanc de Moming (3557m) which can be reached by a short climb from the Mountet Hut. In calm weather this is recommended as a scenic approach route that avoids the crevasses of the Mountet Glacier. The final rock ridge is very sharp and exposed in places, harder than the Normal Route but easier than the Rothorngrat. On the 200m of climbing above the shoulder (L'Épaule), the first tasty morsel is 'La Rasoir' (the open razor), which is overcome by a hand-traverse 700m above the Hohlicht Glacier. The imposing mass of the 'Sphinx' is turned on the right followed by the knife-edged 'Bourrique' and the 40m 'Bosse'. Finally the snow of the summit ridge demands the utmost concentration. These sections remain in the memory because, while climbing them, one can have the delightful experience of embracing members of descending parties, there being no other way of detouring around one another!

The Normal Route

Most ascents are made by way of the South-East Ridge. This steepens dramatically below the summit tower, and this final section (the Kanzelgrat) is bypassed by an unpleasant couloir on the South Face which leads up to the 'Gabel Notch' high on the South-West Ridge (Rothorngrat). Above, a 15m pinnacle blocks the way and beyond this a descending traverse brings one to a slanting crack splitting the slightly tilted 30m 'Biner Slab'. Several pitons are *in situ* and the climbing is III–. If the slab is verglassed, one can make a detour round to the left, cramponing up the névé slope on the Mountet side. After this two squat towers are climbed to reach the top.

The first ascent of this intricate route was made on 5 September 1872 (after careful reconnaissance) by the combined teams of George Augustus Passingham (with his guides Ferdinand Imseng and Franz Andermatten) and Clinton Thomas Dent (with his guide Alexander Burgener). They left the valley at 3 a.m. and were on the summit at 1.30 p.m. A porter accompanied them to the couloir and, based on Dent's account, may have gone to the top though no guidebook records this. The guides equipped the difficult pitches above the Gabel Notch while their clients rested and this greatly speeded both ascent and descent, the only incident being when a dislodged boulder slid through the party as they descended the Biner Slab. This was deflected by Andermatten (injuring him in the process) and, at the last moment, bounced over Imseng, who was unroped at the time.

The Kanzelgrat

The steep upper section of the the South-East Ridge (the Kanzelgrat) was finally climbed on 5 September 1933, after two earlier attempts, by Emile Robert Blanchet and Kaspar Mooser, taking time off from their ceaseless quest for new ice faces to conquer. This provides an excellent rock climb with several pitches of VI+.

*A.J. II p67.

Willi Burkhardt

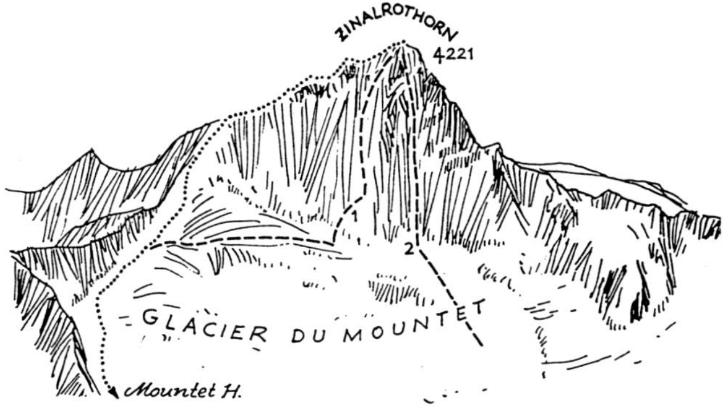

The western aspect of the Zinalrothorn showing the North Ridge (dotted line), the 1965 Theytaz Route (1) and the original West Face route (2).

The Finest Climb

The complete South-West Ridge (the Rothorngrat) is considered by many to be the best climb on the mountain. It was first descended in 1898 by J. Armitage Robinson with Peter Perren and Aloys Krönig, and climbed three years later by C.R. Gross and Rudolf Taugwalder. It sweeps up from the Ober-Rothornjoch as a steep rocky staircase. None of the gendarmes are bypassed, the crux being a fifteen-metre pinnacle which gives climbing of grade IV or V, depending on the line taken. One useful aspect of this ridge is that, after bad weather, it is usually the first of the mountain's main routes to come back into condition.

(above) The West Face of the Zinalrothorn seen from the summit of Blanc de Moming. The Rothorngrat is the rocky ridge on the right with the obvious saddle of the Gabel Notch at its top, below the summit mass.

Somewhere Between Night and Day

This was the title of an article written by the Austrian student Dieter Marchart about his moonlit solo ascent of the Rothorngrat. The writing has a prescient quality as it was published shortly before he met his death while trying to make the first solo ascent of the Eigerwand in 1962.

'All around me it is as bright as day, the moon casting soft echoes of sunlight across the landscape, like a munificent peasant sowing amongst the furrows . . . All at once I am overcome by the feeling that I have left this Earth; I walk a narrow path in space, a path without substance or form, supported by light and shade and fastened to the dome of the heavens by countless glistening threads of stars . . .

(below) Climbers on the South-East Ridge about to start the rising traverse across the South Face to gain the Gabel Notch.

'I become aware of my body, conscious of strength and self-confidence yet knowing, too, the ties which bind me to this Earth, whose countenence I tread with twenty-four sharp steel points at every step.

'At the upper edge of the glacier a move must be made onto the rocks. The ice, never completely in accord with its silent brother rock, has fashioned between them a deep chasm through which wafts a malevolent breath of air. Stretching across, I hang there for a moment, a living bridge spanning two dead worlds. A few short, ice-clad moves and the way ahead lies clear, to easy rocks . . .

'To the east, the day ripens into red banks of cloud. At first just a slight flicker, like a delicate reflection on the

(below) On the rock pitch above the Gabel Notch, approaching the Biner Slab.

Jim Teesdale

Jim Teesdale

silky sphere of a pearl, the clouds grow fringed with pink then adorn themselves with red ribbons for the Festival of Day. A fiery red flower bursts into bloom. The sun. The moon drifts on the horizon, a feeble, stranded little vessel, I sit for a long time and watch the changing of the celestial guard.'

(above) A view south from the summit of the Zinalrothorn to climbers on the foresummit (Kanzel) and a lower group finishing Biner Slab – the crux of the Normal Route.

The Traverse

A complete traverse is often made of the Zinalrothorn, entailing a strenuous day's outing amid captivatingly beautiful and varied scenery. If, for example, one chooses the Rothorn Hut as a starting-point, the Rothorngrat/Normal Route combination has much to recommend it. From the Mountet Hut I would suggest the Rothorngrat/North Ridge traverse. The North Ridge/Normal Route traverse is easier but involves a return trip of about six hours over the Ober-Rothornjoch.

The Face Climbs

The East Face (above the Hohlicht Glacier) is swept by stonefall during the daytime and has acquired a certain notoriety. André Roch, Robert Gréloz and Ruedi Schmidt found, on 6 August 1945, a mixed route of some difficulty up the highest part and two other routes now flank it.

The West Face (above the Mountet Glacier) was first climbed in 2½ hours in August 1878 by Martin Conway, William Penhall and G.S. Scriven with Ferdinand Imseng, Peter and M. Truffer. They followed the summit fall-line in preference to the heavily snow-plastered North Ridge. At such times this may be a logical ascent route, but usually the risk of stonefall on this face makes it too dangerous.

From the far reaches of the Moming Glacier, there rears an 800m rampart of ice and snow – the North Face of the Zinalrothorn. The first ascent was made on 3 August 1939 by Pierre Bonnant and Mlle. Loulou Boulaz from Geneva. Until the 1960s, Loulou Boulaz remained the most successful woman alpinist in Europe, whose climbs included the second ascent of the Croz Spur on the Grandes Jorasses in 1936 (with Raymond Lambert), completed a few hours after the Peters/Meier ascent. The Bonnant/Boulaz route finishes at 'L'Épaule' at 4017m. In July 1958, on the steeper face to the left, a much harder climb (ED) was established by René Theytaz and Adrian and Rose Voillat. Little is known about this ascent but, with sustained ice and mixed work, and rock pitches of VI and VI–, it appears to be one of the hardest climbs in the Pennine Alps!

VALLEY BASES

Zermatt see Rimpfischhorn p91
Zinal see Bishorn p129

HUTS/OTHER BASES

Rothorn Hut 3198m. SAC. South-east of the Zinalrothorn, at the start of the Eseltschuggen crags. 100 places. Staffed from end June to mid-September *tel* 028/ 67 20 43. 4½ hours from Zermatt via the Hôtel du Trift.
Cabane du Mountet 2886m. SAC. Situated north of the confluence of the Mountet and Zinal Glaciers. 115 places. Staffed from 1 July to 15 September *tel* 027/ 65 14 31. 5 hours from Zinal via the Restaurant Petit Mountet (2142m).

NORMAL ROUTE

South-East Ridge and Gabel Notch AD– III– (sections), II, I. 4 hours from the Rothorn Hut. 1050mH. A mixed climb.

RIDGES/FACES

North Ridge AD III+ (sections) and easier. 5 hours from the Mountet Hut. 1350mH. Glacier work then rock climbing.
South-West Ridge (Rothorngrat) D IV, III+. 4 hours/370mH from the Ober-Rothornjoch. A rock ridge.
South-East Ridge Direct (Kanzelgrat) TD– V (crux), IV, III. 5 hours/285mH from the start of the summit tower. A rock climb.
North Face D To 55°. 5 hours/800mH from the base of the route (3 hours from the Cabane d'Ar Pitetta across the dangerously crevassed Moming Glacier). An ice climb.

MAPS/GUIDEBOOKS

See Dufourspitze p99.

Ober Gabelhorn *4063 m*

The Mountet Hut stands in the centre of the 'Couronne Imperial', a magical cirque of peaks comprising Zinalrothorn, Ober Gabelhorn and Dent Blanche together with their satellites Besso, Blanc du Moming, Wellenkuppe, Mont Durand, Grand Cornier and the Bouquetins. From this aspect the Ober Gabelhorn looks particularly attractive, not massive but shapely, acclaimed by globe-trotting mountaineers as the most beautiful peak in the Alps. Yet, as impressive as the gleaming ice of the North Face may appear in its lofty position above the crevasse-ridden Ober Gabelhorn Glacier, it is rarely climbed, and even the old Normal Route up the North-West Ridge (known as the Coeurgrat after a heart-shaped isolated island of rock at its base) also remains the preserve of the individualist.

Lord Francis Douglas's Rebuff

The Ober Gabelhorn should always be remembered as a memorial for Lord Francis Douglas who, a week after making the second ascent, was to die on the Matterhorn. Lord Francis, with his guides Peter Taugwalder (who survived the Matterhorn disaster) and Peter Inäbnit (or Josef Viennin or Vianin), made three determined attempts to climb the mountain in late June and early July 1865. On the first he crossed the Unter Gabelhorn and reached the main peak by the South-East Ridge but had to return through lack of time. On the second they gained the summit of the Wellenkuppe from the Triftjoch but judged the continuation ridge (today's Normal Route) too difficult. Finally on the 7th (with Viennin replacing Inäbnit), they climbed the North-West Ridge to the summit only to find that they had been 'pipped to the post' by Adolphus Warburton Moore, Horace Walker and Jakob Anderegg, who had forced a route up the East Face just one day earlier. One can only speculate at the intense disappointment this must have caused after so much effort. Lord Francis saw that the highest point had no footsteps (Moore having noted its danger during his approach to the summit) but even this schemed against him:

'On this peak, we sat down to dine, when, all of a sudden I felt myself go, and the whole top fell with a crash thousands of feet below and I with it as far as the rope allowed (12 feet). Here like a flash of lightning Taugwald[er] came right by me some 12 feet more, but [Viennin], who had only a minute before walked a few feet from the summit to pick something up, did not go down with the mass and thus held us both. The weight on the rope must have been 23 stone, and it is wonderful that, falling straight down without anything to break one's fall, it did not break too.'

This account must have been written straight after the climb and was found and published after Lord Francis Douglas's death*. A superstitious man might have concluded after these dual rebuffs that his star was not in the ascendant, and that he should 'quit while still ahead'. Douglas did not – he hastened to Zermatt, joined forces with Whymper, Hudson and Hadow, and the rest is history.

*A.J. II, p222

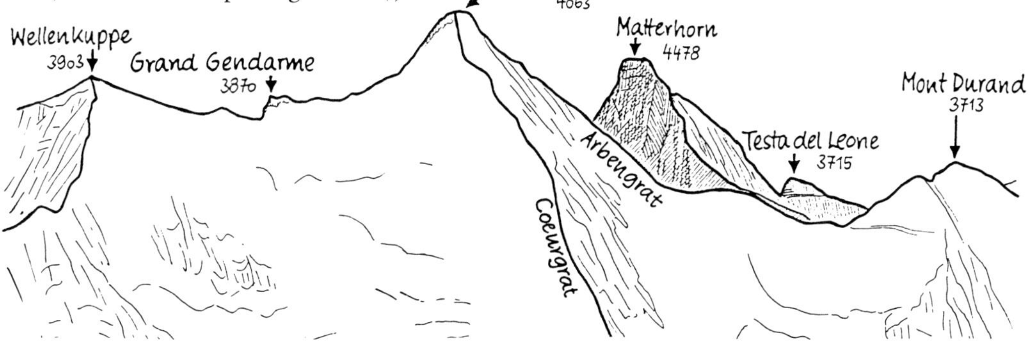

(left) The northern slopes of the Ober Gabelhorn. The Normal Route takes the left-hand ridge with the crux at the prominent step of the Grand Gendarme.

The Other Ridges

The Coeurgrat became the Normal Route but nine years later the West Ridge or Arbengrat was climbed (also approached from the north) by Henry Seymour Hoare and Eustace Hulton with the guides Johann von Bergen, Peter Rubi and Josef Moser. The South-East Ridge (Gabelhorngrat) was climbed by James Walker Hartley, William Edward Davidson, Peter Rubi and Johann Jaun in 1877, a few days before their previously noted Weisshorn ascent.

The final ridge to be climbed was the North-East Ridge which Douglas had studied from the Wellenkuppe. The problem here is a difficult step or tower and this was overcome in 1890 by Christian Klucker and Ludwig Norman-Neruda, who went on to complete the ridge to the summit.

The Normal Route

Evidently the mountaineering fraternity has forgotten the magnificent cirque of Mountet and its elegant Coeurgrat, for most parties set out from the Rothorn Hut to tackle the Wellenkuppe and the North-East Ridge. In 1918 the 'Kluckerturm' (the 'Grand Gendarme' on the North-East Ridge) was rigged with a fixed rope (periodically renewed) by the Zermatt Guides' Association, thereby converting it into the Normal Route.

The climb takes about six hours, half of it being used on the ascent of the Wellenkuppe. Beyond this the snow arête leads down to a depression in the ridge. An eight-metre length of rope hangs from the Kluckerturm, but to reach it involves grade III climbing. The gneiss slabs are often icy and soles find no purchase on the fine-grained rock.

On beyond the tower, after a slight dip, the snow ridge steepens and is often decorated with a fringe of cornices on its left-hand side. The line maintains a respectful distance well to the right and stays on fine consolidated névé as far as the summit region. Thoughout this ascent the sweep of the North Face is a constant companion on the right. The final tower (normally II), if not banked up

Dave Wynne-Jones

John Allen

(above) A view along the North-East Ridge of the Ober Gabelhorn from the summit of the Wellenkuppe, the Grand Gendarme is beyond the intervening col.

(left) Climbers on the steep rocks of the Grand Gendarme (Kluckerturm) – the crucial passage of the North-East Ridge.

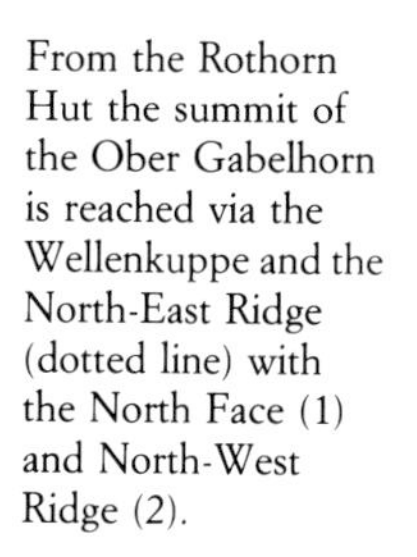

From the Rothorn Hut the summit of the Ober Gabelhorn is reached via the Wellenkuppe and the North-East Ridge (dotted line) with the North Face (1) and North-West Ridge (2).

with snow, can be quite difficult and one comes across the occasional abseil sling, left by traversing or retreating parties.

Descent by the Arbengrat

The Arbengrat provides a logical continuation for parties descending to Zermatt. The Arben Bivouac Hut is perched on a spur leading out from the South Face and at least three hours must be allowed for the descent to there and a further three hours to reach Zermatt. The Grand Gendarme on the West Ridge can be technically outwitted with a double abseil. Problems generally occur in locating the right point at which to move on to the South Face and the ridge is often quitted too soon. The correct place to branch off is on the lower third of the ridge at a diagonal ledge leading leftwards to the South Face. If bad luck still persists, the crevasses of the Arben Glacier force one to resort to complicated evasion tactics.

The South Face

The establishment of the Arben Bivouac Hut in 1977 has not only made the Arbengrat a more popular ascent route but it has also thrown attention on to the 700m South Face. The best line here was made by Percy Farrar and Daniel Maquignaz in 1892. It has a mixed reputation, some maintaining that it is a fine rock climb, others that it is treacherously loose. Certainly the fatal accident that befell the English alpinist Colin Taylor in 1974, when a ledge collapsed just below the summit, seems to support the latter view. However, others have encountered solid gneiss throughout and value it as a long and entertaining rock climb. I spent a day on the face, making the ascent in sunshine and the descent during a break in the weather, and heard no warning note of stonefall! Perhaps luck was with me that day. Despite the fact that the line was often difficult to follow, for me this classic route was pure pleasure; giving grade IV climbing on solid rock with glorious frictional properties.

In 1984 a direct route was established which follows the fall-line of the 'Gabel' up the right-hand section of the South Face. This is known as the 'Überkinger Pillar' and was first climbed, solo, by the German Jürgen Straub.

The 'Gabel' is a feature formed by a pinnacle on the South-East Ridge and the large summit flake, and gave the mountain its name. It can be seen clearly from the east.

The Quiet Men of the North Face

Just after midnight on 30 July 1930 the Austrians Hans Kiener and Rudolf Schwarzgruber left their tent in Zermatt. They took the path to the Rothorn Hut, crossed the Trift Glacier and reached the Triftjoch, thus gaining almost 2000m in height without a pause. The upper part of the North Face of the Ober Gabelhorn glistened in the cold light of dawn as they descended the steep, shadowy slopes to the Ober Gabelhorn Glacier. They struggled up the crevassed glacier to the bergschrund, above which the North Face rises in one concave 400m sweep of 50-55°. But there was no ice, instead they had dreamlike conditions of ideal step-kicking névé. After only two hours the Face set them free with nothing but a straight line of tracks behind them, soon be swept clear by the wind. Towards evening they returned to Zermatt, but not a single, solitary word was heard of their success.

Until 1951 the North Face Route of the Ober Gabelhorn saw only one repeat, after which Wolfgang Stefan hailed it as 'one of the finest ice trips in the Alps'. Once reached, a direct line is followed up the face to below the summit cliffs. As height is gained, the ice becomes steeper and reaches 56° on the upper part. The last forty metres can be avoided on the right up the North-West Ridge or climbed direct on steep mixed ground.

John Allen

(above) A view back to the Wellenkuppe and the Grand Gendarme from high on the North-East Ridge of the Ober Gabelhorn.

VALLEY BASES

Zermatt see Rimpfischorn p91
Zinal see Bishorn p129

HUTS/OTHER BASES

Rothorn Hut/Cabane du Mountet see Zinalrothorn p139
Arben Bivouac 3200m. SAC. On a rock spur above the Arben Glacier and beneath the South Face. 15 places. Always open. 4½ hours from Zermatt, 3 hours from the Schönbiel Hut.

NORMAL ROUTE

Wellenkuppe and North-East Ridge AD– III (one section), II, I. 6 hours from the Rothorn Hut. 900mH. A glacier tour, then mixed (predominantly névé).

RIDGES/FACES

North-West Ridge (Coeurgrat) AD III+ (sections). To 50°. 6 hours from the Mountet Hut. 1300mH. Mixed climbing.
West Ridge (Arbengrat) AD III+ (Grand Gendarme), II+, I. 3 hours/500mH from the upper Arbenjoch (1½ hours from the Arben Bivouac, 3 hours from the Mountet Hut).
South-East Ridge (Gablehorngrat) AD III+. 4 hours from the Arben Bivouac, 850mH. Mixed.
South Face AD IV, III. 6 hours from the Arben Bivouac. 870mH. A rock climb.
South Face (Überkinger Pillar) D+ V (sections), IV, III. 870mH. A rock climb.
North Face D+ To 50-55°. 4 hours/500mH from the foot of the route. An ice and snow climb after a glacier approach.

MAPS/GUIDEBOOKS

See Dufourspitze p99

Dent Blanche *4356m*

In common with other nearby peaks, the Dent Blanche is characterised by a series of sharp ridges separated by difficult and inhospitable faces. With the exception of the Matterhorn, it is the most arresting mountain in the area, appearing dominating and elegant from all quarters. William Hall, viewing it from the Dent d'Hérens in 1863, opined: '. . . the exquisite beauty of the Dent Blanche was even nobler in its general form than the Weisshorn . . . it looked without exception the grandest mountain in the Alps.'

But the most distinctive profile is seen from the west from where the South Ridge (Wandflue Route), and the steep North Ridge and the West Ridge (Ferpècle Arête) can all be studied thoroughly. From this aspect it is clear that the South Ridge, though inconveniently positioned, offers the easiest line of ascent. These days the Dent Blanche Hut (3505m), reached by a long climb from the head of the Val d'Hérens, provides a suitable starting point, but those approaching from Zermatt must use the Schönbiel Hut (2994m) with a correspondingly longer summit climb.

The First Ascent

The first ascent in 1862 was masterminded by the very experienced and strong climber Thomas Stuart Kennedy (not to be confused with Edward Shirley Kennedy). In January 1862 he made a bold winter attempt on the East Face of the Matterhorn, and on 12 July he made an equally audacious bid to climb the Dent Blanche with Peter Taugwalder and his son. They were very nearly successful but high on the ridge, above the Grand Gendarme, the older Taugwalder came close to falling while tackling a difficult rock step and, somewhat chastened, declined to follow Kennedy when he took over the lead. Kennedy duly assembled a stronger team with Jean Baptiste Croz (Michel's older brother) and Johann Krönig as guides for himself and William and C. Wigram. They set out from Bricola on 18 July 1862 in blustery weather and forced their way to the top (C. Wigram waiting on the glacier) in very cold conditions, –20°F being noted on the summit.

The Normal Route

At a rough estimate, eighty percent of mountaineers who climb the mountain use this South Ridge as it is the least difficult route, being on the sunny side of the mountain it clears most rapidly after a break in the weather. From the Dent Blanche Hut, usually full on fine days, a ridge leads to the flat snow-col of the Wandfluelücke (which can also be reached from the Schönbiel Hut with an approach climb that takes three hours longer). At the approximate mid-point of the ridge above, the Grand Gendarme blocks the way. This is turned by a two-pitch traverse on the west side, after which an unpleasant couloir (equipped with iron stakes for abseiling and belaying) leads back to the ridge. The next main step is turned on the right using a horizontal ledge. The steep rocks which follow (turned on the left) decide the success or failure of the undertaking: they face away from the sun and are often covered in a thin layer of ice. The rock difficulties now ease off but the ridge may be corniced on its eastern side in the final section to the summit cross.

Early Repeats

The next ascent of the mountain, by John Finlaison with Christian Lauener and Franz Zurflüh (1864), also with the Bricola approach, was by the somewhat hazardous South-West Flank and the next four ascents followed the same route.[1] Later a Zermatt approach (using the Schönbiel Hut) that took in the whole South Ridge from the Col d'Hérens became the favoured way for a period. The

1. *A.J.* VX. p64

John Allen

(left) Dent Blanche from the west. The Normal (Wandflue) Route takes the right-hand ridge, the Ferpècle Arête goes directly to the summit. The North Ridge is in profile on the left beyond the North-West Face.

(top right) The Grand Gendarme on the South Ridge.

(bottom right) The Grand Gendarme is turned on the left across steep slabby rocks after which it is possible to regain the ridge.

Dave Wynne-Jones

next new line was on the South-East Face and was climbed in 1874 by Edward Robson Whitwell with Christian and Johann Lauener.

The Four Asses

One of the great episodes in the history of the mountain took place on 11 August 1882 when John Stafford Anderson and George Percival Baker, with the experienced guides Aloys Pollinger and Ulrich Almer, climbed the East Ridge. Approaching from the Mountet Hut they took twelve hours for what turned out to be a very sustained and difficult climb, initially over rock towers and then along a very sharp snow arête poised above the North Face. They arrived on the summit at 3 p.m. with no little relief as Anderson described:[2]

'Our first proceeding was to shake hands all round, then Almer, grasping the situation in its entirety, exclaimed in a loud and solemn manner *"Wir sind vier Esel"'* [We are four asses], a sort of concentrated summary of the day's proceedings which it has since been suggested to me by a friend, who I need hardly say is *not* a member of the AC, might be appropriately worked up into a motto for our club.' The ridge, which though hard is very fine, has ever since been known as the Viereselsgrat. A sad footnote to this great climb was that when the four climbers (exhausted and hungry) reached the Schönbiel Hut, they were sustained by W.E. Gabbett and his guides Joseph-Marie Lochmatter and his eldest son Alexander. The following day this party fell from the difficult final traverse on the South Ridge and all were killed.[3]

2. *A.J.* XI p166
3. Many years later it transpired (*A.J.* XL, P183) that this fatal accident, coming after those to Professor Balfour and his guide (on the Aiguille Blanche) and William Penhall and his guides (on the Wetterhorn) all in the summer of 1882, had prompted Queen Victoria to write (through her private secretary) to the British Prime Minister, William Gladstone:

Sir Henry Ponsonby to Mr. Gladstone 24th August, 1882.
Dear Mr. Gladstone – The Queen commands me to ask you if you think she can say anything to mark her disapproval of the dangerous Alpine excursions that have occasioned so much loss of life. – Henry F. Ponsonby

Mr. Gladstone to Sir Henry Ponsonby 25th August, 1882.
My dear Sir H. Ponsonby – I do not wonder that the Queen's sympathetic feelings have again been excited by the accidents, so grave in character, and so accumulated during recent weeks, in the Alps. But I doubt the possibility of any interference, even by Her Majesty, with a prospect of advantage. It may be questionable whether, upon the whole, mountain-climbing (and be it remembered that Snowdon has its victims as well as the Matterhorn) is more destructive that various other pursuits in the way of recreation which perhaps have no justification to plead so respectable as that which may be alleged on behalf of mountain expeditions. The question, however, is not one of wisdom or unwisdom; but viewing it, as you put it, upon its very definite and simple grounds, I see no room for action. My attempt at yachting came to grief, and the chance of renewing it is small. – Yours sincerely, W.E. Gladstone.

Dave Wynne-Jones

Willi Burkhardt

(left) The northern aspect of Dent Blanche. The North Face is in shadow on the left with the North Ridge to its right. The Ferpècle Arête rises above the North-West Face from the centre right.

(right) A north-easterly view of Dent Blanche from the summit of Blanc de Moming. The shadowy North Face dominates the lonely upper basin of the Grand Cornier Glacier.

Tragedy on the Ferpècle Arête

The next major route to be explored was the rocky West Ridge (Ferpècle Arête). This was first *descended* in 1882 by Mrs E.P. Jackson, Dr Karl Schultz, Aloys Pollinger and J.J. Truffer and then climbed in 1889 by Pollinger with his client Walter Gröbli. This ridge was the scene of another terrible accident on 28 August 1899. The noted British rock climber Owen Glynne Jones, F.W. Hill and the guides Elias Furrer, Clemenz Zurbriggen and Jean Vuignier set out to make the ascent. Two-thirds of the way up the ridge they were stopped by a gendarme with a verglassed chimney which Furrer attempted to turn by climbing a steep rock step on the left. This was so hard that it required combined tactics with Jones and Zurbriggen (unbelayed) steadying Furrer from below. At the crucial moment Furrer slipped, knocked off the other two and tore Vuignier from his stance a little way back, breaking the rope. All four fell to their deaths.

Hill was left with thirty-feet of rope and the problem of escape: 'My main feeling was one of astonishment that I was still there . . . the only course open was to attempt to turn the gendarme on the right. This I succeeded in doing with great difficulty, owing to the ice on the rocks and the necessity of cutting up an ice slope in order to reach the ridge. In about another hour I gained the summit . . .' He began the descent but above the Grand Gendarme a snowstorm forced him to bivouac until noon on the following day. He then made good his escape and finally brought the tragic news to Zermatt forty-eight hours after the accident.

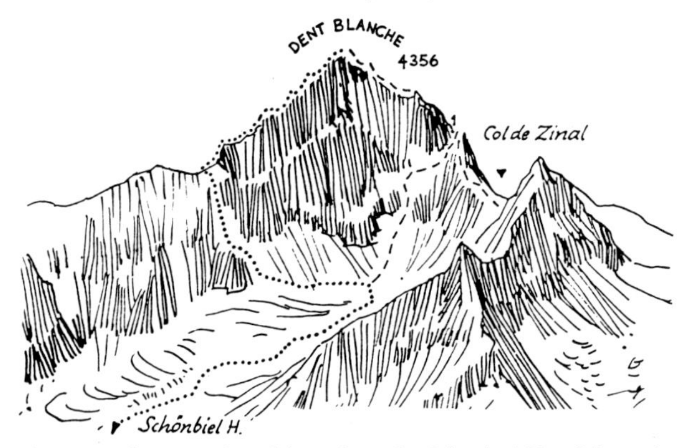

The Normal Route (dotted line) from the Schönbiel Hut follows the glacier of the same name and climbs the South (Wandflue) Ridge. The East Ridge or Viereselsgrat (1) is considerably more difficult.

The North Ridge

The North Ridge of the mountain was not climbed until the 1920s. Ridge is a misnomer as it is broken at half height by a huge and very steep cliff. The first foray on to this formidable bastion was in 1926 when M. Kropf with the local guides Marcel Savioz and Jean Genoud took two days to descend the ridge, mostly by abseiling. This event served to intensify the interest that had been developing and in 1928 two ascents were made. On 20 July, the Cambridge academic Ivor Richards and his wife Dorothy Pilley (Mrs I.A. Richards) with the brothers Joseph and Anthoine Georges made the first ascent, turning the great cliff by a traversing manoeuvre to the right and gaining the upper ridge by a steep rock pitch (well illustrated in André Roch's book *On Rock and Ice*[4]). On 11 August, Dr Maud Cairney with Théophile and Hilaire Theytaz (a trio, who, like the Richards party, had long-cherished ambitions for this project) worked up to the left from the lower ridge, crossing difficult slabs, until they gained the North Face where a mixed rib (which demanded combined tactics at two points) led up to join the final part of the North Ridge. The barrier wall was finally climbed over two days in 1977 by a rope of three with the aid of twenty-eight pitons and two expansion bolts.

The North Face

Although the Cairney/Theytaz line encroached onto the North Face, the first ascent credit for this is accorded to Karl Schneider (German) and Franz Singer (Austrian) who on 26-27 August 1932 climbed the 1000m face by a diagonal line from the bottom left to the summit. Direct lines were established in 1966 (Michel and Yvette Vaucher), and in February 1968 by Camille Bournissen who thus made the first solo and first winter ascents of the face. In 1969, Bournissen, with Cyrille Pralong, straightened out the route on the 850m North-West Face, first climbed in 1934 by Karl Schneider and Ludwig Steinauer.

4. Verlag Amstutz Herdeg, Zürich / A and C. Black, London. 1947.

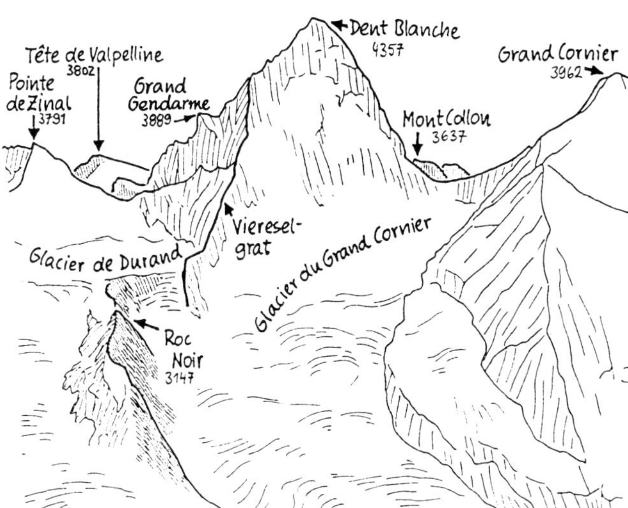

VALLEY BASES

Les Haudères 1443m. A mountain village situated at a fork in the nethermost Val d'Hérens. Access by road from Sitten/Rhône Valley (33km), Post Bus service. Inns, pensions. Campsite *tel* 027/ 83 12 96.

Ferpècle 1770m. On a high pasture in the valley south-east of Les Haudères. Access by road 6km to Hotel Col d'Hérens (*tel* 027/ 83 11 54) Post Bus service in summer. Car-park 3km beyond the hotel at the end of the track by a power station.

Zermatt see Rimpfishhorn p91

Zinal see Bishorn p129

HUTS/OTHER BASES

Cabane de la Dent Blanche 3507m. SAC. On a rocky knoll between the Glacier des Manzettes and the Plateau d'Hérens, west of the lower section of the South Ridge. 40 places. Staffed from 20 July to beginning September. Service of simple meals only in good weather. Approx 5 hours from the car-park at Ferpècle via the mountain inn at Bricola (2415m, reached in 1½ hours).

Schönbiel Hut 2694m. SAC. On the lower terrace of the Schönbiel, south-east of the Dent Blanche. 80 places. Staffed from April to mid-September *tel* 028/ 67 13 54. 3 hours from Furi (cable car from Zermatt).

Mountet Hut see Zinalrothorn p139

Dent Blanche Bivouac 3540m. SAC. Stone-built refuge on the Col de la Dent Blanche. 15 paces. Always open. 6 hours from Ferpècle via Bricola. 4 hours from the Mountet Hut.

NORMAL ROUTE

South Ridge (Wandflue Route) AD III, II. To 35°. 5 hours from the Dent Blanche Hut / 8 hours from the Schönbiel Hut). 850mH or 1662mH. Snow to the ridge, then mixed (mainly rock).

RIDGES/FACES

East Ridge (Viereselsgrat) D III+, III. 15 hours from the Mountet Hut. 1500mH. Rock, Mixed and ice (tricky cornices).

West Ridge (Ferpècle Arête) D+ IV (sections), III, II. 7 hours/ 850mH from foot of the ridge. Rock and mixed.

North Ridge TD+ V+/AI(crux), V, IV+ and IV. 10 hours/820mH from base of route. Mixed and rock.

MAPS/GUIDEBOOKS

See Dufourspitze p99

Matterhorn *4477 m*

And so we come to the Matterhorn. From Italy it looks merely abrupt and difficult as reflected in its title 'Monte Cervino' or 'Stag Mountain'. It is from the east, north and north-west that the mountain appears as a sharp peak. The menacing West Face broods above the Tiefmatten Glacier, perhaps justifying the 'Lion' appellation given to the ridge that rises on the right. Although from most positions the mountain appears as a sharp point, the summit is actually a ninety-metre arête linking the Swiss and Italian summits, broken by a prominent notch, and forming one of the mountain's finest features.

The Drama of the Early Ascents

While the other great peaks of the Pennine Alps were steadily mastered as the 'Golden Age' approached its zenith, the Matterhorn stood aloof and inviolate. From the first serious attempts in 1858, there had been fourteen failed bids (mostly from Italy) of which Edward Whymper was involved in eight and the Val Tournanche guide, Jean Anthoine Carrel, in six. In 1862, a party led by John Tyndall and including J.J. Bennen and Carrel had come close to success on the Italian Ridge, reaching the shoulder (later named Pic Tyndall) below the final summit mass. Bennen's death in 1864 denied Tyndall his favourite guide and the field was thus left to Carrel and Whymper – driven men, both obsessed with the peak, and prepared for anything to capture the first ascent.

At this stage nationalism intervened. Unknown to Whymper, a group of Italian notables led by the politician Quintino Sella, stirred by foreign successes on Italian peaks, had decided that the Matterhorn must be climbed by Italians. Carrel was chosen to lead the attempt and Felice Giordano was charged with organising and financing the venture.

In June 1865, Whymper, and the leading French guide Michel Croz, launched yet another attempt, this time up a couloir on the South-East Face. When this failed, Croz departed to an engagement with Charles Hudson and Whymper, guideless (few of the Swiss guides would consider the Matterhorn), hastened to Breuil hoping to team up with Carrel, only to be mysteriously frustrated.

Giordano (from his Breuil hotel) wrote to Sella:

'I have tried to keep everything secret, but that fellow, whose life seems to depend on the Matterhorn, is here, suspiciously prying into everything. I have taken all the competent men away from him, and yet he is so enamoured of this mountain that he may go up with others and make a scene. He is here, in this hotel, and I try to avoid speaking to him.'

All the elements were building towards triumph and

(left) At the foot of the Hörnli Ridge of the Matterhorn with the East Face and the Furggen Ridge on the left.

(right) The Matterhorn from near Gandegg to the east with the Italian Ridge in profile on the left.

The eastern flank of the Matterhorn with the Hörnli Ridge (dotted line), the East Face (1) and the Furggen Ridge (2).

Willi Burkhardt

tragedy and the events were to unfold with a drama and sensation that stunned the world. The Italian guides under Carrel set out and Whymper learned that he had been misled. At this point he met Lord Francis Douglas (fresh from his Ober Gabelhorn ascent) and the pair (with the guides Peter Taugwalder – father and son) decided to mount an attempt on the hitherto neglected Hörnli Ridge. Returning to Zermatt they found Hudson and Croz, with the inexperienced Douglas Hadow, with the same objective in mind. The two groups combined and climbed the ridge on 14 July 1865. From the summit they gazed down on Carrel's team near the Shoulder on the Italian Ridge, trundling rocks down to attract their attention in an act of unrestrained triumphalism. Then they began the descent, but on the steepest section, poised above the North Face, Hadow slipped, knocking off Croz, and dragging Douglas and Hudson from their stances. The rope broke and the four fell to their deaths, leaving Whymper and the traumatised Taugwalders to make their sad descent to Zermatt with a tale of triumph and tragedy that horrified and scandalised the world.

These events are well-known and have been written about in countless books, the most notable being Whymper's great classic *Scrambles Amongst the Alps* and Guido Rey's *The Matterhorn*. The accident, the broken rope, and the other factors that led to the tragedy, were minutely analysed for years in both the popular press and specialist journals. Perhaps the soundest judgement was made in 1918 by Percy Farrar in the *Alpine Journal* (Vol. XXXII). He noted that in normal circumstances Hadow's inexperience would easily have been balanced by the skill of Hudson and Croz. The error was in roping up as one party and then the ordering of the team:

'But the real cause of the accident was not the slip made by Hadow, not the breaking of the rope, but the want of coherence in the "fortuitously" formed party.

'The great lesson to be learned from the occurrence is to undertake no serious expedition with a large party. Even among good men it engenders a false sense of security and, most certainly, inattention and irresponsibility.'

The Italian guides were totally demoralised. Giordano urged Carrel to try again and with the Abbé Aimé Gorret and two waiters from a local inn – Jean-Baptiste Bich and Jean-Augustin Meynet, he finally climbed the mountain three days later. Carrel and Bich overcame the final tower by a difficult traverse across the West Face to reach the Zmutt Ridge which led them to the top. The direct rock pitches used today were climbed in 1867 by the brothers Jean-Joseph and Pierre Maquignaz, and are now equipped with fixed ropes and a rope ladder (the 'Échelle Jordan') provided by Leighton Jordan, the first amateur to follow the straightened route.

Fame and Notoriety

Both the Italian and Swiss guides were accutely aware that the mountain climbed represented a potential tourist bonanza. Huts were soon established on the two routes and fixed ropes added at the difficult sections. The main repeat ascents took place in 1868 and thereafter the guides and hoteliers steadily exploited the mountain's fame, its reputation enhanced by the publication of Whymper's book in 1871. The combination of the sensational events surrounding the Matterhorn's first ascent

Willi Burkhardt

(right) One of the lower rock towers on the Hörnli Ridge where it is necessary to go on to the East Face.

Wil Hurford

and its singular appearance from all quarters, but particularly from Zermatt, has ensured a worldwide fame that has lasted to this day. In 1964 the Munich magazine *Alpinismus* conducted a poll among leading climbers to decide which was the most beautiful peak in the world. The Matterhorn ranked alongside Fitz Roy, Mont Blanc, the Grandes Jorasses and Machapuchare, but after Alpamayo and K2. How much value can be placed on this is a matter for discussion, but few will disagree that the Matterhorn exudes a powerful and enduring character though sadly this is not matched (on most routes) by the quality of its climbing. Of all the routes, it is the easier ones which have claimed the most victims. It is estimated that a total of five hundred people have come to grief on the peak, the great majority on one of the two Normal Routes. After a rapid drop in temperature and falls of new snow the mountain changes its character, and slow parties descending the Hörnli Route often get into difficulties and, after forced bivouacs, die of exhaustion or hypothermia.

The Zmutt and Furggen Ridges

The easiest of the ridges is the North-East or Hörnli Ridge, the route taken on the first ascent. Slightly harder, more complex, and considerably more interesting is the South-West or Lion Ridge, the usual line of ascent from the Italian side. The North-West or Zmutt Ridge is graded rather higher and has no fixed ropes. It is three kilometres long, has an average gradient of 37° and is the only Matterhorn ridge with a snow section. Here the steepness of the climbing is less important than the conditions encountered, particularly on the Tiefmatten Slabs and the Galerie Carrel yet, for the capable climber, the Zmutt is probably the finest route on the mountain. It was climbed on 3 September 1879 by Albert Frederick Mummery with his guides Alexander Burgener, Johann Petrus and Augustin Gentinetta. On their way to the mountain they met William Penhall, Ferdinand Imseng and Louis (or Ludwig) Zurbrücken who had been forced down by bad weather after a high bivouac on the ridge. The Mummery party completed the route, while the Penhall team, after a brief rest in Zermatt, rushed back up the mountain but had to settle for a harder but less elegant route up the West Face reaching the summit just one hour after the Mummery group. Alessandro Gogna commented on these climbs in his 'Matterhorn Commentary' in *Mountain 36*:

'So it was that both the Zmutt Ridge and the West Face fell in the same day, ascents made with purely mountaineering motives, uncomplicated by issues of patriotism or utilitarianism. . . . to me these ascents were the most impressive of the century.'

Burgener and Mummery went on to more triumphs the following year, crossing the dangerous Col du Lion and then (with Benedict Venetz) making the first attempt on the Furggen Ridge. However they judged the upper section too hard and prepared to traverse off to the Hörnli Ridge, across the stone-strafed slabs of the East Face as Mummery relates:

'[Burgener suggested] . . . that it would be well to drink our Bouvier and consume our other provisions before any less fitting fate should overtake them. . . . Looking back on that distant lunch, I have little doubt that Burgener fully realised that a rollicking self-confident party can dodge falling stones and dance across steep slabs, in a manner, and at a pace, which is impossible to anxious and disheartened men. His object was fully attained . . . we were soon springing across the slabs . . .

(left) The Matterhorn and the Dent d'Hérens seen from the summit of the Mettelhorn to the north-east. The intervening spur leads from Zermatt to the Unter Gabelhorn.

Dave Wynne-Jones

Bill O'Connor

(above left and right) Key sections on the Hörnli Ridge: the Moseley Slab and the first fixed ropes of the summit block.

our leader would brook no hesitation . . . his "Schnell nur schnell" hurried us ever forwards. An occasional rap on the head by a splinter of ice or the hurtle of a great stone, as it spun playfully between the various members of the party, most thoroughly accentuated Burgener's admonitions.'

It was not until 9 September 1911 that Mario Piacenza, with Jean-Joseph Carrel and Joseph Gaspard, forced a route up the final walls (IV) somewhat to the left of the true ridge line which in 1941 succumbed, with sixth grade climbing, to Alfredo Perino with Luigi Carrel and Giacomo Chiara.

The Hörnli Ridge

One should not imagine that this most popular route will give pleasant ridge climbing on splendid rock. The contrary is the truth: it is loose, inelegant and sometimes dangerous, yet somehow the position, history and length of the climb combine to invest it with an indefinable stature. Despite its teeming crowds it is still a great climb on one of the finest peaks in the world. After the horrors of a night spent in the hideously overcrowded Hörnli Hut, the climb begins with scrambling and walking terrain to the left of the crest, over rocky steps not infrequently bombarded by salvos of stonefall. Some distance higher, one scrambles across the 'Moseley Slab' and up a rocky rib. Above, on an airy vantage point, stands the Solvay Refuge, named after the Brussels industrialist, Ernst Solvay, who paid for its construction in 1916. The going becomes steeper. The 'Upper Moseley Slab' that follows is where the American, Dr William Moseley, fell to his death in 1879 while descending after insisting on untying from the rope of his three companions.

The next landmark is the Red Tower, which is turned on the left. The ridge leading up to the Shoulder is bedecked with fixed ropes and iron rungs and a chain.

Bill O'Connor

Bill O'Connor

(above) Climbers ascending fixed ropes of summit block seen from the Shoulder on the Hörnli Ridge. The first ascent party avoided the steep rocks by a move right on to the North Face where the fateful accident took place during the descent.

(far left) The Solvay Hut.

(near left) The Swiss summit of the Matterhorn.

Dave Wynne-Jones

Dave Wynne-Jones

Views on the Italian Ridge of the Matterhorn: (above) The Whymper Chimney with its iron chain; (below) Looking up from the Savoia Hut; (top right) On steep face below Pic Tyndall with the pinnacles of the Crête du Coq below.

Dave Wynne-Jones

Dave Wynne-Jones

The first ascent party traversed off from here on to the North Face – the point where the tragic accident occurred. The passage across the dizzy heights of the magnificent crest is unforgettable – unless, of course, the experience is diluted by the sight of heavy traffic coming in the opposite direction. Michel Vaucher, in his book *Alpes Valaisannes*, sums things up as follows:

'The Normal Route to the top of the Matterhorn is easy . . . but only for climbers who have trained well for it.'

The Italian or Lion Ridge

The hut situation on the Italian Ridge is even poorer than on the Swiss side. The Rifugio Savoia takes sixteen and the Rifugio Carrel, built in 1969 by the Matterhorn Guides (and often occupied by them), has forty-five bunks. The Rifugio Abruzzi lies four hours' walk below. The demands made on the climber on this route, which offers the most solid rock of all the Matterhorn's ridges, are greater than on the Hörnli. The approach route is long and sometimes threatened by stonefall. On the ridge, ropes are fixed at difficult points. Without these artificial aids, the Italian Ridge would be more difficult than the Zmutt and entail grade III free climbing.

Just above the hut the first rope hangs over a steep step. The pinnacles on the 'Crête du Coq' are avoided by ledges on the right which lead to the *mauvais pas* traverse which is also safeguarded by a rope. Hereabouts one can find the initials of Carrel and Whymper scratched on the rocks. 'The Shroud' (Linceul), a small, right-angled patch of snow in the process of shrinking, points the way to the continuation of the route, which climbs its left-hand side to the 30m long 'Grande Corde'. At the 'Cravat', a white ledge slung around the upper part of the Shoulder, the first hut ever built on the Matterhorn (1867) clings to the slope.

From the shoulder of Pic Tyndall the Tyndall Ridge provides the link with the final peak. The ridge is nearly vertical, becoming narrower and more exposed as it climbs up to the 'Enjambée'. A wide, bridging move across the notch and more comfortable ground follows. At this point the first ascent party traversed across the West Face by 'Galerie Carrel' to the Zmutt Ridge, but nowadays one takes hold of the fixed ropes on the 'Scala Jordan' and then places one's trust in the ladder hanging from the off-balance passage until a final heave on the rope leaves the way clear to the Italian Summit.

(left) Below the summit block. The climber has just passed the 'Enjambée' and is approaching the 'Galerie Carrel', the difficult traverse line to the Zmutt Ridge on the left.

(right) The 'Scala Jordan' where the steep final rock section is fitted with a fixed rope and ladder.

Mike Pinney

The Other Routes

All the major features on the mountain have now been climbed, with several routes on each of the main faces. Most of these climbs are loose and serious. A prodigious pioneer in the later years was the diminutive guide Luigi Carrel, who took part in six first ascents between 1931 and 1953, his most notable climbs being the direct finish to the Furggen Ridge (1941) and the 1200m South Face which he climbed with Enzo Benedetti and Morizio Bich on 15 October 1931. Benedetti described the route:*

'Here [one third of the way up] we discovered our mistake in thinking this route safe from falling stones, for marks which we found on the rocks did not leave us in any doubt. . . . With the rising sun the stones began to fall methodically and we were involved in their unpleasant company during ten hours. We were obliged to proceed by rushes, steering towards big boulders or other obstacles which might afford shelter. But the stones were kind to us and fell only at regular intervals, thus permitting us to pass between successive showers.'

Higher up the cliffs got much steeper, giving greater protection, and by 6 p.m. they were on the summit, having completed at the first attempt an audacious climb that would probably have been suicidal in summer.

Gogna considers this route deserving of greater attention, being 'direct and logical', and it has been compared in both challenge and seriousness to the Eigerwand.

*A.J. XLIV

The North Face

Perhaps the most important and perennially popular face route is the North Face Original which was first climbed on 31 July and 1 August 1931 by the Munich engineering students Franz and Toni Schmid. At the time this was considered very bold and even reckless by some experts, but it was also recognised as a landmark ascent of one of the greatest of alpine North Faces. The pair had to contend with sustained and extremely difficult mixed climbing, certainly as hard, and possibly harder, than that climbed by Welzenbach and Tillmann on the Fiescherwand. After thirty-four hours on the face, with a standing bivouac,

Richard Goedeke

(above) Traffic problems on the fixed ropes of the Hörnli Ridge as ascending and descending parties meet.

they arrived on the summit in an electric storm. More storms followed, and after a painfully slow descent they gained the Solvay Refuge where they waited a further thirty-six hours before judging it safe to complete their escape.

Sensations

Events on the Matterhorn always attract popular attention and at the 1932 Olympic Games in Los Angeles the Schmid brothers had gold medals hung about their necks for their ascent of the North Face.

The first winter ascent of the Schmid route, made in February 1962, by the Swiss climbers Paul Etter and Hilti von Allmen, Austrians Erich Krempke and Leo Schlömmer and the German trio of Werner Bittner, Rainer Kauschke and Peter Siegert, filled the columns of the popular press. Bittner had to have his frostbitten toes amputated. On an August day of the same year, 200 people queued below the summit as there was no more room up there – a situation which is, by the way, not exceptional!

Another media extravaganza followed in 1965 (the year of the Centennial Jubilee of the first ascent) when between 18 and 22 February, Walter Bonatti crowned his incomparable career with a spectacular new route on the North Face.

Even in subsequent years, the sensations were never long in coming. Among other feats, one heard tales of spirited descents of the East Face on skis and, of course, there were further new routes, the most difficult climb to date being the Zmutt Nose which traces a line up the steep cliff to the right of the North Face and was the work of Leo Cerrutti and Alessandro Gogna.

Another sensation was provided by the Chamonix guide, Christophe Profit who, on 25 July 1985, climbed the North Face in four hours. From the Hörnli Hut a helicopter took him to Kleine Scheidegg from where, in bad conditions, he raced up the Eigerwand in eight hours. Then it was off to the Grandes Jorasses where he climbed The Shroud in five hours, thus completing the three great North Faces in less than twenty-four hours. Even the flashy French magazine *Vertical* was outraged, describing the 'feat' as the 'Crime of the Century'. Later, to confound his critics, Profit repeated the climbs (in reverse sequence and in winter) taking forty-two hours.

Food for Thought

I will conclude this Matterhorn miscellany with a note about Luc Meynet, the hunchback from Breuil who was involved in the early struggles on the peak. His personal motto, 'We can only die once!' was a comfort to him both in moments of brinkmanship on the mountain and in the misery of his little herdsman's hut, where he cared for the children of his deceased brother. Meynet took part in countless attempts on the mountain as a porter, and reached the summit himself in wintry conditions, on 12 May 1875 (as porter to Signor G. Corona's party)†. Meynet, a good-natured man and, despite his poverty, always amusing, solemnly affirmed that he had heard the 'Angels of Heaven' singing on the summit and now he could die in peace.

†*A.J.* IX, p446

VALLEY BASES

Zermatt see Rimpfischhorn p91
Breuil/Cervinia 2006m. At the head of Italy's Val Tournanche. Access from Chatillon (24km, nearest railway station, 24km from Aosta). Bus service. Hotels, inns, pensions.

HUTS/OTHER BASES

Hörnli Hut 3260m. SAC. At the foot of the Hörnli Ridge. 50 places. Staffed from 15 June to 15 September *tel* 028/ 67 27 29. 4½ hours from Zermatt via the Hotel Schwarzsee (2584m, 12 places). Cable-lift to Hotel Schwarzsee (first lift from Zermatt at 7 a.m., last lift down about 5.50 p.m.). 2 hours from the Hotel Schwarzsee.
Hotel Belvedere 3260m. Private. Next to the Hörnli Hut. 10 places. *tel* 028/ 67 22 64.
Solvay Refuge 4003m. Emergency bivouac shelter on the Hörnli Ridge. No water. Always open. 10 places. 3 hours from the Hörnli Hut.
Schönbiel Hut see Dent Blanche p147
Oreste Bossi Bivouac 3345m. CAI. At the foot of the Furggen Ridge 100 metres to the north of the Breuiljoch. 9 places. Always open. One hour from the Hörnli Hut. About 1½ hours from the Stazione del Furggen (3492m) by cable-lift from Breuil. 4 hours from Breuil.
Rifugio Duca degli Abruzzi 2802m. Private. An inn situated to the south-west of the Matterhorn on L'Orionde. 40 places. Staffed from 1 July to 30 September *tel* 0166/ 94 91 19 (from Breuil). About 2½ hours from Breuil.
Rifugio Carrel 3835m. Matterhorn Guides. Situated on the Italian Ridge. 45 places. Occasionally staffed in summer. 4 hours from the Rifugio Abruzzi. Information: Societa Guide del Cervino *tel* 01 66/ 94 81 49.
Rifugio Luigi Amedeo di Savoia 3847m. CAI. Near the Carrel Hut. 16 places. Always open. No fuel.

NORMAL ROUTES

North-East Ridge (Hörnli Ridge) AD– III– (sections) II, I. Fixed ropes. 6 hours from the Hörnli Hut. 1200mH. Rock and mixed (above the shoulder).
South-West Ridge (Italian or Lion Ridge) AD III–, II (sections), otherwise fixed ropes. 5 hours from the Carrel or Savoia Huts. 650mH. Mainly rock, with mixed climbing after Pic Tyndall.

RIDGES/FACES

North-West Ridge (Zmutt Ridge) D IV–, III+. To 50°. 9 hours from the Hörnli Hut, 10 hours from the Schönbiel Hut. 1200mH from the foot of the ridge. Mixed.
South-East Ridge (Furggen Ridge) D– IV (Piacenza Route) 8 hours from Bossi Bivouac. 1150mH. Rock and mixed (loose and serious). The direct route is TD VI–, V.
The face routes are all difficult, loose and dangerous undertakings.

MAPS/GUIDEBOOKS

See Dufourspitze p99

Dent d'Hérens *4171 m*

Despite ease of access from the Aosta Hut and the magnificent summit views, particularly of the Matterhorn and Dent Blanche, the Dent d'Hérens simply cannot compete with her more illustrious neighbours for attention and popularity. Thus the mountain has preserved a certain calmness; there is no queuing here, no waiting and no hustle and bustle. It provides a solitary experience on a remote and mysterious peak.

The ice-clad North Face gives the Dent d'Hérens dramatic character, looking particularly impressive from the Schönbiel Hut. The wall is in complete harmony with the surroundings, dropping 1300m to the waves of the Tiefmatten Glacier. After its first ascent in 1925 (by Willi Welzenbach and Eugen Allwein) it was acknowledged as one of the most difficult ice faces in the Alps. In contrast, the Italian flanks above Valpelline and Val Tournanche are less arresting and few could even recall the mountain's appearance from these valleys.

The Discovery of the Normal Route

The Normal Route, which sets out from the Aosta Hut to the west of the summit, crosses the Grandes Murailles Glacier, and follows the general line taken on the first ascent on 12 August 1863. That climb was led by Melchior Anderegg, 'Le Grand Melchior', the most celebrated of all the early alpine guides with a status rivalled only by Christian Almer. Dent d'Hérens, the Zinalrothorn (1864) and the Grandes Jorasses (1868) were his most important mountain first ascents, the Old Brenva Route on Mont Blanc (1865) being his hardest new climb on a mountain already climbed. His clients (who planned the expedition) were William Hall, Florence Craufurd Grove, Reginald Macdonald and Montagu Woodmass. There were two other guides, Peter Perren and Jean-Pierre Cachat. The mountain had been attempted a few days earlier by Edward Whymper, Jean-Anthoine Carrel and Luc Meynet, but they chose (on Carrel's advice, because of his preference for rock) the West Ridge which they found both difficult and unjustifiably loose and Whymper insisted on retreat. In his book Whymper noted ruefully that he had wished to follow the line later taken by Anderegg:

'This was the only mountain in the Alps which I have essayed to ascend, that has not, sooner or later, fallen to me. Our failure was mortifying . . .'

Unaware of this, the Anderegg-led party settled on the line from the Grandes Murailles Glacier, up the slopes of the South-West Face, a climb (as Hall described) that was strenuous but enjoyable:*

'[Anderegg, who] led the whole day, hewed steps the shape and size of Glastonbury chairs, so that . . . I began to have some thoughts of settling myself into one for a snooze. . . . our muscles were called into much more varied play by the rocks that followed, and our intellects strained to find something with which the abomination of their rottenness could be compared. [They were likened to] large slices of wedding cake, piled without very strict regard for order and with the gaps between bridged with almond paste . . . . [Up this with] warping and pushing and hauling we all got on to the ice slope [of the North-West Face] . . . . A series of slabs reared themselves above us which Macdonald declared must have been brought over from the Matterhorn.'

Hall was exhausted by these exertions and higher up decided to rest and wait for the others to complete the ascent.

'I got down the chimney, piled up a few stones . . .

*A.J. I pp210-223

Willi Burkhardt

(right) The summit pyramid of Dent d'Hérens in an aerial view across the head of the Grandes Murailles Glacier. The first ascent party crossed the mixed slopes on the lower left.

Willi Burkhardt

(left) The North Face of the Dent d'Hérens seen from the Wandfluelücke. The West-North-West Face is in shadow on the right and the East Ridge the left-hand skyline.

and put my head into a hole, where I could rest in the shade upon a cool pillow of ice, where my mouth could suck icicles as I rolled from side to side. [A few minutes later Macdonald] had leapt to my side [saying that everyone was on the summit] drunk with delight. He went on to declare that I must go up in turn . . . .' Thus the whole party reached the top.

Route Choice from the Zermatt Side

Easy ways are lacking from the Schönbiel Hut. The icy West-North-West Face has much to commend it but is quite hard, though at no point is it excessively steep. It is possible to skirt many of the obstacles but the séracs on the Tiefmatten Glacier can prove uncomfortable. These are also a factor on the long approach to the Tiefmattenjoch below the West Ridge, so the Aosta Hut is a better base for that route.

The East Ridge

Some people may be attracted by the 2.2km East Ridge. In parts rather loose, it starts from the Col Tournanche where the Benedetti Bivouac forms a useful intermediate base. The ridge was first climbed in 1906 by the Irishman Valentine Ryan with his regular guides Franz and Josef Lochmatter, who used the West-North-West Face for their descent of the peak, thus completing two new routes in one day. The climb is very demanding and it takes at least ten hours to cross its various summits before the Dent d'Hérens is reached. A notable early repeat was made in 1923 by Hans Pfann, Willi Welzenbach and Frau Eleonore Noll-Hasenclever who climbed the Zmutt Ridge (soloed by Pfann in 1906), descended to the Savoia Hut and then climbed the complete frontier ridge over the Dent d'Hérens, and down the West Ridge (two days of climbing).

Routes from the Aosta Hut

The Aosta Hut (2781m) is the best base for the Normal Route but an early start will be necessary. Hardly has one reached the first basin of the Grandes Murailles Glacier than care and attention are demanded: it is best to keep well away from the crags which drop down from the West Ridge as stonefall is a distinct possibility. The bergschrund can present a serious obstacle and the névé and rocky terrain of the South-West Face are often icy. The upper part of the West Ridge is gained by a rising traverse to the left and thereafter about four rope-lengths on snow-covered blocky ground have to be run out to the junction with the North-West Ridge which leads to the top.

If the whole West Ridge is the objective one must be capable of tackling grade IV rock climbing at the four-thousand metre mark as the rock (III+) can be verglassed. One can, according to preference, avoid the blocky blade of the ridge by climbing its North-West flank, a manoeuvre that will be essential if the rocks are badly verglassed. The ridge was first climbed on 18 July 1873 by Giles Puller with Jean-Joseph, Pierre and Emmanuel Maquignaz and Louis Carrel.

The North Face

In 1923 the first climbers to explore the face were the Australian-born scientist and early Everest pioneer George Ingle Finch with Guy Forster and Raymond Peto. After long study Finch had devised a route to reach the great slanting snow terrace which spans the complete face (above the ice cliffs). This involved crossing a dangerous bergschrund and lower icefields and ribs on the North-West side which had to be climbed on a moonlit

(near right) Descending a rocky section where the West Ridge joins the North-West Ridge a short distance below the summit.

(far right) The West-North-West Face – negotiating the lower icefall and climbing the upper ice face to join the West Ridge.

Dave Wynne-Jones

Dave Wynne-Jones

(above) The West Face of the Matterhorn seen from the summit of the Dent d'Hérens. The Zmutt Ridge is on the left, the Italian Ridge is on the centre-right and the Penhall Couloir is prominent in the centre of the West Face.

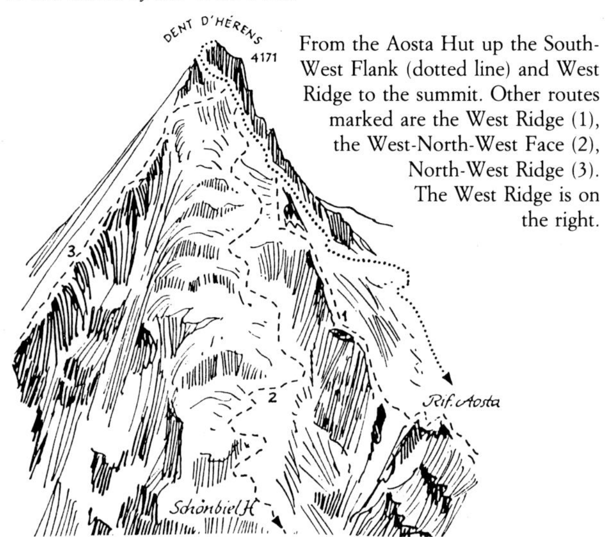

From the Aosta Hut up the South-West Flank (dotted line) and West Ridge to the summit. Other routes marked are the West Ridge (1), the West-North-West Face (2), North-West Ridge (3). The West Ridge is on the right.

night for maximum safety. This accomplished, the terrace was reached by an elaborate descending and traversing manoeuvre. At its top end a gaping bergschrund barred the way to the slopes leading up to the East Ridge which was only overcome by precarious ice climbing, but by 11 a.m. they were on the East Ridge. To this day the feature known as the 'Finch Terrace' commemorates his bold plan.

Two years later Welzenbach and Allwein, profiting from Finch's experience and Welzenbach's own observations from his East Ridge climb, made their famous direct route, spending thirteen hours on the face. On this climb the main problem is finding a way through the complex of ice cliffs and then negotiating the awkward mixed ground on the face below the summit. They were confounded by the difficulties in the ice labyrinth and forced to desperate traversing manoeuvres as Welzenbach described in the book *Welzenbach's Climbs*†:

'I first tried to climb the traverse but I immediately realised the fruitlessness of this task. . . . An excellent idea then occurred to me: I would attempt to overcome the pitch by a rope traverse. For what purpose had we learnt such technical skills in the rock regions of the Eastern Alps? . . . I pushed my feet against the extreme edge of the gangway and laid my weight on the rope . . . my body moved gradually to the left, my hand reached a slight crack, I jammed my fist into it and swung across [and] . . . called Allwein to follow . . . and couldn't help laughing at his flabbergasted expression, "How did you get across there?" he asked in amazement. I replied somewhat maliciously without divulging the secret. For all that he made short work of it . . . .'

This climb soon became a prestigious objective. The most capable ice climbers of their generation followed in the steps cut by the master: Karl von Kraus (1930, twelve hours); Walter Stosser and Fritz Schutt (1930, ten hours); the 'mountain vagabond' Hans Ertl with Friedel Brand (over two days in 1931); Karl Schreiner, the Viennese hot-shot Rudi Fraissl, and the Swiss rope of Leo Graf and Frei who made the eighth ascent in 1933.

†*Welzenbach's Climbs* by Eric Roberts (West Col, 1980)

Polish Climbers on the North Face

The tenth ascent of the North Face fell to Georg Haidukiewiecz, a Polish doctor from Zakopane, and his fellow countryman M. Nischa. The Poles also had a hand in the first winter ascent, which was made by a 'European Rope' from 14-17 March 1964 and saw the return of Haidukiewiecz, with Christoph Berbeka; the Zürich climbers Eckard Grassmann, Pierre Monkewitz and Dieter Naef and the Germans Gerhard Deves and Leo Herncarek. The climb turned into an epic. On 18 March, after the summit bivouac, disaster loomed as Berbeka lost his footing, dragging Haidukiewiecz with him 200 metres down the North-West Face. Naef fell, too, but was held by Monkewitz. The Poles suffered broken bones and Deves and Naef remained with them while the others summoned assistance. Four days passed before the injured men were finally brought down. Berbeka died in hospital, Herncarek had all his toes amputated and Naef both feet above the ankles.

This was the second winter disaster. In March 1963 the Italian party of Romano Merendi, Renato Daguin and Guido Bosco disappeared while attempting the face and are presumed to have perished in an avalanche.

The Poles were again active on the North Face on 13-14 August 1971 when Michal Jagiello, Jerzy Milewski and Tadeusz Piotrowski added a manifestly difficult and dangerous route up the left-hand side, finishing to the west of the 'Épaule' on the East Ridge.

VALLEY BASES

Bionaz 1606m. A village in the upper Valpelline, north-east of Aosta (29km). Bus service. Albergo Valentino *tel* 0165/ 7 39 01. Beyond Bionaz the valley road continues to the dam at Lago di Place Moulin (6km).
Zermatt see Rimpfischhorn p91
Breuil/Cervinia see Matterhorn p156

HUTS/OTHER BASES

Rifugio Aosta 2781m. CAI. West of the summit, at the foot of the West Ridge of the Tête de Valpelline. 25 places. Always open. Staffed from 15 July to 30 August *tel* (valley) 0165/ 3 16 96 or 4 35 88. 5 hours from the dam at Lago di Place Moulin (avalanche danger in winter). 6 hours from the Schönbiel Hut via the Col de Valpelline.
Schönbiel Hut see Dent Blanche p147

NORMAL ROUTE

South-West Flank/West Ridge PD+ II(sections). 5½ hours from the Aosta Hut. 1400mH. A glacier tour then mixed.

RIDGES/FACES

West Ridge AD– III+ (sections) III, II. 3 hours/600mH from the Tiefmattenjoch (3 hours from the Aosta Hut). Glacier approach, then rock, finally mixed.
North-West Face AD· To 45°. 7 hours from the Schönbiel Hut, 1500mH. Glacier and ice climbing.
East Ridge D IV, III, II. 10 hours/700mH from the Col Tournache. Rock and mixed.
North Face Exceptionally difficult ice and mixed routes, vertical in places, 14 hours/1300mH. The Finch Route is easier (AD+) but serious as is the North-West Ridge (AD).

MAPS/GUIDEBOOKS

See Dufourspitze p99

Grand Combin *4314 m*

The Grand Combin is not easily seen from afar. When travelling along the road from Martigny to the Grand St Bernard Pass it makes a brief appearance to the left, alien and majestic, and it can also be seen from Aosta but makes little impression. Yet, like Monte Rosa, this is a complete mountain massif, a lone western sentinel of the Pennine Alps with three distinct four-thousand-metre summits (plus a satellite top), all of which would be given full mountain status if the Monte Rosa premise were used. It is from the north, from the vicinity of the Panossière Hut, that the mountain is seen at its best – an ice-clad man-at-arms standing proudly above its long approach glacier, blocking the southern horizon. Its steep southern precipices (when seen from Mont Vélan or the vicinity of the Chanrion Hut) look equally fine, the mountain resembling some huge medieval castle, dominating the surrounding countryside.

Most parties use the Panossière Hut as the base for operations. It was from this side, too, that the first climbers came – Benjamin and Maurice Felley and Jouvence Bruchez, huntsmen from the Val de Bagnes – on 20 July 1857. Their bold route through the 'Corridor' is today's Normal Route which can be conveniently extended to include the Combin de Tsessette (4141m). Yet this climb (and the succeeding four ascents) ended on the Aiguille du Croissant (4243m). For some reason none of these groups continued the short additional distance, with seventy metres of height gain, to reach the true summit – Combin de Graffeneire (4314m). The true first ascent was made on 30 July 1859 by the Swiss engineer Charles Sainte-Claire Deville (who later played a major role in the building of the trans-Canada railway), Daniel, Emmanuel and Gaspard Balleys and Basile Dorsaz. Further west, the Combin de Valsorey (4184m) remained unclimbed until 16 September 1872 when J.H. Isler with Joseph Gillioz climbed the South Face from the Plateau du Couloir.

Willi Burkhardt

A Little Outing on the Haute Route

It was Marcel Kurz who, in 1907, first ferreted out the Grand Combin as a skiers' mountain, in which capacity it enjoys great popularity to this day, most aspirants using the Panossière Hut approach. Frequently, however, it is those skiing the Haute Route who tackle the mountain, using the Valsorey Hut or the Musso Bivouac which can be reached by skinning up the slopes above Col du Sonadon to gain the Plateau du Couloir. The Col du Meitin must then be crossed to gain the north side and, after a height loss of 200m, the mountain can be ascended by the Corridor.

The Normal Route from the north (dotted line) leads through the Corridor and up to the highest point of the Grand Combin. The left flank route on the North-West Face (1) and the West Ridge (2) are also marked.

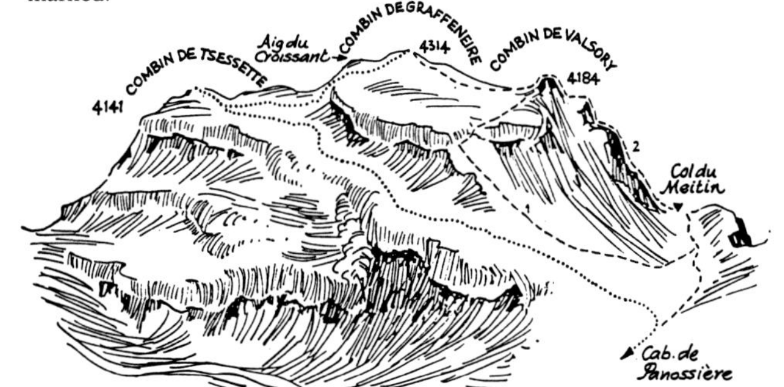

(left) An aerial view of the northern slopes of the Grand Combin taken in early summer snow conditions.

Willi Burkhardt

Running the Gauntlet of the Corridor

Five ski-mountaineers lost their lives in the Corridor in 1959 and one year later, four members of the Swiss Alpine Club fell victim to its unpredictable dangers. This rising glacier ramp on the North Flank of the Grand Combin is threatened by ice cliffs of frightening proportions, and here and there severely fractured. Fresh crack lines glisten a cold blue. Day and night, at unscheduled intervals, the ice thunders down. More than 400m of ascent must be gained by way of this icy ramp and this takes about two hours, at least one of which is spent in the direct firing line, and later the descent frays the nerves again. The climb holds little in the way of real difficulties. Above the Corridor, a long, slanting crevasse is turned on the left. Where the ramp peters out, the tracks meander across flat glacial névé to the Mur de la Côte at almost 4100m. The subsequent 150m slope occasionally calls for step-cutting. After that – just watch out for those cornices! From the Panossière Hut there appears little alternative to the Corridor but Richard Goedeke advocates a subtle route that takes the easiest line on the North-West Flank (well to the left of the 1933 Blanchet/Mooser route) to break through the sérac barrier on the extreme left to gain P.3987. This involves snow and ice climbing of up to 50° but in good conditions it offers a logical and rapid route of ascent.

(above) An aerial view of the South Face of the Grand Combin. The South Face of Combin de Valsorey (taken by the Isler/Gillioz Route) is on the left and the snowy South-East Ridge rises to Combin de Graffeneire from the bottom right corner of the picture. Combin de la Tsessette is the peak on the right.

Routes from the South

The Col du Meitin is best approached from the Valsorey Hut and to reach it a final steep gully has to be climbed. In good conditions this is taken direct, otherwise a detour is made on the rocks bounding the gully on its eastern side. The North-West Face and the Corridor route can be approached from the Col, but the West Ridge, above, though harder than the Normal Route, also offers a tempting means of ascent that is largely free from objective dangers. This was first climbed in 1884 by Charles Boisviel, Daniel Balleys and Séraphin Henry. It sweeps up in three steep rocky steps to the Combin de Valsorey, taking roughly three hours to climb, with a further fifty minutes from the Combin de Valsorey to the main summit.

The South Face

The other climb that deserves consideration is the Isler/Gillioz route on the South Face of the Combin de Valsorey. In good conditions (snow cover but with the rocks standing clear for belaying) this gives a fine and enjoyable mixed climb. Its position facing the sun means that it deteriorates rapidly, and it can be subject to stonefall, so a descent by the Corridor or the West Ridge may be necessary.

One other route of a reasonable grade that merits attention is the South-East Ridge (AD) which rises from the head of the Glacier du Mont Durand (best approached from the Amiante Hut). Though friable, long and quite serious, this offers wonderful views to the Otemma Glacier and the main peaks of the Pennine Alps. It was first climbed on 10 September 1891 by Owen Glynne Jones with Antoine Bovier and Pierre Gaspoz.

VALLEY BASES

Fionnay 1489m. In the upper Val de Bagnes (wildlife reserve). Branch off the Val d'Entremont road at Sembrancher and continue through Le Châble (nearest railway station). 29km from Martigny. Post Bus service. Hôtel Grand Combin *tel* 026/ 7 91 22 or 7 21 23. Campsite in the idyllic Bonatchesse part of the town on the road to Mauvoisin at 1580m *tel* 026/ 7 92 40.

Mauvoisin 1840m. At the top end of the Val de Bagnes, beneath the dam of the Lac de Mauvoisin, 6km from Fionnay. Bus terminus. Hôtel-Restaurant de Mauvoisin, 20 beds – open from May to October *tel* 026/ 7 91 30.

Bourg-St-Pierre 1632m. In the upper Val d'Entremont, 37km from Martigny via Orsieres (nearest railway station). Post Bus. Hotels, inns, pensions. Alpine Garden: laid out by the Geneva Botanist Corevon in 1889 as the 'Alpinum Linnaea', approx 2500 species of plants from the high mountains of the world.

HUTS/OTHER BASES

Cabane de Panossière 2669m. SAC. North of the Grand Combin above the east bank of the Corbassière Glacier. 100 places – staffed in April and May and from July to September *tel* 026/ 7 54 64. 4 hours from Fionnay (winter path from Lourtier over the Col des Avoullions). 3½ hours from Mauvoisin over the Col des Otanes, 2880m. The hut was destroyed by avalanche in March 1988 but is to be rebuilt.

Cabane de Valsorey 3037m. SAC. South-west of the Grand Combin, below the Meitin Glacier. 36 places. Occasionally staffed at weekends *tel* 026/ 4 91 22. About 4½ hours from Bourg-St-Pierre. The last slope to the hut is avalanche-prone in the early part of the year.

Bivouac Biagio Musso 3664m. At the southern base of the Combin de Valsorey. 12 places. Open year-round, gas stoves (no cartridges). 2½ hours from the Valsorey Hut. 5 hours from the Chanrion Hut.

Rifugio Amiante 2979m. On a rocky plateau at the head of the Conca di By. 12 places. Normally locked (keys with warden in Ollomont). Equipped but take stoves. 4 hours from the roadhead at Glacier (1549m).

NORMAL ROUTE

North Flank (Corridor Route) PD To 40°. 7 hours from the Panossière Hut. 1650mH. A serious glacier tour. *As a ski tour:* Deposit skis below the Mur de la Côte.

RIDGES/FACES

West Ridge PD+ III (sections), II. To 45°. 6 hours from the Valsorey Hut to the main summit. 1300mH. Mixed, rock (brittle) and snow.

South Face of Combin de Valsorey PD+ II. 4 hours/650mH from the Plateau du Couloir.

North-West Face (left flank) AD+ To 50°. 4 hours/700mH from the foot of the face.

South-East Ridge AD Short sections of III–, II. 6 hours/1335mH from the Amiante Hut. 7½ hours/1300mH from the Valsorey Hut.

MAPS/GUIDEBOOKS

Landeskarte der Schweiz 1:50,000 Sheet 5003 *Mont Blanc-Grand Combin*. *Pennine Alps West* by Robin Collomb (Alpine Club).
The Alpine 4000m Peaks by the Classic Routes by Richard Goedeke (Diadem/Menasha).

(below) Nearing the top of the Isler/Gillioz Route with the Plateau du Couloir below.

(right) Starting the descent of the Corridor Route.

Wil Hurford

Wil Hurford

The Mont Blanc Group

It is in the granite range of Mont Blanc that the kingdom of the Alps reaches its absolute and overwhelming zenith. Not only because of height and prodigious size, but, as a result of the granite (and other crystalline rocks), the mountains display a particularly savage character where pinnacles, blades, needles, spines, towers and massive buttresses jut provocatively amidst wild glacial cirques, ruthlessly isolated from worldly things.

The climbing on offer here is therefore more challenging than in any other region of the Western Alps. Rock specialists and ice climbers find themselves motivated to produce outstanding performances and mountaineers, with an interest in the high peaks, find their energies fully occupied where even the easiest routes present a significant challenge. The rapid weather changes resulting from Mont Blanc's exposed position at the south-western end of the alpine chain

adds a final element of uncertainty to the equation. Above-average ability and a psyche capable of handling stressful situations are therefore the prerequisites here.

Civilisation eats hungrily at the flanks of the range. Indispensable and unavoidable are the valley bases of the rumbustious Chamonix on the French side, and Courmayeur and Entrèves on the Italian side and the valleys in which these towns spread themselves – the Arve Valley and Val Veni and Val Ferret – form the natural west and east boundaries of the region. The téléphérique system linking Chamonix to Entrèves has also had a potent influence on the development of the region, opening up the expansive snowfields and icefields of the Vallée Blanche and its surrounding peaks to mountaineers and particularly to skiers, with the run down the Géant Glacier and the Mer de Glace to Montenvers being an outstanding attraction. Other téléphériques to the Grands Montets and towards the Aiguille du Goûter have shortened the Argentière and Mont Blanc approaches and the Mont Blanc tunnel now allows easy passage across the range. On the Italian side, apart from the téléphérique to Pointe Helbronner, mountaineers must still accept long hut walks and equally prolonged summit climbs.

These predations remain superficial, however. The great glory of the range is still vested in its climbs – amongst the finest, hardest and most historic routes in Europe – that lure generation after generation of climbers from around the world, a habit that seems unlikely to change.

(previous page) An aerial view of Mont Blanc from the north. Photo: Willi Burkhardt

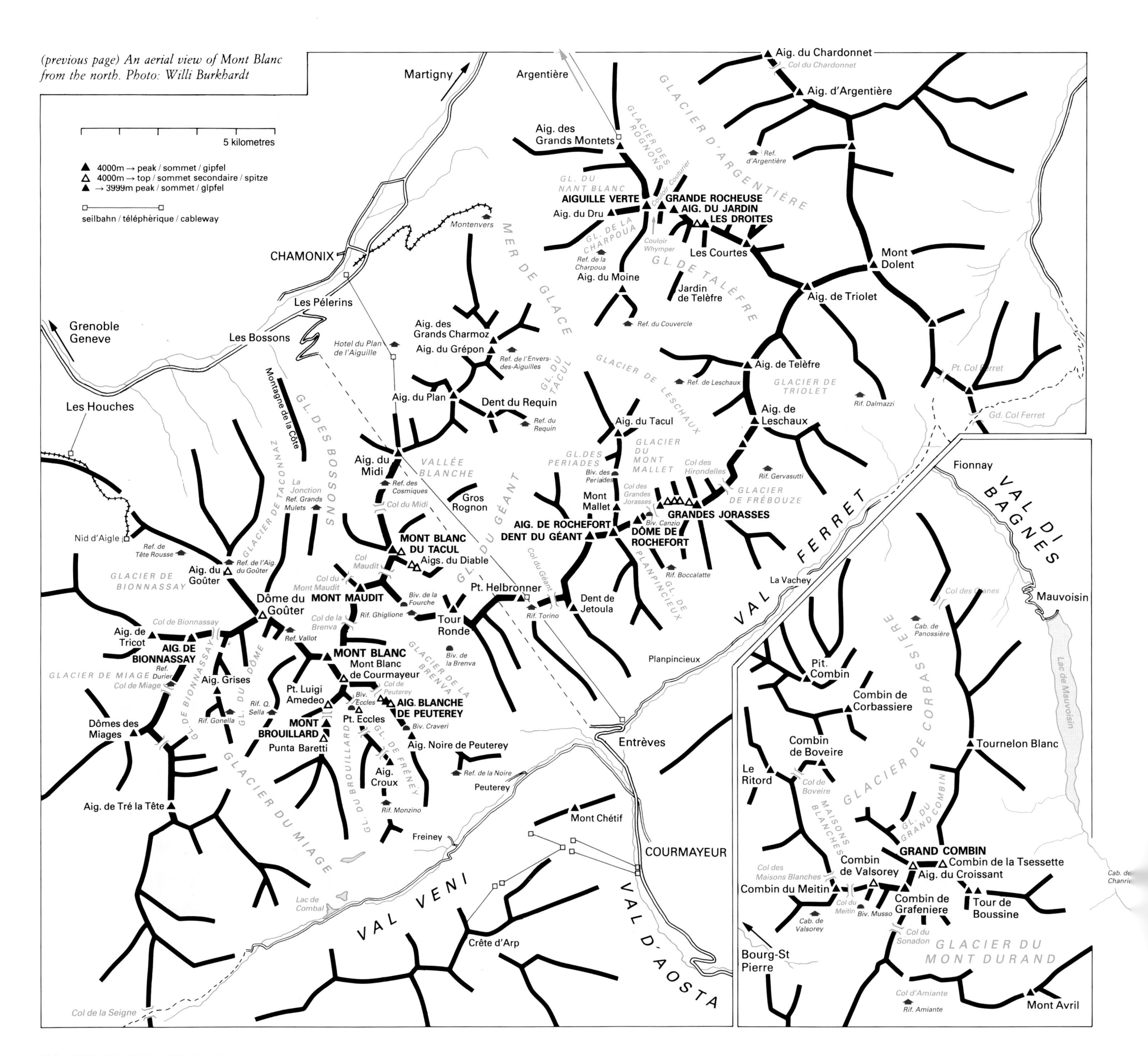

Willi Burkhardt

Les Droites *4000 m*

The most easterly four-thousander of the Mont Blanc range has a height of exactly 4000m. Though undistinguished on its Talèfre side, the face it presents to the Argentière cirque is stupendous. I will never forget the evening which I spent at the Argentière Hut studying that enchanting amphitheatre: a barrier of rock and ice stretching ten kilometres from the Aiguille Verte to Mont Dolent and rising 700-1000m into the skies, the faces seemingly close enough to reach out and touch.

Each mountain has its North Wall, each with an individual character. The North Face of Les Droites is the biggest and hardest – one thousand and sixty metres of ice and rock ribs from the bergschrund to the crest of the ridge and tilted at an average angle of 60°. Its principal climb, the North Face original, is regarded as the finest ice and mixed expedition in the Alps.

The Talèfre Face

The southern side overlooking the Talèfre Glacier is somewhat less savage. Here the serrated summit blade throws down three prominent spurs – the East, Central and West – each offering feasible lines of attack. The approach begins from the Couvercle Hut, which began its life in 1865 as a makeshift howff under a huge leaning boulder. On 16 July 1876, W.A.B. Coolidge with Christian Almer and his son Christian jnr climbed across the Central Spur to gain the West Spur which they followed to the West Summit (3984m). Three weeks later, on 7 August, Thomas Middlemore and John Oakley Maund guided by Henri Cordier from Chamonix and the Grindelwald men Johann Jaun and Andreas Maurer, climbed the East Spur to the main summit (their third major climb in a week,

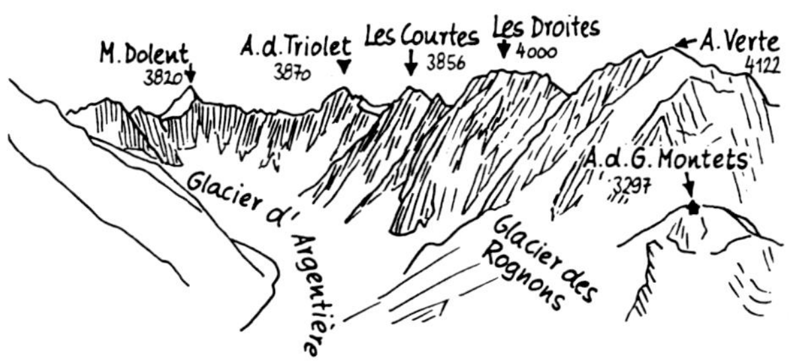

(above) An aerial view from the north-west to the Argentière Glacier basin.

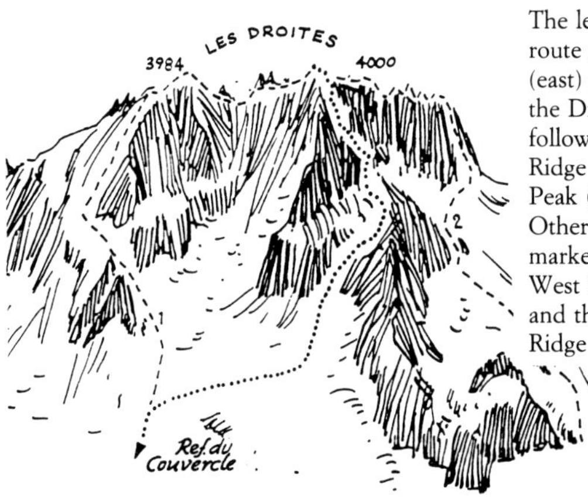

The least difficult route to the main (east) summit of the Droites follows the South Ridge of East Peak (East Spur). Other routes marked are the West Ridge (1) and the East Ridge (2).

following routes on the Aiguille Verte and Les Courtes). The ascent was uneventful but on the descent Oakley Maund described the following hair-raising incident:*

'. . . we heard a roar far above and on looking up saw two enormous rocks coming with great bounds straight for us. We made a rush across the couloir as fast as we could go, as one touch from such blocks would have been instant annihilation. Cordier slipped and fell, dragging Middlemore down with him. I anchored and went flat on my face, as did Maurer who was next in front of me. There was rush of wind followed by a shower of snow and the rocks were past! One mass, which must have weighed a ton, struck just above where Cordier slipped from and passed close over his head. I looked round and saw Jaun spread-eagled on his back, while his hat was flying down the couloir. I thought he was killed . . . but in a moment . . . he looked round and, picking himself up, shouted to Maurer, *"Schnell zu den Felsen!"* I need not tell you that very little time was lost in acting upon his advice.'

The most handsome outing for the medium grade mountaineer is the Droites Traverse, best made from east to west. The distance between the summits is a mere 500m, but the climbing time, with a number of pitches of III to tackle, is at least 5 hours. The summits were linked (west to east) in 1904 by L. Distel and Hans Pfann. In 1905 the complete traverse, starting at Col des Droites and finishing at Col de l'Aiguille Verte, was done by E. Fontaine with Jean Ravanel and Léon Tournier. This ridge formed part of an incredible six-day, multi-peak ridge climb in August 1992 by François Damilano. Starting up the Grands Montets Arête of the Aiguille Verte, he traversed Les Droites, Les Courtes, the summits of the Talèfre and Leschaux to the Grandes Jorasses and Rochefort Ridge. From the Fourche Hut he climbed Mont Blanc, crossed the Bionnassay and finished on Dômes de Miage.

*A.J. VIII, p299

(right) On the western summit crest of Les Droites.

G. Perroux (Damilano archive)

The Normal Route

Les Droites calls for competent climbing on mixed ground, with variable rock and the few *in situ* pitons so that the climb still presents a raw challenge. From the Couvercle Hut, the approach up the Talèfre Glacier passes left of the scree-covered 'Jardin de Talèfre', and brings one to a corner-like snow gully left of the East Spur. If the bergschrund is easy the rocks on the right of the couloir will probably be snow-covered, or vice versa. Further up, shaky blocks perch on the ridge, and a short upsweep of snow requires the use of crampons, which then have to be taken off again before negotiating the rocks which finally provide a passage up to the highest point.

(left) Aiguille Verte and Les Droites seen across the Chamonix Aiguilles from the Aiguille du Midi.

VALLEY BASES

Chamonix 1037m. In the Arve Valley, 39km from Martigny (rail service), 86km from Geneva (rail service), 59km from Aosta. Hotels, inns, pensions. Youth Hostel at Les Pèlerins, *tel* 50/53 14 52. Campsites in the surrounding area. Information Office of the Club Alpin Français (CAF) at 136, Avenue Michel Croz *tel* 50/ 53 16 03.
Argentière 1257m. 8km from Chamonix in the upper Arve Valley. Bus and rail service. Hotels, inns, pensions. Campsite on the southern edge of town.

HUTS/OTHER BASES

Refuge du Couvercle 2687m. CAF. On the south-east slopes of the Aiguille du Moine. 120 places. Staffed in the summer months *tel* 50/ 53 16 94 (self-catering room available). 3½ hours from Montenvers (1909m) which can be reached by rail from Chamonix.
Refuge d'Argentière 2771m. CAF. On the right-hand side of the Argentière Glacier. 80 places. Staffed in the ski touring season and in the summer months *tel* 50/ 53 16 92. 1½ hours from the top station of the Grands Montets téléphérique (3297m) which starts at Argentière. 5½ hours walk from Argentière.

NORMAL ROUTE

South Ridge of East Peak (East Spur) AD III. 7 hours from the Couvercle Hut. 1350mH A glacier tour, then mainly rock. *Descent alternative* Follow the West Ridge to Brèche des Droites (3944m). Abseil piste down a couloir on the south side to the Talèfre Glacier. Danger from avalanches and stonefall.

RIDGES/FACES

East Ridge AD III. 5 hours to the Col des Droites, then 3 hours/500m to the summit. The continuation to the West Summit (AD) takes 3 hours with a further 3 hours to descend via the West Ridge and Col de l'Aiguille Verte. Mixed and rock climbing.
Argentière Face Routes All the routes on the North Face and North-East Face are hard and serious expeditions that usually require at least one bivouac.

MAPS/GUIDEBOOKS

Institut Géographique National 1:25,000 (Top 25) Sheet 3630OT *Chamonix*. Landeskarte der Schwiez 1:50,000 Sheet 5003 *Mont Blanc – Grand Combin. Mont Blanc Range*. Vol 2 by Lindsay Griffin (Alpine Club). *The Alpine 4000m Peaks by the Classic Routes* by Richard Goedeke (Diadem/Menasha).

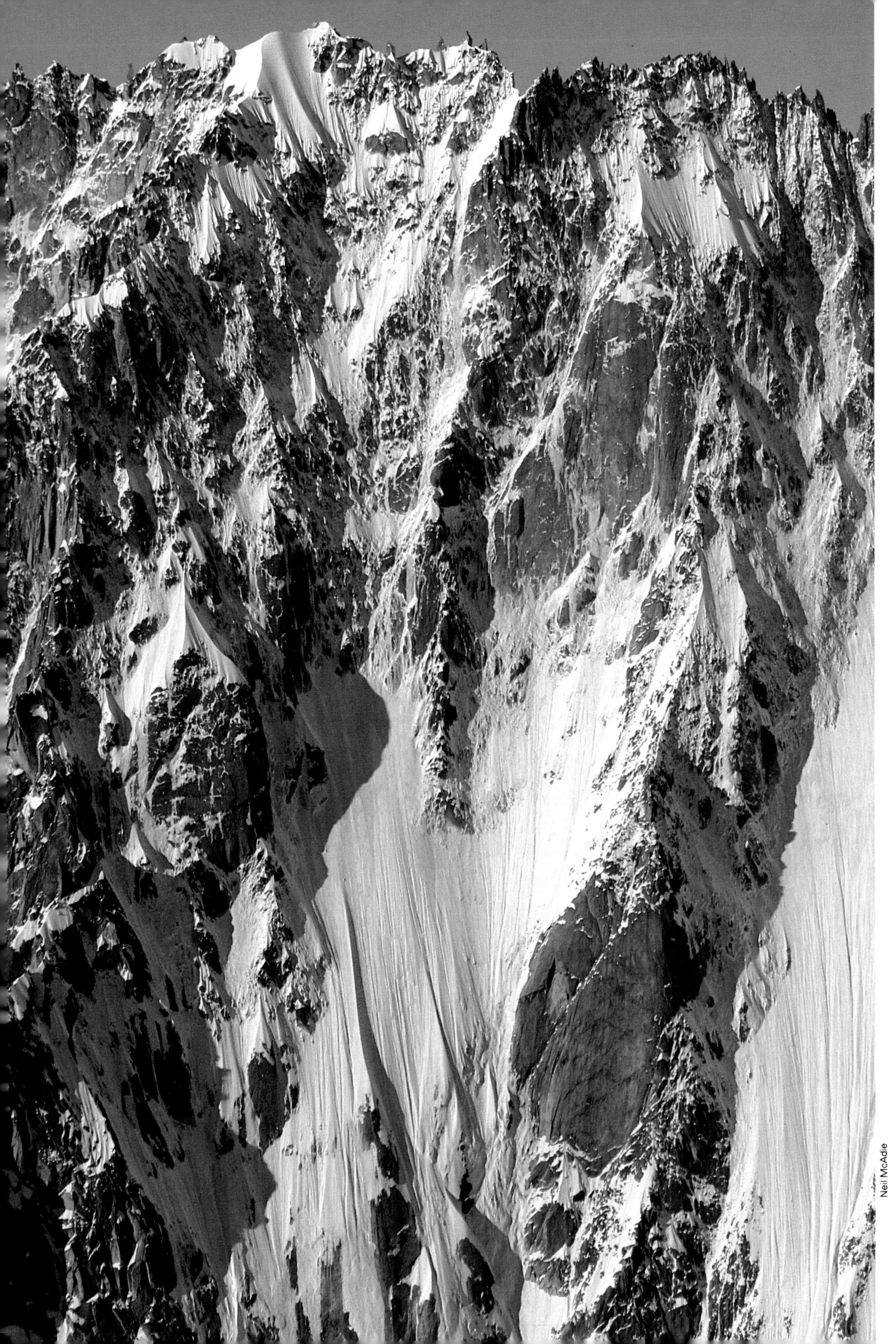

The History of the Argentière Flank

The first climbers to overcome this gloomy precipice (on 31 July 1930) were the Frenchmen Bobi Arsandaux and Jacques Lagarde. They climbed the great central couloir on the North-East Flank, a route which is now an acknowledged winter classic. On 20-21 July 1937 the North-East Pillar (also a highly-regarded classic) bowed to the skills of Fernand Tournier and Christian Authenac. The Pillar now has several alternative starts and variations that can be employed according to taste and prevailing conditions.

On 14-15 July 1952 the North Pillar of the West Summit was climbed by the Parisian Roger Salson with Jean Couzy (who later made the first ascent of Makalu).

With these obvious flanking lines overcome, the stage was set for the North Face ascent. Enter Philippe Corneau and Maurice Davaille, whose performance, over six days in early September 1955, produced the most difficult mixed route in the Alps. Both the second and third ascents took half the time and the route is now done with just one bivouac, its difficulty greatly reduced by the radical improvement in the designs of ice axes and crampons that took place in the 1970s. Prior to this however, Reinhold Messner had climbed the route solo in a scintillating eight hours. Its first winter ascent, completed on 5 January 1971 (by the Swiss – Hans Müller, Hans Berger and Jurg Müller), was a prolonged seige, the fixed ropes going up two-thirds of the face. Four years later an alpine-style winter ascent was made over four days in January by the British pairing of James Bolton and Dave Robinson. In the summer of 1975 Patrick Gabarrou and Jean Marc Boivin climbed the left side of the North Face by a route said to be harder than the Courneau/Davaille line. Both the North and North-East Faces now have a number of additional variations and new routes, yet the basic challenge remains unchanged. Despite this fundamental difficulty there have been very few accidents here, a fact which points to the skill and care of those who aspire to its great routes.

Neil McAdie

(left) A long-focus view of the North Face of Les Droites from the summit of the Aiguille du Chardonnet. The Corneau/ Davaille Route takes the obvious central line, with the North-East Pillar on the left and the Couzy Spur on the right.

Aiguille du Jardin *4035 m*

The Aiguille du Jardin is the shadowy 'outsider' among the four-thousand metre peaks which nevertheless ranks second, after the Aiguille Blanche de Peuterey, in terms of the difficulty of its easiest ascent route.

The climb is tackled from the Couvercle Hut. 'Couvercle' in fact means 'lid' and refers to the slab of rock under which the old hut stands. In 1952, a little lower down, the Club Alpin Français built their comfortable and efficiently-run hotel with its fabulous view of the Grandes Jorasses.

The Aiguille du Jardin is one of the 'youngest' four-thousanders. It was originally included with the Aiguille Verte, and, in common with the Grande Rocheuse, dismissed as a secondary top. Viewed from the Argentière side this seems a reasonable verdict but, from the Talèfre side, the summit rises conspicuously from the ridge crest.

It was Carl Diener who, in 1914, first gave the peak independent four-thousander status in his guidebook to Mont Blanc. The first ascent had taken place ten years earlier, on 1 August 1904, when E. Fontaine, Jean Ravanel and Léon Tournier climbed the peak by today's Normal Route – up the south-east flank and East Ridge. From the summit they then continued along the North-West Ridge to the Grande Rocheuse. A feature worthy of mention on the North-West Ridge is the Pointe Éveline, at 4026m, exactly 37m above the Col Armand Charlet, the trough which divides the Jardin from the Grande Rocheuse. This col was reached by a couloir from the Talèfre Glacier in 1927 by Josef Knubel and the Manchester engineer Eustace Thomas (who climbed all the four-thousanders, including many esoteric tops, over a period of just six years). The couloir gave them a stiff ice climb with a maximum angle of 53°, graded AD+ but only in rare good conditions.

The Aiguille du Jardin – Grande Rocheuse traverse is a mixed climb with passages of grade IV and takes between ten and fourteen hours from the Couvercle Hut. If the Aiguille Verte is included it is best to begin with that, leaving the Normal Route on the Jardin (mainly rock) for the descent.

Other Routes

The North Side remained untouched until 1932 when, on 22 July, Armand Charlet and Jules Simond with P. Dillemann climbed from the Argentière Glacier up to the Col Armand Charlet. Just five days later Karl Blodig soloed the route – up and down. In the 1960s it was the South Face which attracted attention with French climbers establishing difficult routes up its two main rock spurs. The North-East Pillar was climbed on 5 November 1969 by the aspirant guide Georges Nominé who soloed it in 5½ hours.

High Standards on the Normal Routes

No route on the Aiguille du Jardin is easy. There are two standard routes: the East Ridge features sections of grade IV, and the South Couloir of the Col Armand Charlet which leads to the North-West Ridge, can involve ice climbing.

In good conditions, pride of place goes to the East Ridge but the bergschrund at the foot of the couloir which drops from the Col de l'Aiguille Verte can be a stiff obstacle. After three pitches in the couloir (exposed to stonefall) a gully on the left leads to a loose chimney (IV). Grade III and IV rock-climbing follows to gain the East Ridge, which alternates between snow and rock with some splendidly exposed moves.

The normal routes on the Aiguille du Jardin (East Ridge), Aiguille Verte (Whymper Couloir) and Grande Rocheuse (South Pillar). The South Couloir of Col Armand Charlet lies between the Grande Rocheuse and the Aiguille du Jardin.

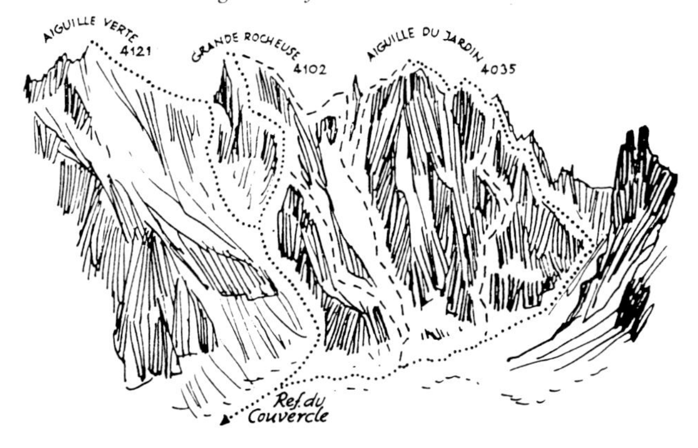

Well-consolidated névé is desirable for the ascent of the 450m ice couloir to the Col Armand Charlet and some seasons it is never climbed at all. July is probably the best time of year and, in an emergency, an escape on to the rocks which bound the cleft on the right-hand (eastern) side can be made. Allow about 3½ hours to the Col. The Pointe Éveline (named after Mlle Éveline Carmichael who climbed it with her guides, Georges Charlet and Anatole Bozon, in 1926) is usually turned on the Argentière side by a narrow snow ridge, but can be climbed direct at grade IV in about three-quarters of an hour. Beyond this a snow ridge and sections of rock climbing complete the ascent.

Blodig's Masterpiece

At 6.25 a.m. on 27 July 1932, Karl Blodig crossed the bergschrund and stood at the foot of the ice gully which rose steeply from the Argentière Glacier up to the Col Armand Charlet. It was three weeks before his seventy-third birthday, an age at which very few men still walk in the mountains, let alone tackle an unclimbed 55° ice couloir . . . solo. (Blodig was unaware of Armand Charlet's ascent a few days earlier.)

In 1911 he was the first person to climb all the four-thousanders, but in 1914 he heard that the Aiguille du Jardin and the Grande Rocheuse had been given independent four-thousander status and he needed them to complete his catalogue.

VALLEY BASES / HUTS/OTHER BASES / MAPS/GUIDEBOOKS

See Les Droites p169

NORMAL ROUTES

East Ridge D IV (several sections), III, II. 8 hours from the Couvercle Hut. 1350mH (5 hours/450m climbing from foot of route. A glacier tour, thereafter mixed. Stonefall danger in the couloir, loose in places.

South Couloir/North-West Ridge AD+ III (sections). To 53°. 8 hours from the Couvercle Hut. 5 hours from the bergschrund. 1350mH (500mH from start of route). A glacier approach, a snow and ice couloir, then mixed.

RIDGES/FACES

North-East Face (Charlet Couloir) D III (sections on summit ridge). To 54°. 6 hours/1000m from foot of the face. An ice climb.

G. Perroux (Damilano archive)

'After crossing the bergschrund,' Blodig recalled,* 'the angle of the snow gully rapidly became greater. I left my long axe above the bergschrund and took my short ice-hammer in my hand. If, previously, I had from time to time ascended in gentle zigzags, I now had to make the turns pretty flat and finally I gave preference to a sideways approach, turning frequently from right to left in order to ease the strain on my ankles.'

Twelve point crampons, so indispensable on today's ice climbs, were unheard of in those days, yet despite this the 1930s are esteemed as the era in which most of the great ice faces were climbed. For nine long hours, that solitary old man toiled his way up the couloir. At the col, exhausted, he slumped down on his sack to rest.

'My fingers were so stiff and cold that I could not manage to open the tin of peach preserve; for hours I had looked forward to this luxury and now I could whistle for it!'

He continued up the East Ridge to the Grande Rocheuse at a snail's pace, returning to the col for his lonely bivouac. The following morning he climbed and descended the North-West Ridge of the Aiguille du Jardin, arriving back at the col by 8 a.m., and then, incredibly, descended the couloir to the Argentière Glacier. Unfortunately, this glittering piece of alpinism was never fully appreciated. Blodig entered these last two four-thousanders in his list as numbers 75 and 76. He later wrote the first edition of this book which contained the following statement that will strike a chord in the hearts of many mountaineers:

'I have become small and modest, for I know how often it was that benign Fate and a mountain's friendly gesture returned me to life unharmed.'

Blodig lived a further twenty-four years, only stopping his work as an oculist in Bregenz at the age of ninety. He was an honorary member of the German and Austrian Alpine Clubs and also, in Britain, the Alpine Club and the Climbers' Club. Geoffrey Winthrop Young added the following tribute to the *Alpine Journal* obituary†:

'Karl Blodig was an alpine pioneer of great initiative and of independent views and character . . . a man of culture and of sociable sympathies, he deserved the almost legendary fame which his long life brought him.'

**German and Austrian Alpine Club Journal* 1932 pp178-182
†*A.J.* LXI, p524

(left) An aerial view of the East Ridge of the Aiguille du Jardin. The tiny figure of François Damilano can be seen descending just to the right of the shadowy chimney in the lower/centre of the picture. The Grande Rocheuse is the snow-capped peak to the left of the Aiguille du Jardin.

Grande Rocheuse *4102 m*

Like the Aiguille du Jardin, the Grande Rocheuse was elevated to the status of an independent four-thousander in 1914. Yet it is less defined than the Aiguille du Jardin and in no way comparable to the Aiguille Verte, and will always tend to be dismissed as just 'one to tick off' on the way to the top of the Aiguille Verte (in a short climb from the Col de la Grande Rocheuse).

The Sunny Side

It would be tempting fate to dismiss the south side of the mountain with the comment that the Grande Rocheuse was merely a satellite peak of the Aiguille Verte: whether on the South Pillar or the Whymper Couloir, the mountain presents rock and ice climbing of a significant standard.

The first ascent was made on 18 September 1865 by the Irish barrister Robert Fowler, with his guides Michel Ducroz and Michel Balmat. Their objective was the third ascent of the Aiguille Verte but, after a start up the Whymper Couloir, they followed the upper section of the South Pillar of the Grande Rocheuse (which Fowler described as a 'little aiguille') and then descended its short West Ridge. Fowler also noted the value of his route for a safer descent. The South Pillar was climbed in its entirety on 8 September 1926 by Madame Carmichael and her daughter Éveline with the local guides Georges Charlet and Anatole Bozon. Today's Normal Route is a combination of the two lines though, in good conditions, the Whymper Couloir might be followed throughout and the mountain climbed by the West Ridge.

VALLEY BASES / HUTS/OTHER BASES / MAPS/GUIDEBOOKS
see Les Droites p169
NORMAL ROUTES
South Pillar AD III, II. 8 hours from the Couvercle Hut. 1420mH. 5 hours/600mH from foot of the route. A glacier tour then rock and mixed climbing.
Whymper Couloir/West Ridge AD III (on the West Ridge) To 58°. 5 hours/600mH from foot of the couloir.
RIDGES/FACES
North-East Pillar D V (one section), IV 18 hours from the Argentière Hut. 1200mH. Mixed and rock climbing.
South Couloir/East Ridge AD+ II+ (on East Ridge). To 53°. 5 hours/600mH from the bergschrund. Ice and mixed.

The Normal Route

The South Pillar is bounded (on the east) by the Whymper Couloir and (west) the South Couloir of Col Armand Charlet. The gaping chasm of the bergschrund below the Whymper Couloir forces the climber to the right and into an ice-hose cut into the torso of the Grande Rocheuse and threatened by stonefall. The route up the pillar is marked by two obvious towers and occasional *in situ* belay pegs but the summit headwall is avoided by a diagonal passage to the left and, in the chimneys which follow, rucksacks and ice axes can hinder progress. The climb is a real grind, and by no means easy. The route joins the East Ridge not far from the summit.

The Northern Flank

The routes on the mighty northern precipices perched above the Argentière Glacier offer stronger meat. The dominating feature is the 1200m North East-Pillar and the ice-chute to the left of this was climbed in August 1895 by Valere A. Fynn and Pierre Goudet, the first guideless climbers to make a new route on the Argentière walls. The pair left the Saleina Hut at midnight with the Aiguille du Chardonnet as their objective, but at the Col du Chardonnet they changed their plans and made for the Grande Rocheuse instead. At 3 a.m. they began the climb, reaching the summit thirteen hours later.

The North-East Pillar, climbed in 1946 by M.A. Azéma and G. Fraissinet, offers a very long mixed route with several sections of VI and one pitch of V, set in a splendid position overlooking the Couturier Couloir.

The epitome of steep ice routes (averaging 75°) was achieved in 1975 by Georges Bettembourg and Michel Thiviergé when they climbed the branch couloir which links the Couturier Couloir to the Col de la Grande Rocheuse, a typical climb of the 1970s in the Mont Blanc range following the improvements in axe and crampon design.

(below) François Damilano descending from the summit of Grande Rocheuse on the first day of his Mont Blanc traverse.

Jean Michel Asselin (Damilano archive)

Aiguille Verte *4121 m*

The mighty massif of the Aiguille Verte (the 'Green Needle') is a tableau full of majesty standing proudly above Chamonix and Argentière, a peak of manifest difficulty. Hanging glaciers and dark, shadowy flanks of ice face to the north and north-west and, on the south, savage rock scenery above the Charpoua Glacier and an equally untamed face above the Talèfre Glacier, just a little more friendly than the others. Thus the Aiguille Verte, difficult on all sides, is one of the most highly ranked four-thousanders.

The Whymper Couloir

One of the least difficult ways up the mountain is by this couloir at the head of the Talèfre Glacier, the 'weakness' selected on the first ascent. This 600m slanting ice corridor, sandwiched between the Aiguille Verte and the Grande Rocheuse, steepens in its middle section to about 58°. Admittedly, the Whymper Couloir should only be considered in reliable snow conditions, and at the end of July at the latest. If it then provides a convenient ladder of steps already hacked in the snow, it's your lucky day, although stonefall from the Grande Rocheuse can never really be ruled out.

Edward Whymper, with his Swiss guides Christian Almer and Peter Biner, descended the whole couloir during the afternoon of 29 June 1865. On the ascent they had quit the couloir low down, beneath the steep section, and worked across to the left to gain the upper part of the Moine Ridge which they followed to the summit.

This was Whymper's last big ascent before the Matterhorn disaster, and it was also one of Almer's most important first ascents in a long and distinguished career. Sadly the aftermath of the climb showed the Chamonix guiding fraternity in its worst light. A local porter had been left at the Couvercle in charge of the tent and food but when the three climbers returned they found that he was about to carry everything down, as Whymper described in *Scrambles*:

'"Stop there! What are you doing?" He observed that he thought we were killed, or at least lost, and was going to Chamonix to communicate his ideas to the *guide chef*.

(below left) A view up the Whymper Couloir from the Talèfre Glacier.

(below) Nearing the top of the Whymper Couloir at dawn.

Dave Wynne-Jones

Denis Mitchell

Willi Burkhardt

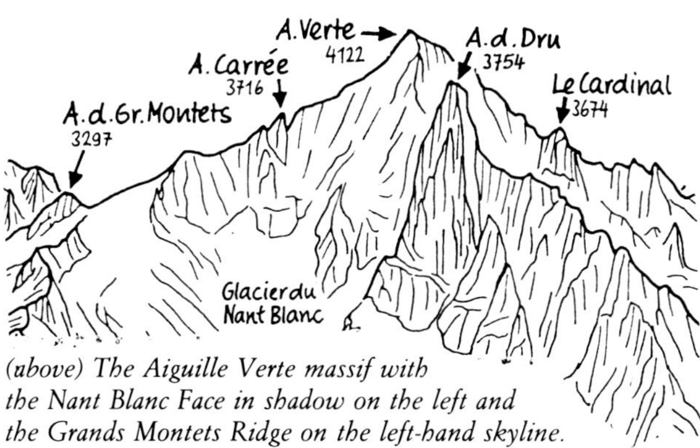

(above) The Aiguille Verte massif with the Nant Blanc Face in shadow on the left and the Grands Montets Ridge on the left-hand skyline.

. . . "Get out the food," we roared, losing all patience. "Here it is," said our worthy friend, producing a dirty piece of bread about as big as a halfpenny roll. We three looked solemnly at the fluff-covered morsel. It was past a joke, he had devoured everything. Mutton, loaves, cheese, wine, eggs, sausages – all was gone – past recovery. It was idle to grumble, and useless to wait. We were light and could move quickly, the porter was laden, inside and out. We went our hardest, he had to shuffle and trot. He streamed with perspiration; the mutton and cheese oozed out in big drops, he larded the glacier.'

Worse was to come. In Chamonix the hotel keepers were delighted and fired a cannon in celebration, but the local guides, notorious for their restrictive practices that compelled climbers to hire them in rotation (regardless of ability), were enraged that two Swiss guides had stolen such a prestigious first ascent. Almer and Biner were goaded in the town's bars and on the streets:

'The *bureau* . . . was thronged with clamouring men. Their ringleader – one Zacharie Cachet – a well-known guide, of no particular merit, though not a bad fellow, was haranguing the multitude. He met with more than

Wil Hurford

Wil Hurford

(above) On the Moine Ridge of the Aiguille Verte.

(above right) The view from the Moine Ridge across the Whymper Couloir (tiny figure) to Grande Rocheuse and Aiguille du Jardin.

his match. My friend [T.S] Kennedy . . . rushed into the fray, confronted the burly guide and thrust back his absurdities into his teeth.

'There was the materials for a very pretty riot; but they manage things better in France than we do, and gendarmes . . . dispersed the crowd. The guides quailed before the cocked hats and retired to cabarets to take little glasses of absinthe and other liquors more or less injurious to the human frame.

'Needless to add, Michel Croz took no part in this demonstration.'

One week later the second ascent was made by Croz and Kennedy, with the clerics Charles Hudson and George Hodgkinson and the guides Michel Ducroz and Peter Perren. They left the Talèfre Glacier at a lower point and followed the Moine Ridge to the summit. This ridge is usually the best option in the high summer when it is clear of snow, and when the Whymper Couloir often glistens with bare ice. It starts from a notch between the summit structure and the Cardinal, which can be reached from either the Talèfre or the Charpoua basins. The climbing on the ridge is II and III, interspersed with patches of snow and with the occasional *in situ* piton.

The Whymper Couloir starts at an angle of about 45°, but steepens to nearly 60° as it rises (54°, according to the guidebook). A dawn start is essential to minimise the stonefall risk, particularly on the descent.

The North Face

The northern flank of the mountain offers two distinct facets the true North Wall and the North-East Face, where the Couturier Couloir immediately holds the eye. First climbed on 2 September 1929 by the noted American geographer H. Bradford Washburn with Georges Charlet, Alfred Couttet and André Devouassoux (the direct line being made on 1 July 1932 by Marcel Couturier with Armand Charlet and Jules Simond), it is nowadays the most popular route from the Argentière amphitheatre and, in the judgement of Pit Schubert, 'comparable to the North Face of the Ortler, but with less threat of falling blocks of ice,' though below the summit cap there is a danger of snow-slab avalanches.

To the right of the Couturier a triangular buttress of rock separates it from the North Face where the main line is the Cordier Couloir. This was climbed on 31 July 1876 by Thomas Middlemore and John Oakley Maund, Jakob Anderegg, Johann Jaun and Andreas Maurer – one of the most respected achievements in the history of Alpine mountaineering, for the 900m couloir is set at an angle of up to 56°. Due to the considerable objective dangers the route sees few repeats.

The Nant Blanc Face

The North Wall is divided from the North-West or Nant Blanc Face by the pinnacled Grands Montets Ridge, first climbed in August 1925 by Pierre Dalloz, Jacques Lagarde and Henri de Segogne. The mixed face above the Nant Blanc glacier is studded with challenging routes leading to the summit of the Aiguille Verte and its western satellites. The main direct line to the Verte (Armand Charlet and D. Platonov, 22 August 1935), deserves more recognition as one of the finest mixed climbs in the Alps, and the harder lines to its right, though serious, also merit far greater attention.

Bill O'Connor

(above) The Couturier Couloir on the Aiguille Verte with the Cordier Couloir on the right and the Charlet Couloir starting up on the left to the Aiguille du Jardin and the Grande Rocheuse.

VALLEY BASES
See Les Droites p169
HUTS/OTHER BASES
Refuge du Couvercle, Refuge d'Argentière see Les Droites p169
Refuge de la Charpoua 2841m. Private. On a rock-spur above the Charpoua Glacier. 15 places. Open all year. 3½ hours from Montenvers (1909m).
Chalet du Col des Montets 3240m. Just below the top station of the Grands Montets téléphérique (from Argentière). No overnight accommodation. *tel* 50/ 54 02 24.
NORMAL ROUTES
South-West (Moine) Ridge AD III, II. To 50°. 9 hours from the Couvercle Hut. 1440mH (6 hours/750mH from the bergschrund). A glacier tour, then snow and ice in the couloir and rock on the ridge.
Whymper Couloir/East Ridge AD To 58°. 9 hours from the Couvercle Hut. 1440mH. (6 hours/630mH from the bergschrund). Glacier approach, then an ice climb.
RIDGES/FACES
North-West (Grands Montets) Ridge D IV. To 50°. 12 hours from the Col des Grands Montets (3233m). 1100mH. Rock then mixed climbing to a névé finish.
North-East Face (Couturier Couloir) D To 55°. 6 hours/900mH from the foot of the route. An ice climb.
North Face (Cordier Couloir) TD– To 56°. 10 hours/1050mH. Ice and mixed. Serious.
North-West Face Direct (Nant Blanc) D+ IV (sections), mostly III. To 58°. 12 hours/1000mH. Ice and mixed. Serious.
MAPS/GUIDEBOOKS
See Les Droites p169.

The Tragedy

One of the worst tragedies in the history of alpinism took place on the upper slopes of the Aiguille Verte on 7 July 1964. A party of five guides and nine aspirants from the *École National de Ski et d'Alpinisme* were completing the Grands Montets Ridge. The weather had been settled for weeks and conditions on the mountain were judged as excellent. Yet at 11 o'clock a huge avalanche swept down the Cordier Couloir and down across the Rognon Glacier. As the veil of snow dust slowly settled, dark points could be made out at the bergschrund. Chamonix was in a state of general alarm and rescue helicopters set out almost immediately. At 11.40 the search parties recovered the first body from the lower slopes of the Cordier Couloir. When a helicopter searched the northern side of the summit zone the observers saw tracks leading to the jagged edge of a snow-slab avalanche just sixty metres below the top.

At three in the afternoon, the last of the victims was recovered: fourteen experienced alpinists had been ensnared on a snow slope of about 45°! It seems likely that they must have walked into a snow-slab zone in close file, carrying loops of rope – a normal practice on such terrain, particularly after settled weather.*

*The guides were Jean Bouvier (one of those that made the first ascent of Makalu in 1955), Charles Bozon (a world class skier), Jean-Louis Jond, Réné Novel and Maurice Simond. The aspirant guides were Adrien Bardin, Xavier Cretton, Michel Leroy, François Lods, Victor Minetto, Jacques Ronet, Roger Tracq, Claude Valleau and Roland Vivet.

Dent du Géant *4013 m*

The Dent du Géant stands in a prominent position in the centre of the Mont Blanc massif, seen from virtually all angles as a true 'giant's tooth' with a particularly wicked tilt when observed from the south-west. In truth the final tower, which juts from a plinth of anonymous rock and snow, has short steep faces on three sides and only on the northern and north-western flank attains real size, looking particularly imposing from the vicinity of the Périades Bivouac. Its architecture is so skilfully crafted by nature that, though actually diminutive by comparison to other rock peaks in the area, it exerts a powerful presence that is impossible to ignore. At the tip of the tooth there are two distinct pinnacles, both the epitome of the fabled sharp alpine needle: Pointe Sella (4009m) and the slightly higher Pointe Graham which fittingly crowns the northern precipices.

The Fight for the Summit

The first ascent of Dent du Géant features four colourful figures from the pantheon of alpine pioneers: Albert Frederick Mummery and his guide Alexander Burgener; the Val Tournanche guide Jean-Joseph Maquignaz (famous for his Matterhorn exploits); and the maverick English climber William Woodman Graham. The peak repelled bids to climb it throughout the 1870s, most of which approached the western end of the Rochefort Ridge from the Col du Géant from where the final tower could be most conveniently addressed. In 1880, Albert Frederick Mummery, a Dover tannery owner, and his guide Alexander Burgener traversed round to the South-West Face and made some progress but were stopped by a band of smooth slabs which prompted Mummery to write the message 'Absolutely inaccessible by fair means!' on a visiting card which he left at the foot of the tower. Soon after this G. de Filippi and Lord Wentworth sought to solve the problem by using rockets to carry a rope between the two summits, and hired a Signor Bertinetti of Turin to direct the ordnance. The first two shots missed the target. On the third firing, the 'party saw the rocket stick fall at their feet but a gust of wind carried back the rope and all subsequent attempts were equally unsuccessful'.*

The main effort took place over four days in July 1882 when J.J. Maquignaz, supported by his son Daniel and nephew Battiste, established a route up the South-West Face, reaching the South-West Summit on 28 July. The following day they conducted their clients, four members of the Sella family (the brothers Alessandro, Alfonso and Corradino and their cousin Gaudenzio) up the same route. Alessandro Sella reported† that at several points they were 'obliged to excavate (or mine) the rock' and at one point they 'were forced to form a ladder by means of our ice axes'. Iron stakes were placed from which they hung 100m of rope. These aids remain to this day in the form of thick hawsers which are periodically replaced. All this paraphernalia, not to mention the 'excavating' and the iron stakes, tended to detract from J.J. Maquignaz's ascent which must have been a very difficult climb for the period, and it is sad that on both this and his direct finish to the Italian Ridge of the Matterhorn we are unable to form a full appreciation of his achievements. After such efforts it is all the more surprising that the guides failed to continue to the highest point on this or either of two repeats shortly afterwards. On 14 August W.W. Graham with the Chamonix guides Auguste Cupelin and Alphonse Payot completed the ascent, climbing half the slab section free (the lower ropes being hidden from view in a groove) and reaching the higher top using

*A.J. IX, p48 †A.J. XI, p72

(left) The Dent du Géant from the Pointe Helbronner above the Torino Hut.

Bill O'Connor

(above) Hauling up the thick fixed ropes of the Dent du Géant as another climber descends by abseil.

combined tactics to ascend a difficult step (Graham, in stockinged feet, climbing on Payot's shoulders).

Thus ended one of the strangest episodes in the history of alpinism. The main players went their separate ways: Mummery and Burgener to their series of major alpine climbs until the former disappeared on Nanga Parbat in 1895 and the latter was killed by an avalanche in the Bernese Alps in 1910; Graham to the Himalayas where he made the first ascent of Kabru (contested) before disappearing into obscurity in the American west; and Maquignaz (with two others) disappeared eight years later on the south side of Mont Blanc.

(below) High on the South-West Face of the Dent du Géant with parties strung out on the Burgener Slabs below.

Other Ascents

The spectacle of a mountain humbled in this manner was not universally appreciated. Karl Blodig, for example, commented (after his ascent in 1899), 'It was the first time in my life that I have returned home dissatisfied from the ascent of a mountain. For I had the disconsolate feeling that I should thank not my strength and skill but, in the main, the availability of artificial aids for the attainment of the summit.'

This attitude was also shared by the Viennese Heinrich Pfannl, Thomas Maischberger and Franz Zimmer. They reached the summit by the North Ridge on 20 July 1900, without using a single piton – a milestone in guideless Alpine mountaineering. In the following years other intricate ways were found to reach the top, the most useful being the very steep route (TD) established on the 130m South Face on 28 July 1935 by Herbert Burggasser and Rudolf Leisz. Though difficult, with some aid climbing, this is so conveniently placed that it is often used as an ascent route in preference to the rope hauling on the Normal Route.

The Normal Route

The Dent de Géant is the most accessible high peak in the Mont Blanc range because of its proximity to the téléphérique at the Torino Hut. The climb can therefore

(below) The view to Pointe Graham from Pointe Sella – a thick fixed rope removes all difficulty from the rock step that W.W. Graham led in stockinged feet to complete the first ascent.

Bill O'Connor

Bill O'Connor

Dave Wynne-Jones

be treated as a single-day outing, indeed it is best not to reach the tower too early as the ropes may be disconcertingly iced. Those who are fit may take the opportunity to climb both the Géant and the Rochefort Ridge on a single expedition, in which case an early start from the Torino Hut is advisable. The mountain has by no means been completely tamed: apart from the approach, up a couloir which is occasionally iced-up, and the delicate traverse from the 'Breakfast Ledge' to the start of the route proper, there are sections of grade III granite to be overcome, one a delightfully exposed arête leading to the ledge beneath the Burgener Slabs and the fixed ropes.

It is best to reach the roped section in mid-morning, any earlier and the ropes will be iced, any later and you will have to queue. The thick ropes are difficult to grip as one hauls, hand over hand, up the steep slabs and walls for 100m. Here and there it is possible to free-climb, and this often seems less strenuous. The climb is very exposed and sensational, particularly on the summit pinnacles where one can look down on Courmayeur 3000m below. It is common to find the summit block festooned with other parties, prompting a wait on Pointe Sella until the higher point becomes vacant. The hole in the head of the summit Madonna was made by lightning, a reminder of the need for a rapid retreat if a storm is suspected! Even in good weather it would be folly to underestimate this route as the summit cliff has all the potential for a miscalculation in the hurly-burly of moving up and down the ropes, and there are several points on the approach climb or during the retreat where one could come to grief. Indeed, in 1895 the celebrated guide, Emile Rey, who was descending unroped, slipped and fell 600m to his death, and in 1953 the great English rock climber, Arthur Dolphin, was killed here in an almost indentical accident.

(above) Descending the Burgener Slabs by abseil after passing late parties still completing their ascents.

VALLEY BASES

Entrèves 1306m. Above Courmayeur in the upper Aosta Valley on the Italian side of Mont Blanc. Railway station at Pré St-Didier (8kms): bus connections. Hotels, guest houses, pensions. 12kms from Chamonix through the Mont Blanc Tunnel. Téléphérique to the Torino Hut and Pointe Helbronner from la Palud, 1360m.

Chamonix see Les Droites p169.

HUTS/OTHER BASES

Rifugio Torino 3372m. CAI. On the Col de Géant. 170 places. Staffed from mid-May to the end of September. Hotel, self-service restaurant *tel* 01 65/ 84 22 47 (from France 1 93 91 65/ 84 22 47). Tunnel access from téléphérique station. Below the new hut is the old Torino Hut (3322m), CAI. 80 places. Staffed all year round.

Pointe Helbronner 3462m. Téléphérique station (from Entrèves-La Palud and Chamonix). Bar. Journey time from Chamonix 1½ hours, service from 6 a.m. to 5 p.m. (July and August).

NORMAL ROUTE

South-West Face AD III (sections), II. Fixed ropes. 4 hours from the Torino Hut, 1½ hours from 'Breakfast Ledge' (on very busy days allow double this time). 640mH (150mH from the 'Breakfast Ledge'. A glacier approach, mixed, then rock.

RIDGES/FACES

North Ridge and North-West Face D IV (sections), III. 5½ hours from the Torino Hut via the Col Supérieur de la Noire (280mH/ 3 hours from the start of the route). Mixed and rock.

South Face TD V, A1. 4 hours/130mH from the start of the route. A steep rock climb.

MAPS/GUIDEBOOKS

See Les Droites p169.

Rochefort Ridge

Aiguille de Rochefort 4001m Dôme de Rochefort 4015m

One of the most prized expeditions in the Mont Blanc massif is the traverse of the Rochefort Ridge, the airy snow arête that defines the frontier between the Dent du Géant and the Col des Grandes Jorasses. The ridge has two four-thousand-metre summits: the Dôme de Rochefort (4015m) at the eastern end, and the Aiguille de Rochefort (4001m), situated about half-way along the crest. In its own way, the structure of the Rochefort Ridge is every bit as unique as that of the Biancograt on the Piz Bernina and its horizonal tightrope walk is incomparable – spiced with the tingling sensation of airy exposure on an exquisitely formed icy crest.

Yet only half of the climbers who begin the ridge continue beyond Aiguille de Rochefort to the Dôme. Few will regret completing the longer expedition: there are higher and more shapely peaks in the Mont Blanc group, but there is only one Rochefort Ridge, and the only true route is the complete traverse. To be absolutely correct the north-eastern cornerstone of the ridge is formed by the Calotte de Rochefort (3974m), but this is generally only visited by those continuing to the Canzio Bivouac Hut at the Col des Grandes Jorasses, with the intention of traversing the Grandes Jorasses on the following day.

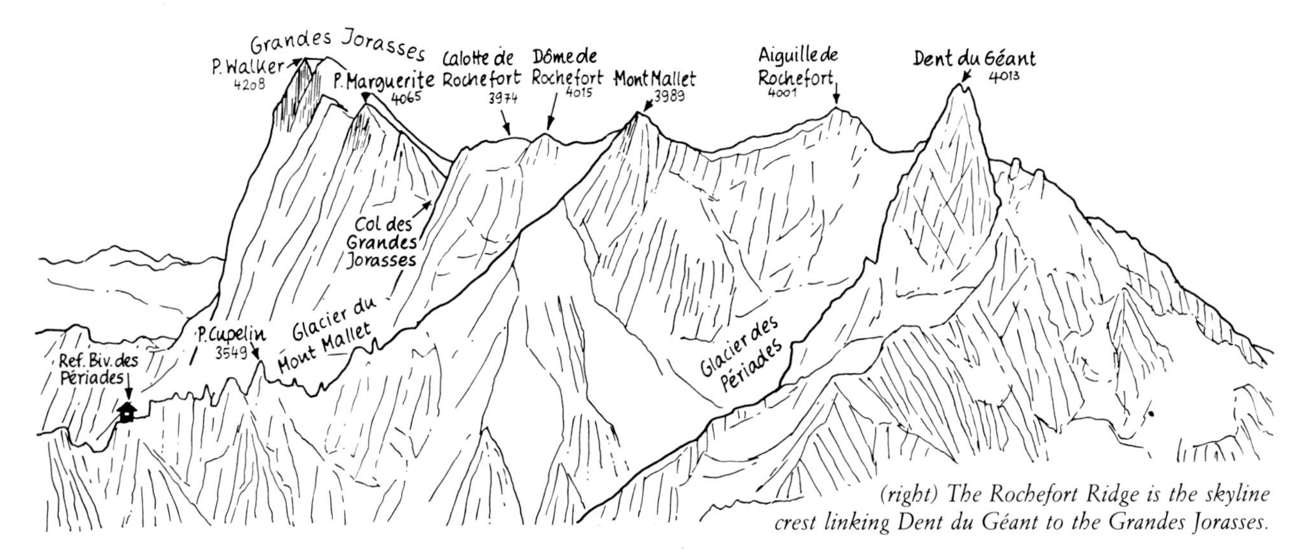

(right) The Rochefort Ridge is the skyline crest linking Dent du Géant to the Grandes Jorasses.

The First Ascents

The two peaks were first climbed from the north on expeditions up the Mont Mallet Glacier: the Aiguille in 1873 and the Dôme in 1881. Both climbs were made by the assiduous Mont Blanc explorer James Eccles with his regular guides Michel and Alphonse Payot. The linking ridge (east to west) was first traversed from the Aiguille de Rochefort to the Dent de Géant in 1900 by Ettore Allegra with the guides Laurent Croux, Pierre Dayne and Alexis Brocherel. The complete ridge from west to east with the extension to the Dôme was traversed three years later by Karl Blodig and Max Horten, and extended to the Col des Grandes Jorasses in 1909 by M.C. Santi and V. Sigismondi.

Other Routes

A number of routes have been made up the flanks of the ridge, generally icy mixed climbs on the northern side (including the 700m North Face of the Aiguille), and long friable rock ridges on the south. The most interesting lines are the original Eccles Route on the North-West Face of the Dôme (AD) and the remote and beautiful North Buttress of the Calotte (AD) which was climbed by Pierre Chevalier and Marcel Sauvage on 11 August 1928. Either climb might be considered as a preliminary to an east/west traverse of the ridge, the size of the bergschrund at the head of the Mont Mallet Glacier being the determining factor. The North Ridge of Mont Mallet (AD) offers another route from this direction. For these three climbs the Périades Bivouac or the Leschaux Hut will be needed as a base.

Along the Dream Ridge

When tackling the Rochefort Ridge from the Dent du Géant one will usually be planning to return by the same route. The main concern will therefore be whether to extend the expedition to include the Dôme de Rochefort. This will be determined by conditions and the speed and stamina of members of the party. For the full itinerary you should plan for at least seven hours out and six hours back and bear in mind that the return trip should be made as early as possible before the snow has softened too much. The final decision can be made at the Aiguille de Rochefort, when the weather conditions may have become less ambiguous. Although the Rochefort Ridge does not involve any particular technical difficulties, the ascent does presuppose the safe use of rope and ice axe, perfect mastery of cramponing techniques and the required degree of experience at four thousand metres in the Western Alps.

Karl Blodig described his traverse with characteristic enthusiasm:

'The ridge appears foreshortened and quite insignificant, but becomes more interesting the further it is followed. At times it is a narrow blade of snow, the flanks to each side losing themselves in the vertiginous depths, along which we must balance, slowly and carefully, in the steps we have cut. At times we are required to chop away a delicate cornice before stamping solid footholds in the powdery snow.'

They overcame the steep descent of the first summit by Horten first belaying Blodig down the slope, who then reclimbed the pitch, cutting steps as he went, before belaying Horten down and finally descending himself.

John Allen

The pair then 'raced along the narrow knife-edge, like men possessed'. After crossing the Aiguille (by a rising traverse to gain a shallow couloir on the right) it soon became obvious that the stretch to the Dôme was rather easier than the first section of the route and, after turning the Doigt de Rochefort (3928m) on the left, they were soon grappling with the snow-covered summit rocks before finally stepping on to the crest of the Dôme de Rochefort just before midday.

Nowadays fine weather sees one party after another moving along the ridge, a hundred and more climbers are not an unusual sight. All are drawn by its magnet-like attraction – the wonderful experience of climbing on a tenuous edge between heaven and earth.

(left) Climbers set out along the Rochefort Ridge from the Dent du Géant, its South Face towering above the start.

(below) At the eastern end of the Rochefort Ridge – a section of rock arête beyond the Dôme de Rochefort on the way to the Col des Grandes Jorasses.

Bill O'Connor

(right) Climbers returning along the Rochefort Ridge from the Aiguille de Rochefort.

The Rochefort Ridge (dotted line) runs from the Dent du Géant, across the Aiguille de Rochefort to the Dôme de Rochefort. The Aiguille can also be climbed from the Requin Hut, or the Leschaux Hut via the North Ridge of Mont Mallet.

VALLEY BASES

Entrèves see Dent du Géant p182.
Chamonix see Les Droites p169.

HUTS/OTHER BASES

Rifugio Torino/Pointe Helbronner see Dent du Géant p182.
Bivacco Ettore Canzio 3818m. CAI. On the Col des Grandes Jorasses. 6 places. Always open. 7 hours from the Leschaux Hut, 3½ hours from the Périades Bivouac. 10 hours from Planpincieux via the Rifugio Boccalatte. 2804m.
Refuge-bivouac des Périades 3450m. CAI On the Les Périades ridge between Brèche des Périades and Pointe Sisyphe. 4 places. 3½ hours from the Leschaux Hut up the heavily crevassed Mont Mallet Glacier.

NORMAL ROUTE

Aiguille de Rochefort, West Ridge AD II (sections), To 50°. 6 hours from the Torino Hut. 800mH (250mH on the ridge itself). A corniced snow/ice arête.
Dôme de Rochefort, South-West Ridge PD I (on summit rocks). 2 hours from the Aiguille de Rochefort. 250mH. A snow ridge with some rock climbing.

RIDGES/FACES

Calotte de Rochefort, North Face (Chevalier/Sauvage) AD 8 hours from the Leschaux Hut. 3½ hours/400mH from bergschund of face. Mixed and ice.
Dôme de Rochefort, South Ridge AD IV– (final chimney), III, II. 11 hours from the Rifugio Boccalatte (Grandes Jorasses Hut).
8½ hours/850mH from the start of the route. Mixed and rock. The most worthwhile route on the Italian side.
Dôme de Rochefort, North-West Face AD 6 hours from the Leschaux Hut. 1½ hours/450mH from bergschrund. Mixed.
Aiguille de Rochefort, North-West Face TD To 70° (average 55°). 10 hours/700mH from the foot of the face. A serious and difficult ice and mixed climb.

MAPS/GUIDEBOOKS

See Dent du Géant p169

Hans Wagner

Grandes Jorasses *4208 m*

A chain of five summits above four thousand metres crown the haughty head of the seemingly unapproachable Grandes Jorasses, the most impressive single mountain bastion in the Mont Blanc group. From east to west they are: Pointe Walker (4208m), Pointe Whymper (4148m), Pointe Croz (4110m), Pointe Hélène (4045m) and Pointe Marguerite (4066m), with Pointe Young (3996m) completing the line-up – an imposing spectacle indeed and for me the most exciting in the whole of the Alps. The wall rises almost 1200m from the Leschaux Glacier, is about one kilometre long and seamed with gigantic spurs of rock and terrifying couloirs. This is the savage and shadowy stage upon which the highest Alpine aspirations are enacted.

Defended by this savage north face and equally problematic eastern and western flanks, the narrow line of linking glaciers on the southern side formed the only feasible point of attack for the first explorers. Here is another case where the formal credit is accorded to the successful party after an earlier attempt had resolved most of the difficulties. The 'moral' first ascent in this case should surely be credited to Edward Whymper with his guides Michel Croz, Christian Almer and Franz Biner who, after careful reconnaissance, reached Pointe Whymper at 1 p.m. on 24 June 1865. Whymper considered traversing to the main summit but abandoned the idea because the weather was deteriorating and the linking ridge was too icy. Their ascent was uneventful but during the descent all four climbers were caught in a minor avalanche from which they jumped clear just before it 'fell into a yawning crevasse, and showed us where our grave would have been if we had remained in its company five seconds longer'. A few days later a group of five Courmayeur guides, led by the enterprising and ambitious Julien Grange, repeated the ascent to learn the route – a venture which greatly impressed Whymper. In September 1867 Christian Almer made another ascent with Hereford Brooke George and two others but, in their attempt to reach the higher summit, they were frustrated by poor visibility. On 30 June the following year the Canadian-born Horace Walker with Melchior Anderegg, Johann Jaun and Julien Grange (employed merely as a 'porter', though his knowledge of the climb must have been invalu-

The Grandes Jorasses from the south-west, showing the Normal Route (dotted line), the approach to the Col des Grandes Jorasses (1), the line of the traverse (2) and the South-East Face (3).

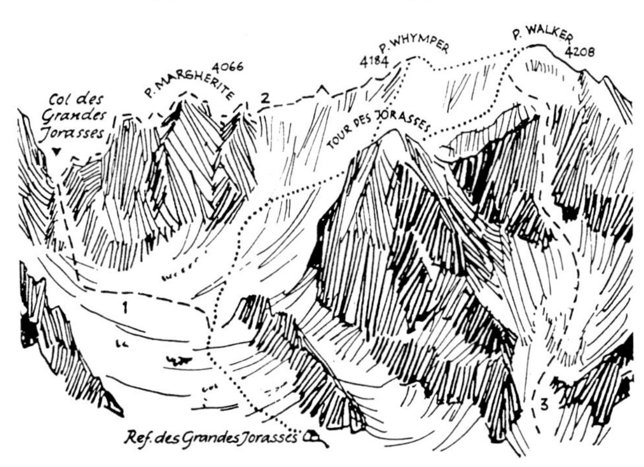

(left) An aerial view of the North Face of the Grandes Jorasses.

(below) A dusting of snow accentuates the features of the South-West Face of the Grandes Jorasses seen from Dent de Jetoula.

Bill O'Connor

(left) At Pointe Walker on the Grandes Jorasses.

able), quit the Whymper route below the final ridge and traversed the glacier basin to its east to reach the parallel ridge which led easily to the higher summit – Pointe Walker.

The Normal Route

The line that Whymper's team pioneered is complex, weaving a way through the crevasses and avalanche areas, using ribs of rock where necessary to avoid sérac zones. Many climbers who descend it after completing one of the North Face climbs speak of it with wide-eyed respect, relieved at having escaped from the mountain in one piece. The zone of crevasses above the hut should be reconnoitred the day before the climb and a decision made whether to climb the 40° ice gully to the right of the Rocher du Reposoir or to follow its rocky spur to the snow above. In good conditions the ice gully is to be preferred. Stonefall (and avalanches in early summer) threatens the traverse to the east across the upper Grandes Jorasses Glacier which gains the 'Whymper Rib' at half-height (old fixed rope). Crossing the glacier basin beyond to gain the spur of Pointe Walker also has manifest dangers, and many climbers elect to climb the Whymper Rib direct – in dry conditions a nice climb on slabby rock. From the Pointe Whymper the linking ridge to the Pointe Walker is corniced and crampons have to be strapped on again. After a steep drop down to a notch, a straightforward snow ridge leads up to Pointe Walker. This detour takes somewhat longer than the line climbed by the first ascentionists and requires a total of about ten hours from the Jorasses Hut.

High Above the Clouds

A traverse of the 1400m West Ridge from the Col des Grandes Jorasses is a middle grade affair, harder than the Normal Route and, though easier than the North Face excursions, a tough route. As it is all at the four-thousand-metre level, its length and difficulties are most keenly felt with rock climbing on predominantly solid granite and several pitches of grade IV. There is some mixed ground beyond Pointe Croz. The individual peaks were climbed as follows: Pointe Croz in 1909, probably by Fräulein Eleonore Hasenclever, Wilhelm Klemm, Felix König and Richard Weitzenböck; Pointes Marguerite and Hélène in 1898 by the Duke of Abruzzi, with Joseph Petigax, Laurent Croux and César and Félix Ollier (the peaks are named after the Duchesses of Abruzzi and Aosta). These ascents were made from the south. Pointe Young was gained in 1904 by Valentine Ryan and the Lochmatters during an attempt to traverse the complete ridge. The failure of such a strong team no doubt made the ridge an alluring prospect for Geoffrey Winthrop Young and his companions, Humphrey Owen Jones and Josef Knubel, making their successful climb on 14 August 1911 all the

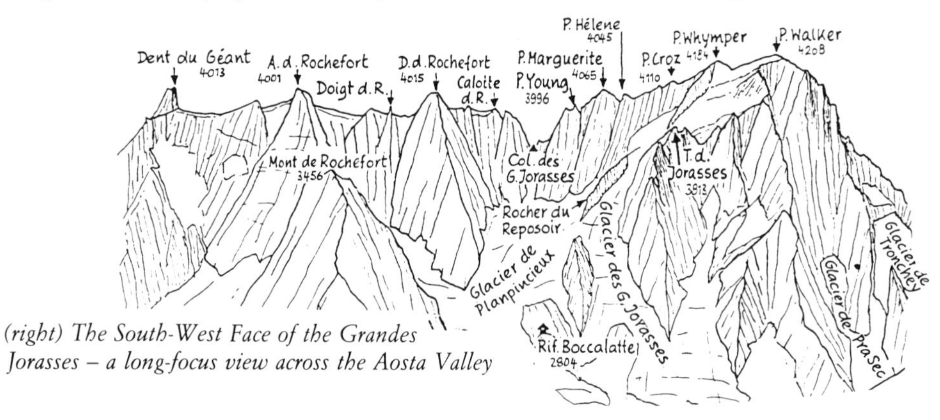

(right) The South-West Face of the Grandes Jorasses – a long-focus view across the Aosta Valley

Willi Burkhardt

Willi Burkhardt

(above) The East Face of the Grandes Jorasses above the Frébouze Glacier, with the Tronchey Arête on the left and the Hirondelles Ridge on the right (the line of light and shade) rising from the Col des Hirondelles.

sweeter. Luck was on their side when Jones fell and pulled off Knubel in an icy chute below the col but, as Young described, 'our leader seemed rather braced than otherwise by the headlong plunge.' At the col 'a chilly, rayless sunrise was there to meet us . . . the air smelt and tasted of frosted flints . . . . The whole face [above the col] was a uniform frown of slab, one and undivided; we wandered perpendicularly up it, on a dim and alarming line. From time to time Josef looked down on my dolorous wriggles with half quizzical gravity; the look which betrayed, I feel sure, his real opinion of the motions of all mortals upon mountains, always excepting those of the adored Franz Lochmatter, and some few of his own'. They pressed on and finally reached Pointe Whymper five hours after leaving the col, a very fast time.

The Hirondelles Ridge

Young's expedition was designed to link up with the North-East or Hirondelles Ridge which the trio (plus Laurent Croux) had descended three days earlier, having found the upward climb too difficult. This great ridge repelled scores of attempts but was finally climbed in 1927 by Gustavo Gaja, Sergio Matteoda, Francesco Ravelli and Guido Alberto Rivetti, guided by Adolphe Rey and Alphonse Chenoz. Rey's lead of the climb and its crucial pitch, a crack in the wall above the U notch, was considered by Alessandro Gogna 'a remarkable piece of climbing for the period . . . a significant step forward in standards in the Western Alps'.*

The Tronchey Arête

Pointe Walker throws out two major ridges to the south.

The South-West or Pra Sec Ridge was climbed in 1923 (Francesco Ravelli, Guido Alberto Rivetti and Evariste Croux). The South-East Ridge (Tronchey Arête) was completed in 1936 by Titta Gilberti and Eliseo Croux. This climb is rarely repeated but offers fine and solid rock pitches which reach a climax in a splendid position on the crucial third tower, high on the mountain between the vertiginous South and East Faces.† These great faces also boast major climbs. The East Face was overcome by Giusto Gervasutti and Giuseppe Gagliardone in 1938, and the complete South Face was climbed by Alessandro Gogna and Guido Machetto in 1972.

The North Face Challenge

The struggles on the North Face have been documented in countless books. After forty attempts by various parties over the course of five years (including three fatalities), fortune eventually smiled on the German pair of Rudolf Peters and Martin Meier who, on 29 June 1935, gained the summit of Pointe Croz by the Central Spur of the Face (the Croz Spur).

The battle for the Walker Spur now began, with the most accomplished alpinists of the day vying for success. Ultimately it was the Lecco aces, Riccardo Cassin, Gino Esposito and Ugo Tizzoni, who captured what was by then universally acknowledged as the finest alpine challenge. They completed their three-day ascent on 6 August 1938. It is now estimated that this, the most popular route on the North Face of the Grandes Jorasses, and perhaps the most prestigious route in the Alps, has received about a thousand ascents.

There are now over a dozen routes on the face but none better than the two original lines. The most popular of the rest is the great ice sheet of 'The Shroud' which was first climbed over ten days in January 1968 by René Desmaison and Robert Flematti. The route is 800m with 65° ice climbing and grade V rock sections. Other climbs have been made by Japanese, British, Polish, Italian, German and French parties pointing to the international importance of this stupendous face.

Old Values Tumble

On 17 March 1976 Jean-Marc Boivin topped out on the Hirondelles Ridge after a four-and-a-half hour ascent of The Shroud, having earlier in the day climbed the North Faces of the Verte (Grassi Couloir), Droites and Courtes. This was an early example of the 'enchainment' craze where several routes are climbed one after another (assisted by helicopters, parapente or hang-gliders).

Further audacious 'feats' followed in the 1980s. Eric Escoffier from Lyon raced up the Croz Spur, to be met on the summit by Christophe Vaillant with a two-man

*From Gogna's article 'Grandes Jorasses Commentary' *Mountain* 26 (March 1973) which gives a good overall summary of the history of the mountain.
†*A.J.* LIX, pp323-331.

VALLEY BASES

Planpincieux 1579m. A little village in the Val Ferret to the south of the Grandes Jorasses, 3.5km from Entrèves and 6km from Courmayeur. Bus service. Campsite, *tel* 0165/ 8 92 53. 'Albergo' where the track to the Jorasses Hut branches off.

Chamonix see Les Droites p169.

HUTS/OTHER BASES

Rifugio Gabriele Boccalatte e Mario Piolti (Grandes Jorasses Hut) 2803m. CAI. On a rognon on the Planpincieux Glacier. 25 places. Staffed from 15 July to 30 August. 4 hours from Planpincieux. (The hut is named after two Italian climbers who were killed by stonefall on the South Face of the Triolet in 1938).

Bivacco Ettore Canzio 3816m. CAAI. At the Col des Grandes Jorasses. 5 places with blankets, clean and tidy. About 6½ hours from the Boccalatte Hut. 7 hours from the Leschaux Hut.

Refuge de Leschaux 2431m. CAF. Facing the Grandes Jorasses above the eastern bank of the Leschaux Glacier. 15 places (often overcrowded). Staffed in July and August. 3½ hours from Montenvers.

Bivacco Gervasutti 2363m. CAI. On a rock island in the Frébouze Glacier above and west of the SSE Spur of P.3657m. 12 places (mattresses, blankets). Always open. 4 hours from the roadhead at Val Ferret.

NORMAL ROUTES

Pointe Walker: South-West Face AD– II. To 45°. 8 hours from Boccalatte Hut. 1400mH. A glacier climb on ice and snow.

Pointe Whymper: South Rib AD– II. To 45°. 8 hours from the Boccalatte Hut. 1380mH. A glacier climb with a rock finish.

RIDGES/FACES

West Ridge D IV, III, II. 6 hours/500mH from the Canzio Bivouac. Rock and mixed on a pinnacled ridge.

North-East (Hirondelles) Ridge D† V (one section) IV (sections). 10 hours/750mH from the Col des Hirondelles (4 hours from the Leschaux Hut, 3 hours from the Gervasutti Bivouac). Abseil 'piste' (for The Shroud). Mixed with some hard rock pitches.

North Face: Croz Spur TD+ V+, V (several pitches) IV. To 58°. 18 hours/1150mH from the foot of the face. Rock and mixed. Stonefall danger in lower section.

North Face: Walker Spur ED VI–/A1 (several pitches), V+, IV+, III. 1½ days/1200m from the foot of the face. Rock and mixed. Stonefall danger on lower slopes, particularly after storms.

North-East Face: The Shroud ED V (exit pitches). To 65°. 15 hours/800mH. A sustained ice climb. Danger from falling stones and ice in lower section.

MAPS/GUIDEBOOKS

See Les Droites p169

hang-glider. At noon the two of them took off for the flight down to the Walker Spur, which Escoffier climbed during the afternoon.

Christophe Profit's link-up of the North Faces of Jorasses, Eiger and Matterhorn in both summer and winter (see Matterhorn chapter) brought the 'enchainment' idea to an incredible level of physical and technical achievement.

Willi Burkhardt

Bill O'Connor

Bill O'Connor

(top right) Looking steeply up the South-West Face of the Grandes Jorasses. On the left the Grandes Jorasses Glacier sweeps round the Tours des Jorasses. The Pra Sec Ridge rises from the centre right with the Tronchey Arête beyond.

(near right) On the summit slopes of Pointe Walker with Pointe Whymper in the background.

(far right) On the descent from Pointe Walker – at a steep glacier couloir, running down the side of the Whymper Rib.

 AIGUILLE BLANCHE DE PEUTEREY

Aiguille Blanche de Peuterey *4112 m*

The Aiguille Blanche de Peuterey, with its three tops – Pointe Seymour King (4107m), Pointe Güssfeldt (4112m) and Pointe Jones (4104m) – is the hardest and most serious of the four-thousand-metre peaks to reach and then escape from. It is the centrepiece of the Peuterey Ridge, one of the world's great alpine climbs, perhaps the finest and most scenically impressive way of climbing Mont Blanc.

The problems of access and escape on the Aiguille Blanche, together with its climbing difficulties, deter many ardent collectors of four-thousand-metre peaks. This is not a mountain to embark on lightly! The most logical way is to take in the peak during an ascent of the Peuterey Ridge – thus avoiding an otherwise hazardous descent, but this is a very taxing expedition and even then one must always plan for an escape as the weather on Mont Blanc can change rapidly.

The Early Ascents

No mention of the history of this mountain would be complete without first noting the remarkable ascent of Mont Blanc by James Eccles, Michel Clement Payot and Alphonse Payot on 31 July 1877.* They gained the upper basin of the Frêney Glacier from the Brouillard Glacier by crossing the Innominata Ridge and descending the slopes below Col Eccles. They then climbed a steep couloir to gain the Peuterey Ridge above the Grand Pilier d'Angle and reached the summit of Mont Blanc de Courmayeur just under nine hours after leaving their bivouac below Pic Eccles. This route passed close to the North-East Ridge of Aiguille Blanche and provided the key to its first ascent. On 14 August 1880 Georg Gruber (the Austrian Consul in Geneva) with Emile Rey and Pierre Revel set out to repeat the Eccles route but, in error, they descended from the Col de Frêney into the lower Frêney basin from where they were compelled to make a somewhat hazardous (because of stonefall) ascent of a rognon/buttress set into the glacier (Rochers Gruber) to gain the upper basin. Above this they were forced to bivouac at 4400m before finishing the climb by the upper slopes climbed by the Eccles party.

In the summer of 1882 the Cambridge professor Francis Maitland Balfour and his Swiss guide Johann Petrus were killed while attempting to climb Aiguille Blanche using the Gruber/Rey approach to the Col du Peuterey (significantly Rey had declined to join them). Their bodies were found in the lower basin just to the right (east) of the Rochers Gruber. The clues suggested that they were descending at the time of the accident, so it is possible that they reached the col and tackled the peak.†

The successful ascent was made on 31 July 1885 by Henry Seymour King, Emile Rey, Ambros Supersaxo (King records Supersax) and Aloys Anthamatten. From a bivouac above the Col de Frêney they gained the upper Frêney basin by a route roughly the same as that taken by Eccles (thus avoiding the Rochers Gruber). From Col de Peuterey they ascended the northern slopes of Aiguille Blanche, turned Pointe N.W. and Pointe Centrale and at 2 p.m. reached the apparently untrodden summit of Pointe S.E. (the official summit, despite the fact that the central

*Eccles's account of this climb is in *A.J.* VIII, p410, and the history of all early attempts on Mont Blanc from the Brouillard and Frêney basins is fully chronicled by T. Graham Brown in *A.J.* LII, p254-267 and *A.J.* LIII, pp48-58 and pp144-156.

†This accident is discussed in detail in *A.J.* XI, p90, in Dr Seymour King's account (*A.J.* XII, p433), and finally in H.O. Jones's account (*A.J.* XXIV, p277) where its position is marked on a photograph.

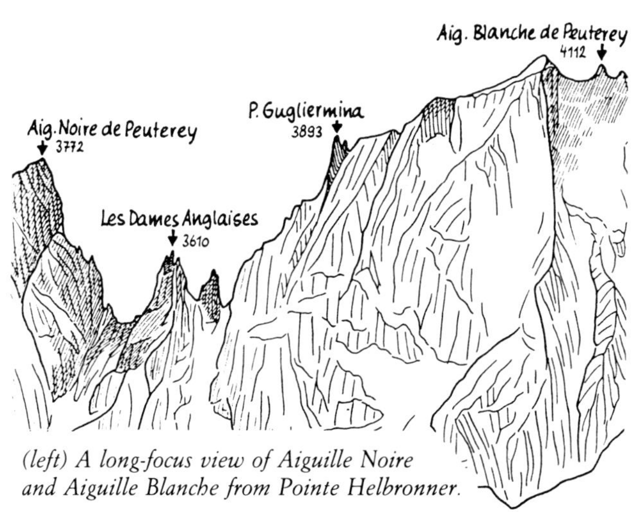

(left) A long-focus view of Aiguille Noire and Aiguille Blanche from Pointe Helbronner.

Dave Wynne-Jones

(below) At the shoulder below the final ridge to Pointe Seymour King, looking down the South Ridge to the Pointe Gugliermina.

Willi Burkhardt

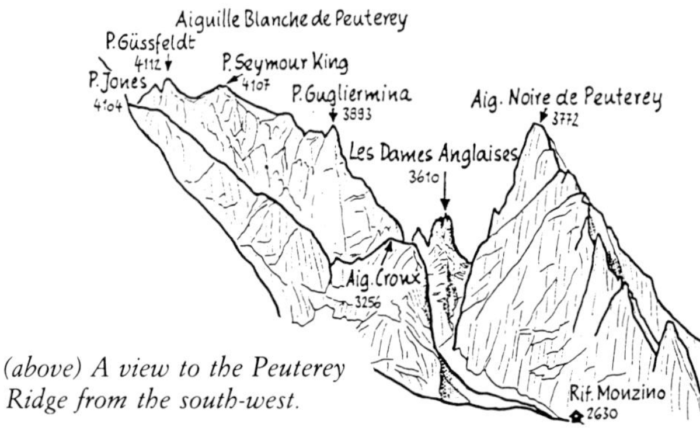

(above) A view to the Peuterey Ridge from the south-west.

peak is five metres higher) which was duly named Pointe Seymour King. They returned by the same route.

The next climb of note was made on 15 August 1893 when the Berliner, Dr Paul Güssfeldt, with Emile Rey, Christian Klucker and César Ollier ascended a very hazardous couloir on the Brenva flank, crossed the summit, descended Seymour King's route to the col and thence continued up the Peuterey Ridge, also bivouacking at 4400m. On the Brenva flank Güssfeldt's party was certainly lucky as a major stonefall swept the couloir just after they had quit it. Güssfeldt was fifty-two when he made this ascent, and the climb took four days. There were two bivouacs on the route, and another night was spent at the hut that then existed on the Rochers Rouges, after which they descended to the Grand Plateau, crossed the Dôme du Goûter and returned to Courmayeur by the Dôme Glacier route.

The final historic ascent on the mountain was made on 16 August 1909 by Humphrey Owen Jones with Laurent Croux and his son Laurent jnr. From near the Rochers Gruber they climbed directly up the South-West Spur to the Pointe N.W. (Pointe Jones). Commenting on all of these ascents in an addendum to Jones's report (*A.J.* XXV, p520) Percy Farrar noted:

'The evolution of these expeditions, among the greatest ever carried out in the Alps, is exceedingly interesting, nor will the names of the great guides who rendered their employers such brilliant service be readily forgotten, least of all that of the Italian, Emile Rey, who played such a leading part in the expeditions of 1880, 1885 and 1893.' Sadly Rey was killed on the Dent du Géant in 1895.

The North Face

The elegant ice flank of the North Face deserves mention as some parties use it to climb the mountain in preference to the Monzino Hut approach. It was first climbed on 4 September 1933 by Renato Chabod and his porter Amato Grivel (an alternative route to the right was added in 1952) and in good conditions provides a superb way to the top set in the most splendid surroundings.

The Peuterey Ridge

Today's Normal Route starts from the Monzino Hut and crosses the Frêney Glacier much lower down by a route from the Col de l'Innominata and then follows a couloir to the Brèche Nord des Dames Anglais. This approach was first done in 1928 by L. Obersteiner and Karl Schreiner when they made the first ascent of the conventional Peuterey Ridge route. At the brèche the Craveri Bivouac forms a welcome advance base where one can gather one's energies for the demands ahead.

The longer Peuterey Ridge Intégrale which incorporates a traverse of the Aiguille Noire was first done on 28-31 July 1934 by Adolf Göttner, Ludwig Schmaderer and Ferdinand Krobath (who used the East Ridge of the Noire). The harder and more elegant way using the South Ridge (V and VI) was climbed by Richard Hechtel and G. Kittelmann on 24-26 July 1953. This is probably the most demanding climb in the Alps, in terms of stamina, seriousness and length.

The Normal Route!

The steep 'walk' to the Monzino Hut is equipped in places with cables and ladders. After this a further seven hour slog is needed to reach the Craveri Bivouac with the

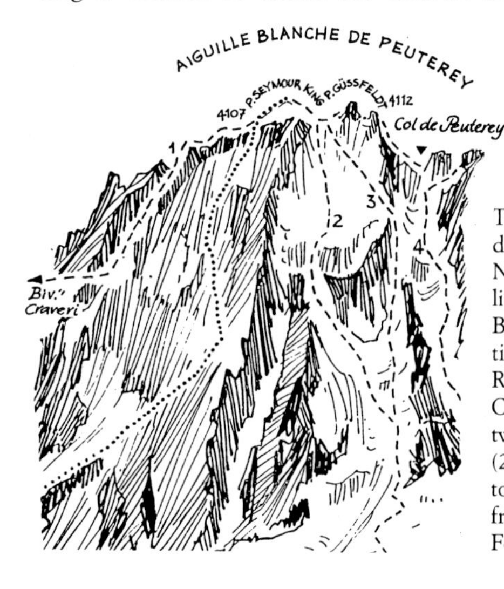

The Aiguille Blanche de Peuterey with the Normal Route (dotted line) from the Brenva Bivouac, the first section of the Peuterey Ridge (1) from the Craveri Bivouac, the two North Face routes (2 & 3) and the climb to the Col de Peuterey from the Col de la Fourche (4).

John Allen

(left) *The North Face of Aiguille Blanche with the Col de Peuteréy on the right.*

(lower left) *Pointe Güssfeldt from Pointe Seymour King.*

(lower right) *Below the Rochers Gruber on the lower Frêney Glacier.*

infamous Frêney Glacier in between. The day before we were there, Lionel Terray had found himself beneath a collapsing ice tower the size of a house. Terray survived his injuries, but his Dutch client was freed from the grip of the ice only ten years later. On the glacier, the ominous creaking of the séracs sent a chill shudder down my spine. Once this jumbled chaos of horizontal and slanting crevasses is negotiated, an ice gully several hundred metres high blocks the way, complete with a guarding bergschrund and the accompanying howl of stonefall (there are alternatives to the left). From the top of the couloir the climb follows the South-East Ridge. This involves 600m of mixed climbing with pitches of III and one passage of IV. The summit should be gained within six hours from the bivouac. From here anything from eight to twelve hours is needed to reach the summit of Mont Blanc by way of the highest ice face in Western Europe.

Denis Mitchell

Denis Mitchell

VALLEY BASE

Freiney 1589m. In the Val Veni. Campsite. 9km from Courmayeur. Access by road to Chalet du Miage. 1569m. Turn right to the shepherds' huts close by.

HUTS/OTHER BASES

Rifugio Franco Monzino 2561m. Association of Courmayeur Mountain Guides. Between the Frêney and the Brouillard Glaciers. 60 places. Staffed from 15 June to 25 September *tel* 0165/ 80 35 53. Winter room (sleeps 6) always open. 3½ hours from Freiney.

Bivacco Piero Craveri 3490m. CAAI. At the Brèche Nord des Dames Anglaises. 5 places. Always open. 7 hours from the Monzino Hut. AD+. To 45°. Ice and mixed. Serious.

Bivacco della Brenva 3200m. CAAI. On a rognon in the Brenva Glacier, north-east of the Aiguille Blanche. 5 places. Always open. 6 hours from Entrèves. F+. Glacier climbing.

Bivacco Giuseppe Lampugnani (Eccles Bivouac) 3850m. CAAI. On the South-West Ridge of Pic Eccles (4041m). 6 places (blankets). 7 hours from the Monzino Hut. PD. Ice and mixed.

Bivacco Crippa 3640m. Guides Association of Courmayeur. On Pic Eccles slightly below the Bivacco Lampugnani. Sleeps 9.

NORMAL ROUTE

South-East Ridge D+ IV (section), III. 6 hours/650mH from the Craveri Bivouac. Mixed and rock.

Continuation down North Ridge and up Peuterey Ridge D+ To 50°. 16-20 hours from the Craveri Bivouac. 1320mH. Mixed and ice. Serious and remote.

RIDGES/FACES

North Face TD– To 55°. 8 hours/700mH from the foot of the route. An ice face.

MAPS/GUIDEBOOKS

Institut Géographique National 1:25,000 (Top 25) Sheet 3531ET *St Gervais*. Landskarte der Schweiz 1:50,000 Sheet 392 *Courmayeur*. *Mont Blanc Range* Vol. 1 by Lindsay Griffin (Alpine Club). *The Alpine 4000m Peaks by the Classic Routes* by Richard Goedeke (Diadem/Menasha).

Willi Burkhardt

Mont Brouillard *4069 m*

Mont Brouillard and Punta Baretti stand slightly apart from the huge bulk of Mont Blanc, the Col Emile Rey forming a neat division between these satellites and the massive buttress of the Brouillard Ridge. Strictly speaking this 'Mountain of Mists' and Punta Baretti are mere bumps on the long South Ridge of Mont Blanc that have somehow, like the south-western satellites of Monte Rosa, managed to attract full four-thousander status. Nevertheless, it is clear that these mountains, in common with the other minor summits on the south side of Mont Blanc, offer rich scope for activity for the connoisseur and allow interesting perspectives of their greater neighbours. After all, the standard route on Mont Brouillard does climb a 600m ice couloir, pockmarked by stonefall and set at an average angle of 50°, and this at the end of a six-hour approach to the unstaffed Quintino Sella Hut which is a significant glacier expedition in its own right.

The Climb from the Sella Hut

The route from the hut, which makes a downwards traverse across the riven Mont Blanc Glacier, follows the same line as the approach to the Brouillard Ridge, sharing with this the ice couloir which comes out at the Col Emile Rey. In the early summer conditions are usually good, but against this should be weighed the danger of avalanches. In high summer, hard bare ice may be a feature. A night-time start is therefore essential.

The couloir leads directly to the Col Emile Rey, from where it is a mere fifty-nine metres in vertical height (three pitches) to the summit block. When dry, the slabby rocks are swiftly overcome, with the occasional sidestep to the left and right of the crest of the ridge and scattered patches of ice – a reasonable diversion (in terms of time and effort) for those who have arrived at the col before dawn with the Brouillard Ridge as their main target. This happened on the first ascent of the Brouillard Ridge from the Col Emile Rey, made on 9 August 1911 by Karl Blodig, Humphrey Owen Jones, Geoffrey Winthrop Young and Josef Knubel, when Young and Knubel climbed Mont Brouillard in just nine minutes from the Col. They embarked on the steep cliffs at the beginning of the main climb at just after 5 a.m. (to minimise the risk from stonefall) and reached the summit of Mont Blanc six hours later. The ridge is 1.8km long and involves 900m of ascent including two 'up and down' sections. The Brouillard Ridge is shorter and marginally easier than both the Peuteréy and Innominata Ridges, with its main problems concentrated below and above the col. Nevertheless it enjoys the reputation of being a serious, strenuous and lengthy expedition and one of the finest routes on Mont Blanc.

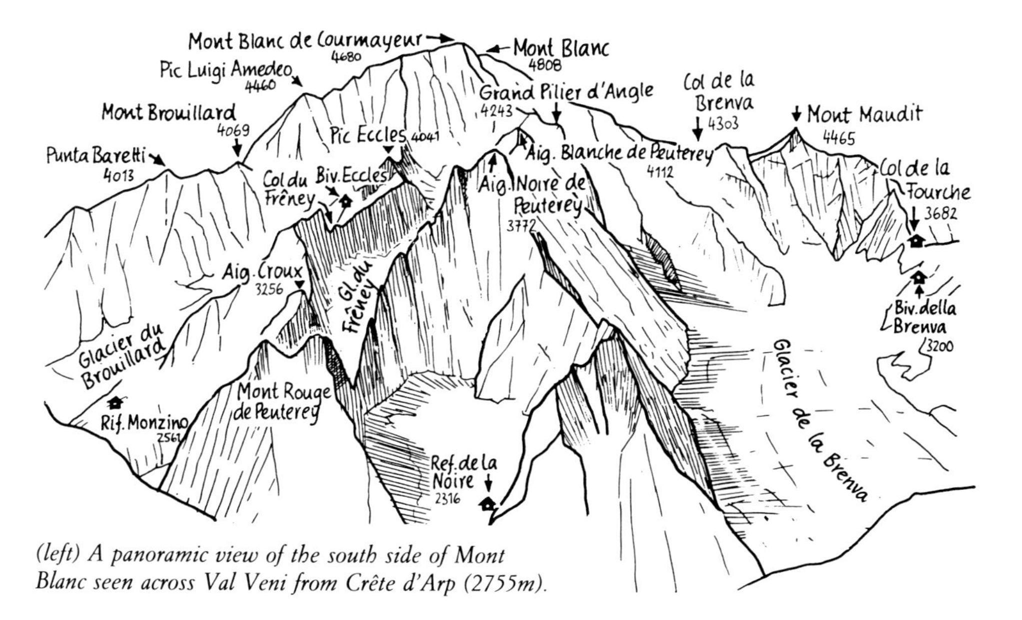

(left) A panoramic view of the south side of Mont Blanc seen across Val Veni from Crête d'Arp (2755m).

(above) A view from the Aiguille de Tré la Tête to the South-West Face of Mont Blanc rising above the Mont Blanc Glacier. The Brouillard Ridge is on the right and the Rochers du Mont Blanc are on the left.

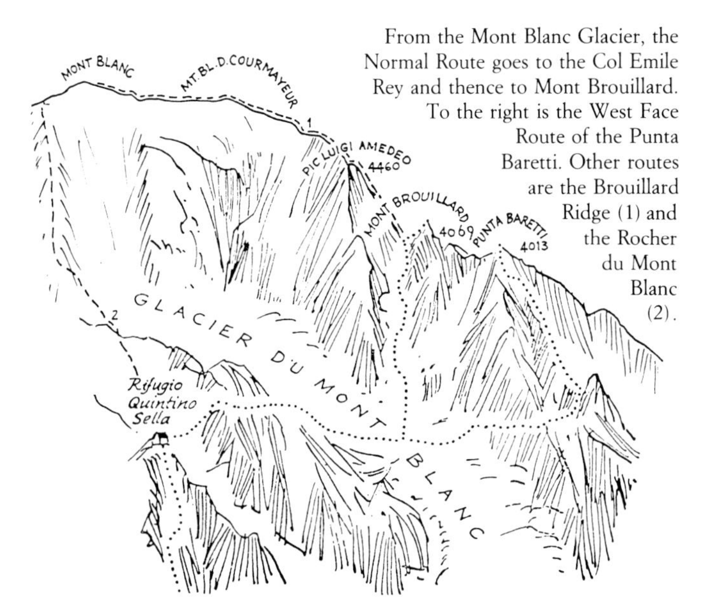

From the Mont Blanc Glacier, the Normal Route goes to the Col Emile Rey and thence to Mont Brouillard. To the right is the West Face Route of the Punta Baretti. Other routes are the Brouillard Ridge (1) and the Rocher du Mont Blanc (2).

Who Was First?

It seems very likely that Martino Baretti and his guide Jean-Joseph Maquignaz were mistaken in their belief that they had climbed both Punta Baretti *and* Mont Brouillard on 28 July 1880. They had approached from the south-west and may have confused the various tops. Karl Blodig always doubted this claim and on 10 July 1906 he effectively disproved it. Setting out from the Mont Blanc Glacier with Oscar Eckenstein and Alexis Brocherel, he gained Col Emile Rey and climbed the North Ridge to the highest point. They saw no sign of previous human presence, even though loose slabs of rock could easily have been used to construct a cairn – common practice in those days. A subsequent visit showed that Baretti's timing for the linking climb was half that required.

A Useful Alternative

The great German climber Fritz Wiessner climbed here in 1958 with E. Bron. They ascended a rock rib on the West Face (to the right of the approach couloir) which has several difficult pitches. This might be used for ascent if the couloir is out of condition, and once ascended could serve as a descent route (see Guide Vallot – Route 304). There is also an AD mixed climb up the West Face of Punta Baretti (1907, Karl Blodig with Laurent and Anthoine Croux).

VALLEY BASES

Lago Combal 1935m. In the Val Veni (campsite) 12km from Courmayeur. Small access road.

HUTS/OTHER BASES

Rifugio Quintino Sella 3371m. CAI. Situated above the nethermost corner of a western branch of the Mont Blanc Glacier. 10 places. Always open. 8 hours from Lago Combal.

NORMAL ROUTE

North Ridge AD II, I To 50°. 5 hours from the Sella Hut. 750mH from the Mont Blanc Glacier. An ice route.

South Ridge and North Ridge of Punta Baretti PD I. 1 hour from Mont Brouillard. Mixed and snow.

RIDGES/FACES

West Face D V (one pitch), VI, III. 8 hours/750mH from the start of the route. A rock climb.

MAPS/GUIDEBOOKS

See Aiguille Blanche p195.

Aiguille de Bionnassay *4052 m*

As one plods up the Dôme du Goûter during an ascent of Mont Blanc, the elegant blade of the East Ridge of the Aiguille de Bionnassay appears to the south-west and figures can sometimes be seen making slow progress along its razor-sharp crest. A traverse of the Aiguille de Bionnassay, which involves a descent of this East Ridge and a climb up the West Ridge of the Dôme du Goûter, is now frequently used as a spicy preliminary to an ascent of Mont Blanc – a truly magical expedition of ice and snow arêtes at great altitude.

A First Ascent in a Thunderstorm

The northern flank of the mountain, with its 1200m of ice slopes guarded by hanging glaciers, makes a particularly powerful impression when viewed from the Tête Rousse. For advanced ice climbers the original North-West Face (AD), plus the direct finish, is a natural early-season Normal Route with an average angle of 40° but with isolated steeper passages to 55°. Yet this was the face that provided the route for the first ascent on 25 July 1865. It was the project of the enterprising Florence Craufurd Grove, who two years earlier, while pointing out the grandeur of the northern slopes of Mont Blanc to 'three young ladies and their highly respectable father', noted the slanting glacier leading up the Aiguille de Bionnassay. 'It occurred to me that an alpine expedition . . . might be made by ascending that untrodden mountain and passing along the fine arête to the gentle sloping banks of the rounded Dôme.' In 1865 Grove was back in Chamonix with the London brewer Edward Buxton and Reginald Somerled Macdonald, both of whom also had designs on the mountain.*

'I communicated our plan to our two sturdy guides, Jean-Pierre Cachat, an excellent iceman, and Michel-Clement Payot . . . . I cannot say that they entered warmly to our scheme . . . the Chamouni guide is a true conservative. He clings to a protective tariff . . . content with his walk through life if it lead him over the well-worn footsteps of Jacques Balmat.' Nevertheless, the following morning saw them trying to find a safe way up the face but the obvious icy difficulties of the upper face (the present-day North-West Face) deterred them: 'The ice in all its gaunt blue nakedness [was] raked by showers of grape . . . I have never been able . . . to assent to Buxton's proposition that showers of stones materially vary and enliven the dull monotony of an ice slope.' They therefore headed for the West Ridge, gaining it at the saddle by the Aiguille de Tricot (3665m), and continued up the

*Grove's entertaining account, and Buxton's description of the Miage Glacier descent, are in *A.J.* II pp321-341 and there is further material in Grove's obituary *A.J.* XXI p244. Lloyd's account of the 1926 climb is in *A.J.* XXXIX pp25-35.

Bill O'Connor

(right) The North and North-West Faces of the Aiguille de Bionnassay. The Aiguille de Tricot is the minor peak on the right.

John Allen

(above) The Miage Glacier provides a convenient approach to the Durier Hut from the south.

(right) From the Col de Miage the South Ridge leads directly to the Aiguille de Bionnassay. The East Ridge leads off to the right to the Col de Bionnassay, the upper exit of the Grises Route and the Dôme du Goûter.

West Ridge, ploughing through snow softened in the morning sun. As they approached the summit the weather deteriorated and it began to snow, and their axes emitted 'a quaint humming sound, something musical in tone, but nevertheless evil to hear, for it told us that we were now in the very heart of the thunderstorm'. A descent of the East Ridge was now out of the question but at the summit the snow curtain lifted for a few minutes and 'we could see the marvellously thin arête fall away in a huge curve . . . a glorious flying buttress that appeared absolutely semicircular . . . the most terrific thing I had ever seen in the Alps, but I am perfectly aware that a highly exaggerated impression [can be gained] of a ridge seen by half-frozen men in the middle of a tremendous storm, from the summit of a virgin peak'. Fearful about returning down their ascent route, they found a series of couloirs down the South-West Face, and after an icy and dangerous bivouac reached St Gervais at noon the following day. Here, relieved and hungry, they sought a mid-day lunch at the elegant Spa Hotel:

'Very cold was our reception at that refined watering place. The high breeding which we are justly told to expect on the Continent caused many a glance of supercilious wonderment to be directed at our soiled garments and thick boots . . . a shudder of subdued horror ran through the polite assembly, whereat Buxton remarked . . . that it was astonishing to find so much iciness in people who obviously had so little to do with cold water. All through dinner we were made to feel that we were not in our proper place; and many a time would a fair-haired *Fräulein* turn around with her knife still between her rosy lips, or a stately *Graf* pause ere his fingers had completed the circuit of his half-cleaned plate, to gaze with haughty contempt on the three Englishmen who, with true insular arrogance, thought themselves justified in sitting down to a midday *table d'hôte* in flannel shirts and knickerbockers.'

John Allen

(left) The old Durier Hut on the Col de Miage since replaced by a metal box.

There was an interesting aftermath to this great climb. As they waited in Chamonix for the weather to improve, they encountered a disconsolate young Peter Taugwalder (fresh from his escape on the Matterhorn) and hired him as a porter. However, Jean Baptiste Croz had also just returned from Zermatt 'emaciated and almost crazed at the loss of his brother'. A vicious whispering campaign soon developed against the Taugwalders and Cachet and Payot came to their employers with 'an abominable accusation' and refused to climb with the young porter. Buxton noted: 'We cared nothing for Taugwald[er], and should have much preferred to leave him and keep our guides, but as we could not desert him in such a strait, we were obliged to pay them and let them go.' Cachet eventually returned and they secured Jakob Anderegg to make up the party for the next expedition, when they attempted to reverse Adams-Reilly's 1864 route. Quitting the West Ridge of the Dôme too early, they ended up in the heavily crevassed and séracked Dôme Glacier basin where they made a somewhat dramatic descent.

The West Ridge from the Col de Tricot was climbed in 1911 by Fräulein Eleonore Hasenclever and Fräulein H. Wirthl with M. Helff, K.G. von Saar and Richard Weitzenböck. The complete North-West Face, with the icy upper slopes that had deterred Grove's party, was first

John Allen

John Allen

(above) Precarious climbing along the sharpest section of the East Ridge of the Aiguille de Bionnassay on the descent to the Col de Bionnassay.

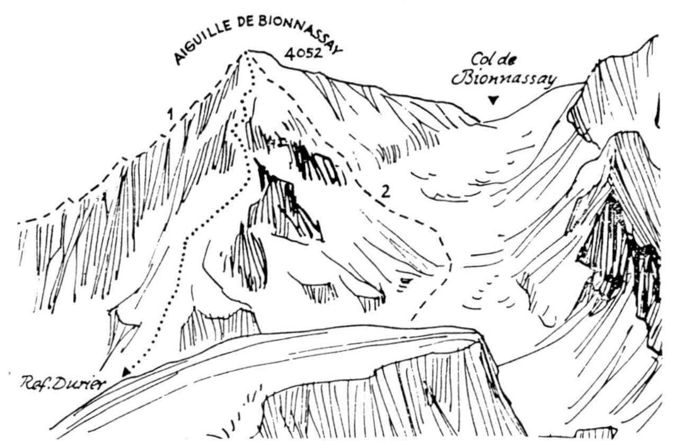

The majority of ascents from the Durier Hut follow the line of the South Ridge (dotted line) from the Italian side. Other routes marked are the Tricot Ridge (1) and South-East Face (2).

climbed in 1926 by the millionaire businessman Robert Wylie Lloyd with his guides Adolf and Josef Pollinger.

The Normal Route

The mountain was climbed for a second time in 1885 when the French trio of Paul Vignon, Henri Devouassoud and Alexandre Balmat approached by the southern Miage Glacier and finished up the South-East Face. Today's standard route of ascent, up the South Ridge from the Col de Miage, was climbed in July 1888 by the Austrian diplomat, Georg Gruber, with his Swiss guides Andreas Jaun and Kaspar Maurer. This long snow and rock ridge gives an impressive mixed climb. At one stage a traverse on to the South-East Face is made along a narrow ledge. When this gangway is snow-covered or icy the rocky South-West Face may provide a better alternative. A question mark also surrounds the steep slope leading to the summit – bare ice can make this a very disturbing climb.

The South Ridge (with its high hut on the Col de Miage) provides the ideal prelude to a traverse to the Dôme du Goûter and Mont Blanc. This will involve a descent of the very sharp East Ridge which is often icy and difficult. Climbers had spotted the possibility of a traverse to Mont Blanc from as early as 1864, when the Irish cartographer Anthony Adams-Reilly with John Birkbeck, Michel Croz and others, bypassed the Aiguille and

Bill O'Connor

(left) Looking back to the Aiguille de Bionnassay from the West Ridge of the Dôme du Goûter. The South Ridge is on the left and the East Ridge runs behind the climber on the right.

VALLEY BASES
Lago Combal see Mont Brouillard p198.
Tresse 1000m. A small village in the Vallée de Montjoie on the western side of the Mont Blanc range on the RN202, 10km from La Faver in the Arve Valley (nearest railway station). Bus service. Inn.
Les Houches 1007m. In the Arve Valley, 8km south-west of Chamonix; bus and rail services.
HUTS/OTHER BASES
Refuge Durier 3349m. CAF. A few metres below the Col de Miage (west side). 8 places. Always open. 6 hours from Lago Combal or 8 hours from Tresse.
Refuge de Tête Rousse 3167m. A privately-owned mountain inn west of the Aiguille du Goûter on the Bionnassay Glacier. 50 places. Staffed from end June to end September *tel* 50/ 58 24 97. Téléphérique from Les Houches to the Hôtel Bellevue (1790m). From here take the La Fayet rack railway to the top station (2372m). Then 2¼ hours to the hut.
NORMAL ROUTE
South Ridge PD+ II+. To 45°. 5 hours from the Durier Hut. 710mH. Mixed climbing.
RIDGES/FACES
East Ridge AD To 40°. A narrow corniced snow and ice ridge. 2 hours/150mH of ascent from the Col de Bionnassay (but usually climbed in descent).
West Ridge (Tricot Ridge) PD III, II. 10 hours/1050mH from the Col de Tricot (2 hours from the Hôtel Bellevue). A very long mixed route.
North-West Face AD+ Average 40° (but with sections of 55°). 8 hours/1200mH from the foot of the face (1½ hours from the Tête Rousse Hut). A steep glacier tour with an ice-face finish.
North Face Direct TD+ IV, III. To 53° (average) but with sections to 65°) in places. The first ascent took 19 hours! 1100mH.
MAPS/GUIDEBOOKS
See Aiguille Blanche p195.

reached the Col de Bionnassay from the Col de Miage and then climbed to the Dôme du Goûter. Grove's party certainly had designs on the East Ridge, Vignon's party tried it but found it too hard and it was finally negotiated (after an ascent of the South Ridge) by Miss Katherine Richardson with her regular guides Emile Rey and Jean-Baptiste Bich. It was a true arête with about 100 metres on ice which they overcame by *à cheval* tactics. They arrived at the Dôme du Goûter at 1.30 p.m. and reached Chamonix five hours later to complete an astonishing sixteen-hour expedition of over twenty kilometres and 2500m of ascent from their start at the foot of the south Miage Glacier.†

The North-West Face

While the North Face (first climbed by Bertrand Kempf and Claude Laurendeau on 30-31 August 1953) ranks among the most difficult ice walls in the Alps and is rarely climbed, the classic North-West Face enjoys increasing popularity. However, it should on no account be underestimated, even with modern equipment. It is a steep glacier so there are regular places to rest on the lips of crevasses, which also reduce the feeling of exposure. Nevertheless, this is a serious expedition of over 1000m and if the ice is hard even the more modestly angled sections become demanding. Conversely in new snow there will be arduous trail-breaking and increased avalanche danger. In 1968, for example, the face claimed four lives in one accident. Steep, bulging glacier routes are, quite simply, an incalculable risk.

†There is a full summary of early Bionnassay ascents and a report of Miss Richardson's ascent in *A.J.* XV p150 and background information in Miss Richardson's obituary *A.J.* XL p160.

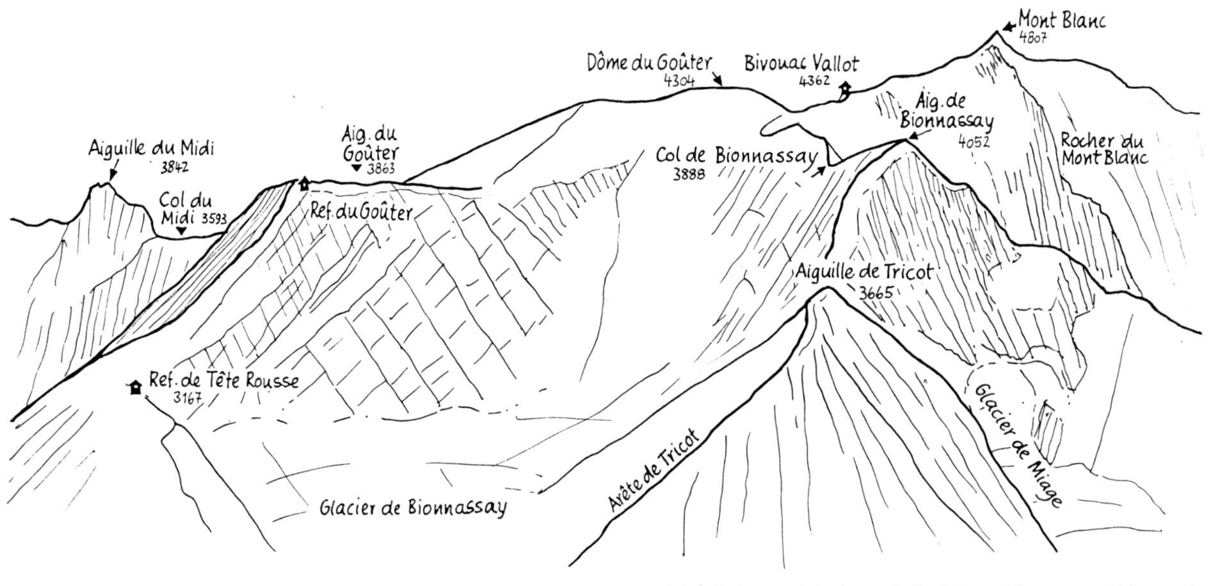

(right) An aerial view of the Mont Blanc massif from the west.

Mont Blanc *4807 m*

The 1986 Summer Festival in Chamonix celebrated the Bicentenary of the first ascent of Mont Blanc. This had been made on 8 August 1786 by the twenty-nine year old doctor Michel-Gabriel Paccard, son of the Notary of Chamonix, and Jacques Balmat, a twenty year old crystal hunter.[1]

The pair arrived together on the summit at 6.25 p.m. – the 'Pole of Western Europe' had finally been reached!

The ascent had been inspired by the enthusiasm and inducements of the wealthy Genevan scientist Horace-Benedict de Saussure who, after he first visited Chamonix in 1761, offered a large reward for anyone who could discover a route to the summit. The first serious attempts (1775, 1783, 1784 and 1785) took the spur of Montagne de la Côte and then followed the great valley formed by the Bossons and Taconnaz Glaciers that heads straight for the summit up the northern flank. During 1784 an alternative way up the North-West Ridge and over Aiguille du Goûter was also discovered, and advanced to the Dôme du Goûter by Jean-Marie Couttet and François Cuidet. In June 1786, two expeditions set out to compare the length of these two routes and they met in the vicinity of the Col du Dôme and advanced to a point roughly where the Vallot Hut now stands before descending. At this point a curious incident took place. One of the party that had used the glacier approach, Jacques Balmat from Les Pelerins, hung back and was left on the mountain. During his solo descent in a snowstorm and the gathering gloom, he was forced to bivouac and next morning returned to Chamonix. Later he teamed up with (or was hired by) Dr Paccard, who had also studied and reconnoitred the mountain. The two planned to make an attempt together with no other support. Accordingly, over the period 7-9 August the climb was made, surely one of the boldest and most spirited ventures in the whole history of alpinism. Balmat's night on the mountain gave them both the confidence to press on at a late hour in the knowledge that they could survive a bivouac but, with good snow conditions, they made a rapid retreat, descended the glacier in moonlight and regained the Montagne de la Côte by midnight.

The climb both delighted and inspired de Saussure and he immediately made preparations for his own ascent, enlisting Balmat's assistance. In June 1787 Balmat climbed the mountain for a second time with Michel Cachet and Alexis Tournier, and on 1 August de Saussure, with a party of seventeen guides led by Jacques Balmat, set out and made his stately ascent of the mountain that had so long been the object of his desire. Above the Grand Plateau they took a line above the Upper Rochers Rouges (rather higher than the Balmat/Paccard route) and for many years this route, the *Ancien Passage (supérieur)*, became the accepted way up the mountain.

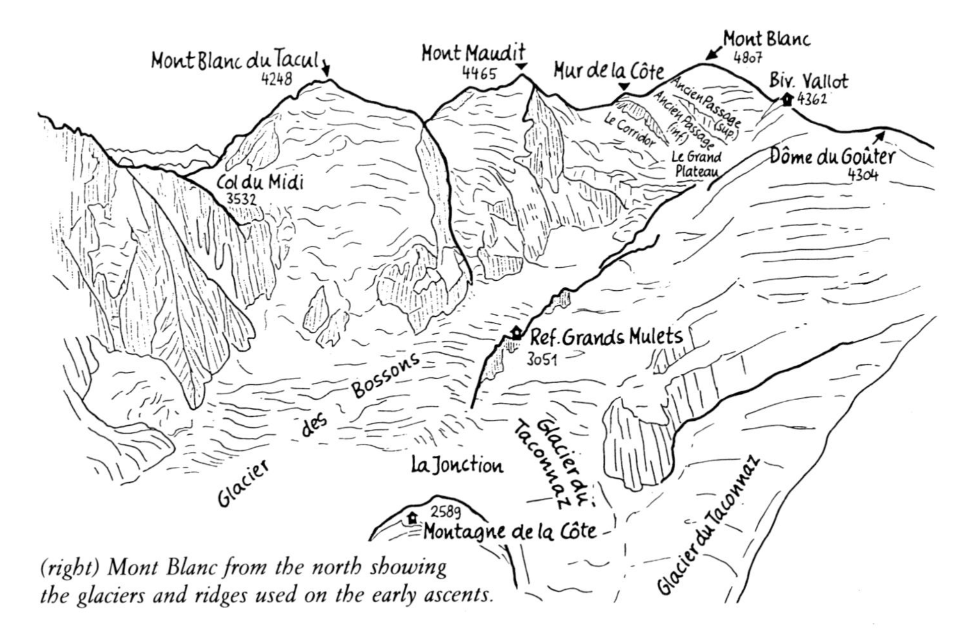

(right) Mont Blanc from the north showing the glaciers and ridges used on the early ascents.

For de Saussure, who was already a respected scientist, this climb and his subsequent scientific reports and book formed the climax of a great career and made him world famous. Sadly the details of the *first* ascent rapidly became obfuscated, mainly as a result of the machinations of a jealous journalist. Balmat's role in the discovery of the crucial route to the top, and indeed in the inspiration of the whole climb, became greatly exaggerated, at the expense of Dr Paccard's part. The controversy curdled into a long-running mountaineering scandal, which took nearly two centuries to resolve.

Balmat was later honoured by Vittorio Amedeo III, the King of Savoy and Sardinia, and Balmat and de Saussure are immortalised in stone by a statue erected in Chamonix, but Paccard's part in the original ascent was eclipsed until the 'Paccard Movement' of scientists and mountaineering historians ensured that his role was fully recognised. A bust to his memory was unveiled in Chamonix in 1932.[2]

The *Ancien Passage*

During the following years nine further ascents were made by the *Ancien Passage* but in poor conditions it was dangerous, as emphasised by the avalanche that swept away Dr Hamel's party in 1820 (when three guides died). In 1827 a lower and rather safer traverse – the Corridor Route (climbed by Charles Fellows, William Hawes and nine guides) – linked the Grand Plateau to the Col de la Brenva from where the steep slopes of the Mur de la Côte were taken, and this became the standard ascent route for a period.

The First Ascents by Women

In 1838, Henriette d'Angeville, after making out her last will and testament, set out for Mont Blanc in the care of

1. The early history of Mont Blanc is highly complicated – the best summaries are in: *The First Ascent of Mont Blanc* by Gavin de Beer and T. Graham Brown (London 1957); *Mountaineering in the Alps* by Claire Elaine Engel (London, 1971); *Savage Snows* by Walt Unsworth (London, 1986). These books also contain detailed bibliographies of important books and the key *Alpine Journal* articles on the subject which examine all aspects in great detail.
2. *A.J.* XLIV, p340.

Jim Teesdale

(above) A photomontage looking across the Bossons Glacier to 'La Jonction', the rock outcrops of the Grands Mulets with the Dôme du Goûter and the Aiguille du Goûter in the background.

six guides and six porters. Mademoiselle H. was the first guided lady tourist to reach the summit, although the first woman ever to set foot on the top was a twenty-three year old farm girl from Chamonix, Marie Paradis, who, in the summer of 1809, was persuaded to make the climb by Jacques Balmat and his two sons for commercial reasons.

Pioneering the Other Normal Routes

For nearly seventy years the heavily crevassed Bossons Glacier/Corridor or the *Ancien Passage* remained the only way up Mont Blanc and a cumbersome 'closed shop' developed among the Chamonix guides forcing large numbers of guides at a fixed tariff on those who wished to make the ascent. In the 1850s, many climbers were growing frustrated by this restrictive system and were seeking ways to avoid it. It was thus as much for this reason, as for normal exploratory curiosity, that new ways up the mountain were developed.

The first route from Italy was made in 1855 when James Ramsay and a group of Italian guides reached the Col du Midi via the Col du Géant. The following day they crossed Mont Blanc du Tacul and Mont Maudit and climbed the upper slopes of Mont Blanc to a point above the Mur de la Côte where, to Ramsey's 'great disgust', the guides (Joseph-Marie Chabod, Pierre-Joseph Mochet and Joseph-Marie Perrod) decided that the route was established and that they would go no further. A hut was soon built on the Col du Midi and the climb was formally completed in 1863 (R.W. Head, Julien Grange, Joseph-Marie Perrod and Adolphe Orset), but it became clear that it was too long to attract mass popularity and the search continued for a shorter way.

Meanwhile attention was redirected at the Goûter Route (then called the St Gervais route) which the guides had half climbed in 1786. In 1854 the unguided group of Charles Hudson, Edward Shirley Kennedy, the Smyth brothers (Christopher and James Grenville) and Charles Ainslie, reached the Col du Dôme and then dropped down to the Grand Plateau and ascended the mountain by the Corridor Route. The natural finish to the Goûter route up the Bosses Arête was done in 1859 using the Grands Mulets approach, and the complete ridge from the Aiguille du Goûter was done in 1862.[3]

The search for a better route from Italy continued with attention now directed to the Brenva Face. After

3. E. Headland, George Christopher Hodgkinson, Charles Hudson, G.C. Joad with Melchior Anderegg, François Couttet and two other guides did the Grands Mulets/Bosses Ridge and the complete Goûter Route (with the Bosses Ridge finish) was done by Leslie Stephen, Francis Fox Tuckett, Melchior Anderegg, Johann Josef Bennen and Peter Perren.

Bill O'Connor

Richard Carter

John Allen

(above) As the first rays of sunlight touch the rocks and ridges around the Vallot Hut as groups of climbers begin the final climb up the Bosses Ridge to the summit of Mont Blanc.

(far left) Hastening across the notorious Grand Couloir of the Aiguille du Goûter.

(near left) The Vallot Hut.

careful inspection from both above (from the Corridor Route) and below, Adolphus Warburton Moore, Horace Walker and his father Frederick, George Mathews and the guides Melchior and Jakob Anderegg mounted an attempt on the inclined spur on the right hand side of the face. The climb gave sustained difficulty to men without crampons and other modern ice equipment. The ice arête (led by Jakob Anderegg) was hard and exposed and forced the climbers to adopt *à cheval* tactics, and finally they were faced with a great wall of ice barring the way. Moore commented 'Our position was, in fact, rather critical. Immediately above our heads . . . a great mass of broken séracs . . . There was no use going to the left, – to the right we *could* not go, and back we *would* not go.' There followed a very tense passage working up to the right through the creaking sérac barrier where Melchior Anderegg 'with a marvellous exercise of skill and activity' led them to safety and jubilant success. This was one of the great climbs of the 'Golden Age', though, as Moore reflected, 'as regards practical utility [the route] has few advantages over that by Mont Blanc du Tacul. But it has one merit . . . that of directness. It is also incomparably more interesting and exciting. I trust therefore that someone will be found sufficiently enterprising to give it another trial.'[4]

The south-western flank above the Miage Glacier now seemed the only place where a route might be found. In 1868 Frederick Augustus Yeats Brown teamed up with Julien Grange who had been involved in both the Brenva (as porter) and Col du Midi climbs. 'I found a rough, tough, ugly, stumpy, red-haired, good-humoured, hot-tempered, broad-shouldered, pocket Hercules of a fellow who hung his head and blushed, and put his thumbs in his waistcoat-armholes when you spoke to him. . . . he opened his heart to me. His pet plan was to attack [Mont Blanc] by the Glacier de Miage and the Dôme . . . . Who could help falling in with such an idea. A new and possibly short route up Mont Blanc was worth trying for . . .'[5]

The result was a very bold new route that crossed the Dôme Glacier from the Aiguilles Grises and forged directly up the South Face to the Dôme du Goûter, but sadly it was too steep and serious to establish any lasting popularity.

Four years later a better way was found on this south-western flank that was less serious, easier and more direct. This was the Rocher du Mont Blanc route that gains the summit ridge from the head of the Mont Blanc Glacier. This was climbed, with typical efficiency by Thomas Stuart Kennedy with his powerful guides Johann Fischer and Jean Anthoine Carrel (the latter having been summoned from Breuil by telegraph). Julien Grange, no doubt to his intense frustration, was hired only as a porter ('next morning we gave Grange a bottle of wine to comfort him on his way back with the luggage'[6]). The trio then briskly ascended the mountain by the Rocher, reaching the summit in a storm from which they just as efficiently extricated themselves by descending the Corridor Route. This climb established itself for several years as the Normal Route from Italy to Mont Blanc and the Quintino Sella Hut was built to support it. But being both steep and (later in the day) subject to stonefall it was not suitable for descent, and climbers still had to go down to Chamonix. A convenient descent back to Italy was finally discovered in 1890 by Achille Ratti – who later became Pope Pius XI – who, with his four guides, found a way off the West Ridge of the Dôme du Goûter to gain the upper part of the Dôme Glacier and the Aiguilles Grises. Though longer, this was far less demanding than the Rocher du Mont Blanc route, and, with the establishment of a convenient hut (now the Gonella Hut), soon usurped the Rocher route to become the accepted Normal Route from Italy.

4. *A.J.* II, pp369-381.
5. *A.J.* IV, pp261-269. Others in the party were Daniel Chabot and Joseph-Ferdinand Lalle. This article is credited to Frederick A.G. Brown. It is clear that this was actually Frederick Augustus Yeats Brown who made the second ascent of the Grandes Jorasses (with Grange) a week earlier (CAI Bulletino 3). The Italian article notes that Brown was the brother of the British Consul in Geneva (a misprint for Genoa) who was Montagu Yeats Brown. The 'G' being (presumably) a misreading of 'Y' by the *A.J.* editor. Brown's entry in Grange's Führerbuch confirms this – the Y in his signature being easily mistaken for a G.

The Lure of Mont Blanc

With four main routes of ascent established the mountain awaited the mass popularity of the twentieth century. The fascination with Mont Blanc is fuelled by the superlative 'highest', a charismatic word which draws thousands to the area, summer after summer. There is probably no climber who has not, at least once, felt the desire to climb it. Indeed the mountain's sheer bulk and overpowering height and the manifest difficulty of its great glaciers and ridges exudes a unique challenge that no other alpine peak can match. Though the modern network of téléphériques have shortened some of the approaches, Mont Blanc remains insidiously dangerous, and the rapid breaks in the weather can turn its high slopes into a merciless hell. Even the easy hut approaches hide enormous dangers. Every summer, one hundred mountaineers fail to return alive from this peak, and it is estimated that between 6000 and 8000 people have lost their lives on Mont Blanc – more than on any other mountain in the world.

The Normal Routes

There are now four established Normal Routes although none of them can be described as 'normal' in the conventional sense being both high and very long:

1. *Goûter Hut – Bosses Ridge* This is the route which sees most ascents. Technically the least demanding, it is nevertheless the most dangerous.
2. *The Traverse from the Aiguille du Midi* Predominantly climbed in descent, from the summit of Mont Blanc, it is also used as a route of ascent and features ice climbing up to 50°.
3. *The Bossons Glacier – Grands Mulets – Bosses Ridge* The first choice for ski-mountaineers; technically comparable to Route 1, but heavily crevassed and still involving some 1750m of height-gain from the highest hut. Only about 10% of the total ascents of this route are made in summer. An alternative to this is the Corridor Route which links with the upper part of the Aiguille du Midi approach.
4. *Gonella Hut – Grises Route by the Dôme Glacier – Bosses Ridge* The easiest route from the Italian side, but more difficult than Routes 1 and 3. Fewer crevasses than on Route 3.

6. *A.J.* VI pp168-174.

From the Goûter Hut

A combination of téléphérique and tramway from Les Houches, or the complete 'Tramway du Mont Blanc' from St Gervais, takes one to Nid d'Aigle (the Eagle's Nest), from where a two-hour walk leads to the mountain inn at Tête Rousse. The 650m climb from here to the Goûter Hut, though unspectacular, is seriously endangered by stonefall and has one of the most hazardous sections of all the normal routes. The couloir traverse is the worst part, a section protected by fixed ropes, and in the afternoons especially the rocks whirl and crash down the infamous gully, mostly let loose by careless parties climbing or descending the loose rib above. Some days the crew of the rescue helicopter are kept constantly occupied, and it remains a mystery why those who are responsible for such things do not establish a safer route up the neighbouring rib.

The oppressive conditions in the tin box of the Goûter Hut have now achieved widespread notoriety; the pool of mattresses is booked up for days in advance and sleep is best accomplished in an upright position. At about 3 a.m. there is a general stirring and the six hour climb begins (four hours if you are fit and acclimatised). The first goal is the Dôme du Goûter first along a narrow

(opposite page) On the upper slopes of Mont Blanc: the Bosses Ridge (upper and lower left); on the summit (top right); descending the north-east towards Mur de la Côte, Mont Maudit and Mont Blanc du Tacul (bottom right).

Jim Teesdale

Jim Teesdale

Jim Teesdale

Jim Teesdale

ridge then by a broad swathe of path. The Vallot Hut, perched on a rock bluff above the Dôme, is a dilapidated lightweight metal refuge which has saved many a person's life over the years. Then there is the steep sweep of the Bosses Ridge where strong winds can make it hard going. Concentration is required on the narrow, airy crest of the 100m summit ridge. One often meets parties descending here which forces evasive action akin to tightrope walking. Finally, there is the summit which has been pursued so ardently – a wide, expansive snowfield flecked with hard scales of frozen ice.

By the Grands Mulets – the Winter Route

This is a route to do earlier in the year when many of the crevasses are covered. But even the walk to the hut from the téléphérique at Plan de l'Aiguille is not easy. 'La Jonction', where the Bossons and the eastern arm of the Taconnaz Glacier meet is a confusing maze set with bizarre towers of ice, where tracks are repeatedly obliterated by collapsing séracs. In the summer months ladders are usually placed across the bigger crevasses, but extreme caution and alertness is still required. A handrail of iron rungs helps the final climb to the Grands Mulets Hut and, in the skiing months of May and June, the futile search for a place to sleep.

Beyond the hut the zone of crevasses continues. The climb past the Petit Plateau, the steep slopes of the Montées, the Grand Plateau and finally to the Col du Dôme (4237m) seems interminable. Half an hour beyond the col is the Vallot Hut (where skis should be left) from there a further two hours is needed to reach the summit. In my experience, the upper part of the ski descent from the Vallot Hut to the Plan d'Aiguille two thousand metres below is a powder-snow dream; further down, the hard snow often turns it into a nightmare.

The first ski ascent was made in February 1904 and the mountain was traversed on skis in April 1924. The first winter ascent of the mountain is also worth noting. This was made on 31 January 1876 by the wealthy Miss Mary Isabella Straton with her guides Jean Charlet and Sylvain Couttet. It was her fourth ascent of the mountain. Shortly after this Miss Straton married Jean Charlet who had been her guide during her fifteen years of alpine climbing. Later both their sons climbed the mountain, the eldest, Robert Charlet-Straton, being just eleven years old when he made the ascent.

(left) A long-focus view of the Brenva Face from Pointe Helbronner. The Frêney Pillars are obvious on the left, rising beyond the Peuteréy Ridge.

The Italian Approach

Media difficolta is how the Italian guidebook grades the approach to the hut alone, situated in the secluded primeval world of the Dôme Glacier, In 1968, the guides equipped one very steep section of the path to the Gonella Hut with cables and ladders, which in the Dolomites would give this *via ferrata* status. It goes without saying that on this route, too, the crevasses lie in wait, and séracs strike fear into the climber. The Frontier Ridge which leads to the Dôme du Goûter is reached to the east of the Col de Bionnassay. At the Dôme we meet those on the way up from the Goûter Hut and accompany them for the slog up to the Vallot Hut and the final two-hour climb to the summit.

The Brenva Face

This mighty Mont Blanc face is at its most impressive when viewed from the Tour Ronde to the east, a thirteen-hundred-metre wall of ice and rock rising steeply above the Brenva Glacier. In addition to the previously described Old Brenva Route, or Brenva Spur, which is nowadays a much respected classic, the other routes on the face also merit attention. More difficult, and with considerable objective danger, is the Sentinelle Rouge route which takes a direct line to the summit of Mont Blanc. This was climbed on 1-2 September 1927 by the British pair, Thomas Graham Brown and Frank (Francis Sydney) Smythe, an efficient partnership 'of convenience' who climbed without guides. The same pair were also responsible for the magnificent Route Major (6-7 August 1928), which lies beyond the notoriously dangerous Great Couloir which must be crossed to reach it. Brown also climbed the third great climb on the face, The Pear, which makes straight for the summit of Mont Blanc de Courmayeur. He was accompanied on this ascent by the guides Alexander Graven and Alfred Aufdenblatten.

These routes have all had solo and winter ascents. One interesting recent feat was accomplished by Marc Batard who climbed three of these classic routes in one night – the Major in four hours, descent by the Sentinelle Rouge in ninety minutes and a finish up the Brenva Spur. His only companion was the full moon. Another notable feat was the ski descent of the Brenva Spur in 1973 by Heini Holzer, who first climbed the route solo in ski boots, with skis strapped to his rucksack, taking four hours from the Col de la Fourche – in itself a remarkable achievement.

The Three Great Ridges

Three great ridge routes on the South side of Mont Blanc – the Brouillard, Innominata and Peuterey Ridges – pre-

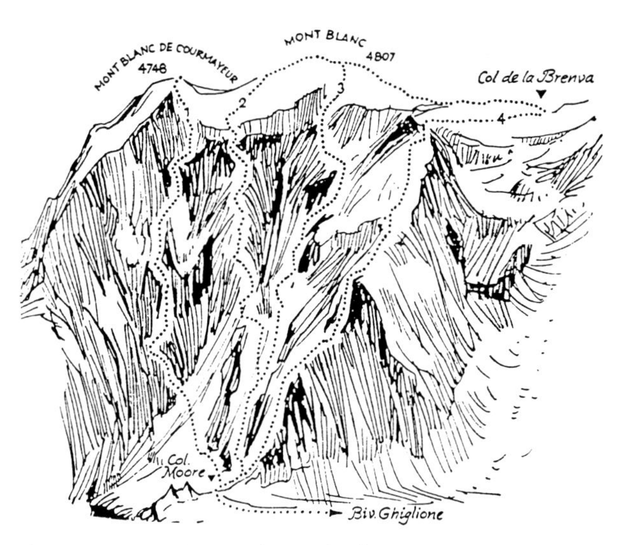

The Brenva Face of Mont Blanc with The Pear (1), Route Major (2), Sentinelle Rouge (3) and the Brenva Spur (4) marked.

occupied the leading climbers in the 1890s and the early years of this century, and provided the mountain with three great middle-grade climbs (to add to the Brenva Face classics).

The Brouillard Ridge (see Mont Brouillard chapter), first climbed in 1911, is the least difficult of the trio. On the ridge the 4469m Pic Luigi Amedeo (first climbed in July 1901 by the Italian brothers Guiseppe and Giovanni Battiste Gugliermina with Joseph Brocherel) is a summit to which some accord the status of an independent four-thousander. As it is almost exclusively climbed during a Brouillard Ridge ascent, if widely endorsed as such, it would become (along with the Aiguille Blanche) the most difficult four-thousand-metre summit.

The most popular and the finest of the three ridges is the normal Peuterey Ridge route from the Monzino Hut (see Aiguille Blanche de Peuterey chapter). This was first done in 1927 by Obersteiner and Schreiner, though the Güssfeldt party of 1893 had traversed Aiguille Blanche on the way to Mont Blanc de Courmayeur using the dangerous Brenva approach, and the upper part of the ridge was climbed by the Eccles party in 1877.

The last, and in many ways the most interesting and challenging of the three, is the Innominata Ridge. This had been a target for a number of ambitious climbers from as far back as 1864 when John Birkbeck and party explored the Brouillard Glacier basin. Thereafter there were attempts by the parties of: Agostino Durazzo (1872); Rev. A.G. Girdlestone and Capt. W.E. Utterson-Kelso (1873); T.S. Kennedy and T. Middlemore (1874). Also in 1874 was the notable attempt by J.A. Garth Marshall with his guides Johann Fischer and the ubiquitous Ulrich Almer. Sadly, during their descent, at about midnight, just as they were about to leave the glacier, a wide snow-

Bill O'Connor

(above) The Brouillard and Frêney Faces of Mont Blanc seen in winter conditions from Mont Chetif above Courmayeur.

bridge collapsed and all three men fell into a crevasse. Marshall and Fischer were killed but Almer survived and returned to tell the tale. After reaching Pic Eccles (4010m), they had made a really determined bid to force the climb and may well have reached the Third Step before retreating at about 4 p.m.[7]

After this the face was examined at close quarters by Eccles in 1877 but he eventually selected the Peuterey Ridge for his successful ascent (albeit based on an Innominata approach). Attempts by the Gugliermina brothers in 1915 and 1916 were stopped at the First Step. Finally, on 19-20 August 1919 the ascent was made by Capt. S.L. Courtauld and Edmund G. Oliver with Adolf Aufdenblatten and Adolphe and Henri Rey. They bivouaced just above the Col du Frêney, started at 6 a.m. and reached the summit at 4.20 p.m. The route traces a right-to-left dogleg to work through the obstacles and gain the Brouillard Ridge, the main difficulties being on the lower rock towers above the Col Eccles where, at a critical point, Adolphe Rey was forced to employ combined tactics. The climb was repeated, with some difficulty, in 1921 by the Gugliermina brothers with Francesco Ravelli and Lucien Proment.[8]

The Great Faces

The three great rock faces of Mont Blanc – the Brouillard Face, the Frêney Face and the walls of the Grand Pilier d'Angle (together with its adjoining very steep ice wall) are now seamed with very difficult routes that are largely beyond the scope of this book. Virtually all of them belong to the age of modern alpinism that became the dominant force after the Second World War. A few highlights should be mentioned however:

The Frêney Pillars

These fabulous granite pillars dominate the upper basin of the Frêney Glacier. The Right-hand Pillar was ascended in 1940 by Giusto Gervasutti and Paulo Bollini – a classic climb described by Pit Schubert as 'a mixed route of great style'.

The route avoided the main challenge, however – the great Central Pillar – and it was not until the 1960s that this began to preoccupy the leading climbers. A determined attempt in 1961 led to one of the most harrowing tragedies in alpine history when, one by one, the top alpi-

7. *A.J.* LII and LIII 'The Early attempts on Mont Blanc du Courmayeur from the Innominata Basin' by T. Graham Brown (serialised).
8. *A.J.* XXXIII p129 and XXXV, pp87-92.

nists Antoine Vielle, Pierre Kohlmann, Robert Guillaume and Andrea Oggioni died of exhaustion during a desperate retreat (using the Rochers Gruber) in an unrelenting storm. The other members of the party, Walter Bonatti, Roberto Gallieni and Pierre Mazeaud, were lucky to escape with their lives.

Soon after this tragedy an Anglo-Polish team of Don Whillans, Chris Bonington, Ian Clough and Jan Djuglosz were at grips with the crucial 'Chandelle' section that had stopped the Bonatti party. They were closely pressed by the Franco-Italian rope of Réné Desmaison, Pierre Julien, Yves Pollet-Villard and Ignazio Piussi. After a dramatic struggle when Whillans took a twenty-metre fall, Bonington finally climbed the critical chimney, Whillans followed and, as the sun set, Clough and Djuglosz prusiked up a rope dropped from above. The first four reached the summit the following day, followed a few hours later by the second ascent party who also avoided the crux section by prusiking up a rope left by Clough.

Bill O'Connor

(left) *At the Ghiglione Hut on the Col du Trident, the main base for climbs on the south-eastern side of Mont Blanc.*

Grand Pilier d'Angle

The 4244m Grand Pilier d'Angle (or the Eckpfeiler as it was called by Paul Güssfeldt) buttresses the upper Peuterey Ridge above the Col du Peuterey. It hit the Alpine headlines in 1957 with Walter Bonatti and Toni Gobbi's conquest of the 700m East Face. In 1971 this sustained mixed climb was effectively upstaged by an even better route just to its right, climbed by Walter Cecchinel and Georges Nominé – now much valued as a high standard classic.

Bonatti also showed his pioneering skills on the icy North-East Face that forms the right flank of the upper Peuterey Ridge. His route here, which he climbed with Cosimo Zappelli in 1962, appeared the epitome of seriousness at the time but the face now boasts several equally challenging routes and is highly regarded for its fine ice and mixed climbing.

The Brouillard Face

Here again Bonatti was first on the scene and in 1960, in the company of Andrea Oggioni climbed the left-hand Red Pillar – now a respected high altitude rock climb. The Right Pillar was climbed in 1965 and the Central in 1971.

VALLEY BASES

Chamonix see Les Droites p169
Entrèves see Dent du Géant p182
Les Houches see Aiguille de Bionnassay p202

HUTS/OTHER BASES

Refuge de Tête Rousse see Aiguille de Bionnassay p202
Aiguille du Midi 3842m. Téléphérique station. Self service restaurant (no accommodation or bivouacking). Journey time from Chamonix ½ hour (also from Entrèves). Service from 6 a.m. to 7 p.m. (July and August) and shorter times in other seasons. No link to Pointe Helbronner from October to April. Ask at the information office about hut accommodation at the *Cosmiques Hut* on the Col du Midi.
Rifugio Torino see Dent du Géant p182.
Rifugio Franco Monzino/Bivacco Craveri see Aiguille Blanche p195.
Rifugio Quintino Sella see Mont Brouillard p198.
Bivacco Lucia e Piero Ghiglione see Mont Maudit p218.
Refuge de l'Aiguille du Goûter 3817m. CAF. Just north of the summit of Aiguille du Goûter. 100 places. Staffed from end June to end September *tel* 50/ 54 40 93. Dormitory with room for 16 and cooking facilities always open. 3 hours from the Tête Rousse.
Refuge Vallot 4362m. CAF. On a rognon south-east of Col du Dôme. Emergency bivouac with 25 places. Always open. About 3 hours from the Goûter Hut.
Refuge Grands Mulets 3051m. Private. On the northern spur of the Grands Mulets surrounded by glaciers. 68 places. Staffed in the ski season and in summer *tel* 50/ 53 16 98. Self-catering room. Winter room (sleeps 20) always open. 5 hours from Plan de l'Aiguille (2300m téléphérique station, reached in 9 minutes from Chamonix).
Bivacco Lampugnani/Bivacco Crippa see Aiguille Blanche p195.
Rifugio Gonella 3071m. CAI. On the west bank of the Dôme Glacier. 40 places. Staffed from 15 July to 30 August *tel* 0165/ 8 93 69. Old hut with room for 16 always open. 5 hours from Lago Combal (1935m 12km from Courmayeur in the Val Veni).

NORMAL ROUTES

North-West Ridge from the Goûter Hut PD I To 35°. 6 hours from the Goûter Hut. 1060mH. Snow ridges.
North Flank from the Grands Mulets Hut PD– I To 40°. 8 hours from the Grands Mulets. 1760mH. A glacier tour. *As a ski tour:* Leave skis at the Vallot Hut.
North-North-East Approach from Col du Midi PD+ I+ (on Mont Maudit). To 48°. 11 hours from the Aiguille du Midi. 1450mH. A snow and ice route.
South-West Approach from Gonella Hut PD+ I To 38°. 9 hours from the Gonella Hut. 1800mH. A glacier tour, then snow and ice ridges.

RIDGES/FACES

Brenva (East) Face – Brenva Spur D– III (sections). To 50° (average 40°). 10 hours from the Bivacco Ghiglione (Trident Hut). 1300mH. A snow and ice route.
Brenva Face – Sentinelle Rouge D III, II. To 55° (average 47°). 14 hours from the Bivacco Ghiglione. 1300mH. Ice and mixed climbing.
Brenva Face – Route Major D+ V (sections), IV, III. To 57° (average 48°). 16 hours from the Bivacco Ghiglione. 1300mH. Ice, mixed and rock.
Brenva Face – The Pear TD– IV, III. To 60°. 16 hours from the Bivacco Ghiglioni. 1300mH. Mixed, ice and rock.
South Face – Innominata Ridge D IV (sections), III. To 54°. 12 hours from the Bivacco Lampugnani (Eccles Hut). 960mH. Mixed and ice.
South-East (Peuterey) Ridge D+ IV (sections), III, II. To 55°. 18 hours from the Bivacco Craveri. 1500mH. Mixed and ice.

MAPS/GUIDEBOOKS

See Aiguille Blanche p195

Mont Maudit *4465 m*

Mont Maudit's western and northern flanks, overlooking the Bossons Glacier basin, are defended with hanging glaciers and rock buttresses but the upper névé slopes provide smooth going for those making the high-level traverse between Mont Blanc and the Col du Midi. On the traverse the crucial Col du Mont Maudit on the North-West Ridge tempts climbers to bypass the summit, which is a pity as the fine views of the Brenva Face and the Aiguilles du Diable, as well as tantalising glimpses down the South-East Face richly reward the additional effort. The mountain can be climbed from the Aiguille du Midi in six hours but the trip may seem an anticlimax unless an ascent of Mont Blanc forms the finale.

An Overlooked First Ascent?

The early travellers on both the Corridor and the Mont Blanc Traverse do not seem to have considered the mountain important enough to visit the summit and it was not until 12 September 1878 that the top was reached – Henry Seymour Hoare and the lawyer/diplomat William Edward Davidson with their Oberland guides, Johann Jaun and Johann von Bergen, followed the corniced South Ridge as a diversion from the Corridor Route during their ascent of Mont Blanc. On the Col du Midi approach the natural route takes the 250m North-West Ridge from the Col du Mont Maudit. This was credited to the descending party of George Morse and Emile Rey after a fiftieth birthday ascent (for Rey) of Mont Blanc in 1895. This was to be the great guide's last completed climb before his death on the Dent du Géant and Morse sadly noted that 'Three days later a fateful slip on some easy rocks brought his career to an untimely end . . . one of the most brilliant modern guides, one of the keenest for new expeditions, and one of the best companions on the mountainside, met his death almost within sight of his own home . . .'.*

The rather more difficult North-East Ridge from Col Maudit was climbed on 31 July 1898 by J.S. Masterman with the brothers Albert and Benedict Supersaxo during an ascent of Mont Blanc from Col du Midi.

The Frontier Ridge

The dazzling rock scenery of the 800m south-eastern precipices – a roughly-hewn and challenging structure of couloirs, arêtes, spurs and faces possessed of a simple and primitive beauty – is Mont Maudit's greatest treasure.

Of all its lines it is the 1600m South-East Ridge which catches the eye, the celebrated Frontier Ridge which cries out as the natural route of ascent. This was first climbed on 2-4 July 1887 by the Austrian brewer Moritz

*A.J. XVIII p215

Mont Maudit was traditionally climbed from the Grands Mulets, but is now more commonly ascended during a traverse from Mont Blanc to the Col du Midi.

Jim Teesdale

(left) Mont Maudit in a long-focus view from Pointe Helbronner.

(right) The west flank of Mont Maudit seen from near the Vallot Hut. The Corridor is the obvious snow ramp leading up to the right behind the rock buttress on the right, with the 'Ancien Passage' on the extreme right.

Dave Wynne-Jones

von Kuffner with the ebullient Alexander Burgener and Josef Furrer. The second ascent was made in 1901 by the Italians E. Canzio and F. Mondini with Henri Brocherel, and the third in 1911 by the controversial Winchester College schoolmaster R.L.G. (Graham) Irving with two of his ex-pupils, Harry Tyndale and George Leigh Mallory. Irvine's contemporary account of the climb merely noted its quality but later, Mallory, apparently prompted by the death of friends on the Western Front in 1916, wrote a highly emotional article of his ascent of this great climb – begun at dawn at the Col du Géant with a finish in *the last moments of daylight* on the summit of Mont Blanc – the final paragraph of which is particularly revealing:†

'A breeze, cool and bracing, seemed to gather force as they plodded up the long slopes, more gentle now as they approached the final goal. He felt the wind about him with its old strange music . . . . Rather than thinking or feeling he was simply listening – listening for distant voices scarcely articulate . . . [the summit] a place where desires point and aspirations end; very, very, high and lovely, long-suffering and wise . . . *Experience*, slowly and wonderfully filtered; the last a purged reminder . . . And what is that? What more than the infinite knowledge that it is all worthwhile – all one strives for? . . . How to get the best of it all? One must conquer, achieve, get to the top; one must know the end to be convinced that one can win the end – to know there's no dream that mustn't be dared. . . . Is this the summit, crowning the day? How cool and quiet! We're not exultant; but delighted, joyful, soberly astonished . . . . Have we vanquished an enemy? None but ourselves. Have we gained success? That word means nothing here. Have we won a kingdom? No . . . and yes. We have achieved an ultimate satisfaction . . . fulfilled a destiny . . . . To struggle and to understand – never this last without the other; such is the law . . . . We've only been obeying an old law then? Ah! But it's *the* law . . . and we understand – a little more. So ancient wise and terrible – and yet kind we see them; with steps for children's feet.' This provides a useful addition to 'because it's there' and some clue, perhaps, to Mallory's state of mind on that final day on Everest eight years later.

This ridge cannot be recommended too strongly though, even today, it is treated rather disparagingly – as a sort of consolation Brenva Spur – it is one of the most worthwhile routes of its kind in the whole of the Mont Blanc region. The difficulties vary between III and IV and a minimum of seven or eight hours will be required for an ascent from the hut on the Col du Trident.

†'Pages from a Journal' France, Autumn 1916 *A.J.* XXXII pp148-162

(above and right) A sequence of pictures on the lower part of the Frontier Ridge – the section up to, and round, the Point de l'Androsace.

John Allen

Dave Wynne-Jones

Dave Wynne-Jones

John Allen

Bill O'Connor

Bill O'Connor

(above) Above Point de l'Androsace on the Frontier Ridge.

(above right) The steep north-eastern slope below the Col du Mont Maudit on the Midi/Mont Blanc traverse.

(lower right) Mont Blanc from north of Col de la Brenva.

Those climbers in search of peace and quiet will find the Cretier Route on the South-East Face interesting. Put up in 1932 by Renato Chabod, Amilcare Cretier and L. Binel, its original start was straightened out in 1937 on the second ascent. The face has at least six more major climbs – all in the higher grades.

VALLEY BASES

Chamonix see Les Droites p169

Entrèves see Dent du Géant p182

HUTS/OTHER BASES

Aiguille du Midi see Mont Blanc p213

Rifugio Torino see Dent du Géant p182

Bivacco Lucia e Piero Ghiglione (Trident Hut) 3690m. CAI. On the Col du Trident (South-East Ridge). 18 places. Staffed occasionally (20 June to 20 September). Always open. 3 hours from the Torino Hut (ice to 50° on the approach). About 400m to the north-west on the Col de la Fourche is the *Bivacco Alberico e Brogna (Fourche Bivouac)* which is in a state of disrepair and has not been in use – due to subsidence – since 1988.

NORMAL ROUTE

North-East Approach to North-West Ridge PD I. To 50°. 6 hours from the Aiguille du Midi. 920mH from the Col du Midi. A glacier tour. *As a ski tour:* Leave skis at the Col du Mont Maudit.

RIDGES/FACES

North-East Ridge from Col Maudit AD To 45°. 3 hours/430mH from Col Maudit. Mixed and ice with some cornice danger. Scenic and interesting.

South-East (Frontier) Ridge D IV, III. To 45°. 10 hours/850mH from the Trident Hut. Mixed, rock and ice climbing.

South-East Face (Cretier Route) TD– IV. To 50°. 10 hours/650mH from the foot of the face. Mixed, rock and ice. Harder than the Brenva classics.

MAPS/GUIDEBOOKS

See Aiguille Blanche p195

Mont Blanc du Tacul *4248 m*

In earlier times this was a very remote peak, protected to the north and west by steep broken glaciers and to the south and east by rocky bastions rising from the upper snow basin of the Géant Glacier. Originally its ascent involved a very long approach up the Geánt Glacier or across the Col du Géant to gain the Col du Midi where a makeshift hut was established in 1863. The Courmayeur guides, in their efforts to establish a route to Mont Blanc from Italy, may well have climbed the peak during their explorations, either in 1854, or on their successful foray (with James Ramsay) in 1855. The official first ascent took place one week later, on 5 August 1855, when the Reverend Charles Hudson climbed to the summit as a breakaway from a party making another attempt on the Midi approach to Mont Blanc.*

The Advantages of the Téléphérique

The establishment of the téléphérique to the Aiguille du Midi made the climb from the Col du Midi highly accessible and very popular. The traverse to Mont Blanc – the most magnificent, and longest Normal Route to the 'Monarch' – takes about ten hours in ascent but is generally done in reverse, descending from the summit of Mont Blanc, during which the summits of Mont Maudit and Mont Blanc du Tacul can be conveniently visited. Ski-mountaineers, on the other hand, might elect to grab themselves a quick summit with a three-hour climb up the 700m North-West Face as a preliminary to the unique run back down the Vallée Blanche to Montenvers. There are also many who are quite content to climb the peak for its own merits. The téléphérique allows these options and also brings Mont Blanc du Tacul's many fine routes above the Géant Glacier within easy reach.

*Hudson, accompanied by Edward John Stevenson, and the brothers Christopher and James Grenville Smyth, were attempting the Midi route to Mont Blanc just four days after their first ascent of the Dufourspitze (where the guides had played a secondary role). No guides were involved on this climb, additional personnel being Edward Shirley Kennedy, Charles Ainslie and the fifteen-year-old G.C. Joad (one of Hudson's pupils). With the exception of Joad, all were climbers of long experience. After a miserable bivouac on the Col du Midi the attempt on Mont Blanc petered out in poor weather and Hudson took the opportunity to climb the lesser peak.

The Easy Way Up

The Normal Route is actually not that easy. From the icicle-hung galleries of the Aiguille du Midi station the initial, very exposed, descent down the North Ridge is protected by cables, and a ladder of snow steps drops down to the glacier. An easy traverse takes one below the sun-baked granite slabs of the popular rock routes of the Midi's South Face to the Col du Midi. Here a bergschrund bars the way on to the North-West Face and is often free of surplus glacial snow, particularly in the late summer. In earlier days the guides used to equip this passage with a wooden ladder, but after it had been repeatedly thrown into the crevasse, the Chamoniards began to doubt the wisdom of this service to their clients.

Keeping to the right, a zone of séracs is gingerly negotiated and the wide track then leads up to the West Shoulder. If the conditions allow, those on skis can make a rising traverse to the left from the centre of the face to reach the summit pinnacles of Mont Blanc du Tacul direct. A word of caution here: after heavy snowfall this

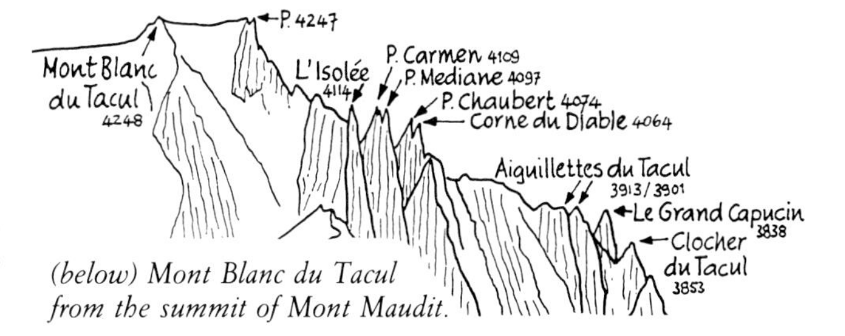

(below) Mont Blanc du Tacul from the summit of Mont Maudit.

Richard Carter

Willi Burkhardt

Bill O'Connor

(left) The northern flank of Mont Blanc du Tacul seen from the Aiguille du Midi. Mont Maudit and Mont Blanc are the peaks on the right. The Normal Route up the North-West Face (lower photo) is prone to avalanche in poor conditions.

face is liable to avalanche and there have been some nasty accidents and several fatalities.

Extremes

The East and North-East Faces are seamed with routes exclusively in the upper and very highest levels of difficulty. A brief list of some of the classic climbs hereabouts would include the Gervasutti Couloir, the Boccalatte Pillar, the Gervasutti Pillar, the Jager Couloir, the Super Couloir and of course, on the satellite rock pinnacles at the foot of the face, numerous climbs including the magnificent big wall routes of the Grand Capucin.

In recent years the previously overlooked gable of the North Face, which is particularly convenient for the téléphérique, has been developed and routes like the Contamine/Mazeaud and the Chére Couloir now enjoy great popularity. The téléphérique access has enabled climbers to treat the ice couloirs and rock pillars of Mont Blanc du Tacul as a virtual high altitude 'klettergarten' and standards have soared as a result.

The Classic

These extreme climbs will be of little interest to the 4000m enthusiast, whereas the Diable Ridge certainly will be. Despite all modern discoveries it retains a well deserved reputation as 'one of the finest ridge climbs in the Mont Blanc region, considerably more difficult than the normal Peuterey Ridge', according to Pit Schubert.

The climbing on the 700m long ridge – the South-East

VALLEY BASES

Chamonix see Les Droites p169
Entrèves see Dent du Géant p182

HUTS/OTHER BASES

Aiguille du Midi see Mont Blanc p213
Rifugio Torino see Dent du Géant p182

NORMAL ROUTE

North-West Face PD To 40°. 3 hours from the Aiguille du Midi. 650mH. A glacier tour.

RIDGES/FACES

South-East Ridge (Diable Ridge) D+ V (one pitch), IV, III. 9 hours/700mH from the start of the route (1½ hours from the Torino Hut). Mixed and rock.
Boccalatte Pillar D+ on the easiest line and in ideal conditions) V, IV, III (if at all snow-covered it gets much harder). 8 hours/800mH from foot of route.
Gervasutti Couloir D+ To 55°. 7 hours/850mH from foot of route. An ice route with some objective danger.

MAPS/GUIDEBOOKS

See Aiguille Blanche p195.

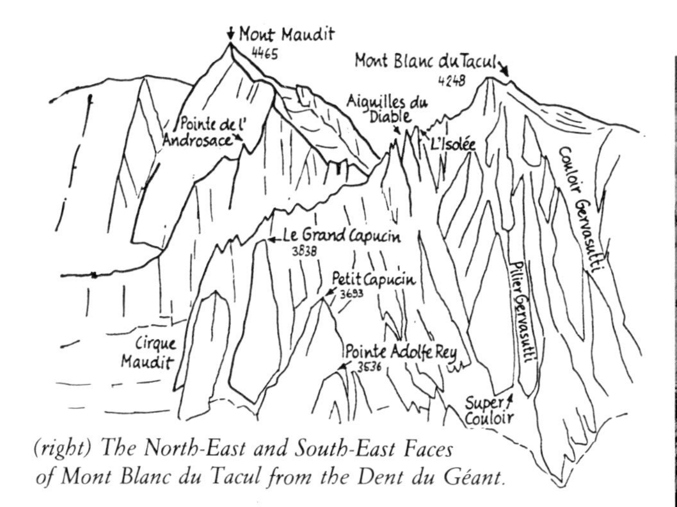

(right) The North-East and South-East Faces of Mont Blanc du Tacul from the Dent du Géant.

Ridge of Mont Blanc du Tacul – is on numerous sharp rocky towers, all of which are four-thousand-metre *tops*. Many purists feel that they should have full *peak* status, being considerably more assertive than, say, the Balmenhorn or Mont Brouillard. The pinnacles are Corne du Diable (4064m), Pointe Chaubert (4074m), Pointe Médiane (4097m), Pointe Carmen (4109m) and L'Isolée or Pointe Blanchard (4114m). There is also an East Summit (4247m) but that is a genuine 'top'. All of these pinnacles had been ascended ('Armand Charlet had led the first ascents of four of the five' – O'Brien) and the traverse of all of them in one expedition was finally made on 4 August 1928 by Charlet, who had been hired by the Americans Miriam O'Brien and her husband-to-be Robert Underhill to lead an expedition Charlet had proposed, Georges Cachet making up the party. The key pitch proved to be on L'Isolée, a grade V passage which Charlet thought slightly easier than the Knubel Crack on the Grépon (though it is 700m higher). Charlet led this, using a jammed ice axe for aid at the critical part (now protected with pitons). Indeed no pitons were used anywhere on the climb; as O'Brien noted, 'In all the years I climbed with Armand, I never saw him use a piton for anything except roping down.' Those who followed this route (which is now well pitoned) have cast doubt on this claim.†

The rest of the climb gives a grade II to IV excursion, all of it above the four-thousand-metre level, with some daring abseil manoeuvres – some as long as forty metres. If one is pressed for time L'Isolée can be bypassed. The 100m East Dièdre of Pointe Médiane (4097m) will provide granite enthusiasts with a truly cosmic experience!

†Miriam Underhill's book *Give Me The Hills* (London, 1956) gives a full description of this climb and includes a four plate photo sequence of Charlet leading the difficult pitch with not a piton in sight.

(right) The North-East Face of Mont Blanc du Tacul from the Gros Rognon. The Gervasutti Couloir is on the right, with the Gervasutti Pillar and the Aiguilles du Diable on the left.

John Allen

Bill O'Connor

Index

A NOTE FOR THE ENGLISH LANGUAGE EDITION This is an adaptation of *Die Viertausender der Alpen* (Rudolf Rother, Munich, 1989). That book had a portrait format which resulted in many of Willi Burkhardt's photographs running across the page split. There was also an accompanying booklet (inserted in a sheath in the cover) with a set of annotated topographical line drawings by Sebastian Schrank showing the important features on the main landscape photos. An earlier set of stylised sketches showing the described routes and other important climbs was retained in the text.

The English language edition has been redesigned on a broader format to avoid splitting the main pictures. The booklet is omitted and a selection of Schrank's drawings have been brought into the main text to supplement traditional sketches. A number of new topographical drawings and route sketches have been added in the style of the original versions to depict detail on the many new photographs. Multilingual maps have been added for each of the major ranges and these are annotated to match the proper names given on the definitive IGN and Landeskarte der Sweiz maps. Thus glaciers are rendered as Glacier, Gletscher or Ghiacciaio according to their country or language area of origin, and the same applies to huts, mountains and passes. For ease of reading the terms Glacier, Pass and Hut have been used in the main text but the official titles of huts are recorded in the tabulated notes.

The text itself has been substantially adapted to include much additional history and anecdote drawn from English language journals and books. This has been woven into the text on behalf of Helmut Dumler whose personal stamp remains on the book with his own anecdotes, a full range of technical advice on the climbing and ski mountaineering possibilities and the original Austro/German historical commentary which drew heavily on Karl Blodig's original book. The book now has an Anglo/German flavour which may, at times, seem curious.

ACKNOWLEDGEMENTS The authors and publishers would like to thank all of those who have contributed to the English-language version of *Die Viertausender der Alpen*. The initial translation was made by Tim Carruthers and then edited and adapted by Ken Wilson assisted by Petra Sluka, Pippa Musselbrook and Janis Tetlow. Additional editorial assistance and advice was provided by John Allen, Gino Buscaini, Christine de Colombel, Robin Collomb, Margaret Ecclestone, Sheila Harrison, Richard Hale, Wil Hurford, Silvia Metzeltin, Geoff Milburn, Chris Russell, Mirella Tenderini, Walter Theil, Walt Unsworth and Dave Wynne-Jones. The maps were produced by Don Sargeant. We would also like to thank Jocelin Winthrop Young for permission to use quotations from *On High Hills* and various *Alpine Journal* articles by his father, and Robin Collomb for permission to quote from *Welzenbach's Climbs*.

The photographic collection is built around Willi Burkhardt's large-format mountain landscapes, a number of which were taken specially for this new edition of the book. Additional photos have been provided by John Allen, Jean Michel Asselin, Richard Carter, Ted Dance, Colin Foord, Richard Gibbens, John Gillham, Richard Goedeke, Wil Hurford, Neil McAdie, Denis Mitchell, Alan O'Brien, Bill O'Connor, G. Perroux, Mike Pinney, Doug Scott, Jim Teesdale, Hans Wagner, Dave Wynne-Jones. Other photographic assistance was provided by John Cleare, Tim Cumberland, François Damilano, Joss Lynam and Jim Yearsley. The individual photo credits are given next to each illustration and each photographer's total contribution is listed below [abbreviations – *t* (top), *b* (bottom), *l* (left), *r* (right), *tr* (top right), etc. (2) denotes the number of pictures on one page by one photographer]: John Allen – 16, 18(2), 30, 35(*t*), 39, 44(*t*), 47, 48(3), 51(2), 59, 62, 63, 64, 66(*tr*), 69, 71, 72, 73(2), 74, 78(*t, br*), 989(2), 102, 116, 118(*b*), 125, 142(*r*), 143, 144, 153(*br*, 184(*l*), 195(*t*), 198, 200(2), 201(2), 207(*br*), 217(*tl*), 218(*l*), 221(*t*); Jean Michel Asselin – 173; Willi Burkhardt – front cover, 1, 2/3, 4/5, 6, 9, 15, 17, 20, 21, 24, 25, 26(*l*), 27, 28, 29, 31, 32, 35(*b*), 36, 37, 41, 42, 44(*b*), 46, 53, 54/55, 57, 58, 60, 65, 76, 77, 78(*bl*), 81, 82(*b*), 83(2), 84, 87, 88, 92, 93, 94, 101, 103, 104(*t*), 106, 107, 108, 110, 111, 112, 114, 115, 117, 121(*b*), 122/123, 124(*tl*), 126, 127, 128(2), 131, 132, 135, 137, 141, 146, 147, 148, 150, 157, 158, 161, 162, 164/165, 167, 168, 175, 178, 186, 189, 190, 192, 194, 196, 203, 205, 210, 214, 220(*t*); Richard Carter – 105(*t*), 113, 207(*bl*), 219; Ted Dance – 160; Colin Foord – 10(*r*), 11, 12(*l*); Richard Gibbens – 13, 14; John Gillham – 23; Richard Goedeke – 26(*br*), 86(*l*), 96(*t*), 133(*r*), 134(*b*), 156; Wil Hurford – 19, 34(*bl/br*), 38(2), 79(*l*), 80, 97, 98, 104(*b*), 134(*t*), 151, 159(*l*), 163(2), 176(2); Neil McAdie – 170; Denis Mitchell – 79(*r*), 174(*r*); Alan O'Brien 91; Bill O'Connor – back cover, 10(*tl,bl*), 12(*r*), 26(*cr*), 96(*bl,br*), 118(*t*), 119(*tl,tr*), 121(*t*), 124(*tr,b*), 152(*r*), 153(*t,bl*), 177, 179, 180(2), 184(*r*), 187, 188(*l*), 191(3), 199, 202, 207(*t*), 212, 213, 218(*tr,br*), 220(*b*); G. Perroux – 169, 172; Mike Pinney – 82(*t*), 155; Rudolf Rother – 45, 49; Doug Scott – 34(*t*); Jim Teesdale – 50, 61, 68, 70(3), 75, 90(*l*), 99, 100, 105(*b*), 109, 119(*b*), 138(2), 139, 206, 209(4), 215; Hans Wagner – 185; Dave Wynne-Jones – 40(2), 66(*tl*), 67, 86(*r*), 90(*r*) 129, 133(*l*), 142(*l*), 145(2),152(*l*), 154(4), 159(*tr,br*), 174(*l*), 181, 183, 193, 195(*bl,br*), 216, 217(*bl,r*).